Queen of
Bebop

Queen of Bebop

The Musical Lives of Sarah Vaughan

ELAINE M. HAYES

An Imprint of HarperCollinsPublishers

QUEEN OF BEBOP. Copyright © 2017 by Elaine M. Hayes. All rights reserved. Printed in the United States of America. No part of this book may be used or reproduced in any manner whatsoever without written permission except in the case of brief quotations embodied in critical articles and reviews. For information address HarperCollins Publishers, 195 Broadway, New York, NY 10007.

HarperCollins books may be purchased for educational, business, or sales promotional use. For information please e-mail the Special Markets Department at SPsales@harpercollins.com.

FIRST EDITION

Designed by Paula Russell Szafranski
Frontispiece by Michael Ochs Archives/Stringer/Getty Images

Library of Congress Cataloging-in-Publication Data has been applied for.

ISBN 978-0-06-236468-5

17 18 19 20 21 LSC   10 9 8 7 6 5 4 3 2 1

For Marisa Wittebort.

Her strength and courage have been an inspiration.

Yes, she was Divine, the true origins of that word. To see the future. Which is what Sassy was singing. For the diggers Sassy's voice was an instrument expressing the exact sensuousness of our hearts. How fantastic that was, how she swooped and bent the beauty of it, ascending like our hopeful vision, the emotional touching of our would-be rationalized reflections . . . what we had picked up trying to dig the world.

Amiri Baraka, "Sassy Was Definitely Not the Avon Lady"

Contents

Prologue   1

Part I: An Artist Is Born, 1924–1947   9

1   "There Was No Sign of Any Kind of Voice"   15

2   "Ah *Mon Vieux,* This Chick Is Groovy!"   37

3   "I'm Not Singing Other People's Ideas"   65

4   "The Most Talked About Voice in America"   83

Part II: A Star Is Born, 1948–1958   99

5   "The Girl with the Magic Voice"   107

6   "She's Vaughanderful. She's Marvelous"   129

7   "Sarah Vaughan and Her Pygmalion"   145

8   "Sarah Vaughan Is Finally on the Way to the Pot of Gold"   163

9   "The High Priestess of Jazz"   183

PART III: A Career Is Reborn, 1959–1990   213

10   "They Say You Can't Teach New Tricks to
        Old Dogs—So Get New Dogs!"   219

11   "The No. 1 Singer of a Decade Ago"   243

12   "I'm Not a Jazz Singer. I'm a Singer"   265

13   "Here I Go Again"   283

14   "The Marian Anderson of Modern Jazz"   299

15   "I'm Just Coming into My Prime"   321

        Epilogue: "The Greatest Vocal Artist of Our Century"   357

Acknowledgments   367

Notes   371

Index   403

Queen of Bebop

Prologue

Sarah Vaughan was my crossover moment. As a classical pianist and violist, then aspiring music historian, I never listened to jazz (or much popular music, either) until I discovered Sarah in 1994, thanks to a college roommate. We listened to her often, as we chatted, played cribbage, cooked, and cleaned our apartment, and while I don't remember the rules of cribbage, I do remember my first impressions of Vaughan's voice. Like so many before me, I was drawn to its sheer beauty. Her tone was exquisite, full and rich like velvet or oozing honey, yet agile and supple, almost light as air. The classical musician in me appreciated her impeccable pitch and time as she tossed off one virtuosic passage after another. And she was a true contralto, able to jump, glide, and swoop between notes at the top and bottom of her four-octave range, all with a stunning precision and ease. But she was more than an amazing voice. I was equally captivated by her musical mind. How she took a song apart, then put it back together again, adding her own unusual harmonies, dissonances, and embellishments. She was always improvising, flirting with the spontaneous and unexpected, and as a classical musician beholden to the score, I was intrigued by this too.

But most of all, I admired the sheer force of her presence. She could silence a boisterous crowd by simply beginning to sing. If she forgot a lyric, she'd thrill her audience as she ad-libbed a new one, using it as a launching pad for new flights of fancy. If she stumbled over a speaker, she kept on singing, unfazed. She always remained in control—of her voice, her ensemble, and her audience. When I listened to Vaughan, I heard excellence, a true mastery of her craft. I heard a strong, confident, and independent woman. As a young woman just beginning to find my way in the world, I valued these qualities. I wanted to be that kind of woman. Although decades separated us, not to mention differences in race and class, I identified with Vaughan and the power of her voice. The more I listened, the closer I felt to her. I felt as if she were singing directly to me, expressing with her voice my hopes, dreams, and disappointments. She possessed an uncanny ability to tap into universal human experiences and create intimacy in her performances—the impression that there was an emotional connection, a real bond, between her and her audience.

So I continued to listen. I added Sarah's jazz sisters—Ella, Billie, Anita, Peggy, and Nina—to my playlist, discovering the unique power and brilliance of their voices. Then I turned to the jazz instrumentalists: Louis Armstrong, Charlie Parker, Miles Davis, Dave Brubeck, Chet Baker, Charles Mingus, John Coltrane, Herbie Hancock, and on and on. My musical horizons expanded. Gone were the rigid highbrow/lowbrow values instilled by my German immigrant grandmother that privileged classical music above all else. I crossed over, embracing not only jazz but rhythm and blues, gospel, world music, and even cheesy pop tunes from the 1950s, which I not so secretly adore. As I transformed myself into a jazz and pop music historian, I stretched myself intellectually, exploring the fields of gender, race, and cultural studies that this new direction involved. It all began with Sarah Vaughan. Her singing was a passport of sorts that opened up my world.

Time and again, Vaughan fans have told me that she was also their entry point into jazz. And as I've studied Vaughan, coming to understand the scope of her talent and legacy, it has become clear that over the course of her forty-seven-year career, she brought countless listeners to the world of jazz. Her singing changed the outlooks of musicians, critics, disc jockeys, and run-of-the-mill fans. When she first burst onto the scene in the 1940s, she left her fellow musicians, especially vocalists, gasping in amazement at her daring innovations and vocal dexterity. It had not occurred to them that the human voice could be used this way. In the 1950s, as she found success as a pop artist crooning ballads, many white Americans heard her for the first time. They were intrigued and explored her jazz singing. Decades later, when she began performing with symphony orchestras, she introduced another new audience, this time classical music lovers, to the wonders of her voice and jazz. She was their crossover moment too.

Sarah Vaughan was a jazz singer par excellence. During her lifetime, she epitomized everything that jazz singing stood for, and in the decades since her death in 1990, she has often been mentioned alongside Ella Fitzgerald and Billie Holiday as one of the best jazz singers of all time. Vaughan would have been flattered by the praise and happy that her legacy endured, but she would have been dissatisfied with its specificity. As she evolved as a musician, she increasingly rejected the label "jazz singer." She found it too confining, too narrow a description of what she did and how she thought about music.

"I'm not a jazz singer. I'm a singer," she insisted during an interview with the jazz publication *Down Beat* in 1982, reiterating a stance she first took in 1960. "I don't know why people call me a jazz singer, though I guess people associate me with jazz because I was raised in it, from way back. I'm not putting jazz down, but I'm not a jazz singer. Betty Bebop [Carter] is a jazz singer because that's all she does. I've even been called a blues singer. I've recorded all kinds of music, but [to them] I'm either a jazz singer or a blues singer." She definitely did not consider herself a blues singer, though she often infused her singing with the blues. "What I want to do, music-wise," she concluded, "is all kinds of music that I like, and I like all kinds of music."[1]

Vaughan did not want to be categorized, pigeonholed, or contained, as a musician or as a woman. "Music has too many labels," she told critic Max Jones in 1981, revisiting a familiar theme. "I call it all just music. . . . And I hate being labelled."[2] This rejection of labels, paired with her faith in music, defined her worldview. As a young black girl growing up in segregated Newark and then as a black woman traveling an often intolerant world, Vaughan understood the power of labels and stereotypes. She understood their ability to strip her of her individuality and humanity, to define and limit her, and, ultimately, to dictate how she should sing. Because musical labels describing genres and styles are often linked, in the public's imagination, to the racial identity of the performer, she realized that these labels influenced how an audience would interpret and perceive her singing. Vaughan and her contemporaries also understood that labels reflected the larger power dynamics of society as a whole. As music historian Guthrie Ramsey Jr. plainly explains, the act of categorizing "tells us who's in charge and running the show."[3] And Sarah Vaughan always wanted to run her own show. She wanted to sing her own way, constantly pushing back against the record executives, concert promoters, and club owners who tried to change her. She spent her entire career defying expectations, forging her own path so that her creative vision and voice could be heard. Vaughan didn't want to be known exclusively as a jazz singer, or a blues, gospel, pop, or even opera singer, either, though she had the versatility and talent to fit into any of these niches. Nor did she want to be known simply as an exceptional black singer. She wanted to be an extraordinary singer. That's it.

Given Vaughan's dislike of labels, it's safe to say that she would have also disapproved of the title of this biography: *Queen of Bebop*. While she was proud of her contributions to the style of jazz known as bebop and considered bebop "good music," she likely would have felt that this title emphasized only one facet, just a few years, of her incredibly varied, almost half-century-long career. Yet Vaughan's early years immersed in bebop informed the rest of her career; they shaped her worldview and her approach to music making. And in the seventy-five years since Vaughan first collaborated with her fellow beboppers in the 1940s, the development of this style has emerged as a pivotal moment in jazz history. Unlike the hummable tunes and danceable rhythms of its predecessor, swing, America's popular music during the war years, bebop was characterized by an expanded, often dissonant harmonic palette, a more complex rhythmic language, wickedly fast instrumental lines, and brash virtuosity. In short, bebop was not for dancing, it was for listening to. It was art. Those wildly adventurous and innovative bebop musicians began to imagine jazz's language for musical abstraction. And, indeed, bebop changed the status of jazz in the cultural imagination, transforming it from a popular or vernacular music into high art.[4]

Jazz historians have extensively chronicled the lives and accomplishments of bebop's founding fathers: Dizzy Gillespie, Charlie Parker, Thelonious Monk, Bud Powell, and others. The attention is merited. They were all giants, the brilliant kings and princes of bebop. But Sarah Vaughan was a giant too. She was bebop's queen. She was one of the only women working in the trenches in the early days and the first vocalist to introduce bebop singing to the world. (Ella Fitzgerald, who came of age during the swing era, also incorporated bebop aesthetics into her singing, but this would happen later.) Vaughan, in fact, became popular before her instrumental counterparts and played an important role in introducing them to a wider audience. Yet Vaughan's role and contributions to bebop have often been overlooked. And her genius, unlike that of her male colleagues, remains undervalued and underexamined. *Queen of Bebop* seeks to remedy this.

Vaughan, however, was much more than the queen of bebop, or a jazz singer. She played the piano and organ. She sang spirituals and gospel music. She became a pop star in the 1950s. In the 1960s and 1970s, she dabbled in yet more pop, soul, funk, disco, and sometimes even rock 'n' roll on her records, although she often disliked the results. She became a master of Brazilian music in the 1970s and 1980s, and she always channeled her inner diva and flirted with her operatic side. Vaughan embraced her self-appointed status as a singer free of labels, slipping between one genre, then another, and back again, all in an effort to create a vocal style uniquely her own. Her way of singing had never been heard before. And she was constantly striving to try new things and reach new audiences. As a result, she had countless crossover moments. *Queen of Bebop* focuses on three. Part I traces her journey from a church girl in Newark to a bebop innovator on the cusp of national fame. Part II explores her emergence as a pop star and how she balanced this new fame and fortune, not to mention the pressures of record executives, with her desire to remain an important, innovative voice in jazz. And part III reveals how she survived the takeover of popular music by rock 'n' roll, remained true to herself, and launched a new phase of her career as a symphonic diva, singing jazz in venues previously reserved for classical music and opera.

Using crossover as a lens through which to examine Vaughan's life in music honors her flexibility as a performer and the breadth of her career. It provides an opportunity to discuss jazz's decades-long quest for legitimacy, its journey from lowbrow vernacular music to highbrow art music, and Vaughan's role in the process, while also acknowledging her pop music, which, until now, has been largely ignored. With her pop singing, Vaughan helped desegregate postwar American airwaves and set the stage for the civil rights activism of the next decades. She challenged contemporary conceptions of race and gender and changed how white Americans understood and responded to black women in song. This approach also offers insights into her private life—how she struggled to balance her status as a professional woman, artist, and genius thriving in the male-dominated world of jazz with society's expectations of her as a daughter, wife, and mother, and how the tensions between these two poles influenced not only her career but also her personal life. Most important, however, a focus on crossover helps unravel the many myths and misunderstandings that still inform how Vaughan's story is told. In their place, *Queen of Bebop* presents a rich, dynamic, and complex portrait of Sarah Vaughan, a woman who, time and again, insisted, "I sing. I just sing."

PART I

An Artist Is Born, 1924–1947

On November 8, 1947, Sarah Vaughan waited in the wings of New York's historic Town Hall as saxophonist Lester Young, the "President of Jazz" or simply "the Prez," tore it up onstage. He played his unique brand of high-energy swing that made him famous in the 1930s. Vaughan hummed along, occasionally shouting out encouragement to the band, as she clapped her hands, throwing in a jitterbug step here and there. The place was hopping with heady anticipation. Electricity filled the theater. It must have been thrilling for the young singer, but nerve-racking too. She was up next.

Since its inaugural concert in 1921, Town Hall had gained a reputation as one of the premier venues in New York City. Vaughan's idol Marian Anderson, the African American opera singer turned civil rights activist, debuted there in 1924, then performed again in 1935 when she returned to the United States after years of touring abroad. Built by suffragists, Town Hall was known for its progressive programming and hosted a series of innovative jazz concerts, including a breakthrough performance by the then-unknown beboppers Dizzy Gillespie and Charlie Parker in 1945. Tonight was Vaughan's opportunity to shine. She had begun her life in music as a choir girl in Newark; paid her dues as a girl singer in the big bands of Earl Hines and Billy Eckstine, where she learned to become "one of the guys"; and then ventured out on her own as a solo act. Although she had sung in New York's small clubs and cafes for several years, her Town Hall debut was a milestone. The concert was sold out, and according to the *Pittsburgh Courier,* a thousand fans had been turned away at the box office.[1] After almost five years in the business, most of it in relative obscurity, Vaughan was immersed in the first crossover phase of her career, and her star was finally on the rise.

To the casual observer, Vaughan could have been mistaken for just another kid hanging around backstage—a fan rather than the evening's final performer. She looked younger than her twenty-three years. She wore a long, slim-fitting white gown with big puffy shoulders and a plunging neckline. It was a stylish dress that epitomized postwar fashion, and it was appropriate for the grandeur of the venue. But it fit poorly and overwhelmed Vaughan. The young vocalist seemed a little out of her element. Town Hall was a regal theater with high ceilings, a billowing red curtain, brass fixtures, and crystal chandeliers. Boasting one of the finest organs in the world and marvelous acoustics, it was on par with Carnegie Hall.

As the Prez launched into the final number of his set that Saturday night in 1947, Vaughan prepared for her Town Hall debut. Applause ushered Prez and his band offstage. Vaughan waited for her cue, then walked to center stage. A bare-bones rhythm section, with piano, guitar, bass, and drums, was clustered behind her. Only the microphone, teetering on its thin stand, stood between her and the fifteen hundred people in the audience. There was no place to hide. The glow of the spotlights illuminated the crowd's expectant faces. Gowns and overcoats rustled as listeners shifted in their seats, leaning forward in anticipation as if to pose the question: Can this slip of a girl fill this cavernous hall?

From the piano came five simple chords, the introduction to "Don't Blame Me." The audience waited until Vaughan, at last, began to sing. But she didn't sing the tune's opening like other vocalists or as it was written—three brisk notes, one for each word in the title. Instead, she drew out these three syllables, expanding them to create an exquisite melisma—a cascade of sound that first went up, then down while punctuating each word with a new twist and turn. Within seconds the audience gasped, whistled, and cooed its approval. Momentum grew as Vaughan exploited every note of this slow ballad, effortlessly bending her voice to change keys and explore unexpected harmonies, all while displaying the impressive highs and lows of her four-octave contralto. Vaughan's voice possessed a maturity, poise, and depth that belied her youthful appearance. It was full, rich, and sumptuous, yet crisp and clear as a bell. By the time she reached the final phrase of "Don't Blame Me," a delightful series of embellished arpeggios, the audience could barely contain itself and burst into applause.

That night, number after number, Vaughan transformed the popular songs of the day with her fresh, innovative approach to singing. Listeners sighed with satisfaction when she launched into "The Man I Love" and "I Cover the Waterfront," her signature tune at the time, then cheered with excitement when she began the up-tempo "Mean to Me." As her set progressed, the audience's applause became more enthusiastic, louder and louder, with more whistles, hoots, and hollers. Vaughan struggled to be heard as she shouted her thanks and appreciation to the crowd between songs. In a surprising contrast to her singing voice, Vaughan's speaking voice was high-pitched, almost squeaky, and unmistakably girlish. For a moment, glimpses of a much younger woman reappeared. But then she turned and shouted directions to the band with firmness and resolve, calling out, "One chorus," then more emphatically, "One!" as the band began "Time After Time." And when the pianist launched into "I Cover the Waterfront," she instructed, "Slow, slower,

slower," insisting that the band reduce the tempo to a crawl. Vaughan commanded respect, and even though she was the only woman onstage, the band listened.

The evening came to a close when Prez and his sideman, the trumpeter Shorty McConnell, joined Vaughan onstage for the grand finale: "I Cried for You." Vaughan called the tune and dove right into the first verse, and as Young took his extended solo, she enthusiastically clapped along and shouted her encouragement: "Come on, Lester!" then "Go on, go on, go on!" When Vaughan finally returned to sing the reprise, she let loose a flourish of seemingly impossible vocal turns and trills bolstered by brilliant harmonic changes. Her singing was a revelation. The elasticity of her voice rivaled that of the finest horn players. She was the perfect complement to Young's relaxed, deliciously lyrical tenor playing. Both had rich, deep, and exquisitely resonant tones; both added nuanced scoops and inflections to their crisp, clean phrasing; and both colored their sustained notes with just a touch of vibrato. Vaughan sang like an instrumentalist, and like the best horn players she played her voice with ease.[2]

The jazz press proclaimed the Town Hall concert a grand success—for Vaughan, but not for Young. According to Michael Levin, a critic for *Down Beat,* "A great vocalist made a great saxophonist sound sick." In contrast to Young's old-fashioned, almost pedestrian performance, "Miss Vaughan only drew raves, some of her astonishingly inventive ideas bringing gasps of amazement from a couple of girl vocalists sitting next to this reviewer. Her tone was impeccable, her taste immaculate, and her stage manner and dress much improved. This girl's singing, after three years of musical if not popular prominence is still a breath of fresh air and a source of jazz inspiration to all who listen to her."[3]

For Levin, his fellow critics, and many musicians, especially vocalists, Vaughan ushered in a changing of the guard. While Young represented the swing era, the soundtrack of the war years, the past, Vaughan embodied everything that was new and modern. Her cutting-edge singing epitomized the very essence of bebop, the avant-garde foundation for modern jazz that would transport the genre from a popular dance music into the realm of abstract, high art. And as Vaughan helped initiate this new chapter in jazz history, she reimagined the way this music would forever be sung. Disc jockeys dubbed her "the new sound," a testament to both the beauty of her voice and her innovations, and in the coming years she would become "the most talked about voice in America."

1

"There Was No Sign of Any Kind of Voice"

Sarah Lois Vaughan's story began twenty-three years earlier in Newark, New Jersey. She was born on March 27, 1924, to Ada and Asbury Vaughan, who had moved north from Virginia during World War I during the Great Migration. After the war, Newark represented a land of promise and prosperity. It was New Jersey's largest city and the embodiment of a bustling, modern metropolis. Tall buildings lined the streets of downtown. Trolleys ferried passengers through the busy commercial district; "the tube" linked Newark with New York and Hoboken; and the airport, built in 1928, soon became one of the busiest in the world. This, along with a recently expanded harbor, ensured that Newark thrived as a hub of international manufacturing and trade.

Laborers from around the world, including southern blacks eager to escape the oppression of Jim Crow, flocked to the city. In addition to better paying jobs, they were drawn to Newark for its promise of desegregated schools, racially mixed neighborhoods, and a well-established, rapidly growing African American community. Between 1915 and 1930, Newark's black population nearly quadrupled, reaching almost thirty-nine thousand—9 percent of the city's population.

Yet upon arriving in Newark, southern blacks learned that the city practiced its own particularly northern interpretation of Jim Crow. Although well north of the Mason-Dixon Line, New Jersey, in fact, had a long history of racial intolerance. It was one of the last northern states to abolish slavery, waiting until 1804 to enact legislation that began a gradual abolition. In 1860, eighteen slaves remained. During the next decade, the state legislature did not support Abraham Lincoln or the Emancipation Proclamation and failed to ratify the Reconstruction amendments to the Constitution guaranteeing equal citizenship and voter rights for all, regardless of race. The state legislature waited until 1875 to enfranchise black men and 1884 to pass laws prohibiting segregation in hotels, restaurants, and public transportation.

Despite the letter of the law, Newark's white community didn't comply, and for nearly eighty years, until the early days of the modern civil rights movement, whites deeply resented black citizenship, denying African Americans the most basic rights and opportunities. They did not have equal access to public services. Local swimming pools were only open to blacks during limited hours when whites were not present. Hospitals remained segregated. Many local department stores did not allow African American customers to try on garments before buying them. And within the workplace, aspiring, hardworking blacks encountered a glass ceiling that prevented them from advancing beyond the lowest paying jobs as unskilled laborers.[1]

Nonetheless, the Vaughans moved to Newark filled with optimism. Ada found work as a laundress. She was paid by the piece and likely earned $15 to $18 a week.[2] Asbury worked as a carpenter for similar, or perhaps slightly higher, wages. Like so many before them, Ada and Asbury settled in the burgeoning African American neighborhood known as "the Hill," a part of the old Third Ward just west of Broad Street and the downtown commercial district. They lived on the top floor of a small duplex at 72 Brunswick Street and probably paid $8 or $10 a month in rent. By 1916, right around the time Ada and Asbury moved to Newark, much of the Third Ward was already a ghetto. Blighted cold-water tenements, many without private baths or toilets, were the norm. Despite these poor living conditions, a tight-knit, vibrant community emerged, one that included immigrants from Poland and Germany as well as Jewish families, remnants from the days when the Third Ward was a Jewish enclave.

Like many working-class African Americans, the Vaughans' lives revolved around their church. They became longtime members of Mount Zion Baptist Church in the nearby Ironbound district and pillars of Newark's black religious community. Predictably, many of Vaughan's first musical experiences took place at Mount Zion. As a toddler, she was so intrigued by the church's organ that she would sneak up to the front of the church to sit with the organist during services. Congregants remember a young Vaughan humming along as her mother sang in the choir. And when she began to peck out her own tunes on the family's piano at the age of seven, her parents turned to the church's organist and musical director for weekly piano lessons, paying twenty-five cents per lesson.

Music permeated the Vaughan household. "Not the kind of music I sing," Vaughan explained in 1961. "They sang the music of God."[3] Asbury also loved to play country songs and blues on his guitar after work. Ada was a talented pianist and singer, and before long she was playing duets with her daughter. When the family was not making music together, they listened to the radio and played records on their Victrola. Although money was tight, Ada managed to set aside enough spare change for her daughter to splurge on the occasional record, even during the height of the Depression. As Vaughan grew older, her family hosted Friday-night musicales for Vaughan and her friends from church and the neighborhood.

Childhood friend Phyllis Brooks remembers climbing the stairs each week to enter the Vaughans' home through their tiny kitchen, then making her way into their equally small living room.

Vaughan's parents retreated to the kitchen as she and the other kids played records and jitterbugged the night away, often with Vaughan accompanying them on the piano tucked away in the corner. "I have no idea how her house became the center of our social life," Brooks explained. "Sarah was a shy girl, very shy, so I guess it just was because the kids were welcome. Her parents were very open and supportive of her and didn't mind the kids gathering there or being dispossessed every weekend."[4]

In 1936, by the time Vaughan was twelve, she was active in music groups at school and played piano for the orchestra and boys' glee club. She also began playing the organ with the junior and senior church choirs during rehearsals and accompanied the junior choir during services. She traded Sundays with Brooks, who studied with the same piano teacher.

Beyond her multi-instrument talent, however, Vaughan was determined to sing. "I always knew I could sing," she told Dick Cavett in 1980. "But when I was little, they always had me playing the organ in church or piano in schools for the choirs, and all that, and I always said, 'I want to sing, y'all.'"[5] Eventually she did join the church choir, though she rarely soloed. "Her voice was very tiny," said Brooks. "She couldn't project much beyond six benches." And Evelyn Greene, a fellow choir member who went on to become a professor of music at Rutgers University, remembered, "Sarah just sang insignificant alto. There was no sign of any kind of voice."[6]

Yet Vaughan persisted. Perhaps she was tired of being pigeonholed as the reliable pianist by friends and choirmasters. Perhaps she no longer wanted to be relegated to the supporting role of accompanist and alto. Unlike sopranos, altos almost never sing the melody; instead, they harmonize with the sopranos, the true focal point of the ensemble. And in the church, soloists were the stars. Vaughan wanted her turn to take the lead, to determine her own path and destiny. She sought more musical freedom and insisted on stretching her vocal cords. This all began when she started to expand her musical horizons—first on piano, then with her voice.

Newark boasted a vibrant collection of regional musicians who played its many neighborhood clubs. In 1938, there were an estimated one thousand saloons in Newark, one for every 429 residents, and many of them offered live entertainment to draw patrons. There was a wealth of musical opportunities beyond the doors of Vaughan's church, but the scene remained deeply segregated. The fancy clubs on Broad Street catered to whites only, and downtown restaurants and hotels were still off-limits for Newark's black community. Except for the black-owned Orpheum Theatre on Washington Street, blacks had to sit in the balconies of Newark's movie halls and major theaters, even when a black artist performed onstage.

Nonetheless, starting as young as the age of twelve, Vaughan and her girlfriends would scrounge together enough money for tickets and sneak out of the house to hear shows at Newark's best theaters. At the Adams Theater, they saw Erskine Hawkins's band and Billy Eckstine singing with the Earl Hines band. At Proctor's Theater, they heard Josephine Baker. After the concert an excited Vaughan and her friends followed the famed singer as she walked down the street, too shy and nervous to approach her. Although Vaughan and her friends were relegated to the balcony, they were determined to have a good time, even if this involved a healthy dose of mischief infused with their own form of social protest. "We used to love it, because we'd throw all kinds of things down below!" Vaughan told Les Tomkins in 1977.[7]

The segregated policies of the white-owned restaurants, clubs, and theaters mirrored the racial politics of the city as a whole. As a child, Vaughan was well aware of the social inequities of her hometown and the hypocrisy that it represented. She understood that Newark's laws forbidding discrimination did not in fact guarantee equality in the face of ingrained, systemic racism. "What I like about the South—they're honest," she reflected in 1977. "They don't like colored people and Jews, and that's it. But I don't think anybody ever really knew about the North—it was just the worst place in the world."[8]

Yet, in the face of the North's segregation, black neighborhoods flourished culturally and socially. Dozens of black-owned and black-friendly clubs and dance halls graced the streets of the Hill in Newark. These clubs were crucial to the black community's economic engine, providing not only models for black entrepreneurship but also much-needed jobs for servers, bartenders, cooks, food distributors, and, of course, musicians, agents, promoters, and, by extension, record and music stores. They represented a bubble of equality, where blacks could relax and congregate on their own terms. It was here where Vaughan would first be encouraged to sing.

By the time Vaughan was fifteen, in 1939, she had completely immersed herself in popular music, defying the expectations of her parents and the church and their preference for classical music, hymns, and spirituals. Friends remember Vaughan rushing home from school to listen to a jazz program on the radio, most likely Bob Howard's fifteen-minute daily on CBS.[9] Howard specialized in jazz-inspired popular music, playing stride piano and singing in the style of Fats Waller. Vaughan loved the show and began imitating what she heard, often sharing her new discoveries with her friends at the Friday night socials. She also learned by ear other popular songs, like "The Bluebird of Happiness," "Danny Boy," and tunes popularized by Ella Fitzgerald, including "Rock It for Me" and "A-Tisket, A-Tasket," Fitzgerald's 1938 breakout hit. Brooks and Vaughan's other friends from church most likely found her new songs intriguing, not just for their popular, secular appeal but for Vaughan's newfound interest in her voice, prompted in part by her growing frustration with the limitations of the piano.

"When I play piano, see, my mind rolls faster than my fingers," she explained to Marian McPartland in 1986. "So, even when I was playing classical music, if I couldn't play that little part I'd sing it. Of course, the teacher didn't go for that." This was not simply a case of poor dexterity or a child looking for shortcuts because she didn't practice enough. Vaughan remained an accomplished pianist throughout her career, despite her insistence to the contrary. Her frustrations were the dissatisfaction of a burgeoning artist struggling to realize her creative identity. "I'm really a singer," she said. "I wish I could play piano like I think, but I can't. My fingers. My mind. I sing faster. I can think what I'm thinking and sing it, but I can't play it."[10]

Perhaps it was impossible to play what she was thinking. She may not have realized it at the time, but the obstacle was not her skill on the piano; rather, it was the instrument itself. The piano, with its fixed pitch and strict adherence to half and whole steps, simply cannot produce the microtones, nuanced slides, and dramatic swoops that soon became a trademark of her vocal style. Vaughan reveled in the freedom that her voice provided, and unlike the piano it presented a collection of exciting, limitless possibilities.[11]

Vaughan's revelations about her voice occurred just as the big band craze swept across the country. Every city had its favorite hometown dance bands and orchestras. Territory bands toured three- and four-state regions, and the big name national acts, like Miller, Basie, Ellington, Calloway, and Goodman, captured the country's imagination. In the 1930s and 1940s these and other name bands all stopped in Newark on their way up to New York City. Live music could be heard every night of the week in the Hill, and to a young Vaughan it felt like a whole new world just waiting to be discovered. Along with her school friends, she learned how to Lindy Hop at the Court Street branch of the colored YMCA, not to be confused with the nearby High Street YMCA, which didn't allow blacks. She frequented the big dance halls like the Graham Auditorium; the Laurel Garden, known for its exciting battles of the bands; and Skateland, where local favorite Pancho Diggs and his orchestra packed the house, drawing crowds of two thousand. Newark's black youth, and on occasion their parents, danced the night away as Diggs burned it up onstage. Even though she was underage, Vaughan also became a regular in the very adult world of Newark's bars and nightclubs, taking in the more intimate jazz presented by their small ensembles.

According to her friends, Vaughan was completely enthralled by the music and would stay to hear the very last song of the evening. Time and again, she missed her 10:00 P.M. curfew, and, not surprisingly, this upset her parents. One can only imagine how they worried about their daughter, their only child, walking home alone late at night, often skirting the Barbary Coast, Newark's red-light district with brothels and after-hours clubs that stayed open long after the taverns and nightclubs officially closed. But this was more than a conflict between protective parents and a young, adventurous teenager asserting her independence. It was also a clash of cultures.

The black church community viewed popular music as a corrupting influence. Vaughan's father saw it similarly, especially when it concerned his daughter. Nightclubs represented the world of alcohol and excess, and many of Newark's clubs had ties to organized crime. Musicians were tainted by these unseemly associations and were often linked, albeit unfairly, to the "sporting life," an illicit world of gambling, drugs, and prostitution that also happened to feature music and entertainment. Although centered in the red-light district, aspects of the sporting life could seep into run-of-the-mill corner bars, and a female vocalist, regardless of where she performed, risked being labeled a "hussy" or "sportin' woman" by church elders.

As much as Vaughan's parents wanted to foster her musicality, they also wanted to safeguard their daughter's reputation and shelter her from these risks. They soon forbade her from attending dances, concerts, nightclubs, or any other popular music performances. According to her mother, Vaughan's father "didn't approve of nothing—her going out of the door."[12] He did, however, encourage his daughter's musical contributions at church. They were a source of great pride for both him and Vaughan's mother, but he did not want his daughter to pursue a career in music, much less a career in jazz. If she insisted, he would have most certainly preferred that she follow the example of Marian

Anderson, the classically trained African American vocalist and a favorite of black Americans. Anderson came to prominence in the 1930s as she toured Europe and the United States, singing recitals of classical music and spirituals like "He's Got the Whole World in His Hands," which appeared on the *Billboard* charts in 1936. Her recordings of opera arias were bestsellers, and in 1939 Anderson sang in her now-landmark open-air concert on the steps of the Lincoln Memorial on Easter Sunday. The concert, attended by seventy-five thousand and broadcast to millions over the radio, with a short excerpt featured on movie house newsreels, was a response to the refusal of the Daughters of the American Revolution to allow Anderson to perform for an integrated audience at Philadelphia's Constitution Hall.

With this concert, Anderson became an instant symbol of the burgeoning civil rights movement and a source of black pride. She was devout, ladylike, and respectable, an embodiment of both high culture and black achievement. In short, Anderson was a race woman, a pillar of the black community, and a model for all black women to aspire to. And should Vaughan choose a career in music, classical music and the life of a concert artist was, according to her father and the church community, the ideal path.

Vaughan didn't seriously explore singing until she transferred from East Side High School, where she had studied stenography for two terms, to the Newark Arts High School her sophomore year, when she was fifteen. Here, even though she never took formal vocal lessons, she made new friends who shared her interest in jazz and Newark's thriving scene.

"I used to play hooky from school to hear music, and at night too," she told British journalist Max Jones years later. Instead of arguing with her parents, she simply snuck out her bedroom window. "I wasn't supposed to be at dances but I was—listening to all of the good music like Ella Fitzgerald and Chick Webb."[13]

All the while, her old church friends and parents had no idea what she was up to. Ada recalled learning about her daughter's exploits from friends and neighbors. "She was sneaking around trying to get out in the nightclubs. She didn't want me to know it." Ada laughed. "Somebody would come in and tell, 'You know I saw your daughter at this place, at this man's night club.' I said, 'You did?!' He said, 'Yes.' He said, 'You know what?' I said, 'What?' He said, 'I would like to have her to work for me.' I said, 'She's only fifteen!'"[14]

Indeed, Vaughan was seen regularly in the Hill's nightclubs and, according to locals, made her unofficial debut at the Alcazar, on Waverly Street, only three blocks from her house. Nicknamed the "Zoo," the Alcazar was one of Newark's most popular black-owned-and-operated bars and a favorite hangout for musicians. The club had a simple setup: a single large room with a modest stage; a huge, double-horseshoe-shaped bar, the club's trademark; a few tables; and a discreet side-door entrance for ladies. At the time, it was still taboo for women to sit at the bar. The Alcazar wasn't fancy—in fact some remembered it as a dingy dive—but the club had a reputation as a well-run and friendly establishment, without fights. And most important, it featured superb music seven nights a week, with matinees on Thursdays and Sundays. Local favorite Leon Eason, a trumpeter and vocalist, led the house band between 1937 and 1940 and often let neighborhood and out-of-town musicians sit in with the band. Of course, one of these musicians was a fourteen- or fifteen-year-old Sarah Vaughan.

Eason's guitarist, Willie Johnson, recalled, "She'd sneak in the side door, and Leon would let her sing."[15] Even though she was welcome at the Alcazar, it took courage for the shy, very quiet aspiring vocalist to step onstage, become the center of attention, and perform for a room full of adults. Alto saxophonist Carl McIntyre, who replaced Eason as house bandleader in 1940, said, "I can recall her coming into the Alcazar when she was just a kid. That's where she got her start. I'd say, 'Sing, girl!' She'd say, 'I'm scared.'" Yet, night after night, Vaughan did go onstage, her desire to sing overpowering her fear, and each time she got a little better, more determined to sing her own way. "All the girls wanted to sound like Billie Holiday," said McIntyre. "She was big time. But Sarah had a style all her own."[16] Although she was a favorite of the musicians, the Alcazar's owner, Pop Durham, would only let Vaughan sing a song or two, and then he'd say, "Daughter, you're nice, but you gotta go."[17]

By the time emcee Thad Howe heard Vaughan in the spring of 1942, just after her eighteenth birthday, she had developed a vocal maturity beyond her years. "The first time I ever saw her was at the Alcazar on Mother's Day," he said. "She was the last one up. I introduced her, and she sang 'I Cried for You.' I stood there dumbfounded. I couldn't believe it. She was just a kid." He concluded, "Golly, she had a voice."[18]

Similar stories played out around town between 1938 and 1942. Locals reported spotting her at the Piccadilly on Peshine Street, the Hydeaway on Halsey, and the Boston Plaza on Boston. She sang, danced, and most important, soaked up anything and everything musical. In addition to their house bands, many clubs hosted regular jam sessions, where musicians could create and explore new ideas, while others sponsored amateur nights that gave ambitious musicians an opportunity to test their chops in front of a live audience. As Vaughan sang at these amateur nights, she became more comfortable performing in front of live audiences. Some have suggested that Frank Tucker, a neighbor and insurance agent, became her first manager, booking her at these and other Newark clubs. During these early years, she also sang for the massive crowds at Skateland, where Pancho Diggs regularly gave young musicians a chance to perform with his big band. "One little girl was always pushed up to do her number," according to Bob Queen, an entertainment reporter for the *New Jersey Afro-American*. "The dancers would always stop and move forward to listen. Her name was Sarah Vaughan."[19]

Vaughan dropped out of school when she was sixteen, sometime during her junior year in 1940 or 1941, as she became more and more immersed in Newark's music scene. Her single-minded pursuit of a jazz education had replaced her formal education. In its place, she embarked on her own very disciplined course of study, a hands-on apprenticeship with Newark's many talented professional musicians. During the day she frequented her neighborhood record stores, like G&R Records on Prince Street or the Radio Record Shop on Market, owned by the founder of Savoy Records, Herman Lubinsky. He catered to a younger crowd and offered private listening booths and bins of nineteen-cent "steals" for collectors. Vaughan studied the latest releases and talked shop with other aspiring musicians. And at night, she continued to hone her craft at Newark's clubs, often staying out until the early hours of the morning.

Importantly, even early on, Vaughan remained open-minded to all kinds of music and took advantage of every opportunity that could further her musical education. After dropping out of school, she sang in a girls' choir sponsored by the National Youth Administration, a WPA work-study program that trained unemployed teens. She earned $25 a month for attending regular rehearsals and public performances. "It was excellent," said Vaughan. "We used to sing in Catholic churches. It was all good for me—anything that happens when you're young, always helps a lot."[20]

By 1942 Vaughan had become a respected member of Newark's jazz community. More experienced musicians recognized her commitment and willingness to learn, and, perhaps most important, her talent as she collaborated and shared her innovative ideas. Despite her youth, she was soon on equal footing with her fellow musicians, a student turned colleague, not a groupie. Vaughan was not a stereotypical teenage girl. She did not obsess about boys, clothes, or her appearance. In fact, biographer Leslie Gourse portrays the teenaged Vaughan as physically unattractive and concludes that the men she encountered in the clubs, whether musicians or patrons, did not consider her a romantic figure. And Gourse speculates that this might have been a good thing. Rather than associating her with looks, as happened with so many female vocalists at the time, musicians took Vaughan more seriously, and this helped her development as an artist.[21] Still, it would be simplistic to attribute Vaughan's credibility within Newark's jazz community solely to her looks, or lack thereof, and her potential as a girlfriend. Instead, jazz musicians took Vaughan seriously because she took herself seriously. Even so, there is something undeniably charming, alluring even, about the spark of new talent, enthusiasm, and unwavering dedication of a burgeoning genius just discovering the power of her voice.

Vaughan had found a place where she belonged, a community of like-minded individuals who shared her passion for jazz. Yet she never forsook her church-girl roots. She continued to play organ and sing in Mount Zion's choir, juggling these commitments with her ever-expanding jazz interests. Eventually, Vaughan's parents realized that they could not stop their daughter's late-night musical pursuits. She was passionate and tenacious, determined to become a jazz vocalist. So they tolerated, begrudgingly, her obsession with jazz, and as long as she honored her responsibilities at church, they looked the other way. It was a truce of sorts.

Vaughan soon outgrew Newark's jazz scene. While she was proud of her Newark roots (she remained a hometown girl until the end, living there until the early 1970s and always returning for charity events when the city needed her), Vaughan reminded people that she lived a mere ten or twelve miles from New York City, the capital of jazz and modern music. "Isn't that fortunate? I could have been from Trenton, you know!" she joked with pianist and radio host Marian McPartland in 1986.[22] Once again unbeknownst to her parents, Vaughan and her girlfriends began making regular trips to Harlem, where she experienced firsthand the latest musical developments and biggest names in jazz. She frequented the Savoy Ballroom, an integrated dance hall featuring legendary battles of the bands, and the famed Apollo Theater.

By the time Vaughan began her pilgrimages to the city, the Apollo Theater had cemented its reputation as the center of black entertainment in New York, if not the world. The theater's now-iconic red neon sign rose up into the sky, like a beacon announcing that the best, most current, and hippest black music could be found here at 253 W. 125th Street. It was the finest theater in Harlem, and according to bandleader and vibraphonist Lionel Hampton, "if you were a black entertainer of any kind—musician, singer, comedian—being a headliner at the Apollo was your proudest achievement."[23]

Built in 1914, the theater began as a whites-only burlesque hall, but in 1934, after multiple transfers of ownership, the Apollo changed formats to showcase almost exclusively black talent. Unlike most venues of the day, it had a fully integrated audience, and it was one of the few theaters to hire black employees backstage. That same year, the Apollo also began hosting its popular amateur contest every Wednesday night. Emceed by veteran entertainer Ralph Cooper, the show began at eight in the evening, with a live national radio feed, syndicated to twenty-one stations across the country, beginning at eleven o'clock. Here, following an audition, an unknown entertainer earned the opportunity to perform while backed by a name band, like Count Basie, Duke Ellington, Chick Webb, Louis Prima, or Louis Armstrong.

The audience at the Apollo was notoriously opinionated and boisterous, and it could be brutal. They were more than 1,500 strong, with the most vocal fans packing the balconies that towered over the stage. If they disliked an act, the audience would barrage the unlucky performer with boos and heckles. Then "Porto Rico," a stock character later known as "the Executioner," would chase unsuccessful contestants from the stage, unceremoniously dragging them away with a shepherd's hook. But if a contestant managed to woo the crowd and went on to win the contest, he or she received a cash prize plus a weeklong follow-up engagement at the theater.

Amateur Night at the Apollo earned the motto "Where stars are born and legends are made." In 1934, an amateur night win launched the career of a young Ella Fitzgerald. According to industry lore, the seventeen-year-old Fitzgerald originally planned to dance during her appearance on November 21, then at the last moment decided to sing instead. She was terribly nervous and faltered onstage, singing off-key. On the verge of being booed off,

Fitzgerald rallied, composed herself, and then tore the place up. As the legend goes, bandleader Chick Webb was so impressed he hired her right then and there, and Fitzgerald was on her way to becoming a star.

Vaughan was eager to try her hand too, and on Wednesday, October 21, 1942, following a rigorous audition process, she sang at the Amateur Night at the Apollo, backed by the "world's greatest growl trumpet king," Cootie Williams, and his band.[24]

The stakes were high. If she failed, she risked public humiliation and, quite possibly, chiding from naysayers back home in Newark. Vaughan didn't boast about her successful audition for the amateur night, nor did she make a big deal about her upcoming appearance. In fact, her old friends from church had no idea what she was up to until the last minute. Perhaps Vaughan was protecting herself, just in case things didn't work out. After all, the Apollo represented the big leagues; the pool of talent was much larger and its audiences a far cry from the friendly crowds at one of her local haunts like Skateland, where the audience stopped dancing and listened, almost reverently, whenever Vaughan stepped onstage. By 1942, she was a fixture of Newark's black music scene, and listeners had literally watched her grow up. They knew and welcomed her. At the Apollo, however, Vaughan was an outsider, an unknown entity, just another contestant for amateur-hour fans to heckle.

Emcee Cooper had his doubts. Based on her audition, he knew that she could sing, but he wondered if she could handle the Apollo's audience and the enormous pressures of the moment. "When I heard she wanted to compete in Amateur Night, I thought about talking her out of it. She seemed so tiny, I thought the roar of the crowd would knock her off her feet," he wrote in his memoir. "Sarah was so thin and so young, I thought she had tagged along with an older brother or sister." She seemed unworldly and naive, like the kind of girl you would find in a small country church choir. "Putting a sweet innocent girl with an angel's voice on that stage and asking her to woo an audience—that would boo a dear relative if she was off-key—is always a risky thing," said Cooper. "It's like asking a soloist in the church choir to sing on a Bourbon Street corner during Mardi Gras."[25]

He also worried about Vaughan's choice of song: "Body and Soul." It was a crowd favorite and indelibly linked to songstress Billie Holiday and saxophonist Coleman Hawkins. Both had recorded iconic renditions of the tune, and both were regular headliners at the Apollo. Cooper feared that Vaughan was about to make a rookie mistake: choosing the signature song of an established and beloved star—much like an aspiring diva on *American Idol* taking on a power ballad of Whitney Houston or Celine Dion. The amateur's rendition rarely passes muster, and as Cooper explained, "the audience could have hummed ['Body and Soul'] in perfect harmony while booing her offstage."[26]

Baritone Billy Eckstine, then singing with the Earl Hines band, was also in the theater. Usually he avoided amateur nights. "Believe me, bedlam is in this joint on Amateur Night, every Wednesday," he told Max Jones in 1954. "You can get water thrown on you . . . anything. So nobody even thinks of going in there." But Eckstine needed to cash a money order. It was after five o'clock, and he thought that Frank Schiffman, the Apollo's white owner and manager, could help him out. Schiffman was out having dinner, so Eckstine decided to brave the melee inside the hall. "I don't know why I went in to the auditorium; it must have been a stroke of fate," he continued. "Well, I'm sitting there watching, when from left field they introduce this little girl, and she's going to sing 'Body and Soul.' She walks out on stage, just a little skinny thing with a brown skirt on. It's Sarah, and she's about seventeen then."

"So help me!" Eckstine exclaimed. "When she opened her mouth I started sliding down in my chair. I couldn't believe this, what I was listening to." He was stunned by the quality of Vaughan's voice—its virtuosity in a performer so young and its beauty in a performer of any age.

Vaughan transformed the tune. Her version of "Body and Soul" sounded nothing like Holiday's. She made the song completely her own, something that had never been heard before, and she was a hit. "Sarah went out and did a job on that audience," Cooper wrote. She charmed the crowd with her lovely voice, her swoops, and vocal acrobatics as she easily (and tunefully) leapt octaves and ninths. "She sang with such poise and precision, if you closed your eyes you'd be sure she was about forty and had just flown in from the Paris Opera."[27]

"She had wrecked the house that night," Eckstine said, and as soon as Vaughan finished singing, he rushed backstage to meet her. "[I] grabbed her, said 'Look here, I want to talk to you.' She was just as naïve and scared as she could be: right away she assumed somebody was giving her a big deal." But it was indeed a big deal for the hopeful vocalist. By 1942, Billy Eckstine had already made a name for himself in the business. He'd just scored a series of hits with the Hines band and was well on his way to earning the moniker "the sepia Sinatra." Plus he was tall, well-dressed, and extremely handsome. Before Vaughan got too excited, however, Eckstine explained that he wanted his boss, Hines, to hear her. "I took her number and everything," he said.[28]

Back home in Newark, word had spread that Vaughan was going to sing at the Apollo, and her friends, neighbors, and entire church all tuned in to hear her on the radio. Members of her congregation must have been surprised to hear their soft-spoken organist singing at the famed theater. Evelyn Brooks, Vaughan's church friend and fellow organist, expressed a common sentiment: "When I heard Sarah, I said, 'Wow! Sarah's singing!' I didn't even recognize her."[29]

Vaughan won the competition that night. According to Cooper, she was the most polished and confident young singer he had ever encountered. "Sarah Vaughan was a superstar in the making."[30]

Perceptions of Vaughan changed after her Apollo performance. The organist and insignificant alto from the church choir, the girl who struggled to project, had become an accomplished vocalist. The aspiring jazz singer, the tomboy constantly underfoot in Newark's clubs, had taken her first big step toward a career in popular music. It must have been a thrilling accomplishment, but it came at a price. She was not following in the footsteps of the beloved Marian Anderson. "My mother was a little disappointed in me," Vaughan said in 1961. "She wanted me to go on in school and become a teacher or a choir director or something 'respectable.'"[31] But Vaughan had chosen another path, and her amateur-night win confirmed her show business aspirations, propelling her further into the world of jazz.

A month later, on Friday, November 20, 1942, Vaughan returned to the Apollo stage, this time sharing the bill with one of her idols: Ella Fitzgerald. Backed by Al Cooper's jump band, Vaughan sang four shows a day, with an extra show on Thursday and Sunday, and earned $40 for the week. "From then on it was shocksville," Vaughan told Marian McPartland in 1986. "I haven't got out of it yet. I was on the bill with Ella Fitzgerald! Oohh."[32]

"[Fitzgerald] stopped me from signing myself away to all of the agents around," Vaughan told reporter Sidney Fields in 1954. "We're friends to this day."[33] Many accounts suggested that Vaughan and Fitzgerald became fast friends. In all likelihood, however, the friendship evolved more gradually. Fitzgerald was notoriously reserved, and Vaughan was still an amateur just starting out. When McPartland asked Vaughan if she met or talked to Fitzgerald during that week, she chuckled, then responded, "Yeah . . . I was very, very, very, very, very, very, very, very, very shy."[34]

As promised, Eckstine told Hines about Vaughan. He explained that he had discovered something extraordinary: a girl singer who, instead of focusing primarily on her looks, could actually sing. He persuaded Hines to check her out during her return engagement at the Apollo. Hines did stop by the theater, although in his autobiography he said that he'd really gone to hear Fitzgerald. Vaughan wowed him instead. Hines admitted that he had been drinking all day, but remembered asking his friend June Clark, "Is that girl singing, or am I drunk or what?" And Clark responded: "No, that kid is singing, boy!"[35]

When the pair went backstage, they found Vaughan sitting on a Coca-Cola crate. Hines approached and offered her a job in his band, and according to Clark, she answered with an eager "Eeh-yuh."[36]

Vaughan, her friends, and her family all knew who Earl Hines was, and it's likely that they knew that Hines also had a reputation for discovering and cultivating new talent. By 1942, Earl "Fatha" Hines was an elder statesman of the jazz world and a celebrity within the African American community. A virtuoso pianist in his own right, he gained national attention in 1928 for his innovative comping on Louis Armstrong's now-classic Hot Five and Hot Seven recordings. Later that year, Hines founded his first big band, the house band for Chicago's luxurious Grand Terrace Ballroom. Hines and the band became household names as they appeared on national radio broadcasts and toured the country, becoming one of the first African American bands to regularly tour in the South. Added to that, the band scored a series of hits in the late 1930s and early 1940s, including the breakout blues "Jelly, Jelly" featuring Billy Eckstine from 1940.

"Now I had told the band about this little chick," Eckstine explained. "How I had never heard anything like it, and the guys were teasing me."[37] As a rule, Eckstine disliked "girl singers," the slang used to describe female vocalists fronting the big bands. "Except for Ella Fitzgerald, girl singers with orchestras were mainly clotheshorses, you know. They weren't picked for their vocal artistry; mainly they were pretty girls who looked good in gowns, and the male vocalists were the ones who carried the songs."[38] As a rule, girl singers were viewed as commercial concessions. Of course, some female vocalists had good voices, but Eckstine believed that even they were too concerned with being cute and not concerned enough about the business at hand, making music. "I mean, they rarely stop to think: this is music, after all; it isn't television," he reflected in 1954.[39] But Vaughan, who soon earned herself the nickname "Sassy," was different. She was a true musician. "When I heard Sarah, she was singing; she didn't care what she looked like, she wanted to sing," said Eckstine.[40]

After hearing Vaughan at the Apollo, Hines conceded that, yes, indeed, she could sing, but he wanted her to join the band during a rehearsal—an audition of sorts.

"So when Sassy comes down to the studio, the band looks at her curiously," Eckstine said. "It was after we had finished rehearsing for the day, and the guys were packing up their horns when she came in, looking young and kind of ordinary with her hair up on top. Most of the guys were doubtful, and some of them said, 'Man, are you kidding?'" Vaughan was nothing like the band's current vocalist, Madeline Greene, a glamorous beauty, who according to Eckstine "couldn't carry a tune in a bucket."[41] Vaughan didn't look the part of a girl singer, but she won them all over as soon as she opened her mouth.

"Do you know this, honey?" Hines asked as he began playing "There Are Such Things," the current No. 1 tune popularized by Frank Sinatra and Tommy Dorsey's orchestra. Vaughan took the mic in hand and began to sing. "You could see the guys stop their packing to stare at each other," Eckstine said. "By the time she had finished, all of them were around the piano—looking at the homely little girl who was singing like this, just wailing."[42] As soon as Hines saw the band's response to Vaughan, she was in. "There it was, my first job," Vaughan told *Metronome*'s Barry Ulanov in 1949. "Period."[43]

Sarah Vaughan made her debut as the Hines band vocalist and second pianist at the Apollo on January 15, 1943. "I was a nervous wreck, sitting up there at that piano," Vaughan said in 1974, "but Earl liked the looks of it. Lord, as much piano as he plays he didn't need me up there for the sound."[44] Hines was a master showman and understood that the presence of a second piano onstage, not to mention three vocalists instead of the usual two, would impress, lending the band an aura of sophistication and grandeur. Their week at the Apollo was a great success. The *Chicago Defender* reported that the show was "one of peppiest and classiest to hit the Apollo" and drew the largest Apollo crowds ever. The theater struggled to get patrons into their seats as lines snaked around the corner. Shows sold out, and the management had to add extra performances.[45]

Vaughan benefited from this exposure. The national black press reported that Hines had hired a sensational new pianist-vocalist, and the *New York Amsterdam News* published an in-depth profile of Vaughan, her first, in their January 30 issue. Proclaiming that she "came, saw, and conquered the Apollo's critical audience better than anyone since the early days of Ella Fitzgerald," they predicted that fame and fortune awaited Vaughan, assuming that she kept her wits about her. "Already, booking agents from the radio advertising agencies and other orchestra leaders are looking her over. A few went so far as to make definite offers but she turned 'em down with the excuse that 'Mr. Hines is handling my affairs and he knows best.'"[46]

As the first Vaughan interview on the record, the *New York Amsterdam News* piece provides glimpses into the young vocalist's mind-set. She is modest, unassuming, and committed to working hard. "People ask me where I studied voice and I can't answer them," she said. "I never figured on singing and I don't know where I got the voice from, if you call it that. I'm a member of Mount Zion Baptist Church, which is pastored by the Rev. Burke. I started singing there in the choir. I can't explain the rest. People started bragging and I kept on trying. I'm going to keep on, too, because I realize that fame is fleeting, if you don't keep on trying."[47]

And she did. After her successful week at the Apollo, Vaughan's trial period with Hines began in earnest. She packed what she would need into a paper bag, met the band at Penn Station, and went on the road. The band, now twenty strong, was a motley crew of new, young talent with a few veterans thrown in. First they headed to Baltimore for a week at the Royal Theater, and then made their way to Chicago for a series of concerts, including a Valentine's Day dance at the Savoy that ended in a case of jitterbug rage. Three thousand dancers had crowded onto the ballroom floor, and, reportedly, one man became enraged when he was inadvertently jostled. He pulled out his gun and began firing. Luckily, members of the band were unharmed, but four dancers required treatment for gunshot wounds.[48]

During Vaughan's early weeks with the Hines band, they continued to carry three vocalists (Eckstine, Greene, and Vaughan) instead of the usual two. But by early March, before they ventured south, the *Defender* reported that Greene had been given two weeks' furlough, without pay.[49] The band left Greene in Chicago with an understanding that they would recall her. That never happened. Vaughan had ousted her predecessor in less than eight weeks, and by the time the Hines band returned to New York for another engagement at the Apollo in April, Vaughan was the band's sole girl singer, earning $65 a week.[50] Her trial period was officially over.

2

"Ah *Mon Vieux,* This Chick Is Groovy!"

If Newark's music scene stood in for Vaughan's high school education, going on the road with Earl Hines and his band earned Vaughan an Ivy League degree. On the surface, Hines's band was just another swing band making the rounds of dance halls and theaters and headlining the occasional society benefit concert. By most measures, it would have been an education in its own right for the novice girl singer. But something else, something extraordinary, was happening in the Hines band behind the scenes. Hines excelled at finding new talent, and by the time Vaughan joined his band in 1943, the roster included the likes of trumpeter John Birks "Dizzy" Gillespie, formerly of the Cab Calloway band, and tenor saxophonist Charlie "Yardbird" Parker, a relative unknown from the Jay McShann territory band, plus Gail Brockman and Shorty McConnell on trumpet, Benny Green on trombone, and Rossiere "Shadow" Wilson on drums.

In hindsight, we know that these musicians were on the verge of changing jazz. During intense jam sessions between gigs and after hours, they embarked on a process of musical exploration—

challenging the known boundaries of jazz and swing, to create the innovative idiom that would become known as bebop, the foundation of modern jazz. And Sarah Vaughan was right in the thick of it.

"It was just like going to school. So that's how fortunate I was," Vaughan said years later.[1] "I was sitting up there shaking in my boots. But that's when I first realized I had something going there. I learned an awful lot from those guys, too. I just learned music, music and more music."[2] The emerging bebop-pers were a studious, intellectual crowd, committed to mastering the fundamentals of swing and music theory and then transform-ing the expected into something entirely new and different. The lilting, very danceable rhythms of swing were replaced by wick-edly fast tempos, complex syncopation, and drummers "drop-ping bombs," unpredictable explosions of sound. Melodic lines spanned the full range of an instrument, or in Vaughan's case the voice, and often incorporated disjunct leaps and bounds. Hum-mable tunes became runs of fast eighth and sixteenth notes filled with syncopation that were then organized into asymmetrical phrases. The established harmonic language of swing grew and expanded to include bold clashing tones and dissonance. And beboppers brought all of this together to craft improvisations that ventured further afield and were more daring and dramatic than those of their swing counterparts. They brought an unprec-edented complexity and rigor to jazz. In short, bebop musicians were developing a new language for musical abstraction, and it sounded innovative, fresh, and self-consciously modern.[3]

"I used to stare at [Parker and Gillespie] in amazement," Vaughan said. "But I used to feel it; you know, [Dizzy and I] used to sit on the stand and we'd get to swinging so much, Dizzy would come down and grab me and start jitterbugging all over the place. It was swinging."[4] Vaughan was fascinated with Gil-lespie's and Parker's complete mastery of their instruments; the speed, agility, and brilliance with which they played; and the unusual harmonies on which they built their solos. She loved the environment of collaboration, innovation, and creativity. The thrill of musical exploration and the enthusiasm of her brilliant peers, who just like her had curious minds and an intense work ethic verging on obsession. Vaughan felt a kinship with her new bandmates.

Most important, however, Sarah Vaughan had the chops to hold her own. The awe and genuine respect she had for her new peers was returned in kind. "She came equipped," Eckstine proclaimed in 1991 as he discussed her earliest days with the Hines band.[5] No doubt her training as a pianist was paying off. "While I was playing piano in the [high] school band, I learned to take music apart and analyze the notes and put it back together again," she explained in 1961. "By doing this, I learned to sing differently from other singers."[6] In other words, she could sit down at the piano and play beautiful progressions while singing and improvising her own countermelodies. She understood harmony and thus had the theoretical and technical know-how, not to mention the vocal mastery, to keep up with Gillespie and Parker.

"[Sarah] was as good a musician as anybody in the band," Gillespie wrote in his autobiography. "She could play the piano, knew all of the chords, and played terrific chords behind us."[7] And she had good ears, meaning that in the spontaneous, free-flowing world of improvised bebop she could hear, not just intellectually grasp, the harmonic changes. This ensured that Vaughan could follow, and often dictate, the musical direction of a piece, regardless of where it went in that particular moment. She had the talent to lead the band.

All bebop musicians needed these skills, and as the movement became more popular, beboppers relied on cutting contests—fierce, testosterone-fueled musical battles with overt displays of virtuosity—to weed out poseurs and bebop wannabes. During after-hours sessions at the now-legendary Minton's Playhouse and Monroe's Uptown House, both in New York, seasoned beboppers tested the mettle of newcomers by transforming popular songs of the day into harmonic obstacle courses. Most musicians were proficient in the familiar, "easy" keys, so beboppers opted for the "harder" keys with lots of flats and sharps. Suddenly, without warning, they would change keys or play each chorus in a new key. One favorite trick treated competitors to a tour of the tonics, with the first chorus in A-flat, the next in A, followed by B-flat, B, and so on. It was a musical tongue twister that required enormous mental clarity and technical prowess. Chorus after chorus, one musician tried to best the other.

Eventually this experimental, after-hours work made its way onto the bandstand. Charlie Parker became revered for his treatment of "Cherokee," a three-minute pop song that he expanded into thirty minutes of lightning-fast riffs and changes that showcased his near machine-like virtuosity. And the slow, romantic ballad "How the High Moon" became an intricate, up-tempo anthem for the progressive beboppers.

But this level of technical proficiency was not the norm, especially for vocalists. Many could not even read music, let alone play an instrument. In fact, early in his career, Eckstine fell into this category too (ironic given his harsh opinion of Madeline Greene and other girl singers). After an embarrassing audition with Hollywood producers, however, he taught himself how to read music and play the trumpet and valve trombone, which ultimately put him in good stead with the beboppers he later considered his colleagues.

On the whole, the bar was set fairly low for vocalists and even lower for female musicians of any kind. Widespread stereotypes perpetuated the notion that women simply did not have the intellect or musical proficiency to match their male, instrumental counterparts. And many musicians, critics, and jazz fans believed that women had no real place in jazz. Rather, they were mere commercial fluff, attractions to draw in less knowledgeable patrons. During the 1940s (and even today), the reality was that most women were not viewed as real musicians. Except for a handful of women, including Sarah Vaughan.

Her colleagues in the Hines band clearly recognized her talent, and soon the critics did too. Upon first hearing Vaughan at the Apollo in April 1943, just months after she joined the band,

British-born critic Leonard Feather, then writing for the magazine *Metronome,* another leading jazz publication, declared:

> It will be a long time before I forget "Body and Soul."
> Toward the end she twisted the melody into a startling
> descending sequence of ninths. Every musician in the au-
> dience at that moment probably thought to himself, my
> God, this girl isn't just a singer. She's a musician. She
> knows changes. And what a quality![8]

The critics were not the only converts; audiences loved her too. Eckstine recalled, "Earl would bring [Sarah] down to sing, and boy, she wrecked everywhere she went."[9]

During Vaughan's first year with the Earl Hines band, she crisscrossed the country more than once. After her successful trial at the Apollo and follow-up stints in Baltimore and Chicago, the band headed off to Boston, then south to Jackson, Mississippi, in March 1943. In April, they journeyed back again to the Midwest for a tour of theaters, this time with blues legend Ethel Waters joining the revue. Then Vaughan and the band finished off the month with another week at the Apollo. Next, Hines and his band headlined an all-star, all-black unit, featuring jump blues star Louis Jordan, in a tour of southern army camps. Between May 7 and June 3, twenty-eight days, the group hit twenty-five bases. Hines's band stayed in the South for the rest of the summer, except for a quick detour to New York for a week at the Apollo in July, and then returned to the Midwest at the end of August for gigs in Chicago and Detroit. Finally, they had a short break, followed by rehearsals in New York and a week at the Apollo, and they were back on the road by late September. The band finished off 1943 with appearances in Washington, D.C., and in 1944 it all began again. It was an exhausting year, but by no means unusual.

Vaughan was eighteen when she went on the road with the Hines band. Except for her clandestine journeys to New York, only ten miles from Newark, she had never been away from home. "Everything was new to me," she told Max Jones in 1981. "I'd never had so much fun. Yes, I had lots of fun in there, and yet I was shocked—scared to death really, 'cos I didn't really know all this sort of thing went on." The smoking and casual drinking that she began as a teenager trying to fit into Newark's music scene had not prepared her for the seedy, very adult underworld of addicts, pushers, and hustlers that Vaughan discovered on the road. "You know, I was just a young singer from Newark."[10]

When Jones asked about her life on the road with the Hines band, Vaughan chuckled and then responded, "Yeah, one girl and sixteen guys; what the hell. What else can I say?"[11] She had little or no privacy and rarely had time alone, away from the men in the band. If they were not rehearsing or performing, they were on their way to the next gig. Popular bands could easily travel fifty thousand miles a year, often making jumps of 200 to 450 miles a night. In the 1930s and early 1940s, buses were the norm. A home on wheels, they provided not only transportation but also a place to eat, sleep, socialize, and at times even practice. As World War II intensified, however, rationing of rubber and gas eventually led to a complete ban on nonessential driving in January 1943. Just as Vaughan went on the road, the big bands started traveling by train, and the life of touring musicians became even more complicated.[12]

Musicians were bound to train schedules and often spent hours, usually in the early morning, waiting for the next train. Then they found themselves on crowded, overbooked trains, standing in the aisles as they clutched their instruments and luggage. By the time they transported themselves and their gear from the station to the next club or dance hall, they barely had enough time to change clothes before going onstage.

For the boys in the Hines band, this was doable. They wore uniforms, usually modeled after a suit and tie. They had short hair and could "clean up," when they had the chance, in a restroom. Vaughan, the sole woman in the band, had a harder time. She was expected to wear fancy gowns and exude an effortless glamour and beauty, an extreme femininity, complete with immaculate hair and makeup. But stockings ran. Gowns creased and crumpled in suitcases, and there was often no time or place to press them, not to mention clean and mend them. While in the Hines band, Vaughan reportedly got a cigarette burn in the back of her only dress, a long, flowing white gown. From then on, she never turned around while onstage, making sure that her backside faced the orchestra at all times.

Being a girl singer required a certain kind of woman, and according to Eckstine, Vaughan fit the bill perfectly: "A girl on the road, man, she's got a tough job, man. . . . She's got to be a certain type of chick. Because when the bus stops [the guys] run to get the rooms. They're going to run all over her. They ain't goin' to pick up her bags. Bullshit to that. She's got to be a strong person and a liked person. If it is one of those broads with her nose in the air, oh, she's in trouble. Sass was perfect on the road with the guys."[13]

"Sarah Vaughan acted just like one of the boys," Gillespie recalled. "She put herself in that position, one of the boys, just another musician."[14] Unlike many girl singers who isolated themselves in the hotel when not working, Vaughan constantly hung out with the band. She ate, drank, and smoked with them; went to the movies with them; played ball with them, ran foot races, and roughhoused with them. If an argument broke out, she'd ball up her fists, ready to box, just like everybody else in the band. And when a separate hotel room was not available for her, she bunked with the guys too.[15] On the long train rides, the band often played cards and dice to pass the time. Vaughan didn't shy away from gambling; she was in on the band's many jokes and pranks; and she even mastered the art of cussing and swearing, earning herself the nickname "Sailor." "I remember Ella [Fitzgerald] never acted like one of the boys; she always played the role of a lady," Gillespie wrote. "But you could say anything you wanted to in front of 'Sailor,' uh, I mean, Sarah. She'd use the same language I used with the guys."[16]

Pianist John Malachi agreed: "Sarah was just so unique, because she wasn't like a lot of girls would have been, that you had to treat her different or something like that." A few days after he began working with Vaughan in the summer of 1944, he remembered sharing a cab with her to the train station in Washington, D.C., as they embarked on their tour of the South. They were both burdened down with luggage, so Malachi, in an act of chivalry, opened and held the door for Vaughan. "And Sarah, this girl that I hardly know, I've just smiled and spoken to on the bandstand a couple of times and at rehearsal, looks at me and says, 'What are you standing up there looking at me for, fool? Go on through the door.'" He did, and as Vaughan followed, she exclaimed, "You damn fool." "It was never an angry thing," Malachi insisted, "but I was more hurt than ever, because I didn't understand that kind of behavior, you know, coming from a girl." He soon realized that Vaughan not only expected to be treated just like the men in the band, she insisted upon it. "You couldn't do anything for her," he recalled in 1983. "You talk about women's lib. She was liberated long before any woman that I know."[17]

Life on the road was difficult anywhere, but conditions became nearly unbearable as soon as black bands ventured down south. Although the Thirteenth Amendment had abolished slavery in 1865, southern blacks still lived within a strict caste system. Jim Crow and its laws of segregation dictated every aspect of their lives: where they could live, eat, work, and go to school, and where and with whom they could socialize; Jim Crow even dictated the rules of the road. Driving etiquette in the Mississippi Delta, for example, forbade black drivers from overtaking cars with white passengers on unpaved roads. A car with a black driver and black passengers might stir up dust that would get on the white passengers in the car it passed. And the laws and social customs of Jim Crow varied from city to city, county to county, leaving black travelers extremely vulnerable as they navigated a constantly shifting landscape of rules and expectations.[18]

Yet black musicians had no choice. Many of the most lucrative gigs, at the best theaters, clubs, and hotel ballrooms in the North, only booked white bands (regardless of their skill level), so even the most famous black bands had to tour the South in order to stay afloat.

Each and every tour of the South brought a series of indignities. Black musicians traveled on segregated trains, performed in segregated clubs, and were not allowed to stay in white-owned hotels or eat at white restaurants. If they were lucky, a white friend, perhaps a manager, might order takeout for them to eat outside, behind the restaurant. But usually black musicians had to search out the black district of town. When kind black families couldn't take them in, they had no choice but to stay in the substandard yet overpriced lodgings that catered to African Americans. According to bassist Milt Hinton,

> A hotel might charge you five or six dollars, and man, it was terrible. One bathroom 'way down the hall. They wouldn't even change the sheets on the bed sometimes. Bed bugs, roach-infested places that they didn't clean up. And they just figured, the hell with it. They didn't have to clean them up, because we had no other place to go. And they were all black-owned. And we really resented this highly, because they knew that they had us. And our same brother white bands were staying in hotels, and the guys were paying two or three dollars a day, in nice white hotels.[19]

And the food was awful: "'axle-grease fried chicken' or dried-up ham sandwiches on even more dried-up bread."[20] During his early years on the road, Billy Eckstine developed the habit of inspecting his sandwiches before eating them to make sure that ground glass, vermin feces, or other contaminants hadn't been added, and he did this for the rest of his life.[21] Making matters worse, producer Teddy Reig described how when bands did get to eat in a restaurant, the owners would "take all the prices down and charge us three times as much. And then the *pièce de résis-*

tance: the promoter would let people in for half a buck apiece to watch us eat!"[22]

The system was not fair, and the inequities that black bands encountered on the road were compounded by the expectations of many southern whites. Although they were eager to enjoy black talent, southern whites insisted that blacks remain subservient. Any transgression, real or perceived, could result in violence, and even death. When Vaughan began touring the South in the 1940s, lynchings still took place, and the smallest breach of Jim Crow laws could set off an angry mob of whites in search of vigilante justice. Black victims were regularly tortured—beaten beyond recognition, dismembered, and burned—often in a carnival-like atmosphere, complete with white onlookers, including families with young children, cheering on the violence. The threat was real. In 1980, Vaughan told pianist Butch Lacy how, while she was working with the Billy Eckstine band in the south, the Ku Klux Klan showed up at one of their gigs, wearing their robes, with guns in hand, and began shooting. Vaughan and the rest of the band ran to their bus, and as they sped out of town, the Klan lined both sides of Main Street, shooting holes in the bus. The band escaped unharmed by lying on the floor.[23]

All African Americans knew the South's history of racial violence, yet many black musicians, especially northerners, experienced culture shock when they toured the South. They simply did not have an intuitive understanding of the South's ingrained racism, and they unwittingly offended southern whites, perhaps by expressing an opinion, asserting too much autonomy and independence, or otherwise stepping out of line. Some musicians, however, deliberately provoked confrontations. They viewed themselves as skilled, highly trained professionals. Many of them had achieved international critical acclaim and were celebrities within the African American and general music communities. They bristled at the treatment from southern whites, rebelled, and stood up for their rights as artists and human beings.

While Vaughan was with the Hines band, Gillespie was attacked in Pine Bluff, Arkansas, during a white dance. The musicians couldn't mingle with the crowd or sit at the bar during intermission, so Gillespie stayed on the bandstand to practice the piano. A white man requested a tune and threw a nickel on the stage. Gillespie refused, threw the nickel back, and kept on playing. Later that night, when the hall was empty, Gillespie used the "whites only" bathroom. As he came out, he was hit on the head with a bottle and grabbed by five men. He struggled and tried to fight back, but he was bleeding and outnumbered. Luckily, Charlie Parker intervened and yelled, "You took advantage of my friend, you cur!" "That was funny," Gillespie wrote in his autobiography, "because I know that peckawood didn't know what a cur was." Still, Gillespie required nine stitches to his head.[24]

Vaughan remembered other moments of defiance, where the tables were turned. "One time we were on a train," she said during her interview for Gillespie's autobiography. "We were coming from down South. You know that train was split, colored and white, segregated. One white fella was sitting by the train door eating chicken, and he threw the chicken bones back in our part."[25] Conditions in the Jim Crow car were substandard and often unbearable. The car lacked air conditioning or heat, making it terribly hot during the summer and cold during the winter. It was overcrowded, especially during the war years when more people used the trains. It was less safe: positioned at the front of the train, just behind the engine, the Jim Crow car took the brunt of the impact in any collision, resulting in more damage and casualties. It was loud, and it was dirty. Soot from the engine flew back into the car, covering everyone with a layer of grime and dust. Conditions were so unpleasant in the first car of the train that white passengers refused to sit there. Black passengers ended their journeys filthy, the musicians among them struggling to look presentable for their next gig. So when that "white fella" began using the Jim Crow car as his personal garbage can, Vaughan and her bandmates were incensed. But they waited until the train arrived in Washington, D.C., the official ending point of Jim Crow. "We had some friends of [Eckstine]'s who came from Washington that used to just travel around with us, just for the hell of it," she continued. "Very tough hustlers from Washington. They didn't say nothing, didn't bother him until we got in. We pulled into Washington, and that's when it all started."[26] The band got off the train and waited for the white man on the platform. "God, it was bloody. They knocked that guy back up in the train. I even kicked him a little bit," a smiling Vaughan elaborated during an unusually candid interview with Dick Cavett in 1980. "Then I ran ahead to see if the police were coming. And they were. There was a grove of them coming. I ran down to tell the guys 'Let's make it.' So as we were going up [the stairs], the police were running down past us to find out what all of the disturbance was. So we got away with that one."[27]

Without Jim Crow, the North was better, but the band still encountered plenty of discrimination. Years later, Vaughan told pianist Mike Wofford, who worked with her in 1979 and 1983, that Philadelphia was one of the worst cities for visiting black musicians. While Vaughan was touring with the Earl Hines band, Hines took the crew to a clothier to buy new uniforms. "They went to this warehouse at the back of the clothing store . . . and the guys' suits in various sizes were on the rack there and they were only able to point to the suit that they felt would probably be the best for them. They couldn't touch them or try them on," Wofford recalled. "I remember Sarah telling me that with a disgusted look."[28]

Another time, Vaughan described waiting for a train after performing at a dance in Wilmington, Delaware, where "they still had the whipping post downtown in the middle of the street," she told Les Tomkins in 1977. Eckstine, affectionately known as "B.," wanted to get his shoes shined, but the white teenager manning the booth refused. "On the station, all the cats were laying out there, sleeping, waiting for the train to come in. So B. walks up, and says: 'Hey, fellows—there's a guy back there who says he don't shine no nigger's shoes!' So the guys said: 'Oh, my goodness. Here we go again.'"[29] In a show of unity, the entire band got up, slowly walked toward the young man, and got in line.

Outnumbered and confronted by a group of fifteen black men demanding service at one in the morning in an otherwise empty train station, the shoe shiner acquiesced. The band quickly retreated. "We left town by foot. Everybody spread out and said, 'I'll see you at the next gig,'" Vaughan said, in a later account of the incident.[30] "Yeah, we had fun doing things like that. It made life's problems bearable. B. was always the little instigator; he liked to start things."[31]

Vaughan, on the other hand, was not a little instigator. Perhaps the confrontational style of Eckstine, Gillespie, and the other boys in the band did not suit her shy, more introverted personality. There was no need to offend or provoke. And perhaps, as a woman, she understood that she was more vulnerable to the advances of strange men and the violence that they might bring with them. Instead, Vaughan, like many of her contemporaries, played the part expected of her. "When we went down South," she said, "if we were supposed to say 'Yessuh' and all that, we would, to keep the peace, but we always had a plan in mind."[32]

Early on Vaughan realized the power of her voice to unite and bring people together. She was able to get southern whites to see and hear her as an individual rather than a racial stereotype—an impressive feat at the time. "Before we left, all those guys were saying: 'Boy, that girl sure can sing,'" she explained. "After we got with 'em, we'd speak in our natural voices, and they'd say: 'Well, there's some good niggers from up North.'"[33]

By the time the Hines band returned north at the end of August in 1943, Billy Eckstine had had enough. "Hell, no! I don't want to go down South anymore, Earl," he said.[34] He had just gotten married and decided to stay put in New York City and work on 52nd Street, *the* hotbed of progressive jazz. Eckstine had aspirations of becoming a solo act, perhaps even starting his own band.

The innovations of the young, up-and-coming beboppers had whetted Eckstine's appetite for the avant-garde, and he wanted to learn more. But Hines was changing directions in favor of a more commercial, novelty-driven band. In September Hines, always the showman, added an all-girl string section, a harp player, and the Bluebonnets, a female vocal quartet that had performed with the unit during their tour of military bases earlier that summer. According to Eckstine, when he put in his resignation, nine other guys followed, including many of the band's most progressive musicians, such as Gillespie, Wilson, Parker, and Benny Harris. Vaughan, however, stayed behind.

Eckstine had spent almost five years with the Hines band and a few years before that working in Buffalo, Detroit, and Chicago.[35] But Vaughan was just eight months into her career as a professional musician. She needed more time to develop and establish herself. Plus, she was under contract with Hines for a year, until January 1944. The Hines band meant job security in a notoriously fickle industry where it was hard for girl singers to find regular work. While there were four trumpets, four or five saxophones, and four trombones in each swing band, there was only one permanent girl singer and many candidates vying for the position. After Hines dismissed Madeline Greene, the vocalist that Vaughan replaced, Greene spent months bouncing between short-term gigs, struggling to find steady employment. Vaughan was smart. She had a good job and kept it, staying on with Hines for another ten months as the band made its rounds of the Midwest and mid-Atlantic states, all while waiting for her next opportunity.

Nine months after leaving Hines, Eckstine had found representation and financial backing to start his own band. He installed Dizzy Gillespie as his musical director, convinced Charlie Parker to join, and then recruited many of his old friends from Hines's band. After three weeks of rehearsals, Eckstine's fledgling band was ready to make its debut in Wilmington, Delaware, on June 9, 1944. But they still needed a girl singer, and that's when Eckstine called Vaughan. Only then, with the promise of consistent work and another opportunity to create alongside her fellow bebop innovators, did she leave Hines to join Eckstine in his new venture.

Billy Eckstine's unit was a magnet for progressive musical talent. In addition to Gillespie, Parker, and Vaughan, drummers Art Blakey and Shadow Wilson; tenor saxophonists Dexter Gordon, Gene Ammons, Lucky Thompson, and Budd Johnson; pianist John Malachi; and trumpeters Fats Navarro and Howard McGhee were all on the band's payroll during its first year. The band's roster, Vaughan's closest colleagues and collaborators, was a veritable who's-who of the emerging bebop movement. The experimentation that began in the Hines band primarily behind the scenes and after hours took center stage. Eckstine's band became the first bebop big band, a designation that has cemented its position in the history of jazz.

Early on, however, the Eckstine band struggled to establish itself, and they had to make money. To do that the band had to tour (ironically, considering Eckstine's disdain) the South. After the gig in Delaware, they headed down to Washington, D.C., then further south into North Carolina, South Carolina, Florida, Alabama, Louisiana, Texas, Oklahoma, and finally Missouri.[36]

After weeks of grueling one-nighters, the band took up residence in St. Louis in late July. Originally, they were booked into the white-owned Plantation Club, but upon arriving at the club on the first night Eckstine insisted that they enter through the front door rather than the back as expected. The club management, a collection of gangsters, was furious and fired the band on the spot, before they had played a single note. Eckstine, thinking on his feet, swapped gigs with George Hudson's band performing across town at the black-owned Riviera Club.

Living in St. Louis in 1944 was an eighteen-year-old Miles Davis. Just out of high school, Davis idolized Gillespie, and when he learned that Eckstine's band was at the Riviera, he picked up his trumpet and hurried to the club. After he hung out at the club for several days, Gillespie asked him to sit in with the band to sub for a sick musician. Davis was simply blown away by Gillespie and Parker. "Sarah Vaughan was there also, and she's a motherfucker too. Then and now," he wrote in his autobiography.

"Sarah sounding like Bird and Diz and them two playing every-thing! I mean they would look at Sarah like she was just another horn. You know what I mean? She'd be singing 'You Are My First Love' and Bird would be soloing. Man, I wish everybody could have heard that shit!"[37] The experience changed Davis's life. In that moment, he decided to move to New York and pursue a ca-reer in music.

Not all audiences were as enthusiastic about the Eckstine band and the new music that they played. "Everybody was star-ing at us a lot during that time," Vaughan said in 1977. "We'd play dances, and people would be standing and staring."[38] Musicians were thrilled, but general listeners didn't know what to make of the crazy rhythms and frenetic solos that the Eckstine band presented. A reviewer in Cleveland lamented that while Vaughan was great as she "chirped 'I'll Walk Alone' in a voice that was soft and pleasing," the band as a whole was "much too noisy," and that the antics of Gillespie were over the top and distracting.[39] Another reviewer, writing about the band's gig at the Riviera in St. Louis, didn't like Vaughan either. "We suggest that Eckstine should get a girl vocalist who looks better in her clothes and is more suitable for his type of ballads," the review read, according to Eckstine. "They were writing about Sarah Vaughan, but never stopped to hear this girl's voice. They were looking at her as a sex object, instead of listening to her sing. That's what we were confronted with!"[40] It was an uphill battle, and, in 1954, Eckstine conceded, "I was losing a lot of loot with the band because—well, it is history now—the people were not quite ready for that type of music."[41] Audiences were still crazy about dancing, and bebop was not danceable. "Only a few, that knew what we were doing, and could understand the rhythm and stuff, would be jitterbug-ging around forever in a little circle in the corner," Vaughan said. "When we played slow tunes, everyone would dance, but once we got back into those fast things, they would stare again." Yet Vaughan insisted that the music they played was not a deliber-ate act of experimentation or innovation. Rather, it was an effort to be artistically true to themselves, to play music that inspired them and educated their listeners. "They call that the bebop era, but I call it the good music era," she said.[42]

Even in the face of repeated rejection and the risk of financial failure, they all continued to put themselves out there, make themselves vulnerable, in order to create new, innovative music that truly expressed their artistic ideals and aesthetic. They looked out for one another, and these experiences fostered an intimacy, trust, and bond not unlike that found in a family. Still, it was difficult being the only woman in the band, just as it might be difficult being the only girl in a family with eight brothers. "It was a very rough band," said Vaughan.[43] "Everybody in that band had a pistol," Gillespie wrote. "If you went down South, you'd better have one and a lot of ammunition. We were musicians first, though, and fun-loving peaceable men. But don't start no shit."[44] Vaughan did not carry a gun; instead, she used her hatpin to protect herself.[45] The violence they encountered on the road, especially in the South, sometimes found its way into the group dynamics. The guys in the band were young, brash, and assertive, and without the calming leadership of Earl Hines, a jazz elder, it's possible that Eckstine's band was more rowdy and raucous. Eckstine in particular had a reputation for being extremely tough. He was known to knock guys out at the slightest provocation. And his treatment of women was notorious. Davis described Eckstine, who was married at the time, introducing his girlfriend of the moment as "my woman." She objected and insisted that Eckstine tell Davis her name. "B. turned around and said, 'Bitch, shut up!' He slapped the shit out of her right there," Davis wrote. The woman was furious as Eckstine laughed at her, then said, "Aw, shut up, bitch. Wait 'til I get some rest. I'm gonna knock your fucking ass out!"[46]

By all accounts Eckstine was more fraternal with Vaughan. In the band she was a musician before she was a woman. But she was still a woman—a very young, relatively inexperienced woman. When she first joined Hines's band, Eckstine remembered, "Myself and guys in the band like Shadow Wilson, Bird and Diz, Benny Harris and Shorty McConnell, we raised Sarah and showed her practically everything that the music business was about."[47] Vaughan agreed. "Not only did I learn much stage presence from Billy, but several other members of the Hines band were like fathers to me," she said.[48]

The guys in the band were her fathers and brothers, and much like a younger sibling, the little sister, she wanted to do everything that they did. Drugs were a part of life on the road. Marijuana, and increasingly heroin, had become essential components of a black hip or "hepster" lifestyle and identity. Drug use provided refuge from a racist world, while acting as a form of protest against a society that did not include them. And as musicians, it symbolized their membership in a unique, insider club, one that valued creativity, spontaneity, and freedom.[49] Vaughan saw musicians using heroin and wanted to try it too, so she finally approached Charlie Parker. "Bird, come on. Help me out, man. You know I want to know what it is. I want to know. I got to know. I got to know. Get me high. Get me some of that stuff," pianist Carl Schroeder remembered Vaughan saying as she told him the story during the 1970s. "No. I can't. I ain't got time—baby, get out of here. Leave me alone," Parker replied. But Vaughan persisted, and Bird continued to refuse, telling her that she did not want to try this. He knew far too well the horrors of heroin addiction. Eventually, however, Parker relented. He took her money, left the room, returned with a syringe, and injected her with it. "So, how does that feel?" he asked. "Oh yes. This is—oh yes. I like this," she said, "I feel good. Mmm mmm." Only later did she learn that Parker had shot her full of water. "Think about the amount of love that Bird showed to Sarah in that. He said he would, but he couldn't bring himself to," Schroeder concluded. "I find that story to be so touching between these immense figures: Bird and Sarah Vaughan. The simple, dignified act of refusing."[50] In 1977, when asked about her days with Charlie Parker, she alluded to his heroin addiction, adding, "I never got that far."[51] But it was well known, especially as her career progressed, that she regularly used marijuana and cocaine.

While the guys were protective of their newest vocalist, nurturing her along as she adjusted to the world of show business, they could also be strict, almost punitive disciplinarians. "Later, when she was in my band," Eckstine said, "if she came late for a job we didn't bother to fine her. I would never fine Sarah if she was late. I'd turn her over my knee and whip her ass. She wouldn't often be late after that. And when she did come in late she looked around cautiously. Because one of us was behind the door to grab her and beat the hell out of her. So Sarah just came up right as a bunch of the guys: just as a musician."[52]

Eckstine is affectionate and good-humored. He seemed proud of his role in Vaughan's early career and her ability to take it, just like one of the boys. Maybe she had to. "They kept me in order," she said.[53] "They would beat me if I didn't listen to them!" Years later, she remembered one instance in particular:

> One time, I was late going to Indianapolis, where the band was playing a dance; I was having so much fun in Chicago, I decided to stay: "I'll see you guys later." When I got there, the dance was just over; I walked in and said: "Hi, guys, Sorry I'm late." So they all formed a circle round me and beat me to death! After getting hit on the arm by fifteen guys, when I left there both my arms were down by my sides. I couldn't move. And I was never late any more. Yes, I could do no wrong in that band. If I did, I would do it no more. I was very fortunate, compared with other girls I've seen in orchestras.[54]

It's hard to know exactly what other girl singers endured in order for Vaughan to consider herself lucky in comparison, but popular stereotypes of the time labeled women in the music industry as "loose women," and, as a result, what is now considered sexual harassment was rampant. Industry men—club owners, bookers, and musicians—often expected companionship and sexual favors from female performers. There were reports of rape from girl singers traveling with otherwise all-male bands, although this aspect of life on the road has rarely been discussed or explored. Vaughan never mentioned this kind of abuse, and pianist Malachi, who often shared a room with Vaughan, insisted that their relationship was always platonic. "Sarah's the kind of person that if she didn't want to be bothered, you had a good fight on your hands," he explained. "She could be just like one of the guys, and the guys did not bother her."[55]

But Vaughan did have her romances. By September 1944, after three months of touring with the Eckstine band, she had become involved with trumpeter Marian "Boonie" Hazel. During a gig in Boston, one of the guys in the band came backstage between shows and said, "Boonie, man, there's a pretty girl back there who just told me to come back here and see if you were in the dressing room. She wants you to come out there." "Oh yeah?" replied Boonie, interested and flattered by the attention. "What's her name?" His bandmate told him. "Okay, tell her I'll be out in a minute," said Boonie. Vaughan was not happy. She looked at him and said, "You go through that door and I'll kick your ass." "Shit," he said, rolling his eyes. He ignored her, put on his coat, and started for the door. "Sarah put her foot in his behind, and they turned around and they went at it in the dressing room!" said Malachi. "And Sarah boxed just like any man, you know."[56]

Sarah Vaughan didn't take any flak. She had clear ideas of what she would and would not tolerate, but it took her time to establish these boundaries with the men she worked and socialized with. She needed to figure out her role in the social hierarchy of the band and what she, as the only woman, should and could expect, and, ultimately, what she wanted. Years later, stride pianist Judy Carmichael remembers Vaughan telling her, "Yes, [Billy Eckstine] was a real snake, but I have to give it to him because he was the one that told [me] I didn't have to sleep with everybody in the band." Vaughan was a woman of few words, but when she did say something, those around her took note. "And she just left it there, and I didn't think she meant it to be heavy," said Carmichael, a white woman who was only twenty-six when she befriended Vaughan in the early 1980s. "It broke my heart. Yes, it was deep."

Reflecting on her own experiences as a young woman entering the world of jazz in the late 1970s and early 1980s and hanging out with the Basie band, Carmichael explained, "You're with
a bunch of guys who are used to getting whatever they want,
because the women are throwing themselves at them." Women
were available for sex, and it was all very casual. "I was a young
golden lock; I could have been taken advantage of," Carmichael
continued. "I was just wandering around with no women men-
tors, no real [mentors]. Sarah was in a way, but she certainly
wasn't saying, 'Look out for this, look out for that.'"[57] Like
Vaughan forty years earlier, Carmichael had to find her own
way. Fortunately, the musicians that she hung out with from the
Basie band respected her as a musician. "The Basie band had a
protective shield around me, because I was so much younger,"
Carmichael explained. "I wouldn't get into the whole thing, and
the word went out that, 'She's not to be messed with. Don't even
hit on her.'"[58]

Eckstine protected Vaughan too. He reminded her that she
was a musician. Sleeping with the guys in the band was not part
of her job description. She had a choice. He also reminded her,
although more subtly, that there was a different set of expectations for men and women. While it was socially acceptable for
men to be promiscuous, Eckstine included, this was not the case
for women. Double standards aside, in his own way Eckstine was
safeguarding Vaughan's virtue. Nonetheless, living and working
in a climate that objectified women and allowed the sexual assault of women must have been unnerving for Vaughan. And it
is ironic that within this world that offered her so much creative
freedom, not to mention the opportunity to explore new places
and people, there were still clear limitations on what she, the only
woman in the band, could and could not do. Her tolerance of
this reality, despite what she may or may not have experienced,
was the price she had to pay for "equality." To be considered one
of the guys, both socially and musically, she had to accept whatever they doled out.

Was there a double standard? Did her male colleagues receive similar punishment for similar lapses in personal and professional judgment? Probably not. Take Charlie Parker. As Parker's drug addiction escalated, his behavior became more and more erratic, and less professional. While in the Hines band, Eckstine remembered Parker pawning his horn and missing more shows than he made, but Hines simply fined him, and the other guys in the band would shame him, explaining that, musically, they needed him. The band just didn't sound right with four instead of five reeds. Parker also had a collection of quirks: he wore sunglasses onstage; he often slept on the bandstand during performances; and he didn't like to wear shoes when he played, preferring instead to rest his feet on top of his shoes. More than once he forgot to put his shoes back on before rushing out front for his solos. And others described him passing out cold during solos. Parker was regularly fined, and occasionally fired, but for the most part bandleaders tolerated his many eccentricities, and, unlike for Vaughan, there are no accounts suggesting that these infractions earned Parker a beating or any other kind of physical confrontation.

In order to survive in Eckstine's band and the music world at large, Vaughan had to fend for herself. She needed to know when to fight and when to let things go. One battle she did choose to wage involved records. While with the Hines band, Vaughan and her bandmates were prohibited from making commercial recordings; concerned that phonograph records were replacing live entertainment and thus causing musicians to lose work, the American Federation of Musicians initiated an industry-wide recording ban on August 1, 1942. By the time she rejoined Eckstine in June 1944, the ban was finally winding down. At last, Vaughan and the other aspiring beboppers could make records. That same month Eckstine signed a yearlong contract with DeLuxe, and *Down Beat* reported that Vaughan and Eckstine would share vocals on the upcoming releases.[59] But nothing happened. Fall became winter as the band toured the Midwest and New England, and even though they had made multiple stops in New York, where the band recorded, Vaughan still had not made her first record. She was tired of waiting and made a fuss. "They were recording, and I was just sitting there wondering how come I couldn't make a record. But [the label] wouldn't let me make none; so I just boo-hooed so. . . . I mean, you could hear me all over the place," she said in 1977. "I cried about it. I cried so bad, till Billy Eckstine said, 'Jesus—let her make a record 'cause this noise is about to kill me.'"[60]

On December 5, 1944, Vaughan finally made her recording debut with "I'll Wait and Pray," and while she had to fight for the opportunity, the band fought for her right to record too. The session included three ballads, all featuring Eckstine; an instrumental number composed by the band's pianist, John Malachi; and a blues-based duet for tenor saxophonists Dexter Gordon and Gene Ammons. Vaughan was set to sing on the sixth and final side. Then the record executives at DeLuxe called Eckstine into their office as the guys in the band took a break. Eckstine returned, with a somber look on his face. "Fellows, come on. Gather around," he said to the band. "Something's come up. Instead of recording Sarah's tune, the tune that she's going to sing, 'I'll Wait and Pray,' they would like for me to do another blues and have Sarah record this on the next record date." DeLuxe wanted to capitalize on Eckstine's popularity in the South. "So nobody smiled or did anything," Malachi said. "All of a sudden, Sarah began to cry, since this is her first record date, and what these people are thinking about is makin' some money, and they're ignoring Sarah altogether. So Sarah began to cry. And to show you how close the band was, how tight and how much they cared about Sarah, everybody said, 'Well, if Sarah don't record, then nobody's going to record. We're not going to record anything else.'"[61] Eckstine turned around, went back to the office, and told the executives. He returned with a smile on his face, and said, "We're going to do Sarah's tune."[62]

In "I'll Wait and Pray," a moody, melancholy ballad by Malachi and trombonist Jerry Valentine, we hear that the foundation for Vaughan's soon-to-be signature style is already firmly in place. As expected, her performance is polished and assured, if a bit stiff. Her voice is beautiful, and her tone full and rich, even though it features less vibrato than she used later in her career. The tempo is deliciously slow, making it clear that Vaughan already had a knack for infusing even the simplest ballads with subtlety and sophistication. She bent some notes and slid between others, hinting at the tune's underlying harmonic structure. But the recording did not reflect how she sang in her live performances.

In 1977, while discussing her vocal style at the beginning of her career, Vaughan explained:

> Oh, I was really going up and down the scale more so than I am now—I've tamed down a lot. Yeah, I think then they wouldn't even know what the hell I was singing, because I was running all through the chords, and up and down and around. But I was in the band with Charlie Parker and Dizzy Gillespie—what else should you do? I was matching up to them—yes, indeed.[63]

Leonard Feather, who had been a big fan of Vaughan's since her early days with the Hines band, was disappointed by the relative tameness and commercial nature of Vaughan's first outing on wax. In his review of "I'll Wait and Pray" for *Metronome,* appearing in the July 1945 issue, he lamented that the record failed to truly capture "the extraordinary richness of her tone and the originality of her conception."[64] This inventiveness and brilliance had prompted him to exclaim, "Ah *mon vieux,* this chick is groovy!" when he heard her perform live at the Apollo with Eckstine and the band in September 1944.[65]

Feather enjoyed his status as a well-connected white critic and prided himself on introducing black talent to white audiences. He was also an aspiring producer and composer who regularly arranged for black musicians to record his material during the sessions that he produced. He then used the pages of *Metronome* to praise his latest finds. It was a major conflict of interest. Black musicians, who had fewer opportunities than their white counterparts, understood this. They also understood that Feather had the power to make or break their careers. Eckstine, Gillespie, and Vaughan disliked Feather, who didn't always have kind words for the band, and resented his influence in the industry. In the early days of Eckstine's band, they sang the following to the tune of "Stormy Weather":

> *I know why, we can't get a gig on Friday night,*
> *Leonard Feather,*
> *Keeps makin' it harder for me to keep this band together,*
> *Talkin' shit about us all the time.*[66]

Of course, when they were with Feather, they made nice and played along, but they viewed him, and white men like him, as a necessary evil of the music business.

Gillespie shared a record demo of Vaughan with Feather in December 1944, and Feather was impressed. In his memoir, Feather remembers running into Gillespie outside the Nola Studio at 52nd and Broadway. "Come upstairs and listen to this," said Gillespie. Feather writes that he immediately realized that Vaughan needed a recording session of her own, an opportunity to be a headliner. So he began shopping her demo around to all the major record labels in New York, but they turned him away without even listening to it. He was shocked. Finally, Feather persuaded Continental Records, at that time headed by Donald Gabor, to give her another shot.

Vaughan's schedule with the Eckstine band kept her busy, but she was free to record on December 31, 1944. She and a pickup band squeezed into the only recording studio available that day: a small, clammy room high up in the RKO building, next door to Radio City Music Hall. Backed by a septet including Gillespie on trumpet, Georgie Auld on tenor, and Feather on piano, she recorded four sides. She earned $20 a side, while Feather, who produced the session, agreed to work for $12.50 a side. Feather also composed two of the numbers: "Signing Off," a straightforward love song, and "No Smoke Blues," a run-of-the-mill blues in the style of Ethel Waters about the impending cigarette shortage.[67] Vaughan gave this blues a competent yet unmemorable treatment. Though there were some people that wanted Vaughan to be a blues singer, early on she knew this genre was not for her.

The highlights of this New Year's Eve Day session were Vaughan's renditions of two bebop staples: "East of the Sun," arranged by Gillespie, and "Interlude," a vocal interpretation of the instrumental standard "A Night in Tunisia," composed by Gillespie. She was the first artist to record "Tunisia," and she brought an easy swinging feel to both numbers. While she didn't include elaborate turns, slides, or embellishments, she did demonstrate her mastery of bebop's expanded harmonic language. In fact, due to its complex chord changes, Gillespie replaced Feather on piano for "Interlude." Vaughan, however, easily navigated the harmonic terrain of both tunes, effortlessly leaping tritones, sevenths, and other tricky intervals. She also demonstrated her ability to grasp the larger musical arc of the pieces, expertly building a sense of tension and momentum that drove the songs forward and then finally resolved in a satisfying conclusion.

Immediately following this recording session, Vaughan went back to work. The Eckstine Band ushered in the New Year with another tour of one-nighters. They headed south through Virginia, the Carolinas, and into Florida, then west across Alabama, Louisiana, and Texas, and they finally landed in Hollywood. On February 1, 1945, they began a month's engagement at the black-owned Plantation Club in the Watts neighborhood of Los Angeles to enthusiastic reviews, then two weeks at the Silver Slipper in San Diego, followed by another string of one-nighters as the band zigzagged its way back east. They arrived in New York on April 1 for an Easter Sunday dance and then headed out on the road again for weeklong theater dates in Detroit and Chicago, a collection of one-nighters throughout Ohio and Kentucky, a week in Baltimore, then back into New York for another week at the Apollo, beginning on May 18. It was the band's third appearance at the Apollo in the past year, an impressive feat for such a new band. It was also Vaughan's last engagement with the band. After nearly a year on the road with Eckstine and the guys, she quit.

According to rumors, Vaughan walked out on the band during a recording session. She hadn't made a record with Eckstine's unit since "I'll Wait and Pray" six months earlier, and she was still waiting for it to be released. Plus, Eckstine had just signed a new, more lucrative contract with National Records.[68] The contract ensured that Eckstine had a showcase for his vocals, and this in turn laid the foundation for his career as a solo act, which he launched in 1947. The label's president, Al Green, disliked working with women musicians. He thought they were too much trouble, and when Eckstine brought Vaughan with him to the studio, Green said, "No broads. No broads."[69] With no recording opportunities on the horizon, Vaughan had come to a dead end.

Records were crucial for an artist's success, especially for black musicians, who had limited access to national radio broadcasts. They relied on records to draw audiences to their live performances, the primary source of their livelihood. By definition, Vaughan played second fiddle in Eckstine's band. He was the headliner, and if she wanted to record more, she had to strike out on her own. Fortunately, before leaving the band, she had already found more recording opportunities. Gillespie invited her to a session with his quintet, which included Parker and drummer Sid Catlett, and on May 11 they recorded a memorable rendition of "Lover Man" for Guild. Then on May 25, while finishing up her week at the Apollo, she had another session organized by Feather, once again for Continental. This time drummer Max Roach joined Gillespie's septet, with Parker still on alto, and together they backed Vaughan on three love songs, most notably her now-classic "Mean to Me." It's hip, swinging, and clearly shows the synergy that Vaughan had with her bandmates, particularly Gillespie and Parker. With the help of her friends, she was steadily building a collection of recordings.

Being a vocalist with a band had its limitations, especially for an ambitious up-and-comer like Vaughan. "I had about two or three arrangements, and I sang those songs to death," she said. "I don't know why, but vocalists in bands never had too many arrangements; those we had, we sang forever. Every night the same songs; if we wanted to do something different, the rhythm section would just strike up, I'd sing, and somebody would blow behind me."[70] But these moments of spontaneity were probably infrequent, perhaps more so since both Parker and Gillespie, her favorite creative partners, had already left the Eckstine band months earlier. Furthermore, after the gig at the Apollo, Eckstine's band was gearing up for another tour of the South.

Vaughan had outgrown her role as a girl singer. It was time for her to move on.

3

"I'm Not Singing Other People's Ideas"

In June 1945 Vaughan took the plunge and launched her career as a solo artist. It was truly a leap of faith—faith in herself and her talent. As a freelancer, she no longer had the backing of a big-name band or the promise of steady work. It was a risky move. Many successful vocalists with celebrity swing bands, like Harry James's Helen Forrest, were able to support themselves in the band, but never quite made it out on their own. If Vaughan succeeded, however, just as she had two and a half years earlier when she competed at the Apollo's amateur night, the possible rewards were tremendous: fame, fortune, and, most important, freedom.

The nine months following Vaughan's departure from the Eckstine band were difficult. Although DeLuxe finally released her first recording, "I'll Wait and Pray," in June, Continental still had not issued the sides from her New Year's Eve session (in fact, they never released "No Smoke Blues" and waited until June 1946 to release "Signing Off"). And records from her most recent sessions with Gillespie would not appear until the fall. Without the benefit of the publicity and exposure that these records would generate, she struggled to find work, landing only a smattering of gigs during this period. Fellow musicians remember seeing Vaughan perform on 52nd Street at the Three Deuces, Famous Door, Onyx, and Downbeat, often as an intermission pianist. Sometimes she sang while accompanying herself on the piano. *Metronome* critic Leonard Feather reported that she opened and closed, both in the same night, at the Spotlight, also on 52nd Street.[1] And John Williams, a baritone saxophonist and former colleague from the Hines band, saw Vaughan outside the Braddock Hotel in Harlem. Located around the corner from the Apollo, the Braddock was *the* place for African American musicians to stay and hang out while working in New York. When she could afford it, Vaughan lived there (otherwise she went home to Newark). According to Williams, he ran into Vaughan during one of her rough patches: "I asked her to come to my room and sing a song for me, and I paid her five dollars to do it."[2] "Man, I always had to scuffle for bread!" Vaughan said in 1955, while discussing her early days as a solo act.[3]

After leaving the Eckstine band, Vaughan also spent a lot of time visiting with pianist Count Basie and his band while they played an extended engagement at the Roxy Theatre during the summer of 1945. "Sassy, as we also called her, and I had become very good pals by that time," Basie wrote in his autobiography. "She was crazy about the band, and she was very friendly with the fellows, so whenever we were in the same town for a while, she used to drop by all the time, maybe every day, and just hang out backstage with them and also in my dressing room." By this point, vocalist Thelma Carpenter had left the band, and Basie was auditioning new girl singers in his dressing room between sets. Vaughan often sat in and offered her feedback. Then one day, after listening to two or three singers, Basie was too tired to accompany another applicant. He wanted to relax before the band's next set. Vaughan stepped in. "I'll play for you," she said. "Why don't you just lie over there and listen and let me play." "Well, if you don't really mind," he replied.[4]

Vaughan played, Basie listened, and then they discussed,

agreeing that they should listen to a few more vocalists. "So this went on for a couple of weeks. She would come by there every day and play for me, so all I had to do between shows was lie on the couch and listen," Basie recalled. "Now all I was thinking about during this time was what a great pal she was to be doing that for me. It wasn't until later on that I realized that all the while I was supposed to be looking for a vocalist I had had one of the greatest singers in the world coming by there every goddam day, playing that piano so I could audition *other* singers."

The old-school swing that Basie's band specialized in would have been a departure from the progressive bebop that Vaughan favored, but the Basie band was famous and extremely busy, and his girl singers got plenty of opportunities to record. It was a good gig. Even though Vaughan was unemployed and clearly interested in the job, she never explicitly asked for an audition. Years later, when Basie asked her "why the hell she didn't say something," Vaughan laughed. "I thought you just didn't want me," she said. "I just thought I wasn't what you were looking for."[5]

There are few printed accounts documenting Vaughan's performances in 1945. She appeared in an All-Star Jazz Concert on June 5 with Dizzy Gillespie at the Academy of Music in Philadelphia. Five months later, she worked with violinist Stuff Smith's trio at the Onyx, and together they recorded "Time and Again" on October 1. Then on November 23, six months after leaving Eckstine, she returned for a week at the Apollo. Frank Humphries's band headlined, with Vaughan appearing at the bottom of the bill, much lower than she ever had as a girl singer with either Eckstine or Hines.

Things began to turn around in December. Bassist John Kirby hired Vaughan to sing with his sextet at the famed Copacabana. It was a real coup for a young singer. The mob-backed nightery was an elite supper club frequented by athletes, celebrities, and New York's high society, and it featured the biggest names in the business. Frank Sinatra, Peggy Lee, and Tommy Dorsey were all regular headliners, and now Vaughan's name was on the marquee too, although she performed in the smaller lounge upstairs instead of the main dining room. The job, however, was far from perfect. "At that time they didn't allow colored people to come into the club," said Vaughan.[6] Just a year earlier Harry Belafonte, then seventeen and a newly enlisted munitions loader in the navy, was banned entry when he brought a date to the club. Belafonte remembered the white bouncer asking him to stand aside as he ushered in one white couple after another. When he asked what was going on, the bouncer replied, "No more seats, buddy." Puzzled, Belafonte then asked, "How come all these other people are getting in?" "They got reservations." Belafonte was humiliated and retreated with his girlfriend in tow as the crowd of affluent whites looked on.[7]

Conditions were not much better for the black performers allowed inside of the club. "We didn't have any dressing rooms: I had to dress at home, do my show, then get out of there between shows, go round the corner, and have a few drinks," Vaughan explained.[8] Other times Vaughan and her fellow musicians pooled their money to hire a cab during the twenty-minute breaks.[9] She didn't stick around for the gig's entire run. After a month, Vaughan quit. "From the outside, it simply seemed that Sarah was temperamental," *Metronome*'s Leonard Feather wrote six months later, while explaining why she left. "The real reasons were probably far deeper rooted. There were more obvious, practical reasons, too. Such as the lack of proper dressing room facilities and the attitude about mixing with customers at the Copa."[10] She took a stand, one that in all likelihood hurt her career. Once again, she was without regular work, and for her principals she had gained a reputation for being testy and unreliable, potential death knells for any aspiring musician.

Although the Copa eliminated its "no blacks" policy in the 1950s, Vaughan's resentment lingered. "You know, you wonder why those things went on like they did. I don't know what music has to do with color, but it does," she said in 1977 when asked about her time at the Copa. "Yeah, it's a dumb world we live in, I think." And when the club finally closed in 1973, Vaughan said that she was glad, adding, "I'm sorry it lasted that long!"[11]

It's easy to dismiss this period of underemployment, a hiatus of sorts, as a minor disruption in an otherwise busy and extremely successful career. But at the time, the months following Vaughan's departure from Eckstine's band must have been worrisome and terribly discouraging.[12] At just twenty-two, she must have feared she was yet another casualty of the music industry; like those of so many other vocalists with swing bands during the war, her career was potentially over before it truly had a chance to flourish.

Even though work had been slow during her first nine months as a solo act, Vaughan continued to make new contacts. While at the Copa she met Howard Richmond, recently returned from the war and eager to set up his own talent agency. He took Vaughan on and, along with the influential white producer and talent scout John Hammond, who had taken a fancy to Vaughan when she sang with Hines and Eckstine, helped her get an audition with Barney Josephson.[13] Josephson was the owner of Café Society Downtown, the most racially progressive club in New York, if not the country.

Unlike the Copacabana, Café Society was fully integrated. Blacks and whites performed together onstage and mingled together in the audience, crowding around the small round tables that packed the L-shaped basement at 1 Sheridan Square in Greenwich Village. Colorful murals à la Matisse and Picasso covered the walls, creating an atmosphere that was contemporary and sophisticated, yet edgy, with a countercultural vibe. Josephson, who was white and began his career as a shoe salesman from New Jersey, opened the club in December 1938 in response to New York's exclusive "high society" and clubs like the Copacabana that catered to it. Billed as "the wrong place for the Right people," Café Society was a haven for New York's intelligentsia, celebrities, members of the press, and other musicians. It specialized in cabaret-style performances of jazz, blues, and folk music, and Josephson prided himself on discovering and developing new talent. In 1939, he introduced Billie Holiday to "Strange Fruit," her protest song describing the horrors of lynching, and encouraged her to perform the now-iconic song at Café Society. And after hearing Sarah Vaughan at her audition in early 1946, he expected to have the same influence on her career.

"She was kind of awkward, rather dowdily dressed, and had a gap between her front teeth," Josephson wrote in his memoir. "But her voice! I had never heard such a voice." Vaughan's audition also made an impression on Café Society darling Susie Reed, a zither-playing white folk singer, then eighteen years old: "I remember the night Sarah Vaughan tried out. I never heard anything like it, and I stayed and listened to her sing. I thought it was the most wonderful thing I had ever heard because she sang like an instrument, a clarinet." Josephson agreed, though he likened her voice to a saxophone and explained, "I hired her then and there."[14]

Vaughan opened Café Society on a Tuesday night, March 5, 1946. Billed as a "Sensational New Song Stylist," she was one of six acts on the program, which included vocalist Josh White, boogie-woogie pianist Pete Johnson, and the house band, led by J. C. Heard. Each act performed a short set, three or four numbers, for a total running time of seventy-five minutes—perfect for encouraging a high patron turnaround at the club. She did three shows a night, at 8:30 P.M., midnight, and 2:00 A.M., with new material in each set.[15] It was a good job with steady pay, and landing a gig at Café Society was a major accomplishment for any young performer. Josephson treated his musicians well, providing them with regular, long-term work and fair wages. Instead of the two- or three-week runs common at many clubs, Josephson hired his musicians for months at a time, sometimes for years. Pianist and vocalist Hazel Scott performed at the café for seven and a half years, pianist Mary Lou Williams more than five, and while Vaughan's tenure at the club was much shorter, she stayed for six months.

"Sarah was not a hit," Josephson wrote in his memoir. "She sings week after week, month after month. People would complain, 'She can't sing. She's not even pretty.' They protest my having her. . . . In general, I would say that Café Society attracted a rather intellectual crowd, knowledgeable about jazz. But they just didn't understand what Sarah was doing."[16] According to Reed, "She did much more then than she did later, improvising around the melody. When she started singing commercially, she was much more on the melody of each song."[17] In 1946, Vaughan's singing was progressive, heavily influenced by her years working with the bebop instrumentalists. The sophisticated passing tones and complex chord changes, plus her tendency to run up and down the scale rather than sing a song straight—the same qualities that made her a favorite of musicians and critics—simply didn't fly with Café Society's patrons.

They ignored her. Night after night, the audience talked over Vaughan as she sang, drowning her out, making it almost impossible for her to be heard. On one occasion Josephson remembered Paul Robeson, the acclaimed actor and civil rights activist, shushing the crowd: "In his melodious baritone, which cut through the chatter in the room, and without getting up, he said, 'Ladies and gentlemen, I would like to hear this lady. Mr. Josephson considers her to be a great talent. Give her the courtesy of your attention if you please.'"[18]

Café Society was an intimate club. It had no stage. Instead, crowded tables surrounded the performer, just a few feet away. Vaughan could see and feel everything happening in the club, and it must have been difficult having to fight to be acknowledged. But her time at Café Society also made her a tougher, more resilient entertainer. It became a test of her determination and artistic integrity.

Years later she recalled John Hammond, the same influential producer who helped her land the job at Café Society, snubbing her during her performances. "Every night he used to come in, sit on the ringside, and read a newspaper," she said.[19] Whether or not Vaughan realized it, Hammond had a reputation for sitting up front, as close as he could possibly get to the music making, and if he liked the musician, he listened intently, engrossed. But if he didn't like what he heard, he ignored the performer and read his collection of newspapers, biding his time until the next act came on. It was a public dismissal, one that could be seen by every patron in the club. And Hammond did not like bebop. "I became afraid about what the future might hold for me," she confided to friend Robert Richards when she told him of Hammond's nightly snubs decades later.[20] Yet instead of cowering or compromising her artistic vision, as many young artists might have when dismissed by an industry powerhouse, Vaughan held her ground. Backed by the boys in the band, she became defiant and laughed at Hammond. "We loved it," she said, "because it would sorta stop the show a bit; wouldn't be too much getting done, due to us being in hysterics."[21]

She believed that Hammond was holding a grudge. "Now, would you believe this!" she told Les Tomkins in 1977. "John Hammond, at that time, wanted to make me a Bessie Smith. I knew the name, but when I was little I really hadn't heard too much about Bessie Smith. So I told him to stick it up his ear. He got a little peeved about that."[22]

It was a risky move, like poking a sleeping bear. The son of a Vanderbilt and a wealthy corporate lawyer, John Hammond came from a position of power and privilege. As an executive at Columbia during the 1930s, he'd guided the career of Benny Goodman, encouraging him to embrace "hot jazz," a move that eventually earned him the title "King of Swing." He also specialized in bringing black talent to the attention of larger, white, mainstream audiences. He's credited with launching the career of Billie Holiday in 1933; reviving the flagging career of the "Empress of the Blues" Bessie Smith herself, also in 1933; rescuing the underappreciated (and underrecorded) boogie-woogie pianist Meade Lux Lewis from an obscurity washing cars in a Chicago garage in 1935; and, in 1936, "discovering" Count Basie in Kansas City and guiding his band to national, and international, recognition. But Hammond's help came with strings attached. He had a reputation for needing to be needed and considered himself a savior of downtrodden African Americans. Despite his liberal, integrationist politics, the black artists he advocated for were not his equals. He expected them to be beholden to him and do what he said. And when they didn't, he could become punitive. In 1938 he reportedly fired Billie Holiday from Count Basie's band when she, like Vaughan, refused to sing the blues. Holiday didn't want to steal the spotlight from blues specialist Herb Jeffreys and opted instead to stick to "rhythm" numbers.[23] According to trumpeter Rex Stewart, a longtime colleague of Bessie Smith, "If you dare criticize him, John Hammond will go out of his way to prevent you from working."[24]

Vaughan's nightly slight at Café Society was tame in comparison, but it still ruffled her feathers. "Imagine somebody doing that, just because you don't want to do what they want you to do," she lamented.[25] Vaughan didn't like being told how and what to sing. She understood that the blues were not for her, but she also did not want to be musically contained or typecast because of her race. "I was a little insulted about that, too, I think," she said. "Back at that time, they thought all colored folk should sing the blues, for some reason or other."[26]

And she was right. When Vaughan appeared on the music scene in 1942, there were very clear rules about which styles black and white musicians could perform. Black musicians were expected to limit themselves to the blues and blues-derived styles, like jazz, while white musicians could perform pop tunes, ballads, and folk songs, as well as jazz, blues, or any other style they wanted. White artists had the freedom of flexibility and the privilege of choice. Their musical choices were stylistic ones, rather than determined by their racial identity. This was not the case for black artists. Many white audiences assumed that black artists should perform the blues, and these expectations were, in large part, created by white record producers and critics. Hammond had a strong emotional investment in the blues and how they reinforced his image of black America. With their earthy sounds, working-class southern origins, and tales of hardship, the blues for him represented black musical expression in its purest, most authentic form. The blues were sincere and innocent—a true expression of natural, instinctive black talent. They epitomized the black vernacular and, for Hammond and many of his white contemporaries, became the only legitimate form of black musical expression.[27]

Vaughan and her fellow beboppers resented this. They did not want to be chained to the blues, which, to them, symbolized both social and musical restrictions. Musically, the twelve-bar blues were melodically repetitive and harmonically limited, usually centered on straightforward I–IV–V chord progressions. With relative ease, beboppers exploded these musical boundaries, crafting elaborate improvisations using their adventurous, often dissonant, harmonic language. Yet they struggled to overcome the larger social and cultural implications of the blues. For beboppers, the blues represented a rural, almost premodern, cultural past, not to mention the primitivist expectations of many whites, including the likes of John Hammond, who sought to pigeonhole black performers. Beboppers wanted to challenge contemporary views of black artistic expression as innate, the product of "natural" talent and instincts. They considered themselves highly trained, innovative artists with a cosmopolitan outlook. In response, Vaughan and her fellow beboppers developed a new form of black cultural expression based on their intellect and mental acuity, an insistence that racial boundaries were fluid, coupled with a contempt for musical labels and categorization. They sought the same freedom and privilege of choice as their white contemporaries, a kind of artistic equality, and in so doing challenged the status quo.[28]

Unlike her male instrumental colleagues, however, Vaughan's relationship with the blues was complicated by gender and what the blues, as sung by black women, represented. Blues women like Bessie Smith, Gertrude "Ma" Rainey, and Ethel Waters, the so-called red hot mamas, sang openly, and often explicitly, about their sexuality, desires, and troubles with men (and women). They condemned domestic violence and other forms of abuse and injustice. Blues women of the 1920s challenged the norms of patriarchy and reclaimed their agency, all while defining their own identities as black women. They were powerful voices of change. But they were also controversial. In the eyes of many religious black Americans, the music of blues women was coarse and vulgar. It was not proper. The black Baptist church worried that the red hot mamas confirmed widely held stereotypes that cast black women as lascivious and wanton. The church, practicing a politics of respectability, promoted, instead, an alternate ideal of black women as ladylike and refined, as pillars of the community and their race. The politics of respectability emphasized temperance, sexual purity, manners, and morals in an effort to counter prevailing white notions of black womanhood.[29] These were the values instilled in Vaughan by her parents. She was a church girl and the daughter of devout Baptist parents, and her family forsook much popular music as unwholesome. Her family didn't listen to the red hot mamas, and their music didn't inform Vaughan's childhood musical vernacular or emerging artistic agenda.

Vaughan confirmed her ambivalence toward blues women in 1949 when she participated in Leonard Feather's now-iconic "blindfold tests" published in *Metronome*. These were drop-the-needle-style tests based on an ideal of colorblind, race-free listening where musicians ranked what they heard. Feather played Bessie Smith's "Young Woman Blues" from 1926, and Vaughan was at a loss. "Julia Lee? Mamie Smith? Around 1930? I have absolutely no feeling for this," she said. Then she recalled a recent gig in Kansas City with a blues singer, who she first mistakenly identified as the late Bessie Smith, who passed away in 1937 following a well-publicized car crash, then corrected herself: "No, I guess it was Julia Lee." Blues women were simply not on her musical radar. "I've always wanted to find out what people see in this kind of thing, I've met so many people who treasure these records," she explained. "But I don't get it. No stars."

At the conclusion of the survey, Feather asked Vaughan about her own vocal influences. "I've never been influenced by any particular favorite singers," she said, a mantra she would repeat again and again throughout her career. She did, however, list a handful a vocalists she remembered listening to as a child. The list included expected candidates, notable black talent of the day like Billie Holiday and Billy Eckstine. It also contained the less expected—an eclectic mix of popular white singers: Frances Langford, a staple of 1930s radio and long-time USO collaborator with Bob Hope; Martha Raye, a swing vocalist known for adding blues inflections to her songs and convincing portrayals of black women in films; Tony Martin, a crooner turned actor; and Jean Sablon, a French balladeer, who, Vaughan confessed, "soothes me more than Sinatra!" "But my favorite singer," Vaughan insisted, "is Marian Anderson—*singer*, I said! One of the greatest compliments I've ever been paid was when someone said I sounded like her at times."[30]

In 1946, however, when pressured by record executives and industry insiders, Vaughan insisted on choosing her own path. She went against type and sang romantic love songs and ballads, up-tempo rhythm numbers, spirituals, and anything else she found musically interesting or inspiring. Of course, Vaughan was not the only black vocalist singing ballads and rhythm songs, but she always did insist on singing the material her way. She sought artistic freedom and equality. But the struggle for self-determination is a difficult, uphill battle. In August 1946, six months into her engagement at Café Society, Vaughan told *Down Beat*'s Michael Levin, "It's been a long haul, Mike. I'm not singing other people's ideas—I'm trying to make a style for myself. At least I'll be different."[31]

Despite these challenges, things finally began to come together for Vaughan during her Café Society run. On May 8, 1946, with the help of her agent, Howard Richmond, she signed her first official solo recording contract with Musicraft, an ambitious yet comparatively small independent label. Founded in 1937, Musicraft first specialized in classical music, then shifted its focus to popular music, especially jazz, during World War II. Mel Tormé, Teddy Wilson, Georgie Auld, Artie Shaw, and beboppers like Dizzy Gillespie all recorded on Musicraft. And Duke Ellington signed with the label on the same day as Vaughan, May 8, after being lured away from Victor with promises of a hefty $100,000 guarantee. Vaughan's advance was more modest: a mere $100 per side, with a promise of recording sixteen sides a year. But her contract pledged to press at least eight hundred thousand records a year, with the goal of selling a million records.[32] In the end, these aspirations proved unrealistic. Musicraft simply did not have the capacity to manufacture and distribute this volume of records. Nonetheless, in the spring of 1946 as Vaughan struggled to establish herself, signing with Musicraft helped lay the foundation for her burgeoning career as a solo act. During her first four months with the label, she recorded and released ten sides—five singles. Unlike her earlier collaborations with Gillespie, Parker, and fellow beboppers, these new releases only hinted at her bebop roots. She sang straighter, with an eye toward a more mainstream, commercial audience. With a steady stream of new records on the market, she began to get her name out there.

During her tenure at Café Society, she also appeared regularly on WMCA's twice-weekly radio broadcast from the club, helping her reach listeners throughout the region. She supplemented her work at the café with special guest appearances at dances and charity benefits presented by organizations like the NAACP and *New York Amsterdam News*. And just as she became more visible within the New York scene, the national jazz press, also centered in New York, upped their coverage of her too.

In July 1946, *Metronome* published its first full profile of Vaughan, nearly four years after she won the amateur-night competition at the Apollo. Complete with a photo, recap of her career, and full discography, the piece introduced Vaughan to the magazine's national readership. It seems as if Leonard Feather, the same critic who helped Vaughan land two of her earliest recording sessions, was determined to convince listeners, especially those who did not understand her singing, what made Vaughan so exceptional:

> Well it isn't any one thing, but a combination of qualities; the ethereally pure tone, her instrument-like sense of phrasing (Sara [*sic*] explains it by saying she's always been crazy about musical instruments and tries consciously to

sing like one), and, best of all, the occasional effects she
achieves, generally toward the end of a song, by spread-
ing one syllable over several notes and suggesting passing
chords with these subtle variations on the melody.

He described her as a "musician's singer," adding, "There are
musicians who are saying that nothing fresher, more inspired and
original has been heard since Billie Holiday first came out of
obscurity."[33]

Down Beat's Michael Levin agreed, and his profile published
in late August proclaimed: "The *Beat* has raved about Vaughan
for some time. In the last six months, her singing has notice-
ably improved, the tone being clearer and rounder, and attack
being even sharper. . . . Add this to her flowing ideas and clarity of conception and La Vaughan for my money is right there
with [Mildred] Bailey, Fitzgerald, and Holiday as the best in the
country."[34]

Unfortunately, the praise and acceptance that Vaughan received
in the relatively tolerant world of jazz did not translate into a
larger acceptance by society as a whole. Two weeks before Levin's
profile appeared in *Down Beat*, Vaughan and her friends George
Treadwell, Naomi Wright, Johnnie Garry, and bandleader
J. C. Heard were attacked after leaving Café Society early in the
morning on Sunday, August 3. George was a trumpeter with
the house band, Naomi was the club's powder room attendant,
and Johnnie worked behind the scenes as a stagehand. A gang
of fifteen white men jumped the group as they entered the subway station nearest the café. The men shouted "Get niggers out
of the Village" as they struck, kicked, and spat upon Vaughan
and Wright, who, believing that the hoodlums would spare the
women in the group, both tried to shield Treadwell from the
most severe blows. The group got past the turnstiles, but members of the gang followed, chasing them down the subway stairs
and into the corridor that led to the platform. "J. C. and I pushed
one guy on the tracks," Garry remembered. "Sarah was biting

and fighting the guy. She got the worst of it."[35] Vaughan and her friends escaped on the next train, but they were hurt. After the attack Vaughan had abdominal bruises, a split lip, and a swollen eye. Still, she felt compelled to return to work. Wright's injuries, however, confined her to bed.

Reports of Vaughan's assault circulated in the nation's black newspapers. The African American community was outraged. Other Café Society musicians had suffered similar attacks, and just after Vaughan and her friends were assaulted, the gang preyed on a veteran of the Tuskegee Airmen, beating him so badly that he required a lengthy hospital stay. Three weeks later bassist Slam Stewart was brutally attacked outside of the Three Deuces when the gang shifted to 52nd Street. The white gang yelled, "No Niggers on this street," treatment familiar to musicians as they toured the South but less expected in the more cosmopolitan North. Vaughan immediately reported the incident to the police, who were already aware of the gang, but black leaders worried that nothing was being done. Prominent citizens wrote a letter of protest to the mayor. Leonard Feather called for more police protection for musicians after hours. The *New York Amsterdam News* decried the attacks as "race terrorism," explaining that Greenwich Village, once a black neighborhood, had become a postwar mecca for southern whites who had brought their hatreds and prejudices with them. The white gang openly resented seeing blacks and whites mix, as often happened at Café Society.[36] It was a brutal reminder that the progressive politics of Café Society did not mirror those of the country at large. If Vaughan wanted to transcend racial categories and become popular among mainstream white audiences, she still had a long road ahead of her.

Vaughan was already a minor celebrity within African American circles. The black press faithfully reported on her gigs—listing not only when and where she performed but also the prestige factor of each venue. Vaughan's engagement at Café Society was her first major booking as a solo act, and the jazz critics loved her, so the black press heralded her run at the café as a great success, despite the mixed reception. But she was just beginning to get attention from white audiences outside of the elite intelligentsia, who so far had been some of her strongest advocates. She finally broke through into the mainstream media in July 1946 when *Time* magazine, likely impressed by Leonard Feather's piece in *Metronome,* included her in a profile of up-and-coming vocalists. Their two-sentence blurb praised her as the "newest favorite" at Café Society, describing her as "the freshest Negro talent since Ella Fitzgerald."[37] Short, but very sweet. It was a start.

As the media paid more and more attention to Vaughan's professional life, they also delved into her personal life. In March 1946, *Down Beat* reported that she had recently wed a former colleague from the Eckstine Band. The *Baltimore Afro-American* soon picked up the story and ran with it.[38] In July, Feather asked her if she had indeed married tenor saxophonist Gene Ammons, mentioning that the two had been close friends when they worked together for Eckstine. Vaughan flatly denied the rumors, declaring that there was "plenty of time yet for marriage."[39]

But, unbeknownst to Feather, she had become increasingly friendly with George Treadwell, one of her companions during the late-night subway attack. Five years older than Vaughan, Treadwell was born in New Rochelle, New York. He played trumpet in the house band at Monroe's Uptown House in Harlem in 1941 and 1942, just as the future beboppers began frequenting the club's jam sessions. He worked in Cootie Williams's band, the same band that backed Vaughan during her amateur-night appearance at the Apollo on October 21, 1942, for almost three years, and finally joined J. C. Heard's house band at Café Society in 1946. At first Vaughan and Treadwell's friendship centered on music and a desire to further their careers. After work, they often went to clubs in Harlem and on 52nd Street. "I think they fell in love on the A train," Johnnie Garry said. "They were drawn together by their shared love of music." Treadwell supported and encouraged Vaughan, becoming increasingly involved in her career. During Vaughan's first recording session as a solo act with Musicraft on May 7, 1946, Treadwell was not present. He was, however, bustling behind the scenes during her next session on

June 14, 1946, and led her July 18, 1946, session, playing trumpet and conducting the George Treadwell Orchestra.

"One night we went out after finishing work—we'd usually go to 52nd Street and make the rounds. George told me again what a great singer he thought I was and that I should have a manager to see that I got the right breaks," a 1950 confessional under Vaughan's byline (but likely written by Treadwell and her publicity team) revealed. According to the piece, which appeared in *Tan Confessions*, Vaughan said, "Why don't you manage me?" Treadwell looked at Vaughan, surprised, then replied, "Sure, Sass, I'll manage you, but it would be even better if we managed each other." The couple got a marriage license the next morning and wed on September 17, 1946. Upon reflection, Vaughan admitted, "I guess the only trouble was that George was very slow in getting around to proposing. Several times I almost proposed to him."[40]

That September, after six months of critical, if not popular, success, Josephson finally released Vaughan from her Café Society engagement. He simply needed to replace her with a more commercially viable act. Vaughan was out on her own again, and although she did not leave Café Society a star, as Josephson hoped she would and as Billie Holiday had eight years earlier, Vaughan did exit the club with valuable experience and plenty of open doors. She finished out the year in New York, keeping busy singing for jam sessions, dances, socialite parties, and clubs throughout the city. In January, she returned to the Apollo. Billed as an "award winner"—she had just won *Esquire* magazine's Jazz Book award for outstanding new jazz vocalist for the upcoming year—and "famous singing record star," Vaughan shared the spotlight with headliner Dizzy Gillespie and his band.[41]

Her career, however, didn't really gain momentum until the spring of 1947. Treadwell had given up his career as a professional musician and was now onboard as Vaughan's full-time manager. After twenty months of freelancing in New York, it was time for Vaughan to broaden her horizons and explore opportunities in a new city.

4

"The Most Talked About Voice in America"

f New York City was the jazz capital of the United States, Chicago came in a close second, especially in the 1920s. After World War I, African American musicians flocked to Chicago from New Orleans and elsewhere. Louis Armstrong, for example, went from being an anonymous sideman to become a big-name soloist after he moved to Chicago in 1924 and recorded his game-changing "Hot Five" and "Hot Seven" sides. Pianist Earl Hines, Vaughan's former boss, had similar success in Chicago. Aspiring white musicians also gravitated to the Midwest metropolis in search of financial security and artistic opportunities; the so-called Chicago style, practiced by Eddie Condon, Bix Beiderbecke, and Jimmy McPartland, originated there, and swing bandleaders Benny Goodman and Gene Krupa were born and raised in Chicago. The city was a creative hub. It boasted thriving club scenes in the black South Side neighborhoods as well as the downtown core and white suburbs. There were plenty of good paying gigs, a strong record label presence, an extensive network of radio stations fronted by outspoken, jazz-loving disc jockeys, and, perhaps most important, enthusiastic, knowledgeable audiences with keen ears for new, experimental music. It was an ideal proving ground for an innovative, cutting-edge artist like Vaughan, who now had a growing number of records to her name.

So when Vaughan opened at the Rhumboogie Club, in the heart of the South Side, on March 21, 1947, she became a sensation.[1] Before her arrival, the club, co-owned by boxing champion Joe Louis, struggled to make ends meet. Drummer Floyd Campbell remembered receiving his paycheck on a Friday with instructions not to cash it until Monday. "But Sarah packed the place every night," he said. "They had to send out for extra chairs to accommodate the patrons." When her original four-week contract ended, Treadwell, embracing his new role as her manager, insisted that the club management more than double Vaughan's pay. "At first they refused," said Campbell. "Then Ziggy Johnson, the show's producer, and I threatened to pull the band out if they didn't agree. They did give her the raise and they doubled the length of her engagement from four to eight weeks."[2] Not too long after Vaughan's run ended on May 15, the Rhumboogie closed its doors for good.

During her run, Dave Garroway, a white DJ at the local NBC affiliate, trekked over to the South Side every night after his midnight show to listen to Vaughan. He fell completely in love with her voice—its beauty, prowess, and ingenuity—and became one of her biggest fans. "People were telling me about him praising me before I knew Dave," Vaughan told *Down Beat*'s Don Gold in 1957.[3] "He actually made me very famous in Chicago," Vaughan told Dick Cavett in 1980. "I was working at a club called the Rhumboogie, and I was making $250 a week. And he used to talk about me on the radio all of the time. Constantly. And I would hear about it. And then when I met him, I was on his show all of the time. My salary went from $250 to $750. And I bought my first car."[4]

During her tenure at the Rhumboogie, Garroway also organized two special concerts showcasing Vaughan, both of which sold out. "The atom smasher in this case was Sarah's singing,"

Down Beat raved in their review of her first Garroway-sponsored concert on April 13. "Sarah's use of her voice is a musical miracle as well as a paradox. . . . Nearly 600 patrons sat enthralled while La Vaughan opened her mouth wide and molded her tones into exquisite phrases."[5] During her second concert, held at the Civic Opera House on May 4, they reported, Vaughan had the "crowd in the palm of her hand," and even though she only sang five songs, she could have gone on all night.[6]

By the end of April, six weeks after arriving in town, sales of Vaughan's records soared in Chicago; she made two guest appearances on Nat King Cole's nationally broadcast radio program; and on May 17, after closing at the Rhumboogie, she was picked up for three weeks at the Sherman Hotel. The Sherman was a grandiose establishment in the heart of the Loop's theater district. In less than three months Vaughan went from singing for in-the-know jazz aficionados at a near-bankrupt club on the South Side to performing for affluent, mainstream audiences, often dubbed "squares" for their lack of hip jazz savvy, in downtown Chicago.

The floor show at the Sherman was part of a revue series featuring up-and-coming recording artists, and freelance disc jockey Linn Burton, another Vaughan devotee, emceed and used his radio program as a promotional tie-in. She shared the bill with three white acts: the Harmonicats, the Herbie Fields orchestra, and pianist Mel Henke. While the *Chicago Defender* hailed Vaughan's appearances at the Sherman as a triumph, explaining it was "the first time an attraction has enjoyed such an elevation in booking," *Billboard*'s review made it clear that Vaughan was still finding her footing with this new, more commercial audience.[7] She struggled to hold the room and to be heard above the chatter of diners. The room was too large, the PA system inadequate, and her singing too esoteric. Vaughan executed "some amazing variations, worthy of the top instrumentalists, but she needs a smaller room and a sharper crowd to register properly," *Billboard*'s Johnny Sippel wrote. "In playing square spots, she'd do well to give out with an occasional novelty to break the routine of just straight standards." Yet she "warmed up the room by the time she finished, hitting especially hard with a smile giving the impression that she's getting a real kick from working."[8]

But Vaughan's rise in Chicago was controversial, especially the role that disc jockeys played in her growing fame. Dave Garroway's admiration was so effusive and consistent that many assumed there was an intimate relationship between the two. "He praised me so much, some of his listeners thought we were married," Vaughan told *Down Beat*'s Don Gold in 1957. "It was the kind of support you can't pay for."[9] And Garroway was but one in a quartet of Chicago disc jockeys advocating for Vaughan. Ernie Simon of WJJD, Eddie Hubbard of WIND, and freelancer Linn Burton, who emceed the floor show at the Sherman, all embraced their roles as taste makers and all used their platforms to voice their enthusiasm, praise, and unflinching support for the promising vocalist. And they played her records all of the time, often at the expense of other artists.

Disc jockeys, the so-called maestros of radio, were growing in importance, popularity, and influence. After World War II, radio transitioned from a national to a local medium. The number of independent radio stations exploded from a mere 56 in 1945 to 916, 44 percent of all radio stations, in 1950. As the role of the national radio networks like NBC and CBS declined, the influence of disc jockeys, especially those affiliated with small, independent stations, skyrocketed. DJs excelled at understanding emerging and niche markets within their communities, and these new markets often centered on what was known as race music. They guided the musical interests of their listeners, introducing them to new music, but also responded to listener requests. (The most popular DJs received copious mail, and eager fans often overloaded telephone switchboards during call-in segments.) DJs developed new, listener-friendly formats, sponsored fan-directed listening clubs, organized popularity polls to rank favorite artists, and worked in tandem with local record stores, placing top-selling discs on high rotation. It was a symbiotic relationship between DJ and community, and the most popular DJs became local celebrities that produced concerts and sponsored civic charities.[10]

Garroway, for instance, forged a partnership with Hudson-Ross, Chicago's self-proclaimed leading record, radio, and appliance store chain. The program notes for Vaughan's April 13, 1947, concert sponsored by Garroway's 11:60 Club included an advertisement listing Vaughan's latest recordings, all of which could be found at one of Hudson-Ross's three downtown locations. And newspaper ads for the store included endorsements from Garroway. An advertisement announcing an in-store appearance by Vaughan on Friday, September 12, 1947, quoted Garroway using what had become familiar rhetoric: "Come and meet Sarah Vaughan, the crystalline, iridescent singing star of Musicraft Records! Get her autograph on any, or all, of those very non-repulsive Musicraft Records which seem alive with little golden sparks. I'll be there too!" He became the store's public voice, promoting Vaughan and his aesthetic agenda, all while selling records and, ultimately, himself. He emerged as a local celebrity, becoming an early television personality in Chicago and eventually the host of NBC's nationally broadcast *Today Show* in 1951.

Members of the established mainstream press pushed back. During Vaughan's appearances at the Sherman Hotel, *Chicago Sun* columnist Dale Harrison, known for his more conservative, "square" tastes, wrote that he simply didn't like Sarah Vaughan and suggested that "the comely Negro chanteuse isn't the great talent they say she is." Angry Vaughan fans wrote letters calling him an "unmitigated moron," another insisted that he was "one of those impoverished souls" incapable of appreciating true art, and another worried that his remarks would keep "a lot of the unintelligent and uninformed squares who read your column" from hearing Vaughan. DJ Ernie Simon leapt to Vaughan's defense, questioning Harrison's musical integrity. Harrison responded with his own ad hominem attacks and dubbed Ernie Simon "Simple Simon." He discussed Garroway too, and although he considered Garroway "one of the less confused jocks," Harrison questioned his enthusiasm for Vaughan and added that "the sense of power which has descended suddenly on the disc maestri has led them sometimes in desperation to touting new singers they believe can be hoisted to the heights with a little platter-playing push." And he concluded, "[Garroway] has given [Vaughan] one of the most determined and persistent buildups any new singer ever had—combining his own persuasiveness with the 50,000-high class watts of NBC's WMAQ." This was indeed a powerful signal: Garroway's reach extended beyond Chicago and its suburbs, and his programs became a favorite of high school and university students as far away as North Carolina and New York.[11]

It's possible, however, that Dale Harrison's dislike of Vaughan and the DJs who supported her was not simply a case of professional jealousy or anxiety that he and his fellow newspapermen were being eclipsed as influential tastemakers. Perhaps Harrison was also uncomfortable with how Garroway and like-minded DJs discussed Vaughan's voice. How they used powerful imagery and rhetoric to frame the listening experiences of their many devoted fans. And how this in turn blurred racial boundaries.

On September 21, 1947, four months after her breakthrough performances in Chicago, Vaughan returned to Garroway's popular radio show on WMAQ, NBC's Chicago affiliate. She had just spent two successful months in Los Angeles, and on her way back east she made another stop in Chicago. She was in the middle of a six-week engagement at Al Sherman's Club Silhouette on the North Side. Garroway emceed at the club, and as he often did, he invited the headliner to appear on his radio show. His broadcasts mixed live, in-studio performances with his musings on art and life. That night he described a man he'd seen with hinges tattooed on his arms and the marvels of modern engineering that created the Bonneville Dam. While introducing Vaughan, he assumed the role of a museum curator or docent and likened Vaughan's singing to a beautiful piece of art. He explained that good art, much like a good book, makes you feel warm, and you feel warmer longer by sharing your discovery with others.

"That is very much the position I am in now," he said. "Here is a girl named Sarah Vaughan, who sings with exceeding grace and transparent beauty. Her voice is rich, moist, and filled with tiny gold filaments. A slim girl on the threshold of one of the great careers in music, I think." Then he instructed his listeners to sit down and "close your eyes and open your mind to a new gossamer sound." He never mentioned Vaughan's race, and instead encouraged listeners to remove sight, and by extension skin color and the physical body (in other words, the visual clues usually used to determine race), from their listening experience. He asked them to set aside their inhibitions and prejudices, to relax and completely immerse themselves in the pleasures of Vaughan's voice.

Then she sang. Backed by piano and studio orchestra, she began with "Tenderly," a romantic ballad by Walter Gross and Jack Lawrence that she recorded two months earlier for Musicraft. It would become a personal favorite of Garroway's, and in those early years he often called Vaughan, asking her to sing "Tenderly" to his wife over the phone. That night her tempo was slow. Her voice was full and deep, near the bottom of her contralto register and enveloped by a languorous vibrato. She sang the last note. Garroway paused and exclaimed, "Now you know it is possible to feel hot and cold at the same time."

"My progressive guest stars, I know, are not supposed to sing two songs in a row. But they are not Sarah Vaughan," he said. "If you have not heard Sarah sing 'It Might as Well Be Spring,' you are about to look closely at the face of beauty." Penned by Richard Rodgers and Oscar Hammerstein for the 1945 film *State Fair*, "It Might as Well Be Spring" won an Academy Award for Best Original Song and became a hit for crooner Dick Haymes. Vaughan recorded it for Crown Records in January 1946 with John Kirby's orchestra, the same band she played with at the Copacabana, and it soon became one of her signature songs too.

She "sings this utterly differently," Garroway explained, reaching the "depths of tenderness" while evoking a "daintiness" and "delicacy" and the "freshness of a yellow crocus."

"That, my starling, is as about as transcendent as we're going to get," Garroway sighed as she finished. Then he gave his radio audience a tutorial on how to listen to Vaughan's bebop-infused singing. He turned their attention to the final bars of the tune, where she improvised and sang wordlessly, like an instrumentalist, outlining the song's chords, often only alluding to the melody. "Did you hear, or could your mind hear as your ear did, the convolutions of image in that later part? Where she does adhere to the framework of the melody but twists and convolutes it in a way never heard before?"

"Sarah, will you breathe into that again?" he asked. Vaughan sang the final verse, once again demonstrating the now-iconic slides, passing tones, and arpeggios she added to the tune's tag. It was a demonstration of the vocal prowess, technical proficiency, and pure tone she was becoming known for, not to mention her unique creative vision and genius. When she finished, Garroway sighed his signature phrase, "Peace."[12]

Vaughan's segment lasted seven, perhaps eight, minutes. On the surface, Garroway simply shared his favorite new artist, an artist he believed paired modern innovation and exquisite beauty, with his listeners. But the way he discussed her voice, the language he used, did not conform to the conventions of the day. Many of his white contemporaries used different language when talking about black female vocalists in an effort, perhaps subconscious, to maintain clear boundaries between the music sung by black vocalists and the music of white vocalists. In a sense, Dave Garroway broke the rules.

In the 1940s and 1950s, it was still taboo for whites and blacks to intermingle, especially in the deeply segregated South, and radio broadcasts, recordings, and jukeboxes presented an unsettling opportunity for this to happen. Unlike live performances, where racial identity was self-evident, sound recordings separated voices from the physical bodies that created them. Race became obscured as disembodied voices interacted with listeners with little mediation. A white singer could sound "black," and a black singer could sound "white." And a white man might listen to the radio and unwittingly form an attachment to a black singer, like Garroway so clearly (albeit knowingly) had. To minimize this danger of listening across racial boundaries, a sonic miscegenation of sorts, white critics developed a code, a way of discussing voices that helped listeners determine the racial identity of the performer, a way to know if they were hearing a black voice or a white voice.

White critics focused on vocal timbre, describing the many nuances of sound that defined a voice's grain and texture, its unique aural fingerprint. They assigned certain vocal qualities and timbres to specific genres and styles, which happened to be informed by race. Just like producer John Hammond, most white critics of the day considered the blues the only true, or "authentic," form of black musical expression, and they equated blues singing with vocal blackness. According to these critics, blues singers like Bessie Smith and Ma Rainey possessed deep, full-powered voices that were throaty, husky, and gritty. Their voices were primal, with an earthy zest. And because they were often referred to as "shouters," blues singers were expected to growl, sob, and belt out their tunes.

Girl singers were their opposite. While plenty of black girl singers worked in the 1930s and 1940s, Vaughan included, the designation "girl singer" became a way for white critics to discuss vocal whiteness. The voices of girl singers were dainty, pure, and warm; smooth and melodic; natural yet refined. The industry also used a collection of bird metaphors when discussing girl singers, referring to them as chirps, chicks, thrushes, and canaries. They chirped, peeped, and warbled. Like birds, they sang softly, sweetly, and eloquently with agile, flexible voices that were light, ephemeral, and buoyant. Of course, the vocabulary developed by white critics to differentiate black and white voices was informed by larger social and cultural constructions defining ideal beauty and womanhood, race and gender. White voices were conventionally beautiful, effortlessly feminine, and ladylike, while black voices were not.

Black critics, however, did not make these distinctions. They didn't have a system of code words to distinguish blues shouters from girl singers, black voices from white voices. Unlike many of their white counterparts, they rarely conflated genre with race. Instead, they worked to break down and expand the labels and stylistic differences that white critics took such care to delineate. Black critics used the same vocabulary white critics often reserved for white vocalists to describe both black and white vocalists. They referred to blues singers as both shouters and chirpers, instilling the blues voice with a lyricism, clarity, and purity, a beauty and grace absent in descriptions written by white critics. In the process, they released the black voice from the confines of the body of the performer, describing blues voices as delicate, light, and effervescent, just like the voices of girl singers.

With their carefully chosen language, many white critics worked to reembody the black voices heard on the radio and sound recordings. By portraying blues singing as a sweaty, physical endeavor that required a throaty, full voice, they encouraged listeners to imagine the body of the singer, which reintroduced race into the listening equation. This created physical and mental barriers, a distance between listener and performer. It discouraged intimacy and closeness. It helped listeners reduce black performers to a collection of stereotypes, which in turn downplayed, and potentially eliminated, their individuality and humanity.

As cultural historian Richard Dyer explains in his discussion of embodiment and race, "Black people can be reduced (in white culture) to their bodies and thus to race, but white people are something else that is realized in and yet is not reducible to the corporeal, or racial." He further explains that "the embodied something else of whiteness" manifests itself in the "spirit"—the possession of a soul, humanity, enterprise, and agency.[13] White performers were more than just their bodies. They were skilled, rather than intuitive, artists with complex worldviews, thoughts, and dynamic emotions, and the white voice was constructed as possessing these attributes too. These were the qualities that made them human. The white voice was endowed with warmth, purity, kindness, and compassion. It became a sonic representation of their spirits. But this was not the case for the voices of black female singers, whose voices typically lacked spiritual qualities.

During his radio broadcasts, Dave Garroway, however, did not reduce Vaughan to her body. He did not describe her singing as throaty or overly physical; rather, it was ethereal, transcendent, and delicate—"a new gossamer sound." It was beautiful and feminine, warm and sensuous, vibrant and brilliant, and strikingly modern, rather than primitive or intuitive. He also endowed her voice with a spirit. At the end of her segment, when he asked her to resing the tag of "It Might as Well Be Spring," he said, "Breathe into that again," invoking powerful biblical imagery. In Genesis, God breathes life into man so that he could become a living soul. Here Vaughan breathed life into her songs. Her voice became a life force, a representation of her soul and spirit. Garroway had in effect granted Vaughan that intangible, almost magical "embodied something else of whiteness." In 1947, he also began calling Vaughan "the Divine One," a nod to another "Divine Sarah," the legendary actress Sarah Bernhardt. In a sense, Garroway elevated Vaughan to the status of a deity, suggesting that like God, the spirit and creator, Vaughan and her voice resided in the heavenly and celestial spheres.

In many respects, Garroway's description of Vaughan's voice more closely resembled those of vocal whiteness than vocal blackness, at least as defined by white critics of the day. This is not to say that Vaughan's voice sounded white or that it wasn't black enough. Her singing, grounded in the bebop aesthetic and years singing in her church choir, was undeniably a form of cultural expression rooted in her experiences as a black woman. Nor was Vaughan beholden to Dave Garroway and other influential white critics like Leonard Feather for her successes. She insisted, after all, on singing the way that she wanted, even in the face of adversity. Rather, Garroway was so captivated by her innovation, the beauty of her voice, and her exhilarating performances that he set his prejudices and preconceptions aside. And by promoting a boundary-free style of listening, one that sought to eliminate racial, emotional, and ultimately intellectual barriers, he encouraged his audience to do the same.

Disc jockeys set the tone for the conversation about Vaughan's voice—beginning in Chicago and then nationally. Fellow Chicago DJ and Vaughan enthusiast Linn Burton started referring to her as "the Vaughan that comes up like thunder" whenever he played her discs. It was a vivid image borrowed from Rudyard Kipling's poem "Mandalay," popularized by its song adaptation "The Road to Mandalay" during the 1920s. The original line read: "The dawn comes up like thunder outer China 'crost the Bay." In Burton's reimagining, Vaughan was the sun: brilliant and dazzling, a symbol of strength, clarity, and life force. She was the dawn and the beginning of a new day—a new era of popular music. Burton's catchphrase had legs, and it was soon adopted by both the white jazz press and the national black popular press.

As she toured, she made the rounds of the local radio stations, just as she had in Chicago, appearing on dozens, and likely hundreds, of disc jockey shows. She would sing, sometimes for an in-studio audience, chat with the disc jockey, plug her most recent releases and current gig, and then, smiling happily beside the DJ, pose for pictures, which then appeared in local and national publications. A town's most popular jockeys often emceed Vaughan's local engagements and sometimes broadcast her concerts live, resulting in even more publicity and exposure. Soon DJs across the country began referring to Vaughan as "the New Sound," an epithet that referred to both her innovative, modern bebop stylings and the quality of her voice: its extraordinary beauty, elegance, and lushness. It was a voice unlike any heard before. Soon advertisements and posters announcing Vaughan's performances billed her as "The Most Talked About Voice in America."

Before her successes in Chicago, Vaughan struggled to find consistent work. After, she was booked solid. As 1947 came to a close, she had been working nonstop since March, ten whole months, and there was no break in sight. Years later, when asked about her grueling schedule early on, Vaughan acknowledged: "Oh, it was rough. You know, you had maybe three or four shows a night during the week, and four or five on the weekends. And we're doing loads and loads of one-nighters, and loads and loads of clubs, and loads and loads of loudness, and loads and loads of drunkenness, and loads and loads of no money. But it was still fun. Now that it's over!"[14]

Her demanding schedule did begin to pay off. In 1947, she emerged onto the national music scene, capping off the year by winning annual popularity polls sponsored by the leading trade magazines. Both the editors and readers of *Metronome* voted Vaughan the best female vocalist, black or white, without a band in their year-end poll for 1947. Readers of *Down Beat* and *Orchestra World* bestowed similar honors; in March 1948, the predominantly black readers of the *Pittsburgh Courier* selected Vaughan as their favorite female vocalist, upending perennial favorite Ella Fitzgerald, and in April Vaughan was voted the most promising female vocalist of the year in *Billboard*'s 10th Annual College Poll.[15] It was an impressive sweep that symbolized both her acceptance by the jazz establishment and a changing of the guard—from the old-school, more traditional swing of the war years to the postwar modernism of bebop. Her *Down Beat* win, in particular, was an upset over the previous year's winner, Peggy Lee, a platinum blonde queen of swing and former darling of Benny Goodman's big band, the same band responsible for making swing music popular with white, mainstream audiences in 1939. In the 1947 survey, Vaughan scored 1,192 votes in the readers' poll in comparison to Lee's 870. Although relatively few readers participated in the polls, the results made national headlines, and the awards, usually plaques, were presented on national radio broadcasts with photos of the award ceremonies circulated in the national press.

As Vaughan's popularity grew, she not only furthered her own career; she also brought more attention to bebop and the cohort of musicians she had worked with in the Earl Hines and Billy Eckstine bands, many of whom still struggled to find a wider audience. On April 18, 1948, she and saxophonist Charlie Parker launched a twenty-one-city tour of concert halls throughout the Midwest and East Coast. Sponsored by Norman Granz's popular Jazz at the Philharmonic series, the concerts focused on bebop and also included tenor saxophonists Dexter Gordon and Flip Phillips, trumpeter Red Rodney, guitarist Barney Kessel, bassist Tommy Potter, and drummer Stan Levy backing the headliners. Importantly, Sarah Vaughan, also accompanied by pianist Jimmy Jones, received top billing. Despite the prominence of Charlie Parker in modern histories of bebop and jazz, in 1948 Vaughan's fame surpassed Parker's. She was the main draw. Ads and marquees listed her name above his. Concert previews made only passing mention of Parker and the other instrumentalists, focusing instead on Vaughan, who, according to the *Cincinnati Enquirer,* was "the nation's number one record personality; with such sides as 'Lord's Prayer,' 'Love Me or Leave Me,' and 'Body and Soul' leading dozens more of her platters."[16] And in reviews it was Vaughan, not Parker, who stood out. "That Sarah Vaughan, by the way, is everything that's been claimed for her. What a goose pimple–raising song stylist she is!" the *Pittsburgh Post-Gazette* proclaimed following her April 22 appearance. The *St. Louis Post-Dispatch* deemed her the "most artistic performer" of the night on April 30.[17] And according to the *Milwaukee Journal-Sentinel*'s reviewer, the troupe's May 4 concert "served to introduce bebop, the newest art form of jazz, to Milwaukee." He acknowledged the contributions of Parker and his instrumental colleagues, "a group of top technicians," then declared Vaughan the star of the evening, concluding, "The show was really stopped by Sarah Vaughan, a brown gal in a white gown that sparkled with sequins. Her voice sparkled even more and frequently went off on the tangents with which Miss Vaughan has insinuated herself among the country's top vocalists."[18]

Time and again, Vaughan's singing introduced new audiences
to the world of jazz and her favorite corner of that world, bebop. Her voice was a gateway of sorts. By 1948, however, she
was beginning to reach beyond this world. Her appeal was expanding and her audience growing. In May, four New York DJs
selected Vaughan, the only African American on the bill, to headline a stage show at the Strand Theatre, one of the city's grand
movie palaces. It was her first show on Broadway, the so-called
Great White Way, and, according to the black press, hundreds
of young fans crowded the Strand's stage door each night seeking her autograph. During the show's two-week run, members of
Vaughan's regional fan clubs presented her with a thoroughbred
boxer they named Vaughanderful and she later renamed Baron
von Ludwig.[19] In August, listeners selected Vaughan to headline
another DJ show, organized by Garroway and his Vaughan-loving
colleagues, at the Chicago Theatre. In November, members of
DJ Graeme Zimmer's Music Makers Club in Columbus, Indi-
ana, selected "I'll Wait and Pray," recently rerecorded by Vaughan
for Musicraft, as their favorite disc of the month, and Zimmer
played it daily. Six months later they voted Vaughan their favorite
girl singer in Zimmer's semiannual popularity poll. She beat out
darlings Doris Day and Jo Stafford. And in perhaps the most unusual sign of her growing popularity, that spring the black press
reported that police were searching for a Sarah Vaughan fan following a robbery at a record store in Atlantic City, New Jersey.
Aside from the cash in the register, the thief limited his spoils
to the store's complete inventory of Vaughan records, some 250
discs.[20]

This changing of the guard also coincided with a larger shift
in both the music industry and American society. As the United
States recovered from World War II, life began to return to normal. Women who had entered the workforce at the call of Rosie
the Riveter relinquished their factory jobs to men home from the
war and resumed their prewar lives of domesticity. At the same
time, a boom in manufacturing generated unprecedented economic growth, newfound prosperity, and a thriving consumer

culture. Fashion became less austere, and more glamorous and sophisticated, as the "New Look" swept across the country. Travel became easier. More people owned cars, and the government built new roads and developed the country's network of interstate highways. These roads, in turn, facilitated "white flight," the migration of financially comfortable white families from crowded cities to the open expanses of newly created suburbs.

As the country's population shifted away from urban centers, so did the patrons for live music. Audiences shrank as radio, then television, became more and more popular. The huge urban dance halls, known for their battles of the bands and hordes of jitterbuggers during the war years, were replaced by smaller, more intimate nightclubs and supper clubs—the perfect venue for trios or quartets fronted by a vocalist. In short, the era of the big band was over and the era of the big-name singer had arrived. Vaughan, with her "New Sound," was poised to take advantage of this changing musical landscape.

PART II

A Star Is Born, 1948–1958

To a passerby, the entrance to New York City's Birdland was unimpressive, inconspicuous even. A simple awning extended onto the sidewalk of Broadway just around the corner from 52nd Street, home of the once thriving "Swing Street." A single word, in stark white letters, adorned the awning: BIRDLAND. The uninitiated would simply walk by. Those in the know, however, stopped. They were drawn to the bright lights flooding from the open door plastered with posters and playbills and, most important, the music that spilled out onto the sidewalk. Insiders knew that the unusual name was, in fact, a reference to the bebop saxophonist Charlie "Bird" Parker and that this was a jazz club. Dubbed the "Jazz Center of the World," Birdland showcased the best in modern jazz. It was the home of the hepcats.

After passing through an entrance resembling a birdcage, patrons descended into the basement club. To the left, behind the long bar and all along the club's side walls, glass cages housed dozens of singing birds. To the right, there was a wall of booths, and in front, a small, slightly elevated stage, barely big enough to hold a piano and drum set. Fifteen tables with red-checkered tablecloths clustered around the bandstand. Behind the tables, along the back wall, was the "bullpen," with rows of chairs reserved for listeners—those who wanted to focus exclusively on music, without the distraction of food, drink, or socializing. For a cover of ninety-eight cents, plus minimum (for those not sitting in the bullpen), patrons could hear three acts on a continuous loop until early in the morning. In all, the club could squeeze in two hundred lovers of jazz.

Birdland opened its doors on December 15, 1949. Vaughan made her debut almost a year later on November 16, 1950, and when she returned for a ten-day stay on Thursday, March 26, 1953, it was her ninth appearance at the club. Vaughan was a favorite at Birdland—both on and off the stage. Owner Morris Levy said that he received more mail requesting her than any other artist he booked. He commissioned portraitist Miguelo Andre to paint a series of murals of Vaughan for the club's walls, and the club's bestselling mixed drink was the Sarah Vaughan cooler.[1] When she returned five months later, management installed a new security door for her dressing room and hired a security guard to watch her designer wardrobe, reportedly worth $10,000.[2] Playing Birdland was like going home, and that night in March more so than usual. She had just returned from two weeks in Paris, the final leg of her first European tour, and it was the eve of her twenty-ninth birthday. Actress Dorothy Dandridge; vocalists Eartha Kitt, Patti Page, and Thelma Carpenter; rhumba man Noro Morales; and a host of society reporters were on hand to help her celebrate. And radio audiences from coast to coast listened in as NBC broadcast her opening night on *Stars of Jazz,* thirty minutes of jazz live from Birdland airing Tuesdays and Thursdays.

"Sarah Vaughan, ladies and gentlemen!" announced NBC veteran Fred Collins. "Thank you. Thank you," she called out above the audience's applause. Then she launched into "I Get a Kick Out of You" followed by a more adventurous "I Cried for

You," two swinging rhythm numbers, both standards from her Musicraft days and both recently reissued by MGM. That night Vaughan was accompanied by her regular pianist John Malachi, mistakenly identified on air as "Jimmy Mordecai" by Collins, and drummer Fats Herd and bassist Wyatt Reuther, both on loan from Erroll Garner's trio. "Wonderful Sarah," said Collins, as she finished singing. "Thank you. Thank you. Thank you," Vaughan shouted again as the crowd clapped, whistled, and shouted their approval.[3]

"But tonight is not a night for crying here at Birdland," Collins interrupted. "All hail fellows well met, welcoming Sarah Vaughan and wishing her a . . . very, very happy birthday! They just brought up here on the bandstand one of the most beautiful cakes I've ever seen in my life, Sarah," Collins said above more applause and whistles. "Thank you very much, darling," a coy Vaughan replied. "I'm umm . . . twenty-one years old." She giggled, and the audience laughed along. "Bless your heart," said Collins. Vaughan giggled again. "Ladies and gentlemen, this is a little bit unusual. But Sarah has done so much for us by way of this wonderful entertainment. Could we make an exception? Tonight you sing to her. I don't think we even have to hit it." They didn't. Led by Collin's authoritative if slightly out-of-tune baritone, the audience enthusiastically sang "Happy Birthday." Then Vaughan, standing next to the multitiered, frosted cake, bent down to blow out the candles, all three of them. "She just blew out the candles," Collins told his listeners in radioland. "All nineteen of them? Twenty-one. Well," he said, playing along with Vaughan's earlier joke. "Three of them!" yelled Vaughan, correcting him. "This is a terrible thing to do after singing 'Happy Birthday' and everything else, Sarah," Collins continued. "But we have about two and a half, three minutes, something like that. Could you do us the favor of singing 'Body and Soul?'" "Alright. Love to."[4]

Vaughan was in the midst of the second crossover phase of her career: her journey from a bebop singer, favored by black audiences and in-the-know jazz intelligentsia, to a pop artist, with a larger, more mainstream following. In the six years since appearing on Dave Garroway's radio programs, she had achieved her first successes on the pop record charts, graduated from a small independent record label to one of the major players, and steadily improved the stature and prestige of the venues where she performed. She still played intimate jazz clubs like Birdland, but she also became a regular fixture of the exclusive supper club circuit, the lucrative movie palaces, and the more elegant concert halls, venues that had often been off-limits to all but the most popular and successful black artists. During these years, Vaughan streamlined her vocal style, reining in her more esoteric mannerisms and harmonic excursions, remnants of her early bebop days with Charlie Parker and Dizzy Gillespie. She did not sing "straighter," per se; rather, she added another layer of polish and sophistication. Her interpretations became more eloquent and seamless, less superficially experimental or avant-garde yet still engaging and compelling studies in vocal improvisation. "Headliner Sarah Vaughan has unique pulling power," *Variety* critic Herman Schoenfeld explained in 1953. "The squarer customers dig her, via her pop disk releases, and she's still caviar for the cognoscenti because of her tricky stylistic attack."[5]

Vaughan, however, had to continue to fight to have her voice heard and sing the way that she wanted. She battled a dysfunctional record label. She endured overbearing record producers, the censure of jazz critics, and the demeaning requests of club owners. Motivated by personal agendas, often with the bottom line in mind, they pressured her to change the way that she sang. Vaughan stood up to all of them, in her own quiet yet firm way. She possessed a keen awareness of her responsibilities as an artist and black woman. She understood the impact of her voice and balked when asked to sing material she found racially demeaning or artistically beneath her. She held firm to her musical vision and integrity. And as the 1950s progressed, she found a way to balance the competing demands of commercial pop stardom with her desire to remain a jazz artist. In the process, she changed the way that white America heard and understood the black female voice while simultaneously presenting an example of black female genius and creativity to the world.

That night at Birdland in 1953, on the eve of her twenty-ninth birthday, demonstrated the high esteem and regard that audiences had for Vaughan. But that same night also revealed challenges in her life offstage. After finishing the NBC simulcast and her last set, after her birthday party, and after schmoozing with the celebrities and fans in the audience, Vaughan and her husband, George Treadwell, went to the Veteran's Club, an after-hours spot in Harlem. When she arrived at 5:25 A.M., the place was packed, standing room only, much like her sets at Birdland earlier in the evening. A young man gave up his seat at the bar, and she sat down, had a drink, and relaxed. Then the man sitting next to her, a twenty-five-year-old newsstand operator named Edmund Johnson, asked if he could introduce Vaughan to his female friend. She declined, telling Johnson, "I am just too tired to meet anybody."

What happened next is unclear. According to Johnson, he thanked Vaughan, turned his back, and continued socializing with his friends. Then Treadwell, standing a few feet away, rushed over and accosted Johnson, "Man, you have insulted my wife." Surprised, Johnson spun around and replied, "Are you kidding, champ? All I asked your wife was to give me a chance to introduce her to this lady with us." Johnson told the *New York Amsterdam News* that he then heard Treadwell mutter, "You are one of these wise guys, aren't you?" "No sense in me arguing with you, man," Johnson said and walked away.[6]

As he turned to walk away, Johnson said that someone held him from behind, and Treadwell lunged forward and smashed a highball glass in his face. Before Johnson could retaliate, a crowd of people pulled Treadwell away. Johnson needed twenty-two stiches in his left cheek and multiple hospital visits. He filed assault charges against Treadwell, and Johnson's lawyer planned a civil suit for $250,000. The police sought Treadwell for questioning and issued a warrant for his arrest, but they couldn't find him. He had disappeared.[7]

Vaughan told a different story. "First of all, let me explain that George is entirely innocent of this assault charge," she said to Alvin Webb of the *Amsterdam News* on Tuesday, March 31, five days after the incident. "He is in Philly now, but I expect him back here tomorrow." When Vaughan gave her comment, she was between sets at Birdland, and earlier in the night she'd done another coast-to-coast simulcast on NBC radio.

"My girlfriend and I were being annoyed by Johnson and his companions and George came over to the bar to reprimand them about molesting us," she explained. "This fellow, Johnson, reached in his pocket as if he were trying to pull out a weapon of some kind, and one of George's friends hit him in the face with a glass. I'm not going to call any names, but I swear to God it wasn't George." After finishing the near-midnight interview, she went back out onstage and according to the *Amsterdam News* began her next set with "Lover Man (Oh Where Can You Be?)."[8]

Treadwell returned from Philadelphia Wednesday night. The police booked and questioned him. He denied any wrongdoing, insisting that he had not assaulted Johnson, nor had he eluded the police, and he promised to provide an affidavit from the man who did attack Johnson.[9] "Guy became abusive," said Treadwell during a press conference at the Theresa Hotel in Harlem. Then he lashed out at the press. "[He] took the position that the newsmen should have come to him before printing the police's and the other guy's story," James Hicks wrote in the *Baltimore Afro-American*. "I have news for George. Every newsman in town was looking for him to get his side of the story. But that's not all. The police were looking for George, too!"[10]

Two weeks later, on Tuesday morning, April 14, 1953, Treadwell appeared in Manhattan's felony court. Johnson did not.

For the second time in a row he failed to appear. Without a witness, the assault charges against Treadwell were dropped. Neither Johnson nor his lawyer could be found for comment; both seemed to have left town for the week. Rumors circulated that Johnson had been "taken care of" and advised "to take a short trip until things cool off."[11]

Treadwell loved publicity, for his wife and himself. In the years since he became Vaughan's manager, he had become a master of shaping her public image and, by extension, his own. He initiated aggressive publicity campaigns that portrayed Vaughan as a stylish and increasingly affluent modern woman who, when she wasn't working, was a domestic homebody. He was a savvy businessman and self-sacrificing, hardworking husband completely devoted to his wife's career. Their marriage was strong and their home life happy. This portrait of traditional gender roles and domestic bliss was, in fact, an important prerequisite for Vaughan's crossover pop successes. And tales of an after-hours bar fight, possibly fueled by jealousy; an arrest after eluding the police; and dates in felony court threatened Treadwell's carefully crafted picture, suggesting that all was not well behind the scenes.

5

"The Girl with the Magic Voice"

In 1948, during the dog days of summer, Vaughan scored her first pop hit: "It's Magic," a sentimental, romantic ballad featured in that summer's film *Romance on the High Seas*. She recorded the tune on December 27, 1947, as part of a year-end push to stockpile new sides before another American Federation of Musicians recording ban began on January 1, 1948. The single, paired with "It's You or No One," also from *Romance*, was released at the end of April. And in August, it finally made its way onto the all-important *Billboard* charts. Once again, the nation's disc jockeys came through for Vaughan. Her recording of "It's Magic" spent eleven weeks, until the end of October, on the "Most Played by Disc Jockeys" chart, peaking at No. 11. Of the hundreds of songs available to DJs in the nation's major markets, there were only ten that they played more often. Boosted by this exposure, in September Vaughan's "It's Magic" made a brief appearance, just two weeks, on the "Best-Selling Popular Retail Records" list. The black press reported that she had sold four hundred thousand copies, predicting that she would soon surpass a half million.[1] And on September 12, Vaughan sang the tune on Ed Sullivan's popular television show *Toast of the Town*.[2] "It's Magic" was, by far, her biggest seller to date, her breakout record, and the culmination of the momentum that had been building for the past eighteen months.

Vaughan was not the only vocalist to find success with "It's Magic." In the 1940s, it was common for many artists to record, or cover, the same tune, and in an effort to maximize sales record companies usually released covers to appeal to each segment of the larger music market: country, folk, race, and, of course, pop, the largest market. "It's Magic" was one of the most popular and most played songs of 1948, with Doris Day, Vic Damone, Dick Haymes, Gordon MacRae, Tony Martin, and the Buddy Kaye Quintet all releasing discs in hopes of finding their niche in the market. Doris Day's cover outpaced them all. The up-and-coming blond, blue-eyed former big band singer made her film debut in *Romance on the High Seas* and performed its signature song. Her recording of "It's Magic" entered the charts in early July, right after the film opened, and stayed there for twenty-one weeks, peaking at No. 2. It was the beginning of her decades-long dominance of both the box office and pop charts.

But Vaughan came in a close second, succeeding, in many respects, against the odds. She was the only black artist of the bunch, and her record company, Musicraft, was small, with less clout and fewer resources than the labels backing her competitors, powerhouses like Columbia, Mercury, Decca, Capitol, and Victor. Vaughan's traction with "It's Magic" was an impressive feat, a watershed moment in her career. It provided an opportunity for Musicraft to realize its lofty sales goals promised Vaughan in her contract two years earlier. And more important, it demonstrated Vaughan's potential to become a viable crossover artist. Unlike the progressive jazz standards that she had become known for, her version of "It's Magic" was a deliberately commercial single designed to appeal to mainstream, predominantly white audiences. Backed by a lush string orchestra, complete with harp interludes, Vaughan sang the melody without her trademark embellishments. The disc showcased the sumptuous beauty of her voice, and audiences, both black and white (and not just whites who considered themselves members of the jazz intelligentsia), liked what they heard. She had more fans than ever, and disc jockeys began referring to her as the "Girl with the Magic Voice." It was a play on words, a reference to the song's title, but also an acknowledgment that her voice was special, unique, and powerful.

Yet Vaughan didn't profit financially as much as she should have from the success of "It's Magic," nor was she able to build on the momentum created by her first pop hit. In the fall, as DJs across the county continued to push "It's Magic," Musicraft was struggling financially. There had been hints of trouble before. In the spring and summer of 1947, as her national profile grew and she became a darling of DJs across the country, Vaughan was forced to take a seven-month hiatus from the recording studio as the label reorganized and scrambled to secure more funding. And now, in the fall of 1948, Musicraft was on the verge of bankruptcy. In October, the label began liquidating its assets, including the plant used to press records; it stopped releasing and distributing new records; and it stopped paying its artists record royalties.

Vaughan's frustration was palpable. "I mean, a long time ago, when I was with Musicraft, I used to go in there to see the guy about the records," she told Les Tomkins in 1977. "He would sit in his big office, and show me the big pictures on the walls of all the yachts he owned." Meanwhile, she was not receiving royalties for the records that she had sold. On September 14, 1948, Vaughan received her usual quarterly statement from the label—minus her royalty check. They owed her $3,117.93, her share of sales from almost eighty-eight thousand records.[3] And due to Musicraft's financial woes, she had fewer records to sell (one possible reason why her cover of "It's Magic" spent only two weeks on *Billboard*'s bestselling list). Excited new fans who had discovered Vaughan on the radio wanted to hear more. But they could not find copies of "It's Magic" or any other Vaughan sides in stores. Record bins were empty because Musicraft could not meet the demand for their most popular, bestselling artist. "Soon after that [Musicraft] went bankrupt!" said Vaughan. "Just when I was passing Doris Day's big hit on 'It's Magic.'"[4]

Her recording career, which months earlier had seemed so promising, stalled. She was under contract until June 1950, and even though Musicraft had breached her contract, they refused to release her. Stuck at a dysfunctional record company, Vaughan sued Musicraft. She requested her back royalties, rights to the thirty-seven masters she recorded for the label, and, most important, a release from her contract. As her lawyers waded through the legal mess, Vaughan continued to tour and make radio and television appearances. Fortunately, her popularity with DJs, combined with the sales of "It's Magic," had captured the attention of executives from the major record companies. They courted Vaughan, and Treadwell, her husband-manager, worked behind the scenes to secure a new deal.

On January 3, 1949, Vaughan secretly signed with Columbia Records. Two weeks later, Musicraft offered to release her from her contract if she waived all rights to her royalties and masters, paid them $10,000, and cut six more sides for Musicraft, all at her own expense.[5] (The label desperately needed new material to release but did not have the funds to produce it themselves.) Treadwell promptly rejected the offer.[6] Tensions with Musicraft escalated again when, on January 20, Vaughan stepped into Columbia's studios to record three sides. She returned five days later to record three more.[7] Vaughan was moving on, with the assumption that she would soon be free from Musicraft, but the struggling label would not let their most popular artist go. Then Musicraft threatened to sue Columbia for breach of contract, and Columbia stopped all work on Vaughan's new discs and waited for her legal troubles to pass; no progress was made for the next two months.[8]

Finally, on March 17, 1949, minutes before Vaughan and her attorney prepared to make her case in federal court in New York, she settled with Musicraft. They agreed to release Vaughan from her contract if she agreed to waive all royalties owed to her for records sold before January 1, 1949—an unknown amount, estimated by industry insiders as somewhere between $7,500 and $15,000; to decrease her future royalty earnings in half, from 5 percent per record to 2.5 percent; to record four new sides for Musicraft at her own expense; and to pay Musicraft $1,500 in attorney fees.[9] Musicraft retained control of all of Vaughan's master recordings. The deal was far from perfect, but Vaughan, after months of inaction and legal woes, was now free to move on with her new label, Columbia. She had successfully cleared another hurdle in her journey to find an audience for her musical vision and voice.

Columbia Records could offer Vaughan opportunities that Musicraft and other independent labels like it simply could not. She now had the backing of a major player in the industry. Columbia, Victor, RCA, and Capitol were the top four record labels, and, after the second American Federation of Musicians strike in 1948, they controlled 90 percent of the market. Columbia was at the forefront of recording technology. Their research and development department had just invested $250,000 inventing the $33^{1}/_{3}$ rpm long-playing microgroove record, which would revolutionize the sound of recorded music and the way audiences heard and consumed music. Columbia owned its manufacturing plants and an unparalleled network of distributors. Unlike other labels, including the struggling Musicraft, Columbia eliminated all middlemen, which allowed them to cut production and marketing costs and maximize profits, all while reaching as many listeners as possible.[10] And Columbia could offer Vaughan more money. The black press speculated that her five-year contract was worth at least a quarter million dollars in future royalties. It was an impressive sum, especially for a black artist, and for many within the black community it validated not just Vaughan and her talent but all black talent. Her contract with Columbia symbolized racial progress. The financial terms of her contract were in fact more modest, and it was for three years, with two one-year options. But it did include a promise to record sixteen sides a year, twelve of which had to be released.

Columbia vice president Manie Sacks promised to rush Vaughan's first Columbia releases to market in record time. Sacks was responsible for bringing Vaughan to Columbia, and during his nine-year tenure at the label he had nurtured along the careers of singers Frank Sinatra, Dinah Shore, and most recently Doris Day, making them all household names. He had a knack for discovering new talent, pairing an artist with the right material, usually sentimental ballads, and then backing her with effective promotion. Sacks used the same strategy with Vaughan. In April, during the buildup to her debut disc, a pairing of "As You Desire Me," a lush, romantic ballad accompanied by a full orchestra, and "Black Coffee," a ballad with blues inflections, he announced that the disc had preorders of more than 150,000 copies.[11] Photos of her controversial studio sessions in January circulated in the press. And Columbia widely distributed the disc to jockeys across the country. They played the record and touted each tune's hit potential. "As You Desire Me" appeared on *Billboard*'s Disc Jockeys Pick chart for three weeks, the maximum allowed any disc, then was replaced by "Black Coffee" at the end of May. On June 27, Columbia released two more discs, followed by more in September, October, and November, all with a similar rollout. And four songs made brief appearances on *Billboard*'s popularity charts.

Vaughan sounded stunning on her new Columbia discs. In 1947, Columbia became the first label to use magnetic tape to record all of its master tapes. Recording on magnetic tape captured more sonic information than cutting a disc directly onto wax cylinders, the technique still used by independent labels like Musicraft, and it was quieter, with less background noise, fewer pops and crackles. The results were striking. Unlike the small, almost boxed-in, old-fashioned sound of her Musicraft releases, on Columbia Vaughan sounded modern. Her voice was fuller, richer, and more dynamic. The bell tones of her upper register were clearer, and the full-bodied tones of her contralto more luxurious and free ranging. Listeners could hear every detail as she sculpted individual notes and subtly used vibrato to punctuate her phrasing. For the first time, many of her listeners, especially those unfamiliar with her live performances, truly heard her voice.

Backed by the clout of Columbia and the increased exposure the label offered, Vaughan's career catapulted to the next level, and, once again, the stature and prestige of her gigs improved. On July 25, 1949, she performed with the Philadelphia Symphony Orchestra at Robin Hood Dell, the orchestra's summer home. She shared the bill with Duke Ellington and his orchestra in a concert praised, especially by the black press, for placing the creative vision of two of jazz's finest artists, representatives of black music, on an equal footing with the highbrow, predominantly white, cultural institution of European classical music. In November, Vaughan achieved another career milestone when she made her first appearances at the Paramount Theatre on Broadway in New York. Another of the famed movie palaces, like the Strand, the Paramount was the biggest, most prestigious pop venue in town, a regular stomping ground for Frank Sinatra, Peggy Lee, and countless other popular white acts. Celebrities attended Vaughan's club dates on both coasts. Executives from MGM scouted her performances at Bop City in New York as they prepared to acquire Musicraft's masters. Her recordings were the now-defunct label's most valuable asset. After hearing Vaughan at the Oasis in Los Angeles, an executive from Twentieth Century Fox sent her a case of scotch and invited her to a sit-down. While nothing came of the meeting, she did sign a contract with Universal International to produce a series of film shorts to be shown in movie theaters throughout the country. She continued her rounds of the DJ radio shows, returned as a guest star on Ed Sullivan's popular variety show, and made appearances on other nationally broadcast television programs, including CBS's popular *We the People*, simulcast coast to coast on both radio and television. Vaughan introduced herself to this national audience. She told her personal story, her journey from a Newark choir girl to Columbia recording artist, and then sang "The Lord's Prayer." Her club dates regularly attracted celebrities, and when she returned to Café Society in December 1949, she merited $2,250 a week plus a percentage of the door—a far cry from the $200 she garnered in 1946.

Vaughan's career clearly benefited from her associations with Columbia, but it is unclear if Columbia benefited in turn. She was the label's marquee black vocalist, signed because she showed crossover potential. It's likely that label executives hoped that she would become their Nat King Cole, who in the 1940s had transformed from a well-respected jazz pianist leading his own trio into a chart-topping balladeer. He scored hits with "The Christmas Song" and "Route 66" in 1946, "Nature Boy" in 1948, "Mona Lisa" in 1950, and "Too Young" and "Unforgettable" in 1951. While her discs did well, Vaughan had yet to achieve the tremendous successes of Cole, and Columbia's pop music division, under the helm of Sacks, was foundering. The label's pop sales ranked dead last among the four major labels. And in the spring of 1950, Columbia's executive vice president Goddard Lieberson began to shake things up. Sacks, an old-school gentleman who came of age during the swing years, was pushed out in favor of a younger, brasher rival with a controversial yet very profitable vision for popular music.

On May 5, 1950, Vaughan returned to Columbia's New York recording studios and was greeted by her new producer, Mitch Miller. He was a cigar-smoking thirty-eight-year-old classical oboist turned artist and repertoire man, recently lured away from Mercury. He sported a mustache and dramatic goatee, and he paired this with an equally bold, often overbearing, albeit charismatic, personality. The previous year while at Mercury, he orchestrated the runaway success of Frankie Laine's "That Lucky Old Sun" and "Mule Train" and was earning a reputation as a hit maker with a new, revolutionary approach to popular music. He invented novelty songs, tunes that incorporated slick, unconventional sounds derived from unusual instrumentation and technological special effects or "ethnic," nonwhite, sounds, and often both. His records for Columbia would feature harpsichords, accordions, wood blocks to simulate a cracking whip, French horns honking like geese, guitarists that sounded like chickens, dogs barking and howling, and hands clapping, not to mention technological manipulations like echo chambers and overdubbing. Miller prioritized the bottom line and felt no shame in appealing to the lowest common denominator.

It's possible that Vaughan let out an amused chuckle when she first saw Miller, aka "the Beard." After all, her fellow beboppers had popularized goatees, along with a distinct bebop look and language eight years earlier. But Dizzy Gillespie and his cohorts used them to signify their hipness, their status as artists of innovative, avant-garde music, and ultimately their distance, both culturally and socially, from the white American mainstream. On Miller, the goatee must have seemed like an affectation of hipness, even a little silly on a white man and industry insider committed to commercialism, especially to someone like Vaughan who increasingly epitomized hip elegance and coolness herself.

Vaughan, however, remained polite and professional, and their May 4 session was business as usual. Accompanied by Norman Leyden's orchestra, she recorded two more romantic ballads, very much in the vein of her earlier Columbia releases produced by Sacks. Two weeks later, on May 18, she led her first (and only) jazz session for the label. Backed by an octet that included trumpeter Miles Davis and was billed as George Treadwell and His Allstars, even though Treadwell didn't play and pianist Jimmy Jones was listed as the session's contractor, Vaughan sang a collection of jazz standards.

"This album was a real mistake," proclaimed *Down Beat*'s reviewer. "Sarah has recorded half the tunes before, in each case better." Jazz critics of the day prized innovation and complexity, a constant evolution of style and ideas, and were frustrated that Vaughan simply rehashed the past. "All in all, spiritless and lackluster sides," the magazine concluded.[12]

Yet *Down Beat*'s critics approved of her next two pop releases.

She recorded the up-tempo "I Love the Guy" and "Thinking of You," a slower, more contemplative ballad, on Thursday, July 27. Backed by a swinging big band, Vaughan incorporated her trademark vocal inflections on both songs, and *Down Beat* praised her. "['I Love the Guy'] demonstrates her fine ear for tonal shadings, as well as the clean simplicity of her best phrasing," wrote the reviewer, adding, "Some of her leapings here would faze a thoroughly agile tenor man."[13] With these sides Vaughan acknowledged her jazz roots and skillfully distilled them for a more mainstream audience. She was singing jazz-infused pop. Columbia pressed the disc and got it into the hands of DJs within twenty-four hours. That Friday night in New York City, WNEW's Martin Block, host of the popular *Make Believe Ballroom,* named "I Love the Guy" the best new recording of the week, and both sides charted during the fall.[14]

In September, Miller followed a similar formula. He produced a brassy arrangement of "Perdido," the Duke Ellington standard adopted by Vaughan as her signature tune during the early 1950s, and backed it with the less enduring, more novelty-focused "Whippa-Whippa-Woo" on the B-side. The tide of critical opinion turned again, as *Down Beat* declared: "Two disappointing sides by a girl who usually never disappoints. *Perdido* doesn't swing, has little of Sarah's usual freshness, indeed gets into banal riffing at points."[15] The mixed responses of jazz critics highlighted an emerging tension between Vaughan and critics who resented her growing profile as a pop, rather than jazz, artist.

Despite the ambivalence of critics, Columbia seemed happy with Vaughan. Two years into her contract, she had proven herself a reliable artist. She consistently garnered praise and airtime from disc jockeys, and her appeal continued to grow. Six of her releases made brief forays onto the *Billboard, Cash Box,* and *Variety* charts, three of them that fall.

Then Columbia raised the stakes. In October, more than a year before her original three-year contract expired on January 2, 1952, Columbia exercised Vaughan's two one-year options. She was now under contract until January 2, 1954. Miller asserted his influence and implemented his strategy for making Vaughan into a star. And it's likely that the tone of their recording sessions changed as he embraced his brainchild: novelty songs—the same hit-making formula he used with Frankie Laine and would soon use to great success with Tony Bennett, Rosemary Clooney, and Jo Stafford.

On December 6, 1950, Vaughan recorded "De Gas Pipe She's Leakin' Joe," an up-tempo calypso-inspired novelty tune. Backed by a brassy big band and male chorus, Vaughan adopted West Indian–accented English and belted her way through the vaguely Trinidadian tune. Her displeasure is audible, and it's clear that she did not want to sing the song. The usually perfectionist Vaughan, known for her perfect pitch, sang out of tune. She was out of sync with the band and choir. And, most telling, midway through the song, she stifled a laugh, perhaps of discomfort or defiance, disbelief that she was contractually obliged to sing a tune she found unworthy of her talent. The lyrics were silly, the harmonic language simple, and the faux Trinidadian patter offensive. At its core, "De Gas Pipe She's Leakin' Joe" used race, stereotypical representations of Caribbean life, as a novelty device. It was a parody of blackness and antithetical to Vaughan's career-long desire not to be typecast or pigeonholed because of her race.

"You can't believe the crap that he had Jo [Stafford] record, tunes like 'Underneath the Overpass,' stuff that just died," recalled Paul Weston, Stafford's husband and the newly appointed West Coast head of A&R for Columbia. "He would be very persuasive, and the artist didn't have much choice. They'd say, 'This is a piece of crap,' and Mitch would say, 'Oh, it's gonna be a hit,' so they'd do it."[16]

Miller was more heavy-handed with Rosemary Clooney. Six months later, on June 6, 1951, she released what would become her first big hit, "Come On-A My House." Based on an Armenian folk song, its arrangement featured both a jazzy, barrelhouse-style harpsichord and a calypso rhythm. Clooney disliked the tune's campy, hodgepodge arrangement and cheesy accent. "I don't think so," Clooney told Miller. She wanted to record "Tenderly," the jazz standard popularized by Vaughan, instead. Clooney admired Vaughan and regularly attended Vaughan's club dates. "Know what I think?" Miller replied. "I think you'll show up because otherwise you will be fired."[17] Clooney was only twenty-two and unestablished. She did not have the clout or confidence to stand up to Miller. Plus, he was used to getting what he wanted. "I know for a fact that Mitch wanted things his way, and in certain instances, it worked. After he finished recording something, he could call the Sales Department and say, 'Ship three hundred thousand on consignment.' I mean, he had that kind of juice," Clooney explained. "I went along with whatever Mitch wanted to do."[18] Years later, she confessed that whenever she listened to "Come On-A My House," she could only hear the anger and frustration in her voice.

One can imagine the negotiations between Vaughan and Miller when he presented her with "De Gas Pipe She's Leakin' Joe." Perhaps Vaughan refused to sing the song. Miller was persuasive, then more insistent. But Vaughan could be stubborn. Did he threaten to fire her too? Years later, she confided to friend Robert Richards that she hated her producer at Columbia and the songs he chose for her.[19] "After all that I did with 'Fatha' Hines and Billy Eckstine, I never was able to understand how the recording people could get those tunes for me," she told Down Beat's Arnold Jay Smith in 1977, her frustration obvious. "But they got 'em. They were the kind of tunes you don't have to go far to get. They are just lying around in piles. A lot of the time the record company owns the tunes or whatever."[20] Miller was known for making minor suggestions to the songwriters bringing him material in exchange for writing credits, which then earned him publishing royalties. Many concluded that this was in fact a form of payback to Miller, a kind of payola, for selecting their tunes.[21] While Miller did not have a writing credit on "De Gas Pipe She's Leakin' Joe," his name did appear in the Columbia records listing the contractors—the musicians, copyist, and arrangers—receiving payment for the studio session.[22] It seems he had a vested interest in its outcome.

In the end, Vaughan recorded a single take of "De Gas Pipe," and there really should have been another. (Miller got five takes out of Clooney before he was satisfied with "Come On-A My House.") Vaughan, however, phoned in her performance, making a joke of the session. It was a kind of musical "I'll show you"— her way of saying: "You can make me sing this, but you cannot control how I sing it. I will not sing it well." And her laugh-it-off approach, similar to her response to John Hammond, the white producer who snubbed her at Café Society because she didn't want to sing the blues, was a more socially acceptable way for Vaughan to channel her anger and frustration. It was probably one of the few options available to her. After all, both she and Clooney were women, and Vaughan was a black woman. Contemporary gender roles, and in the case of Vaughan racial dynamics, dictated that they defer to men. In contrast, Frank Sinatra was more assertive, less compliant. He rejected material, scolded Miller during recording sessions, and stormed out of sessions in disgust. He blamed Miller for his poor sales and faltering career. The escalating tensions between them, culminating with Sinatra's collaboration with the buxom comic actress Dagmar on "Mama Will Bark," a novelty tune with actual dogs barking, prompted Sinatra to leave Columbia for Capitol in 1952. But most women didn't feel comfortable behaving this way. They were used to being polite and deferential. While Vaughan was firm and consistent in her convictions, she was shy, reserved, and, at her core, a nonconfrontational person.

"She was very easy to work with, she was a wonderful artist," Miller, a master at shaping public perceptions, told Ted Fox in 1986. "Except she was married to the wrong guy then. I forget who her husband was, but he always tried to get the songs of publisher friends recorded. I had to give in to him a couple of times. You know you don't have the last word if someone goes to bed with your artist at night."[23] Any problems he might have had with Vaughan he attributed to her husband and manager George Treadwell who, ironically enough, he accused of working the system using the same tactics that he was notorious for.

Despite its many imperfections, Miller held his ground and released "De Gas Pipe She's Leakin' Joe" on January 8, 1951, and he backed it with a full-blown promotional campaign. At the end of December, weeks after Vaughan recorded "De Gas Pipe She's Leakin' Joe," Columbia announced a new, revamped promotion strategy. The label had three lists of disc jockeys: A included six hundred DJs, B five hundred, and C four hundred. In the past, Columbia distributed new records to the jockeys in list A first, and if a record showed promise, the label passed it along to the jockeys on list B, then list C. Under the revised plan, a new release was sent to DJs on all three lists, some 1,500 jockeys, simultaneously. The strategy took full advantage of Columbia's vast distribution network while harnessing the power and growing influence of disc jockeys. It allowed a new record to receive airtime in both big and small markets, giving it more opportunities to find an audience, its niche. Columbia reserved this treatment for its top four artists, all of them white: Doris Day, Jo Stafford, Sammy Kaye, and Frank Sinatra.[24] Vaughan was not included on this list, although she should have been. She was Columbia's leading African American vocalist, their Nat King Cole, and, more important, her contract guaranteed her a "top artist" promotion schedule. Vaughan's attorney immediately filed a letter of complaint, and Columbia made the appropriate arrangements for Vaughan to receive their top-star-spinner exploitation too.[25]

But "De Gas Pipe She's Leakin' Joe" and its flip side, "I'll Know," were flops. None of the trade publications reviewed the single, and it never gained traction with disc jockeys, even after Columbia ran a full-page ad in *Billboard* on February 24. In a sense, Vaughan ultimately did prevail. Her next releases faired only slightly better. On January 17, 1951, she recorded a pair of religious songs. The first, Schubert's "Ave Maria," sung in English, provided a glimpse into Vaughan, the opera singer. In another homage to Marian Anderson, who recorded the tune in 1936, Vaughan's singing was plaintive and reflective, her voice full and open, embellished with precise trills and bends that were unmistakable. The more sophisticated, classical orientation of "Ave Maria" was the perfect foil for the primitivism of "De Gas Pipe," and it's possible that Vaughan requested "Ave Maria" for the January 17 session. (The recording became a personal favorite and was played at her funeral.) And perhaps Mitch Miller suggested the down-home spiritual "A City Called Heaven," a reminder of Vaughan's days in the gospel choir at the Mount Zion Baptist Church, for the B-side. Although she sang it flawlessly, there was nothing uniquely Sarah Vaughan about her interpretation. It could have been sung equally well, or better, by any number of gospel singers. The trade press praised both sides, yet record sales remained underwhelming.

It was becoming clear that Mitch Miller didn't know how to make a black artist into a pop star, how not to use race (or ethnicity) as a novelty device. He was in tune with white, mainstream America, but he struggled to present the creations of black artists in a way that wasn't stereotypical or reductive. That said, Vaughan's Columbia recordings that performed best, those that made brief appearances on the pop charts, incorporated more often than not her distinct vocal inflections. On "I Love the Guy," which spent seven weeks on the charts, peaking at No. 10, she liberally added vocal turns and twists that became more elaborate as the tune progressed. On "Thinking of You," which also spent seven weeks on the *Billboard* charts, she began with a long melisma reminiscent of her opening for "It Might as Well Be Spring" from 1946, and she didn't stop there, incorporating more vocal shadings and inflections throughout the song. She used similar devices on "I Ran All the Way Home," which spent fifteen weeks on the *Cash Box* charts. On "These Things I Offer You," which spent thirteen weeks on the charts, she expanded the wordless humming and vocal range of Patti Page's popular cover. And she did the same on "Just a Moment More." In other words, Vaughan used her voice and trademark inflections to create her own novelty device, one based on her vocal prowess, creative genius, and bebop roots rather than technological gimmicks or simplistic parodies of race and ethnicity.

She presented a sophisticated, nuanced version of black artistic expression, one that was unique to her and that she had honed for mainstream audiences.

Novelty songs remained controversial. Detractors worried that Miller focused too much on gimmicks and in-studio production values at the expense of high-quality music. In fact, time and again, Miller unapologetically stated that he did not care about "good" music. "I'm there to please, not to educate," he told *Metronome*'s editors.[26] He wanted to make money, and according to his critics he was willing to try almost anything to appeal to the masses. The songs Miller produced (he's considered the first record producer in the modern sense of the word) were unabashedly commercial, musically simple, saccharine ditties that by both past and present standards were catchy but often quite terrible. They did, however, tap into postwar sensibilities, defined by nostalgia coupled with a fascination for technology and innovation, and proved financially lucrative. By the fall of 1951, after just eighteen months at Columbia, Miller had increased the label's pop record sales by 60 percent, catapulting them from a dismal last place among the four major labels to first. As the 1950s progressed, Miller emerged as a powerhouse at Columbia, wielding unprecedented influence, and he became a celebrity in his own right.[27] He hosted radio and television shows, including the popular *Sing Along with Mitch* on NBC, a spin-off of his album series of the same name.

Miller's magic didn't work with Vaughan. After his production-oriented novelty tunes, Columbia returned to their old formula. For the next three years, over the course of seven recording sessions, Vaughan recorded primarily romantic ballads backed by lush studio orchestras sometimes supplemented by a choir. She sang of love found and lost and the joys and trials of unconditional, selfless love. The titles of her releases tell the story: "These Things I Offer You," "I Ran All the Way Home," "Out O' Breath," "Just a Moment More," "After Hours" (which she sang in the 1951 motion picture *Disc Jockey*), "If Someone Had Told Me," "Say You'll Wait for Me," "My Tormented Heart," "Lover's Quarrel," and so on.[28] Slow, sentimental, and often schmaltzy, ballads were a mainstay of popular music during the early 1950s. They fulfilled postwar America's longing for an ideal, simple world, one without violence or the atomic bomb, while reinforcing conventional gender roles disrupted during World War II. They were Vaughan's specialty, and she sang them beautifully.

But nothing became a breakaway hit. Columbia's enthusiasm for Vaughan faded, and her visits to their recording studios became more and more infrequent. In 1949, she participated in six sessions, releasing twenty sides. In 1950, five sessions and sixteen sides. In 1951, four sessions and twelve sides. In 1952, three sessions and twelve sides, and in 1953 a single session generating only four sides. Her contract promised that she would record sixteen tunes a year and that at least twelve of these would be released. Columbia was phasing her out. Her final recording date for the label was January 5, 1953, nearly a year before her contract expired, and on October 9, 1953, Columbia canceled her contract, paying out her remaining sessions.

As Vaughan fought for her artistic integrity, to determine how she, a black woman, was represented musically on discs, she also confronted increasingly disapproving jazz critics. The same critics who supported and embraced her early in her career, who held her up as the standard-bearer for modern jazz singing, were turning against her. They deemed her Columbia releases too corny, too saccharine, and too reliant on clichéd string orchestras, and said Vaughan sang them too straight. At first they directed their frustration at Columbia. In response to the straight singing on "Just Friends" and "You Taught Me to Love Again," released May 8, 1950, Down Beat's reviewer wrote, "I presume this is the result of the request of Columbia. I could be quite wrong, of course, but since Miss Vaughan made her reputation singing her own way, might it not be a good idea to let her go on in this fashion especially since she happens to sing quite well?"[29] He wanted Vaughan's jazz roots to shine through. Yet when she released jazz sides, like the big band arrangement of "Perdido" or the small combo album *Sarah Vaughan in Hi-Fi,* the one with Miles Davis, jazz critics didn't like those either.

Their disappointment escalated, and in the fall of 1951 *Down Beat*'s Jack Tracy penned a full-scale indictment of Vaughan and her musical choices, all under the guise of a record review.

> This is not an easy review to write. Because I have been among the many who have sat countless times enthralled by Sassy's marvelous performances. And I happen to have her [Musicraft] records of *It Might as Well Be Spring, If You Could See Me Now* (see review in reissues section), *Don't Worry 'Bout Me,* etc.
>
> But Sarah on this record isn't the same girl—she's too coy, too dramatic, too self-confidently glib. Though her voice has ripened and achieved the maturity hinted at earlier, she misuses it terribly.
>
> Miss Vaughan has all the equipment in the world— let's hope we don't have to continue to turn to records she made five years ago to hear her at her best when she's capable of exceeding those performances right now.
>
> End of tirade.[30]

Tracy's review of her reissued Musicraft masters praised "Sarah's unaffected, wonderfully controlled singing contrasting sharply with her present-day output." He missed the good old days, the spontaneity and naturalness of her early bebop sides. So did Dave Garroway. Six months later, in May 1952, while listening to Vaughan's duet with Billy Eckstine, "I Love You," during one of Leonard Feather's blindfold tests, he lamented that he no longer enjoyed jazz in the same way that he used to.

> I admire Sarah very much, admire her great strength when she first came out. So when the new records come out, I know all the sounds. She's better than she was a year and a half ago, when she was making arpeggios out of chords which is awful hard for a non-musician like me

to understand. But all you have to do to know my opinion is to play *If You Could See Me Now* [from 1946] and take my blood pressure. It would go up.

So here is just the shell of a great talent. Not, I believe a lost talent; I think if they got her out of those sequin gowns and she would let her hair down and have the fun out of music that she had when I first knew her, everything would be fine. I realize this is commercially impractical—the lady would like to make a buck. I'm not doing all the things *I* want to do, either. But there are people who can make the compromise. Like Louis [Armstrong]. But at least Sarah's vocal quality, like Ella's, remains unimpaired.[31]

Since his days championing Vaughan in Chicago, Garroway had made the leap from radio to television, becoming the cohost of NBC's national *Today Show,* where he shared the anchorman's desk with a chimpanzee named J. Fred Muggs. While Garroway was more diplomatic and sympathetic to Vaughan's plight than Tracy, his criticism was the same. The demands of commercialism kept her from being herself. She placed her artistic integrity at risk with these disappointing lapses in judgment. In short, Sarah Vaughan had sold out.

Jazz critics of the 1940s and 1950s, especially those writing in publications like *Down Beat* and *Metronome,* were a small contingent of voices that did not represent the tastes of the music industry as a whole. But they were passionate and outspoken. A collection of like-minded, predominantly white men, they dedicated themselves to the noble task of canonizing jazz, elevating it to the status of a respected high art. This was not easy, and many critics became possessive of "their" musicians, especially black musicians they advocated for early on. This included beboppers like Vaughan, Eckstine, Gillespie, and Parker whose more abstract, cerebral, less danceable, experimental music was for them an ideal highbrow art form. Critics believed that musicians, especially black musicians, had a moral obligation to perform (and record) jazz, and that they should remain untarnished by crass commercialism.

Vaughan was not the only artist targeted by jazz critics. They also disapproved of pianist Nat King Cole's transition from well-respected but underpaid leader of a jazz trio to chart-topping balladeer in the mid-1940s. "For years we did nothing but play for musicians and other 'hip' people. We practically starved to death," explained Cole in 1946. "When we *did* click, it wasn't on the strength of the good jazz. . . . We clicked with the pop songs, pretty ballads and novelty stuff. You know that. Wouldn't we have been crazy if we'd turned right around after getting a break and started playing pure jazz again? We would have lost the crowd right away."[32] And when confronted with the backlash of critics in 1951, as his single "Too Young" topped the charts, Cole retorted, "Critics don't buy records—they get 'em free."[33] When Billy Eckstine dissolved his bebop big band in 1947 to pursue a career as a solo act, the jazz press lampooned him for neglecting his African American roots and fans. He too crooned smooth, romantic ballads, nearly surpassing a faltering Frank Sinatra's popularity in 1950. "Some creeps said I 'forsook' jazz in order to be commercial," Eckstine exclaimed in frustration. "So I saw one of those creeps, a jazz critic, and I said, 'What are you, mad at me because I want to take care of my family? Is that what pisses you off? You want me to wind up in a goddamn hotel room with a bottle of gin in my pocket and a needle in my arm, and let them discover me laying there? Then I'll be an immortal, I guess, to you.'"[34] Eckstine understood the role white critics wanted him to play and how it fulfilled their emotional investment in an idealized artistic purity; the archetype of the tragic genius, here epitomized by artists like the heroin-addicted Charlie Parker; and, ultimately, racial authenticity. Vaughan understood this too. But she was less outspoken and more diplomatic in her dealings with critics.

"I don't pay them any mind," she explained to *Down Beat*'s Nat Hentoff in 1952. "They have a right to say what they think, but I always sing the best way I know how."[35] In the article, aptly titled

"Sarah's Answer to the Critics," Vaughan outlined what would become the guiding principles for her career. "There's nothing necessarily wrong with being commercial," she continued, "but there's a point beyond which you can't go without being ridiculous. People with genuine talent are lowering themselves by continuing to use some of the material that passes for popular songs these days. I just can't. There are some tunes I just won't do." It was a statement of musical integrity and independence, a veiled indictment of the likes of Mitch Miller. She confessed, however, that she'd never made a record, jazz or pop, exactly as she wanted to. And while she was committed to improvising, especially in nightclubs, she understood that audiences in supper clubs and big theaters did not appreciate improvisation, and for them she sang straighter. Vaughan was unwilling to concede to either ideological extreme, the blatant commercialism of Miller or the anti-commercialism of jazz purists, and sought a middle ground. This gave her the freedom and flexibility to pursue her own musical path—one that privileged the music. "Look, what I want to put over to audiences is music," she concluded. "If I don't then to me, I'm a failure. So music is always more important to me than getting with each new hit."[36]

In their fervor to condemn her pop records for Columbia and the growing commercial appeal that they symbolized, jazz critics neglected her live performances. They overlooked what she did night after night, for hundreds and often thousands of listeners. Here, while performing live, she reconciled the competing demands of jazz and pop. She honed her style, incorporating elements from both. During the early 1950s, Vaughan figured out how to be a successful crossover artist on her own terms. She decided what she would and would not do, and how she would represent herself and her race.

6

"She's Vaughanderful.
She's Marvelous"

hank you. Thank you so much, ladies and gentlemen. You
are so wonderful," Vaughan shouted above the applause of
3,500 fans gathered in Ann Arbor, Michigan, on November 15,
1951. They were there to hear the Biggest Show of '51, an oversized, all-star revue headlining Nat King Cole, Duke Ellington,
and Vaughan. "Right here," she continued as the crowd settled,
"I'd like to do my very latest Columbia recording, and I do hope
you've been hearing 'I Ran All the Way Home.'"[1] Released on
October 12, the tune had just made its way onto the charts five
days earlier. Pianist Jimmy Jones eased into the introduction.
Vaughan sighed, then giggled in her high-pitched voice as the
audience whistled and clapped its approval. Then she sang the
melismatic intro low in her contralto range. Silence fell over
the hall as she and Jones bent the languorous ballad's tempo,
first tugging, then pushing listeners through time, ultimately
leading them to the final note, which she punctuated with one
of her trademark vocal slides. Ellington's band launched into
Vaughan's next number, a medley of her old Musicraft classics,
all recently rereleased on MGM, beginning with the up-tempo

"Mean to Me." A brassy "Perdido" followed, and Vaughan's set was off and running.

It was night fifty-six in a marathon of seventy one-nighters. Vaughan had been on the road with the Biggest Show of '51 since September 21, performing once or twice a night, and she had two more weeks to go. At its heart, the Biggest Show was an old-fashioned vaudeville revue complete with music, dancing, and plenty of comedy. It resembled the live preshow entertainment found at neighborhood movie palaces, only it was bigger and much better, lasting over two hours. In addition to its three big-name stars, the show featured five supporting acts: comedians Timmie Rogers, Patterson and Jackson, and Stump and Stumpy; the Marie Bryant Dancers; and the one-legged tap dancer Peg Leg Bates. In total, there were forty-nine performers—many more than local movie theaters could ever afford.

Each night Ellington, doing double duty as emcee, kicked off the show with his classic big band compositions. He introduced the Marie Bryant Dancers, Timmy Rogers, and finally Vaughan. Night after night, she stopped the show, earning multiple curtain calls. "Sarah had what was called the choice spots," explained pianist Jones to oral historian Patricia Wells in 1978. "She'd close the first half. There's no pressure there. Nat Cole was the only one, King Cole was the only one that could close the second half of the show." Vaughan learned this the hard way. On October 19, when the Biggest Show stopped in Pittsburgh, George Treadwell, Vaughan's husband and manager, "made her late on purpose, to see if she could hold up closing the second half. That meant that if she was absent Nat would have to close the first half. Well, he learned his lesson," remembered Jones. Treadwell's machinations failed, and Vaughan floundered. "As much as I admire Sarah, Nat King Cole was a complete heavyweight."[2]

After Cole finished his set, Vaughan returned to the stage for the grand finale: a duet with Cole. Backed by Duke's band, Cole and Vaughan sang "Love You Madly," a tongue-in-cheek ballad. They traded phrases with an easy, swinging camaraderie, much like the romantic banter of a couple in love. Vaughan scatted a few phrases as Cole sang the melody in the background, and here Vaughan's voice was clearly the stronger of the two, easily overpowering Cole. It was an "argument," or "tiff," all done in good fun. They reunited. The music stopped, and their sung banter became spoken. "I love you madly," said Cole, and Vaughan replied, again in her dainty, girlish voice, "Well, I love the hell out of you too, Nat." The audience laughed. "Well, what do you know!" exclaimed Cole. Ellington, joining in the fun, said, "I just couldn't love either of you more madly!" Vaughan giggled along with the crowd. The band began to play again as Vaughan and Cole sung it out together, and Ellington wrapped up the show for the evening.[3]

As soon as the curtain closed, the stagehands broke down the bandstand, the musicians packed up their instruments, the dancers and comedians changed into street clothes, and the entire cast and crew packed themselves back onto the buses to head to the next gig. If they performed only one show that night, the troupe got an early start, usually hitting the road by midnight. If, however, it was a two-show night, they didn't leave until 4:00 A.M. Vaughan and her colleagues would chat, sleep, and eat as the bus made its way to the next town, typically two hundred and sometimes three hundred miles away. "To break the monotony, I drove our bus," said Vaughan.[4] When they arrived, they checked into a hotel, usually in the town's black neighborhood, and got ready for their next show. Then the entire cycle began again. It must have been an exhausting yet exhilarating two and a half months. In 1954, as she prepared for the Birdland All-Stars tour, a mere twenty-nine one-nighters, she said, "It's been a lot rougher. In 1951, we did 70 one night stands. On the 68th, we got a day off in Detroit and we all went nuts with nothing to do."[5]

The tour began on Friday, September 21, with three days of warmups in Boston at the Garden. After lackluster sales, a mere $18,000 for the three-night stint, the show gained momentum as it made stops in Worcester, Providence, Troy, and Newark.

On September 29 they performed two sold-out, standing-room-only shows at Carnegie Hall in New York, grossing $17,000 in a single night. The show continued its trek of one-nighters, bouncing between cities in Virginia, Maryland, Pennsylvania, Connecticut, New York, and Massachusetts, then up into Canada for a week. They set another tour record in Montreal on Sunday, October 7, with $25,000 in ticket sales. They returned to upstate New York, worked their way to Cleveland and Cincinnati; Charleston, West Virginia; Pittsburgh; Scranton; Washington, D.C.; Roanoke; and Richmond as they prepared to travel further South.

The Biggest Show of '51 was a phenomenon, and the music industry took note. In five weeks, during its first thirty-five dates, the show grossed $351,550—the equivalent of more than $3.2 million today. Not only was it one of the first big arena shows of its kind, capable of filling large coliseums and smaller concert halls night after night, it was the first endeavor of its kind to feature an all-black cast, proving once again that black music sold. And as the troupe prepared to venture further south, industry insiders predicted that its upcoming engagements in the Southland would be its "ripest picking to date."[6]

When the Biggest Show of '51 arrived in Atlanta, Georgia, on Friday, October 26, the evening began as usual. The crew set up the stage while the headliners prepared in their dressing rooms. Outside Municipal Auditorium, a crowd of nearly five thousand gathered, and both black and white patrons waited with tickets in hand to enter through the hall's front doors as they usually did in Atlanta. But only the white ticketholders were allowed inside. "Three gruff and menacing white policemen barred the front entrance to Negroes, using profanity and insulting remarks to those who hesitated to 'move on' around the corner," the Associated Negro Press (ANP) reported.[7] Atlanta's Jim Crow laws required that theaters have separate entrances for black and white patrons. But city officials, most elected by narrow margins by black voters, usually followed a more liberal policy at the Municipal Auditorium. They didn't enforce the side-door policy and allowed black and white audiences to enter through the front door together. That night, however, they didn't, and black patrons were furious. It was a step backward in their ongoing fight for equality.

Black concertgoers yelled at the show's local promoters, also black, as they made a path for the white ticket holders. The promoters tried to settle the crowd, but tensions escalated. Thirty minutes before curtain time, A. T. Walden, a prominent civic leader and lawyer who represented both the promoters and the local NAACP branch, announced: "Due to circumstances beyond our control, we regret to ask all colored people to please use the side entrance."[8]

"I was shocked to learn that Negro ticket-holders were being shunted over to a side door entrance," the wife of a well-known doctor told reporters. "Naturally, I would not voluntarily submit to such a humiliation, and I turned to my daughter and said, 'We'll go home.'" "It was the most disgraceful thing I've heard of," a local schoolteacher fumed. "I think it's terrible that any self-respecting Negro would ever voluntarily accept such an arrangement to witness an all-colored cast, sponsored by a Negro at that." And the president of the Atlanta Musicians Protective Association refused to purchase a ticket. "I cannot voluntarily accept segregation of myself or my people," he said. Others refused to buy tickets too, and according to the ANP another four hundred tore up their tickets in disgust.[9]

But 2,500 black music lovers "forgot race pride and accepted the Jim Crow arrangement."[10] They entered the theater and took their seats, along with 1,500 whites. While segregated entrances were uncommon, segregation within the theater was not. Atlanta city ordinances mandated that blacks and whites sit apart from one another using the so-called vertical Jim Crow pattern, which divided the theater in half from the ground floor up. Even though black patrons outnumbered whites nearly two to one and overflowed their designated sections, according to the *Baltimore Afro-American,* whose coverage was more disapproving, "There were 1,500 white record fans with a great big section all to themselves."[11]

Backstage, the musicians didn't know about the Jim Crow–fueled chaos outside until reporters pressured the headliners to comment. An upset Ellington snapped, "I don't want to discuss it." Cole refused to comment. And Vaughan, speaking through her maid, told the reporters, "This is terrible. I'll never come South again." She was upset, indignant even, but practical. When asked whether the show would go on, Vaughan conceded, "Everyone can't be a Josephine Baker."[12]

The famous expatriate was known for her racial advocacy. Baker, whose evocative performances thrilled Parisians during the 1920s, had made headlines two weeks earlier when waiters at the trendy Stork Club in New York refused to serve her, despite her personal invitation from the club's owner, southerner Sherman Billingsley. Outraged, Baker left the club and told reporters, "This is a terrible experience. It is a snub to my color, to my people. It's not just something you can let drop. It is un-American. It is not fair to other Americans."[13] She considered picketing the restaurant but pursued legal action instead. The NAACP stepped in, demanding that the liquor and cabaret licenses of the Stork Club be revoked. Middleweight boxing champion "Sugar" Ray Robinson expressed his indignation and publicly supported Baker too. Baker was bold and a master of using her celebrity in the fight for racial equality. But the stakes were comparatively low. This was one dinner, an after-work gathering of friends, and it did not directly impact Baker's current engagement at the Roxy Theatre in New York.

When faced with racial injustice in Atlanta, Vaughan, Cole, and Ellington had a more difficult decision to make. If they refused to perform, they jeopardized their professional and financial well-being. The show carried a hefty $5,000 guarantee, and the headliners were under contract to appear. "I had no choice but to observe the terms of the contracts," Ellington later explained to the ANP. "Refusal on my part to honor them would bring on suits for breach of contract, as well as other reprisals, the effect of which would have been to put me out of the band business."[14] In short, the livelihoods of the three headliners, not to mention the other forty-six cast members, the show's crew, the staff supporting the stars, and all of their families, were at stake. Plus, Vaughan and her colleagues were entertainers. They didn't want to disappoint the loyal fans who paid hard-earned money to see the show. They wanted to entertain.

The Biggest Show of '51 did go on that night, albeit forty-five minutes late, and the headliners were criticized for their decision. The event's promoter, whose eleventh-hour attempts to undo the segregated door policy failed, deflected responsibility onto Ellington. "If I had been Duke," he said, "I would have refused to play and told the people why; he could afford to lose the money. . . . I couldn't."[15] An outraged black press chastised the show's stars for participating in, and implicitly condoning, such segregated practices. "Unlike the dynamic Josephine Baker," wrote Cliff MacKay of the *Baltimore Afro-American*, "none of the artists appeared to be the least disturbed over the pungent odor of Jim Crow hanging low over the vast hall."[16] Coverage by the black press incorporated a strong editorial slant—one that promoted racial uplift, equality, and justice, while expecting similar social activism from the show's headliners, especially Ellington. He was the elder statesman of the Biggest Show of '51, a towering figure widely praised not only for his musical accomplishments but also for his sartorial elegance and fashion sense. The *Afro-American*, however, described him as wearing "a greasy stocking on his head."[17] It was an unflattering portrayal, one that diminished Ellington while reminding readers that he straightened his hair. The conch hairstyle favored by Ellington, Cole, and dozens of other black artists was very popular, and scholars have since interpreted the practice of hair straightening as a creative response to racial oppression, an expression of a "neo-African" identity that disturbed cultural norms.[18] But in 1951, the *Afro-American* alluded to Ellington's straightened hair as a way to suggest that he pandered and sold out to white interests—that he was not, in fact, a race man committed to racial equality.

But Ellington and the other stars of the Biggest Show were not responsible for the mess in Atlanta. They were in an impossible situation, with impossible expectations, and there were forces much larger than them at work. The white manager of Municipal Auditorium arranged for the segregated entrances and police presence. When interviewed by the black press, he was forthright, almost boastful, explaining that, due to the high price of tickets, he believed the show's audience would be primarily white, so he reverted to the old, usually suspended, City Council Auditorium Committee regulation requiring separate doors. (According to trade publications, ticket prices for the Biggest Show were much lower than comparable shows, and this affordability contributed to the tour's enormous success.) Others speculated that the policy change in fact reflected a power struggle between local promoters. A white promoter, known to have a virtual monopoly on booking Friday nights at Municipal Auditorium (his events always enforced the segregated entrance policy) and aspirations of entering the lucrative field of promoting black acts, schemed, likely with the help of the hall's white manager, to undermine his competitors. Atlanta's black political leaders demanded and received an apology from Atlanta's white mayor, who publicly scolded the auditorium manager for his "unwise judgment." And black leaders used this victory to tackle similar practices at other prominent venues. Atlanta would not repeal its city ordinances mandating segregation in public spaces until 1963.[19]

The controversy followed the Biggest Show of '51 as it completed its tour of the South and made its way back to the Midwest. A week later, when interviewed by the ANP, Charles Carpenter, the show's black manager, was in damage-control mode. He insisted that the unit had done "more to break down discrimination than any other organization." In Tulsa, Oklahoma, four thousand listeners, both black and white, attended the concert. In Columbia, South Carolina, according to Carpenter, "the audience was mixed and in Fort Worth, Texas, all patrons went to the same box office." These were small but tangible steps forward. Carpenter also expressed concerns about the NAACP's practice of protest-

ing African American–headlined shows, worrying that these protests inflicted great harm on the show while accomplishing little
for the race. "The logical thing to do," he said, "is to picket State
capitals where the laws of segregation are made."[20]

Ellington agreed. The controversy in Atlanta dogged him too,
resulting in a new scandal. After a reporter in St. Louis blatantly
misquoted Ellington as saying "We ain't ready yet" for racial
integration, he was forced to set the record straight and reassert his longstanding commitment to racial equality.[21] "In my
nearly 30 years in public life," he responded, "no one has ever
impugned my devotion to the fight for first-class citizenship." He
too disliked that "southern Negroes picketed only Negro artists,
but never protested when white artists came down to play to segregated audiences. Since southern Negroes live under jimcrow
all year round, why do they wait for Negro artists to come before
putting on demonstrations?" He believed that combatting segregation was a full-time endeavor that required money, concluding, "Segregation is sanctioned by law in the south. We'd have to
have new legislation in every state before jimcrow is completely
abolished."[22]

Yes, laws needed to be changed, but so did mind-sets. Little
had changed since Vaughan toured the South with the Hines and
Eckstine bands eight years earlier. Whites, especially southern
whites, had a deeply ingrained emotional investment in white
supremacy and the racism and segregation that it produced. And
change was hard to enact. The unit encountered more racial hos-
tility in Biloxi, Mississippi, as they prepared to perform for the
troops at Kessler Air Force Base. As usual, the entire cast and
crew stayed at a black hotel. Dick LaPalm, Nat King Cole's white
publicist, told Cole biographer Daniel Mark Epstein that members of a white supremacist group abducted him in the middle of
the night. Upset that LaPalm associated so freely and intimately
with blacks, the group's members packed his bags, checked him
out of the hotel, and relocated him to a white hotel. Unharmed,
LaPalm rejoined the unit the next morning. Cole laughed when
he learned of the incident. But as Cole's laughter intensified, be-

coming louder and louder, LaPalm realized that Cole did not in fact find the situation funny. Instead, his laughter released a pent-up rage and frustration with the cruelties of racism. A furious Ellington threatened not to perform. Cole calmed Ellington, arguing that it was unfair to punish thousands of expectant servicemen because of the ignorance of a few.[23]

Time and again, when confronted by racial injustice, intolerance, and segregation, Cole decided to perform. "The important thing is for Negroes and whites to communicate," he explained. "Even if they sit on separate sides of the room, maybe at intermission a white fellow will ask a Negro for a match or something, and maybe one will ask the other how he likes the show. That way, you have started them to communicating, and that's the answer to the whole problem."[24] Cole viewed himself as a facilitator, someone who, with his music, helped bring people, both black and white, together and helped them see one another's humanity and goodness. He hoped to help southern whites to see blacks as people too. But Cole remained pragmatic. "Those people, segregated or not, are still record fans," he told *Jet* magazine in 1956, following an attempted kidnapping by angry whites in Birmingham. "They can't overpower the law of the South, and I can't come in on a one-night stand and overpower the law. The white come to applaud a Negro performer like the colored do. When you've got the respect of white and colored, you can erase a lot of things. I can't settle the issue. If I was that good I should be President of the United States. But I can help to ease the tension by gaining the respect of both races all over the county."[25] Yet many advocates of racial equality remained unsatisfied. They chastised Cole for not doing more with his celebrity, for not being more outspoken and assertive in his disapproval.

Vaughan chose a similar approach. She was a quiet, reserved woman offstage, uncomfortable in the role of outspoken advocate. Like Cole, she used humor to deflect her discomfort and exasperation in the face of intolerance or disrespect. And although acutely aware of the injustices of Jim Crow and other forms of institutional racism, she rarely voiced her frustration by refusing to sing. Instead, she worked within an unjust system, initiating change one small step at a time. She asserted herself and her worldview onstage. Using the power of her voice, she brought people together, showing audiences, both black and white, her humanity and subjectivity, her creativity and genius. "Sometimes it's better to do nothing, just be yourself," Vaughan explained while telling friends about her experiences working the segregated casinos of Las Vegas. "But strongly be yourself. You respect yourself, and bit by bit you force others to respect you."[26]

She did this time and again. In November 1948, not too long after becoming a regular on Dave Garroway's show, she landed a week at the luxurious Fairmont Hotel in downtown Philadelphia. Outside, the marquee read in bold letters: "The Fairmont Hotel Proudly Presents the Divine Sarah Vaughan." Pianist Butch Lacy remembered Vaughan telling him of her experiences at the Fairmont when they returned for a gig at the same hotel in 1980, more than thirty years later. "Oh, man. This is the place," she said, as the memories came flooding back. She told Lacy how she walked inside with her suitcase in hand and approached the front desk and said, "I'm Sarah Vaughan." "Oh, Miss Vaughan, we are so, so thrilled that you would be here and sing for us," the hotel employee replied. "I know you want to go to your quarters and there's a bellboy there who will lead you." The bellboy took her suitcase, directed her downstairs to the basement, and walked down a long, green corridor, passing the kitchen, the boiler room, the laundry room, and other inner workings of the hotel. They finally arrived at a small room at the end of the hall. It was filled with lockers, and in the middle there was an army cot. "That's for you," said the bellboy. The hotel management expected Vaughan, their marquee attraction, to stay in the same room used by their black employees, the help, to change in and out of their uniforms. Vaughan refused. She calmly turned to the bellboy and said, "You take my bag and follow me." "She goes back down the hall and up [the] steps and walks straight out of the hotel and across the street to another hotel," said Lacy. "She used every penny of [the] money that she earned at that hotel to rent the penthouse of the hotel across the street." He marveled at her composure and presence of mind. "She didn't say 'You motherfuckers,' she said nothing." But she still demanded to be treated with respect.[27]

Then again, on December 15, 1950, a year before touring with the Biggest Show of '51, Vaughan opened at Alan Gale's Celebrity Club in Miami Beach. She was breaking new ground, becoming one of the first African Americans to headline at a supper club in the exclusive resort community. Local laws forbade blacks from working or residing in Miami Beach, and before 1950 only a few black artists had appeared as guests of white acts. This changed during the 1950 winter season when two supper clubs, the Celebrity Club and Copa City, revised their policies and actively wooed black talent. While the *Daily News*, Miami's white newspaper, was ambivalent and dismissive of "what pretends to be a new era in Miami Beach," the black press celebrated Vaughan's appearance, proclaiming, "Sarah Vaughan Shatters Ban on Sepia Stars at Dixie Celebrity Club."[28]

Gale, a white comedian who purchased the floundering club in the fall of 1948 to showcase his talents, still headlined the dinner show along with two white supporting acts: a vocalist and brother-sister tap dancing team. Then he turned the floor over to the black talent, for what the *Daily News* disparagingly called a "midnight sepia festival." Beginning at midnight, then again at 2:30 A.M., comedian Timmie Rogers, Vaughan's future Biggest Show of '51 costar, and the dancing Berry Brothers warmed up the crowd, followed by headliner Vaughan accompanied by George Kirby's band. Between shows they were not allowed to mingle with white guests in the club, so they all retreated to a newly constructed room at the back of the club. Finally, early, early in the morning, after Vaughan closed the late show, a car, provided by Gale, ferried Vaughan and her fellow performers back to the black-owned-and-operated Mary Elizabeth Hotel in Miami's black neighborhood of Overtown.

Still billed as the "most talked about voice in America,"

Vaughan exceeded expectations.[29] It was her first engagement
this far south since touring with Billy Eckstine's band in 1945.
Local disc jockeys created buzz and excitement as they enthusiastically promoted her appearances. Reservations filled quickly,
and night after night she sold out.

"I sure would like to do something nice for you," Gale said
to Vaughan. She had reinvigorated his business during her two-
week appearance, and he was grateful.

"I'd like you to let my own people in," she said.

"Okay."

Vaughan invited her friends from Overtown to the show, and
for one night a Miami Beach club was integrated. Johnnie Garry,
Vaughan's longtime road manager, remembered that night too. It
was the first time he heard Vaughan perform "The Lord's Prayer"
a cappella. It was an emotional performance. Time stopped as
she mesmerized her audience and moved many of them to tears.
And when she finished, the audience burst into applause.[30]

Impresario and producer George Wein remembers Vaughan
singing "The Lord's Prayer" at Storyville, his club in Boston,
to similar effect in 1952 or 1953. "We had to close at midnight
exactly in Boston on Saturday nights," Wein explained. "And so
the police sent three or four tough-looking cops to make sure we
shut down at midnight. So I said to Sassy, 'Do me a favor, when
I tell you, you sing a capella 'The Lord's Prayer'—'Our Father
which art in heaven, hallowed . . .' I said, 'and then just go off the
stage after that.' So it was twelve o'clock, the cops started moving
toward the stage, and Sarah sang a capella 'The Lord's Prayer'
and those cops had to stand right in their tracks, they couldn't
move. It was just wonderful and Sarah did such a great job and
she knew exactly what I wanted."[31]

"'The Lord's Prayer' is both my favorite of the records I've
made and the one I consider my best. It's the only record of
mine I ever play—ask George [Treadwell]," she explained in
1950. "I cut it for Musicraft around Christmas time in 1947. Ted
Dale and a 22 or 23 piece orchestra, with strings, backed me.
I'd always wanted to record it, but I thought I had no business

doing it. Marian Anderson had recorded 'The Lord's Prayer,' you know."[32] Anderson had not, in fact, recorded "The Lord's Prayer." Rather, in 1943 she recorded "Sometimes I Feel like a Motherless Child," the B-side of Vaughan's Musicraft release. But Anderson did send Vaughan a telegram of congratulations, which Vaughan treasured, shortly after the release of her recording of "The Lord's Prayer."

"I'd played it before, at church, school, or the 'Y' for the kids, but it was different from what I'd been doing on my records," Vaughan explained.[33] The song was a favorite of her father's, a staple of church services, but few vocalists had recorded Albert Hay Malotte's setting of "The Lord's Prayer." The white opera singer John Charles Thomas, a baritone, recorded it in 1936, followed more than a decade later by Leonard De Paur, a black choral director and composer, leading his Infantry Chorus in 1947. But it was unusual for a vocalist known for jazz and pop to delve into religious music, and Vaughan's disc was controversial. A handful of detractors believed that it was wrong, sacrilegious even, for a secular artist to record serious, sacred music. Treadwell defended Vaughan in the *Philadelphia Tribune*. "Don't they know that Sarah sang in the choir of the Mount Zion Baptist church in Newark for nine years before she ever had any idea of doing popular singing?" he asked. "Regardless of her background, is there anything wrong with a singer attempting a serious work, provided he or she can render a competent performance? Just because Sarah is identified with jazz and popular singing is no reason for her to be barred from doing anything else."[34]

For Vaughan, "The Lord's Prayer" was an expression of her worldview, one grounded in her faith and days as a choir girl in Newark. It was an example of her desire not to be pigeonholed or typecast, her insistence on maintaining her artistic freedom and flexibility, and her delight in defying expectations. "The Lord's Prayer" became a staple of her live performances well into the 1950s. In November 1951, while touring with the Biggest Show of '51, a Newark DJ asked Vaughan why she included religious numbers like "The Lord's Prayer" in her repertoire, and she simply said, "I like to sing and I like to pray. That way I kill two birds with one stone."[35]

When Vaughan, christened the "Divine One" by Dave Garroway, sang "The Lord's Prayer," she reminded her audiences, both black and white, of their common ground, a shared faith and humanity. It was a message of love and peace, forgiveness and reconciliation, a way to forge a connection with her listeners while infusing her performances with dignity and respect, even in the face of power and intolerance. When Vaughan performed "The Lord's Prayer" in Philadelphia at Robin Hood Dell, Miami Beach at the Celebrity Club, Boston at Storyville, and countless other anonymous clubs and concert halls, she symbolized American democracy and the promise of interracial harmony while simultaneously challenging these democratic principles. As scholar Farrah Griffin explains, in these moments of reconciliation, the black female voice functions as a hinge. For white audiences, black female voices heal a fractured and divided country. They represent an idealized, peaceful vision of America, one that values national unity and racial equality. For black audiences, however, the black female voice is a potent challenge to the status quo. It exposes the larger, more fundamental crisis underlying this spectacle of national unity. Vaughan, like Marian Anderson before her, reminded audiences that there was still much to be done. Even though she was never an outspoken civil rights activist like fellow vocalists Lena Horne, Paul Robeson, Josephine Baker, or Nina Simone, through her singing, Vaughan helped create spaces for resistance.[36]

Her performances of "The Lord's Prayer" joined those of Mahalia Jackson, who recorded it in 1950, and Anderson, who sang it on the steps of the Lincoln Memorial after Martin Luther King Jr. delivered his "I Have a Dream" speech during the March on Washington on August 28, 1963. And in many ways, Vaughan's performances of "The Lord's Prayer" were precursors to the performative prayer so effectively used by protestors during the civil rights movement. In the face of violence and re-taliation, activists knelt down and began to pray, often reciting the Lord's Prayer. In these moments of divine connection, they stopped police in their tracks, just as Vaughan did that Satur-day night at Storyville in 1952. Protestors tapped into a shared faith and collection of values and morals while simultaneously revealing the desperation, absurdity, and, ultimately, violence of segregationists. And as religious historian Tobin Miller Shearer explains, "Black bodies praying in public manifested freedom."[37] Vaughan's singing manifested freedom too. It was how she ex-pressed herself in the face of intolerance and the way she brought about social change, night after night.

But in order to bring about this change, to reach the white au-diences that frequented the swanky supper clubs, hotel lounges, and movie palaces, Vaughan needed to transform her public image. She needed, ironically enough, to cultivate a public per-sona that emphasized her femininity and role as a homemaker. And she needed to look the part. During the Columbia years, Vaughan transformed herself into a glamorous and sophisticated beauty. She became, at least in the public's imagination, a lady in the mold of Grace Kelly, only cooler, hipper, with a touch of attitude befitting her other nickname, "Sassy."

7

"Sarah Vaughan and Her Pygmalion"

Vaughan was busy in her kitchen. She wore an apron, and with spoon in hand she bent over to sample the roast in her oven. This image appeared in a 1949 profile titled "Sarah Vaughan at Home," accompanied by the caption "The 23-year-old singer can bake a cake or whip up a tasty dish if she wants to. She's shown in her sunny kitchen." In other photos from the same profile Vaughan, who was actually twenty-four, almost twenty-five, roughhoused with Baron, her boxer; sat in quiet contemplation on the couch reading a book; worked out musical ideas at the piano; and reviewed a score with her husband George Treadwell before a recording session.[1] It was a charming tableau, a glimpse into her private life, and a striking contrast to the professional side of Vaughan seen by most of her fans. And it was an increasingly important part of her public image and brand.

As Vaughan's popularity grew in the late 1940s and early 1950s, she appeared in more and more profiles celebrating both her successes as a vocalist and her role as a devoted homemaker, hostess, and wife. A profile from 1950 featured more photos of

Vaughan at home, some of them surprisingly intimate. Readers saw Vaughan and Treadwell together in bed; he slept as she perused "funny books." And they saw the couple again the next morning, this time sitting at their breakfast table, where Treadwell read *Variety* as an apron-clad Vaughan looked on. "Her schedule doesn't allow much time for housework, but she does enjoy cooking for her George," the caption explained.[2] In 1952, *Ebony* portrayed Vaughan as the perfect hostess. In the photo piece, "Date with a Dish," Vaughan wore an evening gown, her hair and makeup perfect, as she presented an elaborate platter of three-cornered sandwiches, egg baskets with crab meat, cocktail crackers, and a cheese ball. "Velvet-voiced Sarah Vaughan, charming chanteuse, is an attractive hostess who knows how to provide an equally attractive hors d'oeuvres tray," began the caption for the photo piece.[3] Other profiles extoled her love of cooking (chili was her specialty), comic books, her dogs (her surrogate children), golf, horseback riding, and Dodgers baseball games. The message was clear: despite Vaughan's status as an innovative artist, working woman, and primary breadwinner for her household, at home she was just another doting housewife. And she longed to have children: a boy and a girl. When asked if she planned to retire after becoming a mother, Vaughan said, "I have not given that a thought."[4]

The media's treatment of Vaughan was not unusual. During the 1950s, when writing about women that excelled in male-dominated professions, the press, both black and white, emphasized their roles as wives and mothers. They depicted professional women as extremely feminine and interested in fashion and the domestic arts. It became a way to legitimate a woman's public achievements while reassuring readers that conventional gender roles and heterosexuality remained intact.[5] It reestablished the status quo, the same status quo that Vaughan disrupted every day.

Treadwell possessed a savvy understanding of how audiences needed to see Vaughan and became a master of honing her image. Almost everything in her life, whether public or personal, became fodder for the press. He constantly orchestrated publicity events. Photos of the happy couple out on the town socializing, usually with other celebrities, regularly graced the pages of black newspapers and lifestyle magazines. In 1949, the press greeted Vaughan and her growing entourage of support staff at LaGuardia the first time she flew across the country from Los Angeles to New York. An elaborate, champagne-fueled bon voyage party kicked off her first tour of Europe in 1953. Her birthday parties at Birdland became an annual event. Similar parties marked wedding anniversaries, club openings, and record releases. Society reporters dutifully detailed her wardrobe and jewelry, the gourmet meal she had catered, the celebrities in attendance, and the expensive gifts Treadwell gave Vaughan: diamond rings, mink coats, or new cars, usually Cadillacs. It was all an effort to portray Vaughan as increasingly successful and affluent, as a happily married woman living the American dream.

Sometimes Treadwell manufactured controversy. In the summer of 1948, Vaughan returned to Chicago for seven weeks of engagements. She'd won a local DJ poll, organized by her advocate and friend Dave Garroway, to headline for two of those weeks at the Chicago Theatre, the town's largest, most elaborate movie palace. But her performances were not going well, and her box office draw was lackluster. "She's dying in there," Johnnie Garry, Vaughan's road manager, remembered telling Treadwell. So Treadwell organized for a gang of six hoodlums to throw tomatoes at Vaughan from the balconies. The "attack" sparked outrage. The *Chicago Defender* condemned the "disgraceful episode," reporting that it was the result of petty jealousies over Vaughan's success and Garroway's blatant favoritism. Booking agents were frustrated by the strong hold that Treadwell had on Vaughan's contract. And personal managers of what the *Defender* termed "ofay" singers, a derogatory slang for whites, were bitter because Vaughan crowded out their vocalists during an already sluggish time of year. After the episode, the press covered Vaughan's triumphant return to the stage the next night and the outpouring of support she received from the city's DJs and now-sold-out audiences.[6] And the story of Vaughan's attack had legs, becoming fodder for future profiles. "Headlines!" Garry explained.[7]

Sometimes, however, Treadwell overreached, and his zeal for publicity backfired. Two months before the incident in Chicago, in June 1948, both *Down Beat* and black newspapers reported that two men tried to hold Vaughan and Treadwell up as they walked to their hotel after a gig in Washington, D.C. Fortunately, Vaughan's dog was with them. "Get 'em, Baron!" yelled Treadwell. The boxer leapt at one of the men, Treadwell at the other. Vaughan screamed, alerting the police, who took the two men into custody. Baron's reward? A new diet of steak dinners.[8] It was a cute, catchy story, which *Down Beat* ran on its first page, complete with a photo of Vaughan, Baron, and her latest Musicraft release. But it was also untrue. *Down Beat* discovered that the Washington, D.C., metropolitan police department had no record of an attempted robbery of Vaughan or Treadwell on the date provided by her press agent, Jim McCarthy. The editors of *Down Beat* were furious, decrying phony stories and the press agents and managers who disseminated them.[9]

Vaughan disapproved too. According to friends, she disliked Treadwell's enthusiasm, verging on obsession, for sensational publicity. She was an unassuming woman, shy and reserved. In essence, a very private woman leading a public life. While she needed a boisterous, more extroverted counterpart to interface with the press and industry at large, it must have been difficult for her to have more and more details of her personal life, especially her marriage, put on display.

Unfortunately, as her national profile increased, Treadwell's prominence in her personal narrative increased too.[10] He frequently became the story, the focal point. It began with the occasional profile, like 1948's "The Man Behind the Gal: George Treadwell Quit Band to Pilot Singer-Wife. It Paid Off," and soon escalated. Confessionals, supposedly penned by Vaughan, appeared in African American lifestyle magazines. In 1949, "My Biggest Break" outlined the two most important moments of her career: the first was meeting and marrying George Treadwell, and the second was her appearances at the Chicago Theatre. In this retelling, Treadwell was responsible for landing Vaughan the gig. When crushed by the onslaught of tomatoes, she ran offstage, overwhelmed and terrified, into the protective arms of her loving, always supportive husband. Unconvinced that show business was for her, she cried out, "I'll never sing again!" Treadwell set her right and persuaded her that she must continue. In 1950, *Tan Confessions* published "How He Proposed," and the following year, in "The Man Behind Me," Vaughan outlined everything that Treadwell did for her. He booked her gigs, briefed the press, chose (and sometimes designed) her gowns, had power of attorney, and managed all of her finances. "George almost never rests," she wrote in *Our World*. "George is really a vital part of me. More important than an arm or a leg. He's been behind me since the beginning and I hate to think what things would be like without him."[11]

Despite appearances of a happy marriage and business partnership, their relationship was beginning to crumble. She didn't need Treadwell as much as she had earlier. In 1952, after almost ten years in the business, Vaughan, now twenty-eight, had matured and become more independent and comfortable in her role as a star, and her career was still gaining momentum. Whereas Treadwell once served as her sole companion, she now traveled with an entourage, including her pianist Jimmy Jones, road manager Johnnie Garry, and personal secretary Annette Wilson, later replaced by Modina Davis. That summer, she assembled her first trio, hiring the bassist Israel Crosby, drummer Buzz Freeman, and pianist John Malachi, who sat in for an ailing Jones during a two-year medical leave. She now had a large support network.

Those close to the couple noticed a growing volatility between Vaughan and Treadwell too. Like Vaughan, Treadwell loved being in control. According to friends, he dictated what she wore (as often celebrated in the black press); where she performed; what she did after hours, when not onstage; how she spoke; and who she spoke to. Prone to possessiveness and jealousy, Treadwell didn't want Vaughan socializing with other men at bars, as the after-hours incident following her birthday appearance at Birdland in 1953 so clearly demonstrated. In addition to managing all of her finances, he had her on a strict weekly allowance (although, according to Davis, Vaughan preferred this arrangement). But as her success increased, Vaughan didn't want to be told what to do all of the time. She wanted the freedom to live her life on her own terms. Vaughan was outgrowing the relationship and started to push back. The couple argued more and more. Sometimes she threatened not to go onstage, and sometimes their arguments became physical. Drummer Jimmy Cobb, who joined Vaughan's trio in 1970, remembered staying at the Watkins Hotel in Los Angeles in 1950 at the same time as Vaughan and Treadwell. "The rap was that [they were] fighting all day up in the room," he said. "George used to put her in the closet and kind of smack her around a little, so no one would hear that."[12]

The couple traveled together less frequently. "With George in the office and Sassy on the road, their love affair cooled," explained road manager Johnnie Garry.[13] But Treadwell did make surprise visits to check up on Vaughan as she toured. He'd arrive in town, and when he couldn't find her at her hotel, he'd become jealous, track her down, and, according to Davis, "[sneak] up on her, to see if he would catch her" cheating with another man. Usually, she was just hanging out, relaxing after a long night onstage.[14]

Vaughan and Treadwell likely separated for the first time in the spring or summer of 1952. By the end of the summer, gossip columns in the African American press speculated that all was not well between the couple. Vaughan and Treadwell responded with a strategic photo op together after Vaughan's successful appearance with the New York Symphony at the Yale Bowl in August. "This friendly scene should put at rest the numerous rumors of a rift in the Vaughan-Treadwell association," read one caption, and another proclaimed that Vaughan and Treadwell "are a picture of contentment as they contemplate a rosy future."[15] They would do this time and again. Vaughan stayed in the duplex above her parents' home in Newark and Treadwell moved to an apartment in Greenwich Village. They continued to work together all while maintaining their public façade as the happily married couple. They did this for years.

It's unclear why the couple didn't divorce in 1952. Perhaps they both harbored optimism that the relationship could be saved. Perhaps Vaughan had an emotional investment in remaining married and wanted to avoid the inevitable pain that would come with finalizing her divorce. Perhaps she also understood the value of maintaining a public narrative of a happy marriage and domesticity. It afforded her a certain privacy and freedom to live her life on her own terms. After all, her lifestyle was unconventional. As an entertainer, she worked evenings and weekends. After work, fueled by a post-performance adrenaline high, she went to after-hours clubs to unwind and usually stayed until morning. She smoked, drank, and did drugs. Sometimes she stayed out for days at a time, repeating a cycle of working and partying. The public image of Vaughan as a happy homemaker and homebody, a June Cleaver of sorts, provided a valuable counternarrative to aspects of her life that many in society deemed less acceptable. This was especially important when her world bumped up against the establishment. In 1951, she was arrested during a raid of a private home in Detroit. "We were just having a party last night and we were having a ball when all of a sudden we heard some glass break," Vaughan told reporters. "The door came down and the police came in." The police, concerned that the home was an illegal after-hours club, took her fingerprints and held her for ten hours, during which time she serenaded her fellow inmates.[16] In 1952, Vaughan and Treadwell testified before a Washington, D.C., grand jury investigating the whereabouts of ninety-nine pounds of marijuana that disappeared during a big drug bust the previous year. According to the U.S. attorney Charles M. Irelan, Vaughan was not under investigation, but he believed that she might have information about the missing drugs. She was one of several musicians who appeared before the grand jury that day. In the end, Irelan conceded that her testimony was not helpful. Vaughan and Treadwell shielded their faces from photographers as they left the courthouse, and when asked by the press what she had been questioned about, she said, "They wanted to know whether the sun was shining outside."[17]

In 1953, gossip columnists reported that Vaughan had a new beau, a wealthy businessman from Atlantic City.[18] And in 1957, rumors spread that she and boxing champion Joe Louis were having an affair. After months of speculation, the press finally confronted Vaughan. "This is all very silly," she told the *Baltimore Afro-American*. "I happen to be a married woman!"[19] Vaughan and Louis were not romantically involved, but her status as a married woman did deflect attention from the affairs that she likely had during her separation from Treadwell.

As Vaughan continued to assert her independence and freedom while using her marriage as cover, Treadwell worked to increase his presence in her public narrative. In January 1952, just months before the couple separated, with their relationship deteriorating and his control of Vaughan waning, he launched his most ambitious and enduring publicity campaign.[20] He rewrote her origin story, placing himself at the center. He became the mastermind behind her many successes and the man responsible for quite literally creating the Sarah Vaughan audiences knew and loved.

In his retelling, Vaughan's story began late one night in 1946, near the end of her run at Café Society. Treadwell knocked on her dressing room door, came in, and announced: "Look, Sassy, I got $8,000, here all in cash. It's all the money I've got in the world. Know what I'm going to do with it? I'm taking two dollars of it to buy a marriage license with. The other is going to be put behind Mrs. Sarah Vaughan Treadwell. When I get through with you, I'll bet you won't know yourself. You up for it?"[21]

"I still cannot see what interested George in me at the time, but he later told me he had missed his trumpet parts and had fouled up notes behind me because he 'just fell hard' for me," Vaughan confessed in a March 1953 feature for *Tan Confessions* magazine titled "Dark Girls Can Make It Too!" Even though her name appeared on the byline, it's unlikely that she penned the piece. The profile outlined the key details and plot points for the new publicity campaign, many of which had already appeared, nearly verbatim, in earlier press coverage. "I was still the unglamorous little black girl from Newark in a strange world where people applauded me and considered me not great but odd for the manner in which I did things musically."

"There was also the fact that I was considered nothing much to look at," she added. Early on, a reviewer in the *New York Herald-Tribune* concluded: "She is not exactly handsome to look at, having a toothy face with a flattened ski-jump nose, almost oriental eyes and a low forehead oppressed by a pile of black hair."

"Brother, that hurt!" wrote Vaughan, remembering her reaction to the review. "It was unkind and not calculated to increase my self-assurance. If he had added that I was black, his picture might have been complete. But by now, I am hardened in such things, even though they do not really intend to be cruel when they say them."

Treadwell soon implemented his plan to "fix" Vaughan. "George spent the remaining $7,998 of his life's saving on gowns, special arrangements and a voice coach for me," Vaughan wrote. "One day later on, he came home and told me to get ready to go out. I had stopped asking him where he was taking me or the reason why. We went to a dentist. From there we went to a beauty specialist."

"I looked in my mirror again several months later," she wrote. "I was startled. I hardly knew the person staring wide-eyed back at me. The buck teeth were gone. My face had undergone an unbelievable transformation. Nowhere in that image could I see the little black girl of yesterday whose fear of her color and homeliness had almost turned her into an introvert."

"My figure was streamlined as a result of massaging and beauty treatments. My hair had been trained, finger-waved and done up in such a manner that I could hardly recognize it."

"The elocution lessons George had paid for completed the

metamorphosis," she wrote. "I was a changed person. Completely. Financially and mentally I was divorced from the original Sarah Vaughan, and George had done it all for me."[22]

Treadwell called the new publicity campaign "Sarah Vaughan and Her Pygmalion," and his story of Vaughan's transformation didn't stray far from its inspiration: Ovid's *Metamorphoses*. In Ovid's original Latin, crafted almost two thousand years earlier, Pygmalion is a young sculptor in search of a wife. But he can't find one. After rejecting all of the women in his homeland, he sculpts his ideal woman from ivory and names her Galatea. He falls in love with his creation, prays to Venus to bring his sculpture to life, and then marries her. The story was told and retold for centuries. In 1914, English playwright George Bernard Shaw adapted the myth in *Pygmalion*. Here, phonetics professor Henry Higgins civilized a street urchin named Eliza Doolittle by giving her daily elocution lessons and teaching her how to dress and present herself to the upper crust of British society.

Yet the similarities between Vaughan's new Pygmalion-inspired narrative and its source are uncanny, almost too neat and perfect, especially given Treadwell's tendency toward embellishment and sometimes downright fabrication. Vaughan's "look" did evolve and, by most accounts, improve as she became a more seasoned and sophisticated entertainer in the late 1940s and early 1950s. Friends close to the couple early on, however, doubted that Treadwell had any savings to invest in Vaughan's development and certainly not $8,000, a sizeable sum in the 1940s. When the couple met, Treadwell was a salaried section musician in a band. It was a solid but not particularly lucrative job. Treadwell did not hire a voice coach for Vaughan. "I never took vocal lessons," said Vaughan time and again throughout her career.[23] Nor did she receive elocution lessons, although those close to the couple remembered Treadwell regularly correcting Vaughan's grammar and other aspects of how she spoke, which she found increasingly tiresome. And it's an exaggeration to suggest that Treadwell commissioned special musical arrangements for Vaughan. She developed much of her early repertoire in the trenches with her bebop contemporaries. She often described how she pumped the hand organ as Tad Dameron, a pianist and composer favored by the beboppers, wrote "If You Could See Me Now" in 1946, a tune that she then popularized. And she didn't have a "book" in the traditional sense; instead, she and her longtime pianist and musical director Jimmy Jones played everything by ear, working through their arrangements on the fly.

Other aspects of her transformation story did have a kernel of truth. Vaughan's wardrobe did improve. Her gowns became more sophisticated and stylish, and Treadwell, a very stylish man himself, played a central role in deciding what she wore. He favored bright colors—whites, pinks, yellows, and light greens— that popped against Vaughan's darker skin tone. Treadwell's mother was a seamstress, and early on she likely made or at least tailored many of Vaughan's gowns. Only later, as her fame grew and earnings increased, did she invest in substantial wardrobe improvements. In 1948, the *Chicago Defender* reported that Vaughan recently spent $2,500 on fifteen fashionable "New Look" gowns.[24]

In December 1948, weeks before signing with Columbia, Vaughan visited a dentist to remove the gap between her front teeth. Dental crowns, caps on her teeth, resulted in an even, perfect smile.[25] (But it's unlikely that she underwent "nose-slimming plastic surgery" as reported in later incarnations of the transformation story.)

Vaughan did undergo "beauty salon streamlinings," but they didn't necessarily happen in a salon or spa. Instead, she simply fine-tuned her look as she toured. In the early days, according to road manager Johnnie Garry, Vaughan carried a sponge and a small bottle of Max Factor in her pocketbook. "And that's how we got through those one-night stands, with four gowns and a little makeup in her pocketbook," said Garry.[26] Along the way, Vaughan learned the most flattering ways to apply makeup. And Modina Davis, Vaughan's traveling hairstylist and personal secretary, who joined the team in 1950, remembered trimming and paring down the bulky, often unflattering wigs Vaughan wore, and how these evolved into the short, very hip (and easy to maintain) pixie cut Vaughan sported for much of the 1950s.

Makeovers were (and still are) very common in the entertainment industry. Far too often, they were a prerequisite for commercial success, as was the case for Vaughan. The media regularly commented on the evolving looks and physical appearances of musicians, and they could be terribly blunt and unkind in their assessments. *Down Beat*'s John Wilson took note of Vaughan's improving stage presence and appearance, and cited 1949 as the year that she finally transformed herself from looking "somewhat in the neighborhood of a mess" to being a more glamorous and poised performer.[27] Two weeks later, Wilson wrote a nearly identical review of the blond, blue-eyed Patti Page, describing her stunning transformation from an awkward, chubby kid into a slimmer, more elegant and becomingly gowned woman. He predicted that she would hit it big in 1950, which she did.[28] Helen Forrest, a popular Jewish big band singer, had a highly publicized nose job and dyed her hair blond shortly before leaving Harry James's band to become a solo act in the mid-1940s. In her autobiography, Forrest confessed that she wanted to be more conventionally desirable, especially to James, her charming and often philandering fiancé. The trade press celebrated Peggy Lee's bold new platinum blond look in the late 1940s and fretted about the weight gains of Ella Fitzgerald, Rosemary Clooney, and Dinah Washington. A decade later, Motown's "charm school" taught artists social graces, grooming, and self-presentation, in addition to carefully orchestrating their wardrobes. Makeovers were a normal part of doing business, especially for women, in the music industry.

Vaughan's makeover, however, stands apart. It is unusual in the level of detail revealed (even if much of it is untrue), but more so for the elaborate narrative crafted to tell the story of her transformation and the extent to which the "Sarah Vaughan and Her Pygmalion" story was disseminated. It became a focal point of her press kits that was reproduced nearly verbatim for the next fifteen years, long after Vaughan and Treadwell finally divorced in 1957. It forever changed the way that listeners and many critics thought about Vaughan and her career, and still informs how her story is told today.

While there is value in separating fact from fiction, it is equally valuable to understand what the "Sarah Vaughan and Her Pygmalion" narrative accomplished. The story resonated with mid-century audiences and can provide valuable insights into postwar America's understanding of race and gender.

During the 1950s, the tale of Pygmalion was familiar and compelling, a part of the ethos and larger cultural lexicon. Shaw's *Pygmalion* inspired the Broadway musical *My Fair Lady*. The tale of Professor Henry Higgins's transformation of the street urchin Eliza Doolittle into a high society lady debuted in 1956 with Julie Andrews as its breakout star and was later revived by ingénue Audrey Hepburn in the movie adaptation. And in 1954, the famed plastic surgeon Maxwell Maltz published his autobiography, *Doctor Pygmalion*. Much like Treadwell, Maltz described himself as an artist, a magician of sorts, capable of performing miracles on the visages of his patients. He was a self-styled Pygmalion carving, grinding, and chiseling away the ivory, finally revealing his masterpieces, models of ideal beauty and objects of desire.

George Treadwell was a self-styled Pygmalion too. Vaughan was his Galatea, his creation and ideal woman, an expression of his desires. But his vision was informed by a larger culturally accepted notion of who and what was considered beautiful. After all, makeover stories, by definition, strive toward an ideal beauty, and at this historical moment beauty was defined very narrowly. It was (and still is) the domain of white women. In particular, blond, blue-eyed, slender, and youthful women, who embodied the mores of upper-class, Western femininity.[29] Of course, this ideal cannot exist without its opposite: the "other." The black woman, with her classical African features: dark skin, broad nose, full lips, gapped teeth, and kinky hair.[30] The same markers of racial identity that Treadwell, in his role as Vaughan's Pygmalion, "fixed."

"At first, it still did not make sense for he was asking me to make myself believe I am not black and that I was attractive," Vaughan supposedly wrote in "Dark Girls Can Make It Too!" as she described her transformation and Treadwell's faith in her. "Color hasn't a thing to do with talent," Treadwell told Vaughan. "Just you forget all about it and go out there and make them like you. I think you're good looking. I'm color blind and it doesn't mean a thing to me."

"Dark Girls Can Make It Too!" was a complex tale of race and beauty that explored the emotional trauma of racism while condemning the hierarchy of skin color, a hierarchy that privileged lighter skin tones within the black community. Even though it's likely that Vaughan didn't write the piece, she became a surrogate for all dark-skinned black girls and an embodiment of *Tan Confessions'* assertion that color doesn't matter—talent does. Yet the editors of *Tan Confessions* unwittingly suggested that blackness and beauty were not compatible. It was an unsettling contradiction. By celebrating Treadwell's transformation of Vaughan, they suggested that the best way for a talented black woman like Vaughan to feel confident and succeed was to downplay markers of her racial identity and embrace white ideals of beauty. The publication reinforced this message by flanking the profile with ads for hair straighteners and skin-tone lighteners.

On the surface, Vaughan's makeover reads as an attempt to assimilate, to imitate whiteness by erasing markers of her physical African American identity. This is unsettling, especially seen through our twenty-first-century lens, informed by the "black is beautiful" campaigns of the 1960s and 1970s. There is, however, another way to interpret the publicity-fueled tales of Vaughan's makeover, one that does not rely on discrete definitions of blackness and whiteness, jazz and pop. What if, instead, Vaughan started to reimagine contemporary understandings of race— what it meant to be black, and white, in postwar America, in much the same way as she did with her singing?

Art historian Kobena Mercer addresses similar issues in his study of black hairstyles, in particular those that involve straightening and curling. Instead of viewing them as a "wretched imitation of white people's hair," he suggests that they in fact represent black Americans working in and against existing cultural codes. Black Americans engaged with the dominant white culture while simultaneously expressing a "neo-African" approach to beauty and everyday life, much like Duke Ellington did with his conch hairstyle.[31] It was but one part in a larger process of mastering the modern, cosmopolitan world.

In other words, Vaughan and Treadwell worked within the system. By "mastering" her body, a process magnified by the Pygmalion narrative, Vaughan challenged those critics, like the reviewer for the *New York Herald Tribune* from early in Vaughan's career, who insisted on stereotypical readings of her physical appearance. She overturned these norms and their tendency to pair blackness with the unattractive and ugly, what Mercer refers to as the "distinctions of aesthetic value, 'beautiful/ugly,' [which] have always been central to the way racism divides the world into binary oppositions in its adjudication of human worth."[32] Through her transformation, then, Vaughan acquired a more familiar appearance. She crafted a physical body that better matched the humanity and beauty long perceived in her voice.

Importantly, the storytelling surrounding Vaughan's makeover also changed the way that her voice was heard and understood by linking it to a larger collection of symbols. In addition to the myth of Pygmalion, press coverage of her makeover also included allusions to fairy tales. There were the expected stories of transformation, like the ugly duckling becoming a swan, but also tales of princes rescuing their princesses, including the story of Cinderella, which incorporated both a transformation and rescue narrative. These and other fairy tales celebrate the triumph of beauty over ugliness, good over evil, and lightness over darkness—the same binary oppositions discussed by Mercer. Here, the new and improved Vaughan triumphed over the ugly Vaughan of the past, and in the process moved toward not only greater humanity and familiarity but also an innate, more widely acceptable beauty.

While fairy tales are usually dismissed as harmless stories for children, they have a darker side. They play an important role in defining a community's expectations, mores, and values. They define its social code. According to feminist literary critics, these social codes enforce the more conservative interests of the dominant social group. In other words, fairy tales express patriarchal values. They are stories about marriage and family used to socialize and civilize women while outlining a community's ideals of femininity, sexuality, and womanhood. They are used to control women and undermine their individuality and accomplishments.[33] In the fairy-tale-inspired retellings of Vaughan's origin story, George Treadwell became her knight in shining armor, the dashing prince who saved her from obscurity and the cruelties of racism. And her marriage to Treadwell became the defining moment of her career—on par with and often surpassing her win at the Apollo Theater's amateur night and years on the road with the Hines and Eckstine bands. Marriage was the ultimate act of domestication, and it also reestablished Treadwell as the hero of Vaughan's story.

Yet there is another dark, unsettling side to these fairy tales and the story of "Sarah Vaughan and her Pygmalion," a side that provides insights into the personal dynamics between Vaughan and her husband. Friends described Treadwell as a macho "man's man," and this likely created problems as Vaughan's fame grew and she became more confident and powerful. Perhaps Treadwell was tired of playing a supporting role, always being the man behind the scenes: Mr. Sarah Vaughan. And perhaps the appearance of the Pygmalion-inspired publicity campaign in 1952 reflected an internal power struggle, the tensions building between Treadwell and Vaughan. The story of Pygmalion placed him at the center of Vaughan's success. It boosted his ego, stature, and importance. It helped him reassert his dominance in their relationship, at least publicly, while reestablishing traditional gender roles.

At its core, the story of Pygmalion presents women as controlled, trapped, rescued, idealized, defined, and owned by the men in their lives.[34] Women are tamed and sculpted, in a sense, made to order according the preferences and whims of men. For feminist scholars, the Pygmalion myth and its many retellings are stories about male subjects who, threatened by a woman's independent spirit, vitality, and sexuality, replace her with statues, pictures, and other silent objects.[35] This tale has been used time and again to silence and contain women.

With his Pygmalion-inspired rewriting of her origin story, Treadwell publicly silenced Vaughan and took away her agency too. He accomplished this not by challenging her brilliance as a musician but by honing in on her looks and physical appearance, her body, a point of insecurity for many women, including Vaughan. It was a deeply personal and ultimately hurtful blow. In this light, the story of Treadwell and his "Galatea with a $1,000,000 larynx" is not a romantic story of self-sacrifice and self-improvement.[36] Instead, it is an unsettling story of domestic violence and a crumbling marriage dressed up in the story of Pygmalion, an age-old, socially acceptable narrative that celebrated men controlling, silencing, and dominating the women in their lives. It was a story that condoned violence against women.

While it's easy to portray Treadwell as a villain, he did have a savvy understanding of what American audiences wanted to see, hear, and believe, particularly from black women in pop music. Postwar American audiences, black and especially white, needed Vaughan to be tamed and domesticated by her husband. White listeners needed her, a black woman, to appear civilized and more conventionally beautiful. They needed Vaughan to seem silent, submissive, powerless, and not disruptive so that, ironically enough, they could hear her voice, with its vitality, humanity, beauty, and ability to challenge racial boundaries. By aligning Vaughan's origin story with fairy tales and the Pygmalion myth, Treadwell helped make this happen. And when the story of "Sarah Vaughan and Her Pygmalion" made its way into the white mainstream press in 1954, Vaughan emerged as a pop star, experiencing the biggest crossover success of her career.

8

"Sarah Vaughan Is Finally on the Way to the Pot of Gold"

Having my first smash pop hit gives me a wonderful feeling," Vaughan told a packed house at Birdland in December 1954.[1] She'd recently returned from another successful tour of Europe, her second. This time she added sold-out engagements in Berlin to her stops in Paris, where she appeared at the famed Salle Pleyel on October 11. A tour of the United Kingdom, culminating with a concert at London's Royal Albert Hall on October 24, followed. But before she left New York, Vaughan stepped into Mercury's studios to record "Make Yourself Comfortable" on September 24. Released at the end of October in anticipation of her return home, the single, backed by "Idle Gossip" on the B-side, was selling spectacularly well. By mid-November, just two weeks after its release, "Make Yourself Comfortable" had garnered "unusually enthusiastic sales reports" throughout New England, the mid-Atlantic states, and the Midwest, *Billboard* reported.[2] A week later, it appeared on *Variety*'s list of "Retail Disk Best Sellers," breaking through at No. 25.[3] Five weeks in, during her three weeks at Birdland, it had sold 250,000 copies, and the black press predicted Vaughan was well on her way to "the pot of gold every pop artist hopes for—a record selling a million copies."[4]

This success had been a long time coming. She hadn't had a strong seller since "These Things I Offer You" in the spring of 1951, and its sales paled in comparison to those of "Make Yourself Comfortable." Although making hits was not her top priority, Vaughan understood the value of a successful pop single. "I have more fans now than ever in my life," she told her old friend and advocate Dave Garroway days earlier during an appearance on his national radio show, *Friday with Garroway*. When asked if her new fans understood her jazz sides, Vaughan was diplomatic. "Well, I think they do. But the commercial tunes are taking over. That is the thing now," she said. "Your old albums are still selling well," Garroway countered. "But [they] do not reach the masses," she explained.[5]

A year earlier, in October 1953, after Columbia canceled her contract, Vaughan signed a dual contract with Mercury. She would record pop on the parent label, Mercury, and jazz on EmArcy, their soon to be established jazz subsidiary. She no longer had to compromise. Vaughan could now split her talent in two and experience the best of both worlds: fame and fortune as a pop starlet and the creative freedom of a jazz artist. It was an unprecedented contract. No musician, white or black, had been granted anything like it before. And while it was an artistically satisfying arrangement, it was financially underwhelming. Her new contract did not include a guarantee. Her earnings would rely solely upon royalties from record sales.

The contract went into effect on January 1, 1954, and just as had happened five years earlier with Columbia, Mercury's executives rushed Vaughan into their studios. Weeks later, they issued a single pairing, "Easy Come, Easy Go Lover" with "And This Is My Beloved," followed in February by "Come Along with Me" and "It's Easy to Remember" on the B-side. The sides followed a familiar formula. All were backed by a sweeping, dramatic string orchestra, and, with the exception of the up-tempo "Come Along with Me," they were slow romantic ballads, Vaughan's specialty. She sang beautifully, taking full advantage of her lower range, deep register, full vibrato, and pure tone, but the discs were otherwise unremarkable and far too similar to her Columbia output. And like her Columbia sides, they didn't sell. In May, Mercury departed from the Columbia playbook and released two jazz sides of Vaughan backed by her trio, "Polka Dots and Moonbeams" and the scat-heavy "Shulie a Bop." In July they mixed it up again with a brassy, swinging disc of "Old Devil Moon," reminiscent of her popular Columbia recording of "Perdido," and "Saturday," another crooning ballad. But there was still no significant traction with disc jockeys and record buyers.

Industry insiders understood that Vaughan, and by extension Mercury, needed to end her dry spell and score a big pop hit. The fate of Mercury's new jazz subsidiary depended on it. "Perhaps one reason that Miss Vaughan has failed to come up with a hit recently is that she is bucking the trend to complete simplicity in vocal projection," *Variety*'s Herm Schoenfeld speculated.[6] Her most commercial releases for Mercury were still too esoteric for the pop market, and like Columbia before them, Mercury hadn't figured out how to make their newest acquisition into a pop star. Insiders knew that Vaughan had the talent—was in fact one of the most gifted musicians in the business—but her singing was still too stylized, not quite in sync with the popular tastes of the day. She was at risk of becoming permanently relegated to the jazz sidelines.

Make Yourself Comfortable" cracked the code. "I am crazy about that," Vaughan told Dave Garroway during her appearance on his show in December. "It is a little commercial tune. It is a real cute tune. I like it."[7] Publicly she promoted the record, which just hit No. 13 on the *Billboard* charts, but privately she did not like it. Her road manager Johnnie Garry remembered when Bobby Shad of Mercury gave her "Make Yourself Comfortable" during the recording session. "I'm not going to sing that tune," Vaughan said. "You've got to sing it. We have a contract here," Treadwell reminded her.[8] It is easy to understand why Vaughan found "Make Yourself Comfortable" uninspiring. It was harmonically, rhythmically, and melodically simple. Written by Bob Merrill, the mastermind behind Patti Page's 1953 megahit "How Much Is That Doggie in the Window," "Comfortable" was yet another trendy novelty tune. And given the unpleasant experiences with Mitch Miller and his novelty tunes while at Columbia, Vaughan probably dreaded the session. She sang straight as she told the story of a couple rushing home from a date to smooch. Her interpretation was provocative and filled with innuendo, yet sweet and wholesome at the same time. And like "Doggie," it incorporated a generous helping of overdubbing and echo chambers, technological gimmicks that transformed this otherwise saccharine, rather pedestrian tune into something new and decidedly modern. It was catchy, and Vaughan's voice sounded phenomenal.

According to the *Chicago Defender*, when Mercury's vice president, Art Talmadge, heard the masters for "Make Yourself Comfortable," he immediately ordered an initial pressing of five hundred thousand discs.[9] Full-page ad buys in the leading trade publications followed, and Mercury distributed the disc widely. Both *Billboard* and *Variety* named Vaughan's "Make Yourself Comfortable" a "Best Bet" and published positive reviews, praising not only Vaughan's performance but also the tune's commercial appeal and potential to become a hit. Disc jockeys soon placed the single in heavy rotation.

Sales of Vaughan's "Make Yourself Comfortable" built momentum throughout the winter and continued into early spring, performing well on the *Billboard, Variety,* and *Cash Box* charts. Her recording outpaced all other covers, including Columbia's by Peggy King, which placed a distant second, and its success spawned additional covers. Television personalities Steve Lawrence and Eydie Gormé, future husband and wife, released a charming duet that capitalized on their familiar, affectionate banter. In February, comedian Andy Griffith issued a less charming, more cynical (and sexist) cover for Capitol. He portrayed a man scorned by a scheming, manipulative woman. And most curiously, Eileen Scott, a relatively unknown white singer, released an identical, albeit clumsy and less technologically sophisticated knock-off of Vaughan's arrangement for Gateway, an obscure budget label specializing in covers of hit records. Vaughan's version, however, prevailed and became her biggest seller to date.

In January, as "Make Yourself Comfortable" peaked on the charts, Mercury released a new disc pairing "How Important Can It Be," another romantic ballad, with "Waltzing Down the Aisle," a tongue-in-cheek waltz. Hits beget hits, and the trade press predicted that Vaughan's cover would sell well but face stiff competition from newcomer Joni James, a conventionally beautiful brunette, on MGM and veteran swing stylist Connee Boswell on Decca. Vaughan performed "How Important Can It Be" on variety shows, including Ed Sullivan's *Toast of the Town*.[10] Mercury sponsored a contest asking DJs to sing along with Vaughan's recording on air. The DJ who received the most requests for his sing-along duo won. Bob Dun of KLX in Oakland, California, came in first, followed by Hugh Johnson of WBBW in Youngstown, Ohio, and Ray Wright of KGCX in Williston, North Dakota.[11] In the end, Joni James's cover prevailed, but Vaughan's "How Important Can It Be" still performed well, eventually selling five hundred thousand copies.

With "Make Yourself Comfortable" and "How Important Can It Be," Mercury relaunched Vaughan as a pop artist. Her first four sides as the "new," more commercial Vaughan told a story of an all-American girl in search of a husband. In "Comfortable," she explored the thrills of a new romance, while its B-side contemplated the "Idle Gossip" that accompanies a new affair. Vaughan explained that this time the gossip was true because she had finally found her true love. Her next release asked "How Important Can It Be" that she had kissed other lips and concluded with Vaughan happily "Waltzing Down the Aisle." It was a story line in harmony with contemporary gender roles and sexual mores, and it matched Vaughan's public persona of domestic femininity. Much like a serial novel or film typical of 1950s movie culture, each release ushered in a new stage of Vaughan's hypothetical relationship, and her listeners were there each step of the way. Vaughan sang of universal experiences, her fears, desires, and aspirations—much like one friend confiding to another—and in the process cultivated an emotional intimacy and bond with her listeners. She had always accomplished this with her jazz singing. She was, after all, a skilled, emotionally engaging performer. But now a larger, mainstream, and primarily white audience experienced it too. Her fans, both men and women, black and white, got to know and identify with Vaughan and could imagine themselves as part of her story.

After Vaughan's girl-next-door-in-search-of-a-husband story line finished, her pop persona embraced a new character: that of the bold, sexy temptress. On March 17, as the popularity of "Make Yourself Comfortable" waned, executives at Mercury rushed Vaughan into their studios to record "Whatever Lola Wants," a tale of seduction set to a catchy flamenco. Industry insiders predicted that "Lola," written by current wunderkinds Jerry Ross and Richard Adler for the upcoming musical *Damn Yankees,* would become a big hit, and record labels, both large and small, wanted to get in on the game. At least six artists recorded "Lola" in early 1955: Vaughan for Mercury, along with Dinah Shore for RCA Victor, Carmen McRae for Decca, Ginny Gibson for MGM, Jamie of the Mello Larks for Epic, and the Hi-Los for Starlight. The publisher, Frank Music, promised RCA that Dinah Shore could debut the tune on a nationally televised all-star spectacular broadcast by NBC on Sunday, March 27, the night before record stores began selling her disc. Other labels would have to wait to play, and thus promote, their covers. But Frank Music had changed the clearance date for "Lola" several times, and confusion reigned. Mercury jumped the gun, and DJs throughout the country began spinning Vaughan's "Lola" on Tuesday, March 22, just five days after she recorded the tune but also five days before Shore's big NBC premiere. ASCAP stepped in, and Mercury retreated. On

Friday, in a show of good faith, the label wired forty prominent DJs requesting that they stop playing Vaughan's "Lola" until after Shore's national telecast. They sent similar postcard messages to another two thousand disc jockeys, but few thought the message would arrive in time. Meanwhile, Mercury happily announced that Vaughan's cover would also be available in stores on Monday, March 28.[12]

The race was on. Reviewers liked Vaughan's cover but predicted stiff competition from Shore and Carmen McRae, a relative newcomer to the pop field. Each artist crafted engaging, masterful performances. Carmen McRae's "Lola" is delivered flawlessly, but it is almost cold in its precision—every word perfectly articulated and every note hit precisely on the head. Her voice is crisp, light, and fresh. McRae, a jazz vocalist and pianist by training, sings straight, and her approach is very matter of fact. Shore's interpretation is more sumptuous. She also sings relatively straight but incorporates a deep, full vibrato, microtonal inflections, and vocal slides throughout. In many respects, Shore's interpretation is very Vaughan-esque. Yet unlike the modernity so often associated with Vaughan's singing, Shore's interpretation sounds old-fashioned, overwrought, and almost too mannered. Shore sounds like a nice girl playing sexy, rather than the real thing.

In contrast, Vaughan embodies her role as the seductress. Her Lola exudes confidence. Her voice is full and deep, yet buoyant and never breathy; open and inviting; sensual and provocative, but never coy or lewd. It's feminine and subtle without becoming a parody of womanhood or female sexuality. On the surface, Vaughan sings straight, but in fact she infuses her performance with sophisticated vocal inflections and nuances. She teases with the larger rhythmic and harmonic language, which includes a challenging, exotic-sounding Phrygian mode in the bridge, to create a give-and-take that pulls the listener through each verse. And with each new verse, she adds another layer of vocal complexity to build momentum and intensity. Unlike Shore, who must shorten and lengthen notes, slow down and speed up to accommodate her vocal dramatics, Vaughan always keeps a strict beat. Yet she creates the impression of uncertainty and spontaneity, constantly pushing the boundaries between control and loss of control to produce a delightful tension between the two. From a musical standpoint, Vaughan deftly re-creates the dynamics of any successful seduction. By the time she reaches the final refrain and proclaims "I'm irresistible, you fool / Give in, give in, give in," her success, and the success of her disc, seems a foregone conclusion.

Vaughan's "Lola" is a pop masterpiece. In less than three minutes, she captured the persona of Lola—her motivations and desires—perfectly. In a sense, she became Lola, and she did so in a way that epitomized the ethos of the moment. Unlike Shore's old-fashioned, almost stodgy "Lola," Vaughan's "Lola" is modern and hip, free and easy. It's a brilliant performance. It melded her vocal prowess and technical mastery of music—honed during her years as a jazz artist—with her savvy as a storyteller and interpreter of lyrics.

At last, her skill set and the demands of the pop market intersected. Vaughan's cover became the biggest seller of the three, in spite of Dinah Shore's nationally televised debut. It performed well on the industry charts, peaking at No. 6 on both the *Variety* and *Billboard* rankings, and remained popular throughout the summer. It became an unexpected hit in Morocco. According to international jukebox reports, Vaughan's "Lola" was the most frequently played disc of the spring and summer in Casablanca.[13] Her "Lola" buoyed sales of a compilation album featuring other Mercury artists singing tunes from *Damn Yankees*.[14] Although a lone DJ in Los Angeles banned all versions of the tune sung by women, because they were too provocative, Vaughan's single went on to sell eight hundred thousand copies.[15]

As summer became fall, Mercury continued its strategic release of novelty-driven pop singles that continued to demonstrate Vaughan's flexibility and range. In June, the label issued "Experience Unnecessary," another teasing yet provocative tune, this time with a trendy rhythm and blues influence, backed by

"Slowly with Feeling," a more earnest, romantic waltz. "Johnny Be Smart" and "Hey, Naughty Papa," two more R & B–style tunes, followed in September. And a disc pairing "C'est La Vie" and "Never," both ballads, appeared at the end of October. While none of these were runaway hits like "Make Yourself Comfortable" or "Lola," they sold well, and Vaughan finished the year strong.

In October, Vaughan was ranked the third-most-played female vocalist in the country, behind Georgia Gibbs and Jaye P. Morgan, in *Billboard*'s 1955 Disc Jockey Poll.[16] This momentum spilled into 1956. Her first release of the New Year, the highly anticipated "Mr. Wonderful" from Sammy Davis, Jr.'s upcoming musical of that name, received top exposure from disc jockeys and outpaced much of its competition. And her EmArcy album with tenor saxophonist Cannonball Adderley, *Sarah Vaughan in the Land of Hi-Fi*, a centerpiece of the marketing campaign for the label's new Land of Hi-Fi series, appeared on *Billboard*'s charts of bestselling jazz albums and, perhaps more tellingly, bestselling pop vocal albums too.[17]

Vaughan was in top form, in both the pop and jazz fields, and Mercury rewarded her. In May 1956, seven months before her original contract expired, Mercury cofounder Art Talmadge re-signed Vaughan for another four years. The deal was retroactive to April and, according to trade publications, promised her $500,000 over four years, a dramatic contrast to her original 1954 deal without a guarantee. Though the financial details of her new contract cannot be confirmed, it was a substantial, news-making renegotiation and cited as one in a series of unprecedented deals between the major record labels and their top female stars.[18] Three weeks earlier, Columbia, in a deal described as "one of the costliest contracts" in recording history, re-signed Jo Stafford for five years at $500,000.[19] In full-page ads, Columbia touted Stafford's international appeal and sales of more than thirty-three million discs during her five-and-a-half-year tenure at the label. A week after that, Columbia, following months of negotiations, finalized a new contract with Doris Day for an astronomical $1,050,000 over five years.[20] Day was Columbia's biggest female star. In 1954 and 1955, disc jockeys voted her their favorite girl singer in *Billboard*'s annual polls (Vaughan came in twelfth in 1954 and ninth in 1955); *Down Beat*'s poll of musicians, composers, and directors designated her the "top musical personality" of 1956. In 1956 Day also scored her sixth million-selling single with "Whatever Will Be, Will Be (Que Sera, Sera)." She was also a major movie star and consistent top box office earner.[21]

Vaughan was not in the same league as Doris Day (or, for that matter, Jo Stafford). Vaughan simply did not have the same film, television, and radio platform as Day; few did. Nor did she epitomize the blond, blue-eyed ideal of the American girl next door that Day, often dubbed the "professional virgin," portrayed in both her films and music. Vaughan couldn't. But her new contract for Mercury, with its reported $125,000-a-year guarantee, was still a significant milestone for Vaughan. It solidified her position as an influential power player in the music industry. Vaughan, with her dual contract, had become a cornerstone of Mercury's business model. Her flexibility, vocal mastery, and fresh sound solidified their pop sales, while her expanding appeal, phenomenal technique, and longstanding credentials as a jazz artist were crucial for launching their new jazz label, EmArcy—a source of prestige and, eventually, financial gain for Mercury. Perhaps most important, however, with this deal Vaughan became an African American woman on equal footing, at least financially, with many of her white contemporaries. It was a turning point of sorts for Vaughan and black performers, especially black women.

Mercury treated Vaughan differently than many labels had treated their black talent in the past. In addition to the big paycheck, the unprecedented dual contract, and the creative freedom they represented, Mercury did a better job of selecting tunes for Vaughan than Columbia had. Time and again, reviews of Vaughan's pop releases for Mercury commented on the quality of the material she sang. Her new singles featured, according to *Down Beat*, "some of the best songs written in the last couple of years." In their review of "How Important Can It Be" and "Waltzing Down the Aisle" *Down Beat* critics proclaimed, "Mercury is doing an A-1 job of finding songs for Sarah to sing that utilize her wonderful vocal equipment in a commercial manner, yet won't offend the fans who remember when."[22] And *Billboard* described "Make Yourself Comfortable" as an "out-of-the-ordinary piece of material by writer Bob Merrill," concluding that the "first-rate, light novelty material gives her a chance to get moving in the pop market. Watch this one; it has a chance."[23]

It seems logical; if you give artists strong material, they will make better records that are more likely to sell well and become hits. Yet this was not always the case for black artists. When Nat Hentoff asked Ella Fitzgerald in February 1955 why she never recorded "hot" pop material for her label, Decca, a frustrated Fitzgerald responded: "I don't know myself. Yet I never do get a chance at the songs that have a chance. They give me something by somebody that no one else has, and then they wonder why the record doesn't sell. I'm so heart-broken over it."[24] For years, jazz publications lamented the shortage of "quality" songs and the tendency for record producers to relegate their second-, often third-rate leftovers to critically acclaimed, predominantly black, performers like Ella Fitzgerald, Billy Eckstine, Louis Armstrong, and also Vaughan during her years at Columbia. Instead labels reserved the best material for their white, and in many cases, less talented, performers.

Mercury, however, treated Vaughan more like her white counterparts, especially in the early years of their partnership. They realized it was in everybody's best interest to give Vaughan every chance to compete with her white contemporaries. They wanted hits and gave her strong material—tunes with industry buzz, like "Whatever Lola Wants," and material penned by songwriters with a proven track record, like "Make Yourself Comfortable" by Bob Merrill. Mercury threw Vaughan, often the only black artist covering the song, into the ring with tough competition and then worked to aggressively position her in the market and optimize her exposure, and sometimes they played dirty. The publishers for "Mr. Wonderful," for instance, set a February 1, 1956, clearance date before which covers were not to be released. But, as with "Whatever Lola Wants," Mercury didn't wait. The label leaked the disc to DJs in select markets almost a month early, on January 6. RCA learned of Mercury's plans and rushed Teddi King's disc to DJs for play beginning January 5.[25] When coupled with robust print ads, merchandising campaigns, and carefully timed television appearances, Mercury gave Vaughan a chance at pop success.

Songs with a chance were novelty-driven and used the same techniques developed by Mitch Miller. In 1955, technological gimmicks were still fashionable, as were "ethnic" or vernacular sounds and styles, now with an emphasis on Latin-inspired dances, rhythm and blues, and country and western. That year Rosemary Clooney's "This Ole House," Bill Haley's "Shake Rattle and Roll," and Vaughan Monroe's "They Were Doin' the Mambo" all performed well.[26] In each case, white artists shifted musical identities—their subject positions—by assuming a variety of nationalities, ethnicities, and races. They temporarily entered these other "worlds," shared them with their intrigued listeners, and then returned to their privileged white existences. Black performers were rarely granted this performative flexibility. More often than not, their performances were limited to musical expressions of blackness, be it the blues, gospel or spirituals, or jazz. Pop music historian David Bracket has found that recordings by African Americans that incorporated elements of vernacular blackness, like the sounds of vaudeville and minstrelsy, crossed over onto the pop charts more consistently than those that did not.[27] In other words, for black artists, race functioned as the novelty device of choice. And this is the strategy that Miller used with Vaughan at Columbia.

Here, too, Mercury tried something different. During her success streak beginning at the end of 1954 and extending into early 1956, Vaughan's pop releases featured a diverse collection of soundscapes and musical codes. In addition to "Whatever Lola Wants," she sang other Latin-infused singles like "Johnny Be

Smart," "Never," and "The Bashful Matador." She sang more traditional, jingle-like waltzes too: "Waltzing Down the Aisle," along with "Slowly with Feeling" and "It Happened Again." When R & B–style pop tunes were all the rage, in the summer and fall of 1955, she released "Hey Naughty Papa." These were not blues in the style of fellow Mercury artist Dinah Washington, the Queen of the Blues, but rather of Georgia Gibbs, a white vocalist, also on Mercury, who had scored hits with her covers of LaVern Baker's "Tweedle Dee" and Etta James's "The Wallflower (Dance with Me, Henry)." Throughout it all Vaughan continued to record romantic ballads and standards backed by lush string orchestras, ensembles still associated with white cultural institutions. But these were released as pop albums, not novelty-driven singles. And she simultaneously recorded jazz for EmArcy. Even though Vaughan didn't like many of the pop tunes she recorded, they were an impressive display of her artistic range and flexibility, a testament to her skill as an artist. Through her recordings, Vaughan demonstrated to mainstream America, again primarily white, that a black voice could sound many ways and sing many different styles. She demonstrated that performances by black artists, just like those of their white contemporaries, were indeed performances. They were not set or fixed expressions of an essential racial identity. Black performers need not, and in fact should not, be typecast and restricted to a single style or vocal type.

In her pop songs for Mercury, Vaughan assumed many roles. Her performances did not conform to the stereotypes typically associated with black womanhood, those perpetuated in classic movies like *Gone with the Wind* and *Cabin in the Sky*. In her music, Vaughan was not a maid or mammy, a naive girl or a loose woman. Rather, she portrayed an all-American sweetheart in one song, a jilted lover in another, a devoted housewife in yet others, and a sultry seductress in the still popular "Whatever Lola Wants, Lola Gets." With this collection of roles, as performed in her pop music for Mercury, Vaughan presented the many sides of a woman while displaying a humanity, emotional depth, and complexity so often denied black women by the popular imagination. This was huge.

A closer look at Vaughan's first smash hit, "Make Yourself Comfortable," demonstrates how she accomplished this. Unlike many records from this period, "Comfortable" did not rely on unusual regional or vernacular sounds for its hook. Instead, it incorporated new technologies—echo chambers and generous helpings of overdubbing, the layering of voices using multitrack tape, techniques often associated with white performers like Patti Page or Les Paul and Mary Ford. "Comfortable" is an otherwise simple, formulaic tune: it has two straightforward, easily hummable melodic ideas that alternate AABA, a basic harmonic language, and an equally clear-cut rhythmic language. So what makes Vaughan's cover interesting, and ultimately a catchy earworm, are the various manipulations and permutations of her voice created by technology and the way these multiple voices of Vaughan complement and interact with one another. There are three contrasting "types" or "combinations" of her voice, and each produces a different sound world with a distinct texture, timbre, and mood.

The recording begins with a choir of effervescent-voiced Sarah Vaughans singing in "head" voices that have been altered by an echo chamber. Enhanced by the reverberations of the echo chamber, her voice, or rather voices, sound smooth, light, and airy. They are disembodied as she sings the tune's refrain, "Ooh, ooh, make yourself comfortable," on a dominant prolongation, a harmonic holding pattern of sorts that eases listeners into the performance while creating anticipation for Vaughan's big entrance. Then a full-voiced, solo Vaughan, still accompanied by her choir, begins the song in earnest. Singing in a "chest" voice, she invites her beau in after a date, turns on the record player, and takes the phone off the hook so that no one can intrude. In comparison to the introductory choir, here her tone is fuller and deeper, and within the context of this recording the solo voice seems more grounded. In the contrasting B section, or bridge, the choir drops out and a second grounded voice joins the first. Together the two Vaughans harmonize and blend with one another as the pair asks the hypothetical boyfriend why they hurried through dinner and dancing and left before their movie finished. To make time for smooching, of course. The opening A-section material returns, again with the solo Vaughan accompanied by her choir, as she instructs her date to take off his shoes and loosen his tie. The couple kisses and turns down the lights. The performance concludes with one last statement of the refrain. Now unaccompanied, Vaughan's voice becomes thicker and heavier with a touch of throaty rumble as she slowly sings "Make yourself comfortable" followed by a breathy "baby," which is manipulated and extended using an echo chamber.

Vaughan's "Make Yourself Comfortable" used technology to play with the contemporary vocal codes often associated with black and white voices. She sang the final "baby" of the tune in a voice reminiscent of many of her blues contemporaries, a timbre many white audiences still associated with blackness and embodied performances. But technology transformed this grounded voice into an ungrounded voice separated from the body that created it. It became disembodied. Because of Vaughan's access to the extensive technological resources of Mercury, itself a by-product of her status in the industry at that time, she was able to play with and ultimately reconfigure existing racial vocal codes in the space of a single recording. In other words, although "Make Yourself Comfortable" was a cheesy, schmaltzy tune, especially to our twenty-first-century ears, it was also subversive, pushing back against the accepted norms of the day.

The overdubbing and the layering of voices using multitrack tape in "Make Yourself Comfortable" also explored how technology could change the way audiences sonically perceived a person's individuality and identity. Patti Page popularized the technique with "Confess" in 1948, followed by other hits including "With My Eyes Wide Open I'm Dreaming" in 1950, the oft-cited and maligned "(How Much Is) That Doggie in the Window" in 1953, and "Cross Over the Bridge" in 1954. In a nod to the technological manipulations of Page's voice—the use of overdubbing—when crediting the artists on the disc, producers listed the vocalists as "Patti Page, Patti Page, Patti Page, Patti Page." The *Billboard* and *Variety* charts referred to the Patti Page Trio, Quartet, or Quintet, as appropriate. On these tunes Page often sang in close harmony with herself, with each "Patti Page" assuming a distinct vocal role, much like the individual singers in popular vocal quartets like the Chordettes, whose cover of "Mr. Sandman" topped the charts in 1954. With the help of technology, Page was able to magnify and multiply herself. Each track of Page's voice represented a unique subject, and by layering the voices one could hear the many sides of a person—the complexities and parts that make up the whole. When applied to an African American performer, so often perceived as a stereotype, the use of overdubbing shattered long-standing preconceptions and assumptions. As with Page in her many overdubbed hits, in "Make Yourself Comfortable" listeners could hear multiple voices of Vaughan simultaneously. She demonstrated that black women were not flat or one-dimensional and that a single black voice could sound multifaceted and complex. The same technology also helped shift the cultural space occupied by black female voices in the white imagination. Instead of the primitivism still associated with the blues, and by extension many black voices, Vaughan's voice, especially on tunes like "Make Yourself Comfortable," became associated with the latest technology and innovation. Hers became a voice of modernity, and this was groundbreaking, especially for a black woman.

At the same time, songs like "Make Yourself Comfortable" and "How Important Can It Be" embraced the ethos of the moment. They paired technology with nostalgia to become both sonic and textual realizations of postwar American ideals and values. Americans nostalgically embraced distinct gender roles as women abandoned their wartime jobs in order to become professional homemakers, and men once again became the primary breadwinners. In the process they fortified the institutions of both the family and home, which, it was believed, countered the communist threat from abroad. "Make Yourself Comfortable" is about both the home and conventional gender roles. From a purely textual point of view, the lyrics told the story of a woman welcoming a young man into her home using the common greeting "Make yourself comfortable." And the larger narrative initiated by the release of this single, which related the experiences of a woman in search of a husband, reflected postwar views on domesticity and the acceptable role of women, a role reinforced by Vaughan's own public image, honed by her husband Treadwell, as a devoted wife skilled in the domestic arts. As historian Elaine Tyler May has explored in her study of family life during the Cold War, when confronted by the horrors of World War II and the uncertainties of the Atomic Age, Americans sought security and stability in the modern suburban home.[28] Household appliances, and the consumerism that they represented, played a central role in this process. By making modern homes comfortable and secure, appliances like fully automated washing machines, vacuum cleaners, toasters, and hand-held mixers, as well as hi-fi stereo systems and televisions, came to symbolize the benefits of technology in the Atomic Age. May explains that "science and technology seemed to have invaded virtually every aspect of life, from the most public to the most private."[29] The extensive invocations of technology in "Make Yourself Comfortable," not to mention the subject matter of its lyrics, epitomized these postwar ideals. With the release of "Make Yourself Comfortable" and its successors, Vaughan and her voice invaded the home and became a part of the postwar American suburban life and mind-set.

At the height of the song's popularity, the black press claimed that "Make Yourself Comfortable" received "thousands of spins daily from disc jockeys."[30] It was a bold, if perhaps exaggerated, statement, and it evoked powerful imagery. Americans, both black and white, heard Vaughan and her voice as they drove in their cars, relaxed in the privacy of their living rooms, or cooked dinner in their kitchens. A 1956 review for Vaughan's "The Other Woman" concluded, "Daytime spinners should have a ball with this one. It's a natural lead-in for human-interest chatter aimed at the long-suffering housewife. The canary sings with rich intensity on an unusual ballad, with imaginative lyrics."[31] Vaughan had become an ally and confidant of sorts, another household fixture. Her voice emanated from jukeboxes as Americans ate at the local diner or socialized in restaurants and country clubs. They overheard her singing while shopping at the neighborhood grocery store. And in 1956, patrons of the Grand Union grocery store chain could purchase *Sarah and Dizzy,* an album of reissues from her youthful bebop days. It was one of the few jazz offerings in a new line of bargain hi-fi albums, featuring primarily classical music, sold in the chain's 344 stores throughout the Northeast.[32] During the 1950s, Vaughan's voice became a part of daily life for both black and white Americans. Her voice became a part of the American soundtrack.

Vaughan, along with her African American contemporaries like Nat King Cole and Ella Fitzgerald, integrated the airwaves, initiating a kind of sonic desegregation at a time when the United States was still deeply divided along racial lines. Black Americans encountered the blatant Jim Crow of the South, but also the more subtle yet insidious racism of the North. In the postwar years, as whites fled the diversity of urban centers for the suburbs, often with the help of federal home loans, they actively resisted integration. The majority of white Americans did not want black neighbors. Housing developers and neighborhood improvement associations enacted restrictive housing covenants that forbade homeowners from selling their properties to blacks; realtors and financial institutions told their agents and lenders not to help blacks wanting to buy properties in white neighborhoods; and local governments enacted restrictive zoning laws that maintained segregation.[33]

When black families did move into white neighborhoods, they encountered fierce opposition, and often violence. In 1948, Nat King Cole purchased a home in the affluent, exclusive Los Angeles neighborhood of Hancock Park. The Hancock Park Property Owners Association held emergency meetings to stop Cole's family from moving in. They tried to buy back the house from Cole, offering him an additional $25,000 over the $75,000 purchase price. "How would YOU like it if you had to come out of your home and see a Negro walking down the street wearing a big wide hat, a zoot suit, long chain and yellow shoes?" association members reportedly asked Cole's white manager, Carlos Gastel.[34] Nat King Cole, of course, did not wear zoot suits. He wore immaculately tailored suits, crisp white shirts, and slim black ties. He cultivated an image of polished elegance, sophistication, and respectability, which members of the property association discovered during a meeting with Cole and his wife, Maria. "There it was patiently explained to my husband that the good people of Hancock Park simply did not want any undesirables moving in," Maria wrote in her memoir. Cole replied, "Neither do I. And if I see anybody undesirable coming in here, I'll be the first to complain."[35] Cole, his wife, and two daughters moved in in August 1948. White residents placed a sign on the Coles' lawn that read "Nigger Heaven," and later Cole's daughter Carol remembered someone burning the word "nigger" into their front lawn.[36]

In 1953, baseball legend Jackie Robinson and his wife struggled to purchase a home in Fairfield County, Connecticut, and Westchester County, New York. During their search, showings were canceled, offers rejected, asking prices suddenly raised, and properties mysteriously sold to other families—anything to keep a black family from moving into the neighborhood. Fellow baseball great Willie Mays encountered resistance when he wanted to purchase a home in San Francisco in 1957. And racial violence greeted countless black families across the country when they tried to relocate to white neighborhoods. Local police barred entrances. Protestors bombed homes and destroyed personal property. Riots, often involving thousands, erupted in Cicero, Illinois; Detroit, Michigan; and Levittown, Pennsylvania, requiring the National Guard to step in to restore order.

In 1968, in the wake of the riots in urban centers across the country the previous summer, Lyndon Johnson signed the Civil

Rights Act of 1968, better known as the Fair Housing Act, into law. Residential segregation and discrimination were now illegal. Fifteen years earlier the NAACP had proclaimed housing segregation the central issue in the larger fight against segregation. In the 1950s and 1960s, the attitudes of white Americans gradually began to shift. Many became embarrassed by racial intolerance and the violence so often associated with it, especially how it was perceived abroad. Many white Americans began to see black Americans differently, as potential neighbors.

Musicians like Sarah Vaughan were helping to shift their perceptions. With her singing, she demonstrated the humanity, complexity, and subjectivity of black women. Black women had the same depth of feeling, the same hopes and dreams as everybody else. They knew of the excitement of a new romance, the thrill of a seduction, and the pain of a broken heart. Vaughan had an uncanny ability to sing with an emotional intensity, and her performances prompted strong, visceral responses from her listeners that encouraged feelings of intimacy, closeness, and often empathy. Along the way, she changed how white Americans heard, understood, and interacted with the black female voice. When songs like "Make Yourself Comfortable," often dismissed as inconsequential commercial fluff by jazz purists, entered contested spaces like the home and suburbia, by way of radios, record players, and television sets, Vaughan broke down barriers. As fans ventured to her concerts, she brought different kinds of people together who may not have otherwise met. Her singing, along with that of many of her contemporaries, helped set the stage for the advances of the civil rights movement in the 1960s and 1970s.

9

"The High Priestess
of Jazz"

Vaughan stepped offstage and made her way through the crowded club to Birdland's bar. She'd finished her set and wanted to relax.

"A guy at Birdland was standing at the bar," Vaughan told jazz journalist Nat Hentoff in January 1955. "He kept looking at me and looking at me. Finally he came over and said, 'I'm not buying any of your records anymore! For the first time, you have a hit. You're going to change! I feel it. And I never thought you'd do a thing like that.'"[1] Vaughan laughed as she told the story to Hentoff, but she was frustrated too. The exchange took place a month earlier, in December 1954, during the same three-week engagement at Birdland where she happily announced that "Make Yourself Comfortable" would become her first smash pop hit. "I just looked at him. The man was really serious. Now what can I say? I hate to get into that kind of conversation anyway," Vaughan continued. "I guess he hadn't heard any of the EmArcy sides. Of course, I'll never change. I couldn't."[2]

EmArcy was the newly minted jazz subsidiary for Mercury Records, and thanks to her unique dual contract, she no longer had to compromise her artistic integrity with her commercial aspirations. But the fan's disapproval, masked as concern, was familiar territory. It mirrored the censure and reprimands doled out by jazz critics during her years at Columbia—the same critics who worried that Vaughan had forsaken her jazz roots in favor of ball gowns and commercial success. Even though she disliked discussions about selling out—their reliance on labels like "jazz" and "pop," the collection of values so often associated with these labels, and the assumptions people made about what she, as a black woman and artist, should and should not sing— she understood that those same jazz critics and devotees needed to have the conversation. They needed her reassurances that jazz remained her main priority, her one true love. And her new dual contract presented the perfect opportunity. "My contract with Mercury is for pops and my contract with EmArcy is for me," she told Hentoff. "I *have* to sing jazz."[3]

Vaughan's passion for and commitment to jazz was finally backed by executives at her record label. Fueled by this support, she embarked on a decade of intense creativity and productivity, releasing a series of albums, first on EmArcy (1954–1959) and then Roulette (1960–1963), that have become jazz classics. Her initial releases for EmArcy restored her credentials as an important jazz recording artist and an influential voice of modern jazz singing, while refining the innovation and boldness of her earliest bebop recordings, all recently reissued as collector items. Her new releases paired elegant, deceptively simple crooning with agile, spontaneous improvisations that reminded listeners not only of the sheer power of her voice but also of the brilliance of her musical mind, her genius. And thanks to her pop successes on Mercury, her audiences grew as she continued to bring new listeners to jazz, both in the United States and abroad.

On Thursday, December 16, 1954, following her three weeks at Birdland, Vaughan stepped into Fine Recording Studios to record the follow-up to *Images,* her critically acclaimed debut jazz album on EmArcy. The second album was titled simply *Sarah*

Vaughan. It was late at night. The atmosphere was relaxed and casual. According to Hentoff's description, Vaughan wore slacks and a blouse, and the musicians—her trio, with Jimmy Jones on piano, Joe Benjamin on bass, and Roy Haynes on drums, plus Clifford Brown on trumpet, Herbie Mann on flute, and Paul Quinichette on tenor saxophone—had taken off their ties and unbuttoned their shirts at the collar. Recording director Bobby Shad was at ease too, happy to let the evening unfold naturally, at its own pace. The tensions so often present in high-stakes pop sessions employing dozens of musicians and engineers were replaced by an easygoing camaraderie. The musicians joked and laughed as they rehearsed. Vaughan stood behind Jones with her arms draped over his shoulders, holding the lead sheet as he played piano. They shared a comfortable familiarity born from eight years of making music together.[4] The other musicians looked on, and together they all worked through the head arrangements for each tune, experimenting, adding and discarding ideas as they collaborated. "I get ideas all of the time from my trio while I'm singing. We have a ball together, all of us, and wherever I go or work, they're going with me," Vaughan told Hentoff. "We really have a lot of fun on these jazz sessions."[5]

The music created that night, and on Saturday, December 18, was extraordinary, and many consider *Sarah Vaughan* her best, most iconic album. Her singing was deceptively simple, with a refined, often sublime eloquence. Gone were many of the flashy vocal swoops, leaps, and turns that defined her earlier work. Instead, the nine tunes on *Sarah Vaughan* revealed her voice, laying it bare. She frequently sustained notes, creating a languorous, more drawn-out feel. Listeners can hear the smaller, more subtle turns and slides she added to her phrasing and how she intensified and slackened her vibrato. Each note became a miniature drama filled with anticipation and enticing tension.

And in a nod to her jazz roots, she did something unusual for a vocalist. On the album, she assumed the role of a horn and often sang without words as she harmonized with the other instruments in the ensemble. She paired with Herbie Mann's flute during the introductions and final bars of "Lullaby of Birdland" and "Jim." On "September Song," "I'm Glad There Is You," and "He's My Guy," all the musicians layered their voices together, their musical motives intertwined as the song's momentum built, and then they came together in the final bars for one last flourish. Vaughan fully integrated herself into the ensemble and, together with her fellow musicians, created a seamless progression of tone colors and timbres as each pairing came in and out of focus. Together, they crafted a distinct sonic world.

Sarah Vaughan is full of beautiful, transcendent singing. But equally important are the silences. Those moments when Vaughan chose not to sing and let the music breathe. "April in Paris" begins with Vaughan singing the tune relatively straight. It's a romantic, contemplative ballad and Vaughan sings slowly. She's backed by her trio, but it's really an intimate duet with her longtime pianist Jimmy Jones, who complements her voice with a contrapuntal line, adding complexity and nuance to the tune. Then trumpeter Clifford Brown takes a solo. When Vaughan returns, instead of embellishing the reprise as she often did, she simplifies it even further, parsing the phrases to create shorter, more intense musical statements. She sings the lyric "April in Paris," then pauses, letting the listener savor the moment. As the listener waits, Brown adds a short fill, echoing the musical ideas from his earlier solo. Vaughan continues, singing "chestnuts in blossom," again Brown follows. They trade phrases again and again, until Vaughan and Brown finally come together. Vaughan finishes the tune with Brown noodling behind her, creating more contrapuntal lines. And at the end Mann and Quinichette enter, playing a series of chords, almost like a chorale, as Vaughan sings with them.

"April in Paris," along with every other track on *Sarah Vaughan,* feels like an intimate conversation between Vaughan and the musicians in the ensemble. They stretch out and explore, playing off one another as they make art for art's sake. It's never contrived or forced, but instead relaxed and easygoing, leisurely. "She sings more freely here than even in most of her nightclub appearances," wrote *Down Beat*'s reviewer. "There is less of the emphasis on virtuoso effects and more on the kind of after-hours singing Sarah excels at."[6]

Sarah Vaughan was the kind of album that jazz critics needed Vaughan to sing, and by envisioning her in an after-hours session in their reviews, critics like Hentoff signaled Vaughan's return to her roots and the jazz fold. It signaled her authenticity and integrity as a jazz musician. During the 1940s and 1950s, the idea of the after-hours session had become a romanticized symbol of jazz in its purest, most authentic form. Away from the commercial demands of paying gigs, musicians after hours could be true to their personal artistic visions, creating new, innovative music. And many in the jazz community believed that the real innovations took place behind the scenes, after hours. More than a decade earlier, bebop developed after hours, during intense late-night jam sessions. Virtuosity and masculine bravado reigned, as musicians, almost exclusively men, flaunted their prowess and potency on their instruments. And, for the most part, women sat on the sidelines.

With *Sarah Vaughan*, however, Vaughan was front and center. She reimagined the after-hours session, placing a woman's creative voice at its heart. Instead of sensational displays of individual, often heroic prowess, which can be a distancing experience for listeners, she emphasized collaboration, intimacy, and more subtle forms of vocal prowess.[7] Although critics of the day lauded *Sarah Vaughan* for its absence of "virtuoso effects," her singing on the album was unquestionably that of a virtuoso. It was a study in vocal control: her finely tuned vibrato; her understated vocal turns, those microtonal bends rather than the dramatic, two-octave swoops; her use of vocal placement (where in her throat a sound began) to create the album's tonal palette, the contrasts in color and timbre as she shifted between her roles as soloist and sideman; not to mention the breath control required to sing all of those long, sustained notes. And the intimacy praised by critics was incredibly difficult to achieve. It demanded phenomenal ears and a sensitivity to the musicians around her, paired with the skill, the musical toolbox, to instantly respond. Vaughan's excellence was second nature, and whatever the moment demanded she could create. Her execution was effortless and flawless, and even though she could have blown many of her collaborators out of the water with her vocal acrobatics, she chose not to. Instead, she put forward a different model for virtuosity, one practiced by a woman and vocalist and once again expanded both the technical and expressive boundaries of the idiom. In the process, she set the course for modern jazz singing.

"That's one of my favorite records," vocalist Dianne Reeves said while discussing *Sarah Vaughan*. "I think, actually, that record was *the* life-changing record for me. I just loved it. As a kid, my uncle gave it to me and I couldn't stop listening to it because there's so much stuff on it; so musical." Reeves was in high school in the 1970s and an aspiring vocalist. Like Vaughan, she had a big voice with a broad range, but she didn't yet know how to use it. By listening to Vaughan, she learned. "Sarah Vaughan was the first singer that I'd ever heard that really defined her instrument like any instrumentalist would," explained Reeves. "She actually looked at her voice, and I don't know if she would say it this way or not, and [said], 'It has ability to do this and has the ability to do that. I'm going to put this [in] and keep building it and keep stretching it and exploring it.' To me, she was the first one to really do that [with] jazz vocals." This had a profound impact on Reeves and how she conceived of herself as an artist and creative being. It influenced how she understood her place in the larger musical landscape, a landscape that so often tried to relegate vocalists, predominantly women, the girl singers, to the musical sidelines. "It made me realize more than anything that I'm a musician," she said. "This is the instrument that I play. It just happens to be built in."[8]

The jazz community celebrated Vaughan's return to jazz. For them it was a welcome change from the crass commercialism of her Columbia years. Producer and EmArcy head Bobby Shad, however, viewed all of Vaughan's jazz albums as commercial endeavors. He was a businessman and needed to make money. Shad began working for Mercury in 1951 as their director of artists and repertory, and in early 1954, when tasked with creating a new jazz series for Mercury, he quickly realized that jazz listeners were very particular, discerning customers. He needed to create a separate, distinct jazz label to satisfy their expectations. In early 1954, as EmArcy began to take shape, Mercury had only two artists under contract capable of creating high-quality jazz: Vaughan and blues singer Dinah Washington. As Shad aggressively built EmArcy's list of artists—a catalog that soon included pianist Erroll Garner; trumpeter Clifford Brown; saxophonists Cannonball Adderley, Georgie Auld, and Gerry Mulligan; and drummer Max Roach—Vaughan and Washington served as the front women for the fledgling label. They became the centerpiece of EmArcy's print ad campaigns, and Vaughan's *Images* was one of the label's inaugural releases. Shad also took care to attractively package the new albums, often using photos from the studio sessions for covers, a choice that provided a behind-the-scenes glimpse into the creative process and enhanced the albums' authenticity. Record stores then displayed the covers as "mammoth-sized cover blow-ups on easel stands."[9] And Shad made sure that his artists received a level of exposure similar to their pop counterparts. He sent new albums to approximately 750 jazz disc jockeys, and in 1956 Shad told *Down Beat*, "One of the main points of our program has been an effort on our part to have pop disc jockeys play jazz."[10] By January 1955, four months after the label's launch in October, EmArcy had released 55 LPs and 108 EPs, and in October 1955, as the label completed its first year, EmArcy had cut and marketed another 30 LPs, for a grand total of 85. In less than a year, Shad had solidified EmArcy's reputation as an important jazz label known for releasing excellent jazz.

But he didn't want to stop with jazz fans. Shad believed that there was a market for jazz albums among a wider, more mainstream audience. And, here too, Vaughan was central to his strategy. As her star rose in the pop arena with the successes of "Make

Yourself Comfortable," "How Important Can It Be," and "What-ever Lola Wants," her fan base grew, and the new fans wanted to hear more Sarah Vaughan. Shad wooed them. The deceptively titled *Sarah Vaughan at the Blue Note* had no ties with the famed Chicago club. It was not a jazz album but rather a collection of romantic ballads backed by a lush string orchestra, released, tellingly, on Mercury. But it was accessible, an appealing entrée for her new pop fans. And Vaughan's next releases for EmArcy were decidedly less jazzy, clearly geared toward a pop market. *Sarah Vaughan: In the Land of Hi-Fi,* for one, was a swinging big band album pairing Vaughan with saxophonist Adderley. It epitomized an easy, cool hipness in the vein of Frank Sinatra. In other words, Bobby Shad engineered a reverse crossover moment, using Vaughan's popularity, versatility, and accessibility to bring new audiences to jazz. Vaughan had been doing this for years with her live performances, but now, with her albums for EmArcy, she took it to a new level.

On Monday night, June 3, 1957, Vaughan and the Count Basie Orchestra opened at the Waldorf Astoria's Starlight Roof. As New York's most prestigious, premier venue, the Waldorf regularly showcased the biggest names in the business: Frank Sinatra, Tony Bennett, and Doris Day. It was the first time that either Vaughan or Basie performed there—another career milestone for both. It was also an important moment for jazz. While black artists like Harry Belafonte, Dorothy Dandridge, Lena Horne, and Pearl Bailey had all appeared at the Waldorf in the past, this was the hotel's first "all-negro" show. And it was the first time it showcased jazz.

But in a twist, Vaughan and Basie shared the bill with the Haitian Moon Dancers, a troupe of two men and four women clad in colorful island-inspired costumes dancing production numbers like the West Indian limbo. The Waldorf Astoria management billed the floor show as a "Calypso Carnival" and installed a new, Caribbean-themed decor with exotic birdcages and palm trees fashioned from bamboo. The Starlight Roof transformed into a calming, exotic paradise with the calypso dancers "provid[ing] tropical relief from the jazz session."[11]

"I don't dig this calypso bit," Basie's vocalist Joe Williams told *Jet* magazine.[12] And Vaughan, asked to participate in one of the Moon Dancers' more provocative production numbers, rebelled. "Sarah Vaughan really gave the boot to the Waldorf-Astoria policy and emerged triumphant," Dorothy Kilgallen wrote in the *Washington Post and Times Herald*. "Sensing that the hotel management's attempt to turn her into a 'calypso' performer resulted in a bagel at the dinner show, she staged a revolution, and did her own act for the suppertime guests."[13]

"I just don't feel right throwing my hips around that way," said Vaughan to *Jet*.[14] It's also likely that the calypso tune required that she sing in a faux West Indian patter, much as she had on her 1950 recording of "De Gas Pipe She's Leakin' Joe" for Mitch Miller. That tune relied on a narrowly defined, stereotypical notion of blackness for novelty value. The Waldorf's "Calypso Carnival" was a commercial concession too, an attempt to broaden the show's appeal to the Waldorf Astoria's more staid, conservative (and very white) audiences. These patrons were more accustomed to the folk-inspired calypso stylings of Harry Belafonte than the hip, modern bop-infused stylings of Vaughan, the brassy jump music of Count Basie, or the down-home blues of Joe Williams. But Vaughan, as an artist and black woman, didn't want to perform tropical music (with its associations to primitivism and exoticism) for New York's upper crust, clad in their tuxedos and glamorous evening gowns. She wanted to introduce these audiences to her unique musical voice and artistic vision, which was cosmopolitan, sophisticated, and an expression of black creativity, innovation, and genius. "I believe in just singing what comes naturally," Vaughan told *Newsweek*. "If I can't be myself, I'll drive an elevator or something—which has its ups and downs too. I don't sing rock 'n' roll and I don't sing calypso."

"For a singer whose utterances to the press are generally confined to 'Yes,' 'No,' and 'I guess so,' this statement might be construed as 'Sarah's Law,'" wrote *Newsweek*. It was a bold and unusually frank assessment for the reserved, press-shy singer, yet entirely in line with her long-held aesthetics, her values as a jazz musician, and the care she took with her musical presentation, especially the larger social and cultural message that it conveyed.

"I like old songs best," she explained, standards like "If This Isn't Love," "Over the Rainbow," and "Poor Butterfly."[15] But she made sure that they never sounded boring or too familiar. "Miss Vaughan is a stylist of depth and dimension," *Variety*'s reviewer explained. "She follows an almost pure musical line that has a languid content at times and yet creates its own excitement."[16] She also thrilled them with up-tempo rhythm numbers like the brassy "Old Devil Moon" and a scat-filled "How High the Moon," which, in a wink and nod to the jazz fans in the house, paid tribute to Ella Fitzgerald. And she always sang with mastery and confidence, an ease that allowed listeners to relax and immerse themselves into the beauties of her voice. In the process, she made the complexities of bebop accessible to audiences unfamiliar with jazz. "[The] show is Sarah's, we're just the background music," a modest Basie told reporters.[17]

The show quickly transformed itself, eliminating most of its original calypso elements, to focus instead solely on jazz. And the Waldorf's regular patrons loved it. "Dowagers draped in diamonds were among those who couldn't resist the Basie beat and were on the dance floor every set," the *Pittsburgh Courier* reported. "Their masculine counterparts were swooning with the rest as Sarah bent her lovely tones around some old favorites and even as she 'scatted' some real 'hep' vocals."[18] The show also drew a new demographic to the Waldorf: the so-called "prom set." Younger, "hepper" fans, both black and white, who "dig the jive."[19] During the summer of 1957, with the help of Vaughan and Basie, the Starlight Roof became an incubator for change, a place where musical, generational, class, and, ultimately, racial boundaries began to break down. "This mixture of audiences has created a bit of peering-through-the-lorgnettes as the occasional 'mixed' couples (Harlem and ofay) whirl around the floor," *Vari-*

ety reported. "Although very un-Waldorfian, the Roof's business is jumping especially with the prom kids."[20]

Vaughan and Basie broke attendance records for the Starlight Roof. Less than two weeks into their four-week run, the Waldorf's management extended the package for another two weeks, until July 13, and re-signed them for another five weeks, August 13 until September 18, to finish off the summer season. The successes of Basie and Vaughan at the Waldorf also improved the fates of all jazz musicians in New York. An unusual number of venues began to program jazz, and the local press began to refer to the summer of 1957 as the "Summer of Jazz." Combined with the explosion of new summer jazz festivals, prompted by the success of the Newport Jazz Festival, now in its fourth year, the doldrums of summer, once the slow season, now represented prime time for jazz musicians.[21]

Jazz was in the midst of a resurgence unseen since the heyday of swing almost fifteen years earlier. With the help of performers like Vaughan, Ella Fitzgerald, Nat King Cole, Louis Armstrong, Dave Brubeck, and Stan Kenton, with their versatility and widespread appeal, jazz was growing in both popularity and profitability. Equally important, however, was a perceived shift in the cultural status of jazz. Echoing sentiments first expressed in *Variety,* the black press touted the arrival of Vaughan, Basie, and Williams at the Waldorf, "the ivory tower of chic society," as "the first real surrender to 'jazz,' to a 'beat,' and to the notion that what's good enough for Birdland is good enough for the Waldorf."[22] It was an important moment. Jazz was slowly beginning to shed its associations in the popular imagination with nightclubs and the seedy underworld of drugs, its status as lowbrow folk music, and was ever so gradually emerging as a respectable, sophisticated music worthy of America's finest venues. Jazz, with its origins in black culture and musical traditions, was in the early stages of its journey toward becoming highbrow.

Despite Vaughan's professional triumphs at the Waldorf, the summer of 1957 was a difficult one personally, as her marriage to

George Treadwell came to an official end. In the years since the couple first separated in 1952, they weathered ups and downs, trying to make their marriage work, often under the scrutiny of the press in search of gossip-column fodder. During her appearances at the Waldorf, Vaughan confided to her assistant Modina Davis that she thought she and Treadwell should divorce. "The meetings were too unhappy," said Davis. "They were always fighting."[23] After Treadwell filed for divorce, Vaughan stayed in New York, working the Starlight Roof, and Treadwell traveled to Juarez, Mexico. In early July, Justice Martinez Arrio awarded him a final divorce decree on grounds of incompatibility.[24] Weeks later, Treadwell married Fayrene Williams, a model from Los Angeles. According to reports in the black press, Treadwell gifted his new bride a seven-room ranch home in Englewood, New Jersey. And Williams, now Mrs. Treadwell, became her husband's new assistant in his talent management office.

Vaughan wished the couple well. "No hard feelings," she said. "We simply couldn't or didn't make it so now I hope only the best for his new marriage."[25]

Gossip columns speculated that it would take time for Vaughan to get over her divorce and Treadwell's remarriage, reporting that, following her divorce, associates of Vaughan observed a "strange, thoughtful calm that settles over Sarah Vaughan whenever she's alone for a few minutes."[26] In August, weeks after Treadwell remarried, Vaughan learned that he and Fayrene were expecting a baby. Vaughan and Treadwell had desperately wanted to start a family together themselves, but it never happened. After consulting with doctors, Vaughan learned that she couldn't have children. Upon hearing the news of Fayrene's pregnancy, Vaughan wired her congratulations.

After divorcing, Vaughan and Treadwell continued to work together, and she remained one of his biggest clients. Buoyed by his longtime association with Vaughan, his roster now included her former boss Earl Hines and, for a brief time, Dizzy Gillespie, Billie Holiday, and blues vocalist Ruth Jones, whom he promised a makeover treatment, just like Vaughan's. He also found success with the Drifters, a vocal quintet (sometimes quartet) he created in 1953 and managed through its many iterations. The group, which helped define the sound of doo-wop and gospel-influenced soul, featured an evolving collection of singers: Clyde McPhatter, the group's co-founder; Johnny Moore; Ben E. King; and Rudy Lewis. Early on, Treadwell bolstered the group's visibility by arranging photo ops between McPhatter and Vaughan. After a flurry of R & B hits in 1953 and 1954, the group truly broke through in 1959, with "There Goes My Baby," which peaked at No. 2 on the pop charts. They followed this up with a series of hits on Atlantic throughout the 1960s. But the musicians earned no record royalties. Instead, Treadwell, who owned the copyright to the band's name and shared writing credits with Jerry Leiber and Mike Stoller for "There Goes My Baby," paid his musicians a weekly salary. It was a lucrative setup for Treadwell.

Vaughan's decision to stay with Treadwell's management company was puzzling. As the divorcing couple came to a financial settlement, Vaughan discovered that only $16,000 remained in their joint bank accounts. It's unclear where the money went. She'd worked nonstop for fifteen years, earned hundreds of thousands of dollars in appearance fees and record royalties. The business of being Sarah Vaughan had grown considerably. In 1955, as her pop tunes for Mercury climbed the charts and she earned $11,000 a week, the *New York News* reported that Vaughan had thirty-one people on her payroll, a fleet of cars that included station wagons and four convertibles, a half floor of office space on Broadway in the heart of New York's theater district, a music publishing firm, and a half dozen other enterprises. She also supported her family. Perhaps she was overextended financially. When asked about her newfound fame and fortune in 1955, Vaughan agreed that she had come a long way since her early years. But she qualified her answer, explaining that now she had "no peace of mind."[27]

Her friend Modina Davis suspected that Treadwell was being spiteful and vindictive, that there must have been more money somewhere. After all, he had recently purchased a new home for his bride. And when many in the jazz community learned of the financial settlement, it simply confirmed their beliefs that Treadwell was just another hustler.[28] Vaughan trusted Treadwell completely, and this betrayal, whether gross financial mismanagement or something more devious, must have been heartbreaking. Vaughan and Treadwell each took $8,000 and a car and went their separate ways.

"I want to forget that. I never want to think about that again," Vaughan said when asked about her failed marriage four years later, in 1961. "All George ever did for me was really for himself. You know, nobody wants to print that, but it's the truth, and I wish people would understand that."[29]

Vaughan kept working, maintaining her usual demanding schedule and performing nearly fifty weeks a year, now not because she loved singing and life on the road, which she wholeheartedly did, but because she had to financially. As she rebuilt her life and reestablished her fiscal security, however, Vaughan's musical family—her trio—began to fall apart as well. Bassist Joe Benjamin left in 1956 and was replaced by Richard Davis. And at the end of 1957, after nine years with Vaughan, pianist Jimmy Jones decided to leave to pursue a career as an arranger. Vaughan and Jones had met in 1946, during her first Café Society engagement, and weathered those early lean years together. She often cited him as her favorite pianist. They were musical kindred spirits that complemented one another perfectly, relying on an unspoken communication, an intimacy born through years together. His departure must have been a musical and personal loss for Vaughan. She threw him a farewell party, which, not surprisingly, doubled as a press event. Photos showed Vaughan presenting Jones with a diamond wrist watch, reportedly valued at $750, as his replacement, Ronnell Bright, looked on.[30]

Bright was an up-and-coming pianist from Chicago who had just moved to New York. Born in 1930, he met Vaughan in Boston in November 1957 while playing Storyville. Vaughan knew of Bright through their mutual friend vocalist Carmen McRae, and, as she so often did, Vaughan listened in on Bright's set. "Hey, man, Sarah is sitting at a table right behind you checking you out," Bright's guitarist, Ray Crawford, told him. "I didn't really pay much attention to what Ray said," Bright explained during an interview with Marc Myers. "We played opposite her for about a week."[31]

When Jones moved on, Treadwell invited Bright to a meeting at his offices in the Brill Building. "He said Sarah was deciding between me and Wynton Kelly and that it was down to money," he recalled. "I said it would be [an] honor to play for Sarah and whatever she thought would be fair was fine with me."[32] Bright began work immediately.

Two months into his new gig, Bright found himself back in Chicago at Mr. Kelly's. Vaughan, still a favorite for Chicago audiences, appeared regularly at the club. "Singer draws 'em in like flies to a picnic spread," *Variety* reported on opening night, February 25, 1958, "and her fortnight at this nitery is a happy foregone conclusion for the spot's bookkeeper."[33] It was a routine two weeks in Chicago, until Friday, March 7. After their third set of the evening, Vaughan and her trio of Bright, Davis, and Haynes rushed over to the London House.

The club, under the same ownership as Mr. Kelly's, was hosting a special after-hours recording session for Vaughan's next album on Mercury, a follow-up to her successful live album *Sarah Vaughan at Mr. Kelly's,* recorded that past August. Basie sidemen Thad Jones and Wendell Culley on trumpet, Henry Coker on trombone, and Frank Wess on tenor saxophone joined Vaughan and her trio, creating a special, one-night-only pickup band of sorts. There were no rehearsals, arrangements, or charts. "There was not time," said Bright. "Sarah went out and bought piano sheet music for each musician and passed it out on stage, at 2:00 A.M., just before we started recording. We had to transpose the sheet music to her keys. Everyone had to scuffle."[34]

Including Vaughan. She had not recorded any of the eight tunes before, and most were not staples of her live sets. She, like the musicians backing her, had to think on her feet. She had one take to get it right, and that would become the album *Sarah Vaughan After Hours at the London House.*

"That was an amazing night," said Bright. "Everyone I knew was there: bassist Johnnie Pate, pianist Dick Katz, the guys who wrote 'Detour Ahead' [a song on the set list]—guitarist Herb Ellis and bassist John Frigo. The place was packed." And, for the most part, the evening went well. Vaughan was in fine voice and in sync with her trio, despite their lack of rehearsal time. Basie's sidemen noodled in the background and took the occasional solo, but in a symptom of the session's ad hoc origins they never became fully integrated into the fabric of the ensemble as Clifford Brown, Herbie Mann, and Paul Quinichette had on *Sarah Vaughan* three years earlier. Yet there was a spontaneity and energy in the room, and the audience was engaged and excited.

Bright began the evening's final number: "Thanks for the Memory." Following his introduction, a series of arpeggiated chords, Vaughan entered and sang the familiar lyrics: "Thanks for the memory / Of candlelight and wine, castles on the Rhine." Then she stopped and missed her next entrance. Puzzled, the trio slowed, faded out. "Parthenon. Parthenon. Parthenon," Vaughan said, practicing the word. "I got stuck on the word." She repeated it again and again, each time with greater emphasis, as Bright played filler in the background. "Sarah had sheet music for the song, like everyone else, and was reading the word 'Parthenon,' which was hyphenated," Bright explained. "She was unfamiliar with the word or what the Parthenon was. So she couldn't figure out where the emphasis was supposed to go. She stopped cold and calmly worked it out. That was Sarah, recording session or no recording session. No one on stage was prepared for that, as you can hear from the record. It was a live recording, and Sarah doing that was a little scary. But this is what made the session so exciting."[35]

Bright began again, this time with a new introduction. Vaughan entered, embellishing the tune's opening "Thanks," drawing it out into three syllables, pausing for a new trumpet fill, before she continued. She sailed through the first two lines, and launched into the problematic third. "The Parthenon . . ." she sang and stopped again, unable to gain momentum and flow into the next lyric. "I don't get this word, here," she said. Bright was about to say "Parth-ah-non" to help her but stopped himself, remembering that they were recording live. "Sarah worked her way through it and kept the moment alive," said Bright.[36] "Parthenon," Vaughan said, enunciating the world emphatically. "One more time, then we can go home."

Bright began again, with a third introduction subtly different from the first two. Vaughan entered, singing another extended melisma, mastered "the Parthenon," and successfully made her way through her choruses. A lovely muted trumpet solo followed. But when Vaughan returned, reprising the B section, she soon stumbled and missed another lyric. This time she didn't stop. She winged it, inventing her own lyric on the spot. And as the tune entered its final chorus, she acknowledged the chaos of the evening: "Thanks for the most craziest, upset-down-side-ist recording date I ever had in my life." The audience laughed. Vaughan continued, humming the melody, "Da da da dah. Da da da da dee," her voice growing louder and more determined, until she finally reached the tune's final line. "So glad that it's overrrr . . ." More laughter from the house, followed by a man yelling out "Thanks!" "And thank you," Vaughan sang, adding one last dramatic pause, "So much." It was finally over.

"Y'all go home now," Vaughan instructed the crowd as the band vamped behind her. "Thank you so very much ladies and gentlemen for coming out." It was four in the morning, and the session had lasted less than an hour. The musicians packed up their instruments and joined Vaughan for an early breakfast.

Vaughan was a perfectionist, and it's hard to say if the final product created that night met her exacting standards. She did firmly believe that live performances should have imperfections; otherwise they were simply like her studio recordings, but this was also a recording session. Regardless, it is clear that she loved the process and found the mental gymnastics of it all exhilarating: the spontaneity and uncertainty of the musical unknown; the thrill of venturing out onto a musical precipice, then finding her way back; and the constant exploration and striving for innovation. She pushed herself to create something new and different each and every night and expected the same from the musicians she worked with.

"You had to, or Sarah would hear you trying to do what you already did, which to her would be lazy," Bright told Marc Myers when asked about the three distinct introductions he created for "Thanks for the Memory" that night. It was a common refrain, repeated time and again by the musicians who worked for her. "Sarah rarely did anything the same way twice," Bright continued. "She came up through the ranks with Charlie Parker. It was a badge of honor to do things differently each time. There was no other way."[37]

Even when Vaughan did have a tried and true arrangement, she often went off script. "Sarah would change keys in the middle of a song. She'd go somewhere else, and we'd have to find her," Bright explained. "She taught all of her sidemen ear training. You had seconds to figure out what she was going to do. It became intuitive. But once we were comfortable with her, we'd do the same thing to her. She'd sing in one key and we'd change keys so she'd have to find us. She liked the challenge."[38]

Her bassist at the time, Richard Davis, agreed. "That's what made it so beautiful playing with her," he explained. "She had all that range! She was a monster. I mean that in a positive way. Sarah was like any horn, like a saxophone player. What she did with a lyric, what she did with the sound of her voice, she would bend those notes into five different shapes. One note. Five different shapes! And you say, 'God, what's she gonna do next?' And she could scat her butt off, too."[39]

"This woman was a pure genius," said drummer Roy Haynes.[40] He had worked with saxophonists Lester Young and Charlie Parker before joining Vaughan in October 1953. "It was hip to be with Sarah then," he explained.[41] She was different, with a sound and style all her own, and her musicianship was unparalleled. "She would go up to piano players and tell them what notes to play or what keys to play in, that's not something most vocalists can do."[42] Haynes loved the spontaneity on the bandstand each night, the constant push to be innovative, and the thrill of always testing one's limits. "I, *I*, considered Sarah Charlie Parker," he said. "And she was with him. She was with Earl Hines when I first met her. And then she, well she was very tight with Billy Eckstine. So to me, she was a female Charlie Parker."[43]

In April, however, as Vaughan's band played their first gig at the famed Fontainebleau Hotel in Miami Beach, her trio—her musical family—was about to change again. After almost five years, drummer Roy Haynes gave his two-week notice.

"I stayed too long at the fair," said Haynes when asked why he left the trio. "I enjoyed it. It was happening, and I was enjoying it. I liked the clubs. I wasn't making a whole lot of money, but it was pretty steady."[44] He had started his own family and was entering a new phase of his life. "When I was with Sarah Vaughan, man, I was buying a house then," he said. "My first house, boom."[45] But Vaughan toured nearly fifty weeks a year, with only a short break each summer. In 1955, Miles Davis told critic Nat Hentoff that Haynes "has almost destroyed himself working with Sarah so long."[46] Her schedule was relentless, and when Haynes decided to leave the band in 1958, she was preparing for a four-month tour of Europe. Haynes was exhausted and needed time to recuperate. He wanted to explore new creative directions, and, as he explained, "I wanted to hang with my children."[47] Vaughan was upset. "She barely talked to me," Haynes remembered. "I felt very bad about it, because I had loved her. Some people who didn't know us thought that I had been married to her."[48]

On Friday, April 11, 1958, just days after finishing her week at the Fontainebleau and playing with Haynes for the last time, Vaughan and pianist Bright landed in London. It had been a long flight, made longer by delays. Treadwell, with flowers in hand, greeted Vaughan in the arrivals hall. Mercury's Bobby Shad was there too, hoping to fly Vaughan to Paris that night for a guest appearance at the Mercury International Convention, but her plane arrived too late. Instead an exhausted Vaughan went straight to her hotel for a press conference.

"Miss Vaughan, why are you called 'Sassy'?" asked Maurice Burman of *Melody Maker*. "I really don't know—but I'd like a drink," she answered, fatigue mixing with impatience and irritation at yet another silly question. It was well known that John Malachi bestowed the nickname during her years with the Eckstine band. Her drink, gin and water, arrived, and Vaughan continued, "Al Hibbler gave me my name. I guess you'd better ask him." It was a confrontational interview. She was testy and Burman grew increasingly frustrated. "You're not talking too much are you?" Burman said. "Oh, darling don't be that way," Vaughan replied, softening. "I guess I sing better than I talk—much better. And I'm so very tired. I've sat upright in a plane for 10 hours and 45 minutes, and my spine hurts. I ask you, should I be happy or unhappy?" "Happy, because you have come through it alive," he insisted. "I'm happy to be here," she said. "But all I want to do is to get my first show over. I'm worried and I'm nervous. I guess I'm always worried before I go on."[49]

The next morning, rehearsals began for her first London performances, scheduled for that night, Saturday, April 12, at the Odeon in Leicester Square. With pencils in hand, she and Bright reviewed her arrangements. For the next two nights, two shows a night, she would perform with Ted Heath and His Music, an English big band in the style of Stan Kenton's modern bebop-inspired ensemble. She hadn't found a replacement for Haynes, and her bassist, Richard Davis, wouldn't join her until later in the tour. Bright was the only musician there with an intimate musical knowledge of Vaughan and her preferences. Then Treadwell told Bright that he would be conducting Ted Heath's ensemble during the gigs too. "Oh, man, how am I going to do that? Can they do Sarah's material?" Bright asked Treadwell. "Do like Dizzy: Just kick a leg and the band will do the rest. You have to do it," said Treadwell. "So I did," Bright said, laughing. "Heath's band was great. They knew exactly what they were doing, and they could play."[50]

"Sarah is a knock-out," proclaimed the headline for Max Jones's *Melody Maker* review of opening night. "Each time I hear Sarah Vaughan in person she seems to have got substantially better." Vaughan conquered her nerves and performed fifteen songs during a fifty-minute set. She began with "If This Isn't Love," mixing in standards like "Mean to Me," "Lover Man," and "Tenderly" and newer tunes including "Passing Strangers," her duet with Eckstine that had become a hit in England, and concluding with a scatted version of "How High the Moon." The emphasis was squarely on her, and even though she performed the same set twice a night on Saturday and Sunday, she never sang a song the same way twice. "I can't remember ever looking forward so much to a fourth performance of the self-same programme," a musician from the Heath band told Jones.[51]

After her London concerts, Vaughan did two weeks of one-nighters through England and Scotland, this time backed by another collection of British musicians. Before embarking on a tour of the Continent, Davis rejoined the group and along with Bright and the drummer from Ted Heath's band created a new trio for Vaughan. She spent May at the China Theater in Stockholm, Sweden. More one-nighters followed.

When jazz musicians, especially African American musicians, traveled in Europe, they were greeted with an enthusiasm, respect, and admiration that they often did not receive in the racially divided United States. When Vaughan had arrived in London in 1953 for her first European tour, she was treated like royalty. Representatives from *Melody Maker* met her transatlantic ship and ushered her through customs; fans, bestowing gifts, greeted her train at Paddington Station; and the press tracked her every move, reporting on her rehearsals, state of mind, and, of course, concerts. While jazz, with its roots in black culture, still fought for legitimacy back home, in Europe it was embraced as a sophisticated and important art form. Jazz musicians were skilled, innovative artists. They were celebrities.

Five years later, when she arrived in Amsterdam on Saturday, June 7, 1958, Vaughan performed two high-profile yet very different gigs. She began the evening on the elaborate set of a television studio in Bussum, a small town twenty miles outside of Amsterdam. In the States, Vaughan had starred in a handful of movie shorts and regularly sang a pop song or two as a guest on television variety shows, but she had never appeared in a longer, more in-depth television segment devoted solely to her jazz singing. She sang seven numbers in front of a live studio audience, five of which eventually aired on Dutch AVRO Television's *The Weekend Show*. The camera focused on Vaughan, capturing the subtleties of her body language and facial expressions and revealing details, an intimacy, previously unseen by her European fans. Her eyes were nearly closed as she sang plaintive ballads like her mesmerizing "Over the Rainbow." Tiny smiles were paired with a twinkle in her eyes or raised eyebrow as she prepared for especially difficult vocal turns or twists. Her white sequined mermaid gown swayed as her body internalized the beat, and the subtle movements of her arms defined both the macro and micro beats, especially during her languorously slow ballads. She was confident as she sang, calm and controlled, often serene in appearance.

But then the music stopped and the shy, more introverted Vaughan returned. She became uncomfortable and uneasy, overly aware of the cameras as she thanked the studio audience for their applause between numbers, announced her next tune, or explained a song's history. After the final number of the set, an exhilarating up-tempo "Sometimes I'm Happy," Vaughan thanked the studio audience one last time and blew an awkward farewell kiss into the camera.

Backstage Vaughan and her trio packed up their gear and traveled to Amsterdam for a midnight show at the famed Concertgebouw, home of the Royal Concertgebouw orchestra. Even though the concert didn't sell out, the audience spilled onto the stage, sitting behind the band on risers, creating an intimacy and closeness in the cavernous hall. Vaughan, now wearing a form-fitting strapless black gown with white sequined trim on the bodice, headlined the second half of the concert. She began with her usual set opener, "If This Isn't Love," and effortlessly worked her way through a dozen numbers. Her banter, while still sparse, was more relaxed, and the audience's enthusiasm increased as her set gained momentum, culminating with her usual finale, "How High the Moon." This time, however, tenor saxophonist Don Byas, bassist Arvell Shaw, and drummer Wally Bishop, all featured on the program's first half, joined Vaughan and her trio. With her virtuosity on full display, Vaughan scatted, traded fours with Byas, and urged her fellow musicians on during their solos as the energy in the hall continued to grow.

Vaughan was not perfect during her performance at the Concertgebouw. At times, her voice sounded less polished, and, surprisingly, an occasional note was uncharacteristically ever so slightly out of tune. But the energy of the evening was unmistakable and infectious. The jazz critics in the house gushed in amazement. "Sarah does magic with her voice, and in doing so she astonishes more than many a magician with his tricks. Through her magic she demonstrates a musicality, a refinement of taste and a humanity which many of her classical colleagues can envy her," wrote Kees Diemer in the *Vrije Volk*, concluding, "This miraculous voice sparkled like a diamond in the nocturnal darkness of the Concertgebouw." Michiel de Ruyter of the *Parool* tempered his praise, insisting that Ella Fitzgerald remained his favorite jazz singer, but conceded that Vaughan's concert was "a rare experience." "What one hears is a completely new musical instrument in the shape of a female figure," he wrote. "One must constantly remain aware that in fact one doesn't hear an instrument but a voice. Its range exceeds that of all other singers. Vaughan can color her sound more than anyone. Her phrasing, the rhythmic aspect of her singing, everything makes a purely instrumental impression, and the only sensible comparison possible would have to be drawn with the greatest of the instrumental soloists in modern jazz, a Charlie Parker or a Miles Davis."[52]

Offstage, as the band toured Europe, Vaughan worked to infuse levity and unpredictability into the daily grind. Always a prankster and mischief maker, she devised ways to keep her musicians on their toes, sometimes quite literally. During the European tour, Bright remembers her hiding the trio's shoes moments before their curtain calls, forcing them to go onstage in stocking feet. Turnabout, of course, was fair play and the trio played their fair share of pranks on Vaughan. Tired of seeing Vaughan wear the same pink satin gown night after night, the trio buried it in a box outside. When Vaughan asked about the gown, the trio confessed nothing. Another time, the band prepared to go on in San Remo, Italy. "I would be the first to walk on stage," Bright recalled. "As I'd pass by Sarah in the wings, she'd typically hand me a list of songs in the order she wanted to sing them. But on this night in Italy, as I passed her, she let the list drop to the floor on purpose to see if I'd bend down to get it." Bright did not pick up the list, and he walked out to the piano. "That night we played what I wanted, and Sarah had to follow," said Bright, laughing.

Vaughan never dropped the set list again. But she understood that this kind of fooling around and camaraderie was important. It disrupted their routines, warded off complacency, and ultimately made the music better—more spontaneous, energized, and fresh. It marked her status as one of the guys, just another musician in the band. And it symbolized the trust and closeness between Vaughan and her trio. Just like your family, your band had your back when you went out on a musical limb. "Sarah called me her 'backbone' and was very protective of me and all her musicians," Bright explained.[53]

"When we were on the road together, it was a family, man," said road manager Johnnie Garry.[54] But like any family, especially one spending a lot of time together in unusual, often stressful situations, they had their squabbles and disagreements. Vaughan could be temperamental. While en route to a jazz festival in Knokke, Belgium, she disregarded their travel schedule and almost missed their train. Garry reprimanded Vaughan, and they argued. "I'm the boss, and you're fired, and you can worry about how you're going to get home," Vaughan said. "Are you crazy?" he retorted. "I have all the tickets."[55]

The band arrived in Knokke on time for Vaughan's concert. She performed the first set, and Ella Fitzgerald the second, after intermission. Then they joined forces for a grand finale. "I told Sassy, 'whatever you do, don't let her go into an up-tempo song to start,'" said Garry. "Well, at the end of her set Ella called Sarah to the stage, and began with 'Somewhere there's music, it's where you are. Somewhere there's heaven, how near or far.'"[56] Fitzgerald was singing "How High the Moon," the lightning-fast bebop standard that had become one of her signature numbers. Even though Vaughan scatted her heart out to "How High the Moon" during the finale to her own sets every night, hers was a tribute to Fitzgerald and her now-legendary prowess. "And for the next hour they went at it!" said Gary.[57] "They were taking choruses and scatting. Sassy started singing, 'Ella, baby, I'm leaving,' and Ella sang, 'Sassy, baby, I'm just beginning.'"[58] Back home, black newspapers ran a photo from the festival, with Vaughan looking on, arms crossed and deep in thought with her brow slightly furrowed, listening, as Fitzgerald stood at the mic singing.[59] "Both were swinging so hard that they were sweating," said Garry. "Ella would put Sarah's forehead with a handkerchief, and Sarah did the same for her. The audience was sitting there in amazement."[60]

After the concert, Fitzgerald invited Garry to a party. Vaughan was there too and asked Garry how the finale had gone. "I told you not to let her begin with an uptempo song!" he reminded her. "She kicked your ass!"

Vaughan, the "Divine One," was widely regarded as the queen of ballads. She specialized in songs like "Lover Man," "Tenderly," "Body and Soul," "Over the Rainbow," and soon a new tune by Erroll Garner called "Misty." But Fitzgerald had been the queen of rhythm numbers since her early days with the Chick Webb band and her first hit, "A Tisket A Tasket," from 1938. While Fitzgerald experienced leaner years during the late 1940s and early 1950s as Vaughan emerged as a star, her popularity exploded under the management of producer Norman Granz. He founded the influential Jazz at the Philharmonic concert series and, more recently, the Verve record label, which had released

Fitzgerald's now-iconic and extraordinarily popular collections of the great American songbooks. Granz took control of her career in 1955, and by 1958 Fitzgerald had eclipsed Vaughan in both fame and popularity, and she, "the First Lady of Song," would remain the most visible, well-known jazz singer in the world until the end of both of their careers.

Vaughan's successes in Europe during the summer of 1958 were part of a larger trend. During the previous six months, Fitzgerald, Erroll Garner, Dave Brubeck, Bud Shank, Bob Cooper, June Christy, Oscar Peterson, Benny Goodman, and Jazz at the Philharmonic had all also performed at the Concertgebouw in Amsterdam. The popularity of jazz was surging in Europe, fueled in part by the regular broadcast of jazz on Voice of America, first by Leonard Feather's program *Jazz Club USA*, which debuted in 1952, and then its replacement *Music USA*, launched on January 6, 1955. Hosted by Willis Conover, the program played daily in Europe, Africa, and Asia, usually during peak listening hours. In 1955, thirty million listeners enjoyed jazz in eighty countries, and during the next decade the audience grew to one hundred million.[61] "Last year I sold more records in Europe than in America," Vaughan reflected in 1959. "I guess people are people and cats are cats everywhere, regardless of how they think on politics."[62]

Vaughan's European tour culminated with her appearances at the 1958 World's Fair in Brussels. It was the first expo since World War II, and celebrated the "rejuvenation of civilization from the destruction of war through the use of technology."[63] The fair's most iconic image, the Atomium, a massive model of a unit cell of an iron crystal, with nine spheres each representing a single atom, was, according to fair organizers, a "symbol of a peaceful world." During its six-month run, between April 17 and October 19, more than forty-one million people from all walks of life visited the sprawling five-hundred-acre site. It housed an amusement park; gardens with illuminated dancing water fountains; seventy cafes and restaurants; an International Palace of Science; demonstrations by the Frogmen, deep sea divers exploring a huge tank; exhibits of fine art; countless concerts, including an installation of Edward Varese's groundbreaking *Poème Electronique* in the Philips Pavilion; and pavilions representing the United Nations, Red Cross, and Catholic Church, as well as fifty countries, each sharing their vision for the future. It was a bustling coming together of the world, a momentary thaw in the Cold War, and the impetus behind Vaughan's tour of Europe.

On July 29, 1958, Vaughan and her trio began the first of six nights performing at the American Pavilion during "American Days." She performed twice a night and shared the bill with soprano saxophonist Sidney Bechet, who immigrated to Paris in 1950, and the Newport International Youth Band, assembled for the fair. The U.S. State Department asked producer George Wein, the former proprietor of Storyville in Boston and founder of the Newport Jazz Festival, which he launched in 1954, to present a program representing America's most vibrant musical art: jazz. He excelled at creating programming that demonstrated the diversity and history of jazz. Bechet represented the early roots of jazz in New Orleans, Vaughan the sounds of bebop and modern jazz, and the International Youth Band the future and growing international influence of jazz. Voice of America's Willis Conover emceed. All of the acts returned for the show's grand finale: an ad-lib blues jam session featuring all of the musicians on the program.

"After almost every concert, I'd hang out with Sarah Vaughan and Johnnie Garry, her road manager at the time," Wein wrote in his memoir. "One night, at about one o'clock in the morning, we went to a bar to have a drink, where we received some antagonism from a group of intoxicated Americans who voiced their disapproval of having a black man and woman drinking at the same bar as they did. It looked as if there might be some serious trouble. I'm not a fighting man, but I joined Johnnie in standing up to challenge these drunken jerks. They backed down and left the bar, to my great relief."[64]

It was a chilling reminder of the racial intolerance that awaited Vaughan and her trio when they returned home. It was the same brand of racism that prompted many African American jazz artists, including Bechet, Josephine Baker, Bud Powell, and eventually Nina Simone, to relocate to Europe. And it was a stark contrast to the way the U.S. State Department portrayed America's race relations abroad. Race—the inhumanity of segregation, Jim Crow, and the way that white America treated its black citizens—had long been America's Achilles' heel, a source of criticism from the international community, especially the Soviet Union. Beginning in 1955, as Martin Luther King Jr. led the bus boycott in Montgomery, Alabama, ushering in a new phase of the black freedom movement, the U.S. State Department enlisted jazz to rehabilitate the country's tarnished image. They designated prominent African American jazz musicians such as Dizzy Gillespie, Louis Armstrong, and Duke Ellington as goodwill ambassadors and sent them around the world to promote American freedom and democracy. It was a calculated move that embraced jazz's ever-growing international popularity, a way to use American culture as a more subtle form of propaganda. Performing abroad, black jazz artists became symbols of racial harmony and equality. They represented the ideal of a color-blind American democracy, despite the tensions and intolerance at home. And jazz, with its improvisation, fluid ensemble dynamics, and perceived spontaneity, embodied American democracy and freedom too. For many, jazz was the United States' most important, resonant cultural export.[65]

The American Pavilion at the 1958 World's Fair wrestled with similar tensions. It was the largest international exhibit of American culture during the 1950s, and the State Department wanted it to be a "silent ambassador for American ideals."[66] It was designed to be a testament to America's vision of democracy, freedom, and an enthusiastic embrace of capitalism—all essential to counter the evils of communism, embodied by the Soviet Pavilion, located, conveniently enough, across from the American Pavilion. Surprisingly, however, the American Pavilion also included an exhibition called "Unfinished Work" that addressed the United States' problems and its commitment to fixing them, in particular its problem with race. Displays attempted to explain American racism while discussing the work of the emerging civil rights movement. The exhibit was controversial and was shut down following complaints from powerful southern congressmen offended by the exhibit's portrayal of the unrest in Little Rock, Arkansas, when the federal government mandated that the city desegregate its public schools.[67]

By the time Vaughan, Bechet, and their sidemen took the stage at the end of July, they were token minorities, remnants of the State Department's attempts to present the United States as tolerant, welcoming of diversity, and proud of black culture. It was an idealized, largely unrealistic portrayal, but it was also in many ways an improvement. Unlike the fair's pavilions devoted to the Belgian Congo, which depicted an ideal relationship between colonizer and colonized in the "Congolese Village," a human zoo trading in notions of primitivism and exoticism, Vaughan and Bechet presented an alternative image of blackness to the world, one that celebrated black intellect, creativity, and genius, not to mention modernity.

Vaughan's appearances at the World's Fair represented an opportunity for George Wein too. He believed that the time they spent together that week, plus his willingness to stand up against racism at the bar in Brussels, strengthened his relationship with Vaughan. He hoped it would help him gain her trust, something she rarely bestowed. He'd known her since 1951, when she began singing at his Boston club, Storyville, and even though she could be difficult to work with, she was brilliant. "I worshiped Sarah as an artist. No one could emulate her supreme musicianship and quality of voice," he wrote. "Sarah was already a star, but I felt that she could reach an ever greater audience." In the summer of 1958, Vaughan was seeking new management, and Wein wanted to take her career to the next level, in much the same way as Norman Granz was doing for Ella Fitzgerald.

So one night in Brussels, Wein turned to Vaughan and asked, "Sassy, why don't you let me be your manager?"

Vaughan looked at Wein, puzzled. "How can you be my manager?" she asked. "Aren't you still going with the girl in Boston?"

The girl in Boston was Wein's future wife, Joyce. "It surprised me that this was a deciding factor," Wein explained. "I never had eyes for Sarah Vaughan."[68] He advised Vaughan that mixing her personal and professional lives harmed her career, but Vaughan wanted a manager involved in every facet of her life. Someone to travel with her, share her love of music, and love her. She wanted to re-create the arrangement she had had with George Treadwell, but hopefully this time with a happier-ever-after ending.

Vaughan had just experienced a tremendous decade. With her pop and jazz successes, not to mention her growing international acclaim, it must have seemed that her career, propelled along by the power of her voice, had unlimited potential. But the music industry was on the verge of a seismic shift. Audiences' tastes and consumption habits would change, and everybody in the business—record executives, disc jockeys, and the musicians themselves—would scramble to keep up. Vaughan, along with her jazz contemporaries, would struggle to find where she belonged in this new musical landscape. She would need an excellent manager, someone possessing the business savvy, connections, and clout of a George Wein or Norman Granz.

An early publicity photo of Sarah Vaughan, circa 1947 or 1948. *Michael Ochs Archive/Getty Images*

Below: Vaughan performing as Billy Eckstine leads his band at Pittsburgh's Aragon Ballroom, August 1944. With saxophonist Charlie Parker (*first row, third from left*), trumpeters Howard McGhee and Dizzy Gillespie (*last row, third and fourth from left, respectively*), and drummer Art Blakey. *Charles "Teenie" Harris Archive/Carnegie Museum of Art*

Left: Vaughan singing as saxophonist Charlie Parker solos and Billy Eckstine conducts his band at Pittsburgh's Aragon Ballroom, August 1944. *Charles "Teenie" Harris Archive/Carnegie Museum of Art*

Vaughan, bandleader Duke Ellington, and Billy Eckstine backstage at Carnegie Hall, September 1951. Vaughan and Ellington had just started their tour of seventy one-nighters for the Biggest Show of '51. *PoPsie Randolph/Michael Ochs Archives/ Getty Images*

Vaughan and her audience, early 1950s. *Joe Schwartz Photo Archive/ Getty Images*

Voice of America disc jockey Willis Conover chatting with Vaughan, 1950s. *Courtesy of the Willis Conover Collection at the University of Northern Texas*

Vaughan with vocalist Billie Holiday and guitarist Bulee "Slim" Gaillard at Birdland, 1952. © *Marcel Fleiss/ CTSIMAGES*

Vaughan with producer Bobby Shad and arranger-conductor Ernie Wilkins during recording sessions for *Sarah Vaughan in the Land of Hi-Fi*, October 25 or 27, 1955. © *Herman Leonard Photography, LLC*

Vaughan celebrating her thirtieth birthday at Birdland in 1954. *Courtesy Johnson Publishing Company, LLC. All rights reserved.*

Vaughan and her first husband, George Treadwell, mugging for the camera during her thirtieth birthday party. This was one of many orchestrated public appearances following their separation. *Courtesy Johnson Publishing Company, LLC. All rights reserved.*

Vaughan with her parents, Asbury and Ada Vaughan, celebrating "Sarah Vaughan Day" in Newark, February 11, 1957. The Mount Zion Baptist Church sponsored a testimonial dinner in Vaughan's honor. *Courtesy Johnson Publishing Company, LLC. All rights reserved.*

Vaughan and second husband, Clyde B. Atkins, in front of their Englewood, New Jersey, home during the summer of 1961. *Courtesy Johnson Publishing Company, LLC. All rights reserved.*

Vaughan with her daughter, Deborah, in the recording studio, 1962. Quincy Jones is conducting in the foreground. *Courtesy Johnson Publishing Company, LLC.*

Vaughan accepting congratulations from President Johnson, Prime Minister Sato, and Lady Bird Johnson following her White House performance, January 12, 1965. *Courtesy of the Lyndon Baines Johnson Library*

Vaughan and her trio pose with the president and other dignitaries after performing at the White House. *Left to right:* pianist Bob James, President Lyndon B. Johnson, Vaughan, Lady Bird Johnson, Prime Minister of Japan Eisaku Sato, bassist Larry Rockwell, and drummer Omar Clay. *Courtesy of the Lyndon Baines Johnson Library*

Vaughan singing at New York City's Rainbow Room, September 1968. With bassist Herb Mickman. *Media General Communications Holdings, LLC*

Vaughan backstage at the Rainbow Room. *Media General
Communications Holdings, LLC*

Vaughan playing with her daughter, Deborah, in her Newark apartment, fall of 1968. *Media General Communications Holdings, LLC*

Vaughan and the guys arriving in Nice, May 1974. *Left to right:* drummer Jimmy Cobb, manager and boyfriend Marshall Fisher, Vaughan, bassist John Giannelli, unidentified man, pianist Carl Schroeder. *Keystone-France/Gamma-Keystone via Getty Images*

An excerpt from Vaughan's datebooks detailing her rigorous European tour in 1973. © 2016 *Michiyo Tanaka Fisher*

Conductor Michael Tilson Thomas and Vaughan collaborating
on their symphonic program of Gershwin music, 1970s. Their
partnership culminated with the 1982 Grammy-winning album
Gershwin Live! Tom Copi/Michael Ochs Archives/Getty Images

Vaughan and trumpeter Waymon Reed on their wedding day, June 13, 1978. *Courtesy Johnson Publishing Company, LLC. All rights reserved.*

Vaughan rehearsing with microphone and cigarette in hand, 1980. *Don Perdue*

Opera singer Leontyne Price, trumpeter Dizzy Gillespie, and Vaughan after receiving Lifetime Achievement Awards during the 31st Grammy Awards, February 22, 1989. A month earlier, the National Endowment for the Arts had honored Vaughan as an American Jazz Master. *The LIFE Picture Collection/Getty Images*

PART III

A Career Is Reborn, 1959–1990

"Would you sing 'Broken-Hearted Melody'?" a young couple asked at a nightclub performance in Washington, D.C., during the late 1970s. Sarah Vaughan had released the tune nearly twenty years earlier, in 1959, and it became the biggest hit of her career. "No," said Vaughan, "because number one, we can't do it like the record so you'll be disappointed, and number two, the musicians don't know it."[1] The trio did know the tune, of course, but Vaughan didn't want to sing it. "God, I hated it. I did that in the '50s and everybody loves that tune. It's the corniest thing I ever did," Vaughan explained years later. "They still ask for it and it drives me nuts."[2]

"Broken-Hearted Melody" was a trendy mix of rhythm and blues and rockabilly. Like many of her earlier pop successes, it was musically uninteresting. The melody and harmonic language, what Vaughan cared about most, were simple and repetitive, leaving little room for her to explore. And the lyrics were uninspired. It was a trite tune about a woman taunted by the memory of the song her lost love sang to her. But record executives, as they had time and again during the past decade, pressured her to sing the song. "The record companies always wanted me to do something that I didn't want to do," she explained to *Down Beat*'s James Liska in 1982. "'Sarah, you don't sell any records' they'd say, and so 'Broken-Hearted Melody' came up."[3]

She recorded the tune on January 7, 1958, during a session produced by Clyde Otis, then forgot about it. Eighteen months later, in July 1959, Mercury released "Broken-Hearted Melody," and it became a sensation, making its way up the *Billboard* charts. It stayed there for nineteen weeks, until the end of November, and peaked at No. 7. That same month she was nominated for her first Grammy. Elvis Presley won their category, Best Performance by a Top 40 Artist, from a field that also included the Coasters and Neil Sedaka, but "Broken-Hearted Melody" became one of the biggest-selling discs of 1959. It was her first hit in four years, the biggest of her career, and she had more fans than ever, all wanting to hear "Broken-Hearted Melody." A new wave of momentum propelled her career forward as she did the rounds of supper clubs, theaters, radio and television shows, and soon another European tour.

"I love the fact that people ask for *any* of my recorded songs. I like to sing their requests," she said to Max Jones of *Melody Maker* while on tour in England, in January 1960, at the height of "Broken-Hearted Melody"'s popularity there. "But can you imagine singing the same song at every show in every town in all the different countries? It does get a little monotonous but when you're obligated to people you really have no choice. Look at it this way. The reason you have a hit is because people like the song and buy the record. Then that's the first thing they demand to hear. What are you going to do?"[4]

"My heart really lies with the pretty ballads. For that matter, I like good tunes of every description. I'd love to do a whole album of spirituals, other folk songs, too," she confessed, in what would become a familiar refrain. "But I realize this: if I did only the things I love doing, I'm sure I wouldn't have all the fans I have now."[5]

As time passed, however, Vaughan became less and less willing to indulge requests for the tune. Bassist Herb Mickman remembered a persistent businessman pestering Vaughan to sing "Broken-Hearted Melody" when the band toured Mexico City in 1967. "She hated it," Mickman said. "And he kept bothering her to sing it, and one time he sent up a whole bunch of roses on the stage and said, 'Please sing "Broken-Hearted Melody,"' and she wouldn't sing it. She was very independent.' And she had become more so as the 1960s progressed. "We never did that song. People would call for it and call for it," confirmed bassist Bob Magnusson, who worked with Vaughan in the 1970s. "Here and there, she would do it to appease audiences, but pretty much she didn't want to do it."[6]

"Okay, okay, okay, we'll try it," Vaughan finally said to the young couple determined to hear "Broken-Hearted Melody" that night in Washington, D.C. Longtime friend Robert Richards was surprised by what happened next. "She did a funny run through of it and it was fine and the audience loved it," he reminisced. "And after she was through with it, she sat kind of in a very pensive way, and she said, 'You know, did you ever leave home like on a Tuesday night, and you're just going to go out and hear some music and have a drink somewhere and somehow or another you don't get back home for two days?' And the audience is like 'What?' and she was very thoughtful about this and she said, 'Have you ever had that experience?' and the couple [replied,] 'No, no.' And she said, 'Well that's what "Broken-Hearted Melody" is to me.'"[7]

It was an unusually candid, revealing moment; a dramatic contrast to her customary lighthearted, humorous banter; and a striking comparison. She likened singing "Broken-Hearted Melody" to a bender, losing control as events cascade around you. When you finally do emerge from the haze, days, months, or even years later, you realize that that was neither who you are nor who you want to be. For Vaughan, "Broken-Hearted Melody" brought back memories and experiences that she preferred to forget. It had come to symbolize hard times, difficult years in both her personal and professional lives.

The release of "Broken-Hearted Melody" coincided with some of the most challenging, painful years of Vaughan's life. She remarried in 1958, hoping to finally achieve her happily-ever-after, but as the popularity of "Broken-Hearted Melody" soared, her marriage to Clyde B. Atkins began to crumble. She endured physical and emotional abuse, more financial mismanagement, and a messy, prolonged divorce. And these tensions between Vaughan's personal and professional lives, her insistence on appointing her romantic partners as her managers, would continue to shape the final decades of her career, often negatively.

Singing "Broken-Hearted Melody" also reminded Vaughan of her ongoing conflicts with record executives who, motivated solely by the bottom line, tried to dictate what she recorded. It reminded her that far too often she had not had creative control and autonomy in the recording studio, that she had been forced to compromise her artistic integrity. And these battles would only intensify in the coming years. "Broken-Hearted Melody," with its hints of rockabilly and R & B, was a symptom of rock 'n' roll's takeover of the music industry in the 1960s and 1970s. Audiences for jazz shrank, jazz venues closed, radio switched to a Top 40 format, and record labels dropped jazz artists from their rosters. In fact, for almost five years, between 1967 and 1971, Vaughan was without a contract and didn't step into a recording studio. It was the lowest point of her career. Everything that Vaughan knew and understood about the business had changed, and she struggled to remain relevant.

But she weathered these bad years and came out the other side by doing what she did best: singing. Making music was her salvation. "I found who I was in that time," she told Bob Protzman of the *Akron Beacon Journal* in 1978. "I worked more than I ever did in my life." She emerged stronger, wiser, and more resilient. She had learned from "Broken-Hearted Melody" that a bad song could haunt her for decades and resolved to do her best not to compromise again. "I decided I wasn't going to do something just to get me a hit record," she continued. "If it's consistent with what I feel and believe in, fine."[8] As she had since the beginning of her career, Vaughan pushed back against what was expected of her—by record executives, club owners, and promoters or society as a whole—to do what she, a black woman and artist, wanted. As she reasserted her creative vision and independence, and as she kept on working, her career turned around.

In 1974, in the midst of this career renaissance, Vaughan set in motion her third and final crossover phase. She began appearing with symphony orchestras, first in collaboration with conductor Michael Tilson Thomas and then on her own. The jazz artist and occasional pop star emerged as a symphonic diva. She introduced a new, previously untapped audience, those staid, more traditional music lovers who frequented symphony halls, to jazz and the wonders of her voice. These concerts revitalized her career and fulfilled her childhood dreams of following in the footsteps of Marian Anderson, but on her own terms, while helping jazz along its journey toward legitimacy, its transformation from lowbrow folk music to highbrow concert music.

10

"They Say You Can't Teach New Tricks to Old Dogs— So Get New Dogs!"

'm nervous. Old Baby. I'm awfully nervous. I've never been a bridesmaid before," trumpeter Dizzy Gillespie joked with reporters gathered at Chicago's City Hall.[1] Vaughan had just returned from her tour of Europe, culminating in her appearances at the World's Fair in Brussels, and now, on Thursday, September 4, 1958, she was getting married. Two days earlier, on Tuesday, she and Clyde B. Atkins became engaged. Wednesday the couple went to City Hall for a marriage license, but they needed blood tests first. Vaughan and Atkins then rushed to a lab, and as the happy couple waited for their test results, they celebrated through the night at a nearby South Side club. Thursday morning a tired yet excited Vaughan married Atkins. It was a simple ceremony. Judge Fred "Duke" Slater presided. Atkins's half-brother Carl Irvin was best man, and, of course, Gillespie was maid of honor. Vaughan's parents were not there, nor were Modina Davis, Johnnie Garry, or any other close friends. Art Talmadge, the Chicago-based vice president of Mercury Records, was the only guest. He presented Vaughan with a single orchid.

"After I got divorced from George, I never thought I would get married again," Vaughan said as she fielded questions from reporters after the ceremony. "But here I am."[2] When asked about her whirlwind romance and suggestions that the wedding might be impetuous, she explained that she first met Atkins a year earlier in Atlantic City and that they hung out whenever she played in Chicago. "He used to catch all my shows when I came to town, and we sort of eyed each other when I was singing," she said. "I dug him and he dug me, so we just decided to jump the broom."[3] Then a white photographer asked Vaughan to gaze at Atkins, grin, and roll her eyes. This angered the usually polite Vaughan, and, her patience waning, she snapped: "I'm no comedian. You'd better get your picture."[4]

An impromptu reception at the Archway Supper Club followed. According to the press, as news of Vaughan's marriage spread, she fielded phone calls from friends and fellow musicians. "I just heard about it," vocalist Dinah Washington reportedly said. "Congratulations . . . or should I say 'condolences'?" Washington was on her fifth marriage.[5] She and Vaughan used to commiserate about men, and vocalist Joe Williams remembered their joke: "They say you can't teach new tricks to old dogs—so get new dogs!"[6]

"You're going to love him," Vaughan insisted when she phoned Modina Davis with the news. "Well, but who is he?" asked Davis.[7] Vaughan's pianist Ronnell Bright remembered Atkins from his childhood in Chicago. They lived blocks apart and attended the same elementary and high schools. But no one knew what Atkins did for a living. Atkins told the *New York Amsterdam News* that he worked for *Down Beat,* but he did not. The *New York Times* and *Variety* reported that Atkins owned a fleet of cabs in Chicago. Also unlikely. Other profiles emphasized his athletic prowess, writing that he ran track and played football in high school and later unsuccessfully tried out for the Chicago Cardinals football team. Elsewhere he was described as a sportsman, a hustler of sorts, and a well-known regular of Chicago's nightclubs.[8]

Despite George Wein's warnings, Vaughan soon installed Atkins as her new personal manager, even though he had no musical or industry experience. She leased him office space in the same midtown Manhattan building housing her ex-husband's agency, and Treadwell was not happy. Some suspected jealousy, but it's also likely Treadwell worried about his professional well-being. According to news reports, Vaughan, his biggest client, had a five-year management contract with him, and he did not want to release her. He called in his lawyers, claiming that Vaughan still owed him money for managing her. "He won't get a cent," said Vaughan, according to society columnist Dorothy Kilgallen.[9] The estranged couple eventually came to an agreement, and in February 1959, during her honeymoon in Acapulco, she announced, "I've severed all management connections with my former husband, George Treadwell."[10]

On July 26, 1959, as the couple approached their first wedding anniversary, "Broken-Hearted Melody" began to climb the *Billboard* charts. Even though Treadwell no longer managed Vaughan, he seized one last opportunity to take credit for his ex-wife's success. He claimed that he sensed "Broken-Hearted Melody" would become a hit and persuaded executives to rush Vaughan into the studio, despite the fact that it had been recorded a year and a half earlier on January 7, 1958. Nonetheless, her popularity soared, and the stature of her gigs (and paychecks) took another leap. During Christmas, she returned to the Waldorf Astoria, this time playing their more prestigious Empire Room.[11] The next week, she appeared at the Fontainebleau in Miami Beach, followed in January and February by another tour of the United Kingdom, where "Broken-Hearted Melody" spent months on the charts. And she continued to appear on radio and television programs in England and the United States.

The success of "Broken-Hearted Melody" begot other, albeit minor, hits. "Smooth Operator" spent nine weeks on the *Billboard* charts, peaking at No. 44 in December. "You're My Baby" made a brief appearance in the top one hundred in February, followed a week later by "Eternally," which rose to No. 41 during an eight-week run. "Our Waltz" lingered at the bottom of the charts in May, and "Serenata," her first single for Roulette, spent eight weeks on the charts, peaking at No. 82. Ten months earlier, shortly after Vaughan married Atkins but before the release of "Broken-Hearted Melody," Morris Levy, the owner of Birdland and the impresario behind the lucrative Birdland tours, wooed an unhappy Vaughan to Roulette. She had become restless at Mercury. Although she continued to record stunning jazz albums for the label, including *Sarah Vaughan at Mr. Kelly's*, *Sarah Vaughan After Hours at the London House*, and *No Count Sarah*, the quality of the pop material offered her had declined. Levy promised Vaughan a bigger paycheck and more artistic freedom. On April 19, 1960, after her contract with Mercury expired, she recorded her first album for Roulette, *Dreamy*, a collection of wistful, romantic pop tunes backed by strings.

That May, she landed her first gig in Reno. In June, she performed at Madison Square Garden for a screaming crowd of fifteen thousand.[12] Weeks later, the feature length film *Murder, Inc.*, premiered. Billed as "newcomer Sarah Vaughan," she made a cameo appearance as a nightclub singer in the moody gangster flick showcasing future *Columbo* star Peter Falk. In July, she returned to Las Vegas for the first time since her last string of hits in 1955 for a lucrative six weeks at the Flamingo. Unlike her last appearance, she did not have to sneak out through the casino's kitchen to a trailer between sets. She could now stay in the hotel. She played Las Vegas again in January. And, following a stint at the Cloisters in Los Angeles, she performed on the telecast of the Academy Awards on April 17, 1961.

As Vaughan's career thrived, the newlyweds settled into what appeared to be a life of happy domesticity. In the fall of 1959, as the success of "Broken-Hearted Melody" resolved Vaughan's troubled finances, refilling the bank accounts pillaged by Treadwell, she and Atkins purchased a home together in Englewood, New Jersey. It was a spacious 2,933-square-foot split-level ranch with a two-car garage, four bedrooms, white shutters framing the windows, and an impressive multipaned bay window looking out onto their expansive front lawn. In the back, they had a large, fenced-in yard with rosebushes and old-growth trees. Vaughan paid $50,000 for the home, built in 1950, and reportedly spent another $50,000 on renovations supervised by Atkins. They installed a $450 set of entrance chimes that played "How High the Moon."[13] "I used to eat for a year on the price of what it now costs to ring my silly old doorbell," Vaughan joked in *Time* magazine.[14]

She was living the suburban dream. She had a beautiful home in an affluent neighborhood and entertained regularly. Society columns reported that she welcomed African dignitaries to her home and hired three taxicabs to ferry the Treniers, a popular R & B act, to Englewood so she could prepare them a home-cooked meal. Friends Dinah Washington, Gloria Lynne, Dizzy Gillespie, and Clyde Otis all lived within walking distance. Vaughan was just thirty minutes from her parents' house in Newark and a short ride from Manhattan. During her Waldorf Astoria appearance in December, she commuted in a limousine furnished with a record player. When asked by columnist Leonard Lyons how long it took her to get home, Vaughan answered: "Not long. Just one Count Basie LP and two Miles Davis singles."[15]

Yet, by many standards, this picture of a happy suburban life remained incomplete. Postwar America, with its renewed emphasis on domesticity, home, and hearth, expected a "home" to include a husband, a wife, and their children. Vaughan, now thirty-seven, still wanted children, and on June 14, 1961, she and Atkins adopted a baby girl. Vaughan, casually clad in a white dress, head scarf, and sunglasses, held the two-month-old close as they left the Illinois Children's Home and Aid Society in Chicago. Atkins carried Vaughan's handbag as he walked beside mother and child.[16] During the ride home, Vaughan stared at her new baby in her arms, captivated, as Atkins timidly peered over her shoulder.[17] They named their daughter Deborah Lois.

"This is what I have always wanted. I never had a child before because I was either too busy to take time to have one or because I wasn't happy," Vaughan explained in an *Ebony* profile by Allan Morrison published in September. "My life was being wasted," she said of her marriage to Treadwell. "I knew it wasn't going to last." Atkins represented a second chance at happiness, an opportunity to fulfill not only her longstanding desire to be a mother but also society's expectations that women be nurturers and caretakers. "This baby has brought a lot of happiness into our home," Vaughan continued. "She has made a big difference already."

The cover story featured formal portraits of the family, one with both parents gazing at the sleeping infant, who grasped Vaughan's pinky finger as the new mother looked on with an easy, comfortable smile, as well as candid shots of Vaughan performing her new duties as a mother. She weighed Deborah as her husband and Inez Brown, their nanny, watched; sterilized bottles for formula; put the fussy baby down for her nap; and pushed a baby carriage as she and Atkins surveyed their property. Motherhood suited Vaughan and, according to *Ebony*, brought a serenity and security the famous singer had not experienced before, an unconditional love that until this point had eluded her. "I've had to get used to a lot of things since the baby arrived. That baby has changed my household," said Vaughan. "But I love it."

While *Ebony* celebrated Vaughan's newfound status as a mother, it also reminded readers of her professional accomplishments and Atkins's role as her manager. Photos showed the couple at work in the midtown Manhattan penthouse offices of their company, Progressive Talent. In one, they relaxed on the suite's balcony, gazing out at the Manhattan skyline. In another, Atkins took center stage as he led a staff meeting. He sat in his large leather desk chair, surrounded by his secretary, receptionist, and office manager. And Vaughan, the firm's artistic director responsible for vetting talent, sat by his side. It was a portrait of an equal partnership and marriage, an ideal personal and professional collaboration, reminiscent of the press coverage of her marriage to George Treadwell a decade earlier. Vaughan wanted a partnership of equals, the perfect melding of her personal and professional lives. She wanted to be loved, cherished, and taken care of. But she also wanted to be in charge. "All a woman really wants is a roof over her head and a husband under her thumb," said Vaughan in 1955.[18] And these competing, seemingly contradictory needs would prove to be a difficult balancing act, especially in 1961.

But the enterprise must have been an enormous stress for Vaughan. She was Progressive Talent's biggest, most lucrative client and was responsible for the livelihood of everyone in the room, not to mention her parents, daughter, daughter's nanny, road manager, personal assistant, and the three musicians in her band. While *Ebony* proclaimed the management firm a success, citing its impressive offices and roster of clients, friends remember Vaughan going into the office to check up on Atkins to make sure that he was doing his job correctly. Yet she continued to fund his business ventures, with the hope that he too would thrive and succeed. In December 1959, she financed a trip to South America so that Atkins could negotiate a deal to become the sole United States representative booking tours for a Brazilian impresario. Atkins told the press that he had access to a $250,000 fund that would be used to guarantee artists' salaries, but nothing ever came of the venture.[19] In June 1960, she bankrolled Atkins as he dabbled in club management too, but the Roberts Show Lounge in Atkins's hometown of Chicago failed within two months.[20] Industry insiders speculated that Atkins wanted to try his hand managing a club in Atlantic City next.[21]

In public, Vaughan praised Atkins's skills as a manager, just as she had all of those years with Treadwell, and promoted his services. "Sarah always offered me her help and guidance," vocalist Gloria Lynne wrote in her autobiography. "At one point in our friendship, I was in between personal managers and she recommended her husband, C. B. Atkins. I used him for a minute, but he just wasn't any good at it." Another piece of Vaughan's advice, however, puzzled Lynne. "They used to say Sarah wasn't human, because of her incredible voice. Well, I remember, Sarah told me one time: 'Watch the humans.' I didn't catch her meaning. And this thing really tripped me up," Lynne wrote. "I came home and told my mother, 'Mom, Sarah Vaughan told me to watch the humans!' 'Oh, she's just saying to look out for all those raggedy people,' my mother said, 'you know, nasty, lowdown people.'"[22]

"C. B. was a gambler," pianist Ronnell Bright said. "That was C. B.'s real calling." In December 1959, while en route to Los Angeles, Bright remembered stopping in Las Vegas with the couple. Atkins won $40,000 shooting craps, but he soon lost his winnings and then some of Vaughan's money.[23] As her personal manager, Atkins was responsible for collecting her earnings, and far too often, during engagements in Las Vegas, Reno, and Atlantic City, he simply gambled all of the money away. Thousands of dollars gone. Bassist Richard Davis, who worked with Vaughan for six years, between 1957 and 1963, agreed. "He was a gambler. You could have seen he was somebody you didn't want to be around," he said, adding, "He did not have a respect for the musicians who were behind her."[24] Indeed, the week before adopting their daughter, Vaughan played Basin Street East in New York, and Atkins received a warning from Local 822 of the musician's union following a dispute with her sidemen.[25]

After adopting her daughter, Vaughan did not take maternity leave. Two weeks later, on July 2, 1961, she made her annual appearance at the Newport Jazz Festival, and on July 18, before continuing her usual summer schedule of festivals, country clubs, and benefit concerts, she returned to Roulette's New York recording studios. Producer Teddy Reig told Vaughan that he wanted to present her in a new way. "On this next album I want you to sing naked," said Reig, recounting the conversation for oral historian Edward Berger. "Are you losing your mind?" he remembered her replying. "I want you without all that jive noise," he explained. Her previous sessions had been with Count Basie's band and string orchestras, sometimes with a choir. "Just you and a simple background—whatever you feel comfortable with." "How about guitar and bass?" she suggested. "Great. I want [bassist] George Duvivier," he said. "That's great," she answered. "And I'd like [guitarist] Mundell Lowe." "You got a deal."[26]

"We did it up at 106th Street in what I believe was an old movie theater," Lowe said. "They invited about thirty people, and brought in some tables and checkered tablecloths, food and booze—it was like a nightclub. There was a little platform for Sarah, George, and me. We didn't rehearse; all of the things you hear on that album are first takes. We'd talk about each tune for a minute or so and then just do it. We'd record for a while, then have a drink and do some more. We started at seven and by eleven we'd finished the whole album!"[27] It was one of Vaughan's most intimate sessions, befitting the album's title, *After Hours*. There was a seamless interplay, an easy give-and-take, between Vaughan and the duo backing her. And with this sparse accompaniment her voice was laid bare. She sang "My Favorite Things" as a gentle, caressing lullaby, "Sophisticated Lady" as a sensual cautionary tale, and "Easy to Love" as a hip, swinging invitation to romance. "I felt proud of that album," Lowe said, and it is widely considered one of the finest albums recorded by Vaughan. "Teddy Reig told me later that it was the only album she ever made that made any money."[28]

A year later, in an effort to re-create the magic of *After Hours,* Vaughan recorded its follow-up, *Sarah + 2,* this time with Barney Kessel on guitar and Joe Comfort on bass. And the next day, August 8, 1962, Vaughan returned to the same Los Angeles studio to record a second album, the polar opposite of *Sarah + 2,* a big band session with Benny Carter's orchestra that became *The Explosive Side of Sarah Vaughan.* Producer Teddy Reig remembered the easygoing spontaneity of the music making that day. As the band rehearsed "I Can't Give You Anything but Love," Vaughan paced around the studio, trying to get a feel for the arrangement. When she heard the reed chorus Carter had written for the tune, she started to sing along. "Benny and I immediately looked at one another and decided right there to have her sing the lead part with the reeds," said Reig.[29]

There was, however, more drama on the sidelines. "Whenever Teddy did a session in California, he'd give me a call and I'd drop by," publisher Mike Gould told Berger. "I was at the Sarah Vaughan date where Teddy backed her with only guitar and bass. It was one of those inspired concepts that worked perfectly. He used to have to deal with some pretty crazy situations. And he always kept his sense of humor. I was at another of Sarah's dates where Teddy got involved in a scene with Sarah's then husband, who was not a very nice man. A couple of guns suddenly materialized and Teddy screamed, 'They've got guns and I haven't even got a fingernail file!'"[30]

It wasn't the first indication that something might be amiss in Vaughan's nearly four-year marriage. Despite outward appearances of domestic bliss, friends worried that Vaughan had married a controlling man with a volatile temper and that she herself might be in danger. Shortly after their wedding, as Atkins took control of Vaughan's professional and private lives, he assumed the role of gatekeeper. "Within months, parasites, hangers-on, and even more legitimate acquaintances found that to get to the singer they had to get past Atkins first," Barbara Gardner wrote in a *Down Beat* profile for the March 1961 edition, three months before the couple adopted their daughter.[31] Vaughan became more and more isolated. She stopped calling her friends, and when she walked past their tables at clubs, she would say, "Call me," but her friends could never get through. Vocalists Annie Ross and Carmen McRae both remembered dining with the couple, and Atkins would not allow other women in the group to accompany Vaughan to the restroom. "C. B. tried to tie her up so that nobody saw her but him," said childhood friend Aretha Landrum.[32]

In 1960, Atkins abruptly fired Vaughan's road manager, Johnnie Garry and assistant Modina Davis. Garry remembered getting the call from Atkins while he spent his day off with Vaughan. "Sarah Vaughan was sitting in my kitchen eating, cuz we had been to the golf course, and she had asked my wife to fix her some black-eyed peas and stuff like that," Garry explained in

2007. "So I said to Sarah, 'Your husband just fired me.' She said, 'Well, I'll talk to him.' I said 'No, don't do that. As long as I've been with you and the things we've been through, if you had to talk to him about me, it ain't gonna work.'"[33] Garry became the house manager for Birdland, and Vaughan hired a new road manager. She soon regretted losing Garry and asked him to return, but he refused. "I loved her, but I couldn't go back steady because [it] never work[s]," said Garry. "Not when you go back to a job that you got fired from by someone that shouldn't have fired you. It doesn't work."[34]

Garry worked for Vaughan for a dozen years and Davis almost a decade, and both were friends, trusted confidants, advocates, and integral parts of Vaughan's support network on the road. As she did with her musicians, Vaughan shared an intimacy and deep familiarity with both Davis and Garry, and now that was gone. As Vaughan's circle of friends shrank, she withdrew into herself, becoming more sensitive and defensive, anxious and unsettled offstage. According to Gardner, Vaughan's world centered on Atkins and his approval. "She is openly adoring of him, and obedient to the point of subservience. Often she sits quietly, watching him, hanging onto every word. If he asks her to do anything, she is off like a shot," wrote Gardner. "She is almost childlike in her anxiety not to displease him. If in his absence she goes for a moment against his wishes, she is almost instantly contrite, hoping he will never find out what she has done."

"I guess I'm too sensitive," Vaughan acknowledged. "But I'm so afraid of being hurt. I've been hurt so much." At first glance, Vaughan seemed to be discussing her first marriage to George Treadwell. The wounds from his emotional and fiscal betrayals remained raw. But they were also the words of a woman who did not want to get hurt again. It was a portrait of a woman walking on eggshells, doing everything in her power not to upset her violent husband. Gardner never labeled the dynamics between Vaughan and Atkins as domestic violence, but it was implied. She described a woman who was being abused financially, emotionally, and physically. "[Sarah] was scared to say something because this m.f. was going to knock her under the bed," said friend McRae. "C. B. used to hit her. He thought that was the way women should be treated."[35]

Then Vaughan began missing work. The unusually resilient, healthy vocalist, who rarely called in sick, canceled a prestigious two-night engagement with Duke Ellington at Ravinia, the summer home of the Chicago Symphony Orchestra, in August 1961, two months after adopting her daughter. Media reports cited a brief hospital stay, likely for a minor surgery.[36] In the fall of 1962, she canceled a tour of London, citing another hospital stay. Modina Davis, after Atkins fired her, remembered being called by a club manager when Vaughan failed to show up for her scheduled engagement. Davis believed that she missed the gig because she was too busy fighting with Atkins.

Vaughan did her best to hold her marriage together, but her tenuous grasp on the little control that she had quickly slipped away, and the relationship spiraled out of control. Atkins repeatedly threatened to kill her. On October 18, 1962, she had her husband arrested, and what had been a private struggle soon became a very public scandal.[37]

Earlier in the week, on Monday, October 15, as Vaughan performed in Larry Steele's Smart Affairs revue at the Uptown Theater in Philadelphia, cast members saw Vaughan become upset and emotional. She had received a series of threatening letters and telephone calls, they believed, from her husband. Tuesday night, according to newspaper reports, Atkins confronted Vaughan in her dressing room. He berated her, and another violent argument broke out. Vaughan ran into the street to summon a police officer, who warned Atkins to leave the theater. He returned later that night and was ejected. Wednesday, with the urging of Lionel Beckles, a revue dancer, Vaughan filed a warrant for Atkins's arrest, charging that he had threatened her life both in person and by phone.[38] On Thursday night, October 18, the couple argued again backstage. Officers arrived and arrested a surprised Atkins as Vaughan prepared to go onstage.

Detectives talked to him for three hours; he denied making any threatening calls; and he was released. He spent the night at the Penn Sheraton Hotel in a room registered to his wife, but she never returned.[39]

News of Atkins's arrest spread quickly. Television and radio programs debated the upcoming hearing. Some speculated that Atkins had taken Vaughan's daughter from her.[40] Others suspected petty jealousies. The gossip mill linked Vaughan with a revue dancer and Atkins with his client vocalist Gloria Lynne.[41] By Friday afternoon, several hundred people gathered outside the courthouse, waiting for Vaughan to arrive. "As she stepped from an unmarked police car, dressed in black slacks, a cotton pull-over and a bulky knit sweater, the throng of fans let out a cheer," the *Philadelphia Tribune* reported. Once inside the courtroom, an emotional, nearly despondent Vaughan fielded questions from reporters. An hour later, Atkins entered, and the couple immediately retreated into the chambers of Magistrate Earl Lane. "That's husband and wife in there," Lane told reporters gathered in the courtroom. "And I've given them five minutes to talk it over."[42]

The couple emerged thirty minutes later. When asked if she still wanted to testify against her husband, Vaughan, on the verge of tears, turned to the court bar and said in a hushed, barely audible voice: "I wish to withdraw the charges." She bowed her head and averted her gaze, a grim frown on her face, as Lane lectured the couple and warned Atkins not to mistreat his wife. "You will be brought before me again," said the magistrate, if he or the Philadelphia police learned of more threats. "You two are important people. You should not involve yourselves in such nonsense like this. Now kiss, make up and go home."[43] For the benefit of the cameras, Atkins kissed his wary wife on the forehead. "Go out of that door and act intelligent," Lane ordered, and Vaughan, still on the verge of tears, walked out of the courthouse, arm in arm with her husband.[44]

Judge Lane's inaction was regrettable and, from a twenty-first-century perspective, downright negligent. He ordered a downtrodden, abused woman, who feared for her safety and that of her child, to kiss and make up with her abuser. Instead of advocating for Vaughan, Lane deferred to the laws and social customs of the day, in this case, the institution of marriage, which dictated that a wife should be beholden to her husband, regardless of what happened behind closed doors. In the process, he reinforced the status quo and the sexism and gender inequality that it promoted. In the 1960s, domestic violence, though common, was still widely ignored. Society was in denial. There were no legal systems set up to protect the abused—usually women—or prosecute their abusers. Restraining orders didn't exist until the late 1970s. And there were no support groups or safe houses to shelter abused women either. Domestic violence was considered a private matter, something that should be resolved behind closed doors, within the confines of the family. It was (and, for that matter, still is) a taboo subject, a secret, a source of shame and guilt. By coming forward, asking the police and courts for help, Vaughan unwittingly broke the code of silence. She aired not only her dirty laundry but that of society as a whole, and in the process she invited backlash and public ridicule, more shame and humiliation.

Was the Arrest of Sarah Vaughan's Husband Just a Publicity Stunt?" asked the *Philadelphia Tribune* in a poll of six female readers. Two believed it was, asserting that her ticket sales had been poor at the Uptown. Three believed it was not, insisting that, unlike Dinah Washington, Vaughan did not discuss her marriage in public, nor did she seek publicity. And one was on the fence.[45] In another column, an anonymous courtroom observer condemned the couple's public reconciliation, adding, "I think she looked downright tacky. Whoever heard of anyone going to court wearing slacks? That husband of hers wasn't any fashion plate either. He looked like he had just come out of the poolroom."[46] In a letter to the editors of the *Philadelphia Tribune,* a concerned fan expressed his surprise and disappointment at learning of Vaughan's troubled marriage. He believed that Vaughan and Atkins loved one another and hoped that this incident had all been a mistake.[47] A reporter for the *Baltimore Afro-American* described Vaughan as "pathetic," while a headline in the *Washington Post and Times-Herald,* a white publication, proclaimed "Sarah Vaughan's Sad Story Is Out."[48]

Having her private struggles put on display in the court of public opinion must have been mortifying for the shy, intensely private vocalist. The judge's patronizing tone and the public's victim blaming, all intensified by her status as a celebrity, must have compounded the pain and embarrassment that she felt. And as a race woman, a standard-bearer and role model in the black community, Vaughan was under pressure from many not to make black Americans look bad in front of white Americans. When Vaughan stood up to speak her truth, to protest the inequality and abuse she experienced, she found herself at the intersection of complex and competing forces. She regretted getting the police involved. According to the *New York Amsterdam News,* during the aftermath of the trial, Vaughan told her husband, "If I had any idea that this thing would blow up to this size, I wouldn't have done it."[49]

She did, however, take action. After her public reconciliation in court, Vaughan, summoning emotional strength and courage, prepared to leave her husband. Unbeknownst to Atkins, she took her daughter and retreated to her parents' home in Newark. She hoped to remove her personal belongings from her Englewood home on Thursday, October 25, but Atkins learned of her plans and stopped her. On November 2, she filed for divorce, citing mental and physical cruelty. The petition stated that Atkins had threatened her life multiple times during the previous two years, not only in Philadelphia but also Atlantic City, Las Vegas, Washington, D.C., and Canada. Through her lawyer, she also demanded a full financial accounting of her earnings during the four years Atkins managed her career. It seemed history was repeating itself.[50]

"Sarah was not very sharp about money. She wanted someone else to always handle the money," said bassist Herb Mickman, who worked with Vaughan between 1965 and 1968, during the aftermath of her second failed marriage. Yet who would have taught Vaughan how to be good with money? Her family was poor and likely lived paycheck to paycheck during her childhood. And as a professional woman, not to mention a black professional woman, she had few role models to emulate. "I think she had a bank account in both their names and [Atkins] went to the bank and cleaned her out when he left her," Mickman continued. "And she didn't even have enough money to pay all the plane fares to the jobs, so she had to borrow money, and she borrowed money from this guy Preacher Wells, who became her manager. I think he was her lover also; I think they were together."[51]

Vaughan met John "Preacher" Wells in the fall of 1962, shortly after she left her husband and moved back home to Newark. She frequented a nightclub on Clinton Avenue where Wells worked behind the bar. She was vulnerable, in search of comfort and security after the physical and emotional trauma of her failed marriage, and Wells was available. He was three years her junior and a childhood acquaintance. He'd earned his nickname "Preacher" because as a child he shadowed his uncle, a prominent Newark reverend. The couple soon moved into an apartment in Weequahic Towers, near her parents, and, as was her habit, she installed Wells as her new manager, even though he too had no experience in management or the music industry.

Although Vaughan was moving on romantically and professionally, she and Atkins still had unfinished business, and even though Atkins told *Jet* magazine that he hoped he and Vaughan would reconcile, tensions between the estranged couple escalated.[52] A gossip column reported that Atkins wanted the Englewood house, purchased and remodeled with Vaughan's earnings, and an additional $25,000 in the divorce settlement.[53] Another gossip columnist suggested that Atkins wooed Vaughan with roses and a mink coat, hoping to reconcile.[54] In late December, not knowing the other would be there, both Vaughan and Atkins attended vocalist, friend, and neighbor Dinah Washington's opening night at Birdland. At intermission, Atkins confronted

Vaughan. They argued, and Washington stepped in and tried to calm the couple. The disagreement intensified, and Washington ferried Vaughan backstage to her dressing room. Police escorted Atkins from the premises.[55]

Police intervened again on Friday, January 25, 1963, when Vaughan, accompanied by a patrolman and Preacher Wells, returned to her Englewood home, where Atkins still lived, to collect gowns she needed for her upcoming appearance at the Fontainebleau in Miami Beach. The officer kept watch outside until he heard gunshots from inside the home and broke down the door. He disarmed Atkins, who scuffled with Wells, then arrested both men.[56]

Atkins told a very different version of that night's events. He claimed that Vaughan hired ten "thugs," led by Wells, to raid his midtown management offices in search of her contract, which guaranteed him exclusive management rights for the next four years. "Wells knew that before he could legally become her manager he would have to destroy that contract," Atkins told the *Chicago Defender*. After trashing his office, the thugs proceeded to his home. Neighbors alerted Atkins that Vaughan was moving him out, and he returned home to find men removing furniture from his house. Wells and Atkins fought inside, and Atkins fired two shots at Wells, who fled to an upstairs bedroom as Atkins pursued him. Concerned neighbors called the police.[57]

It was a classic he-said-she-said fueled by money and the powerful emotions of a dysfunctional, violent romance. A partnership with Vaughan bestowed social status, wealth, and power, and Atkins's looming divorce forced him to relinquish all of this to another man. In the end, Atkins was charged with assault with a weapon. He was released on $10,000 bail, pending his February 8 trial. In return, he asked prosecutors to file assault charges against Wells, who was released on $200 bail.[58] And Vaughan returned to the safety of her parents' home in Newark and prepared for a two-week return engagement at the Fontainebleau.

In March 1963 the Internal Revenue Service placed a lien on the couple's Englewood home for nonpayment of back taxes.[59]

Vaughan owed $19,150 in personal income taxes for 1960, the year after the successes of "Broken-Hearted Melody."[60] As her personal manager, Atkins was responsible for her accounting and taxes. "Arrangements have been made to pay off the lien," Atkins told *Jet* magazine. "The government has already received $4500 of it and will get the rest within two weeks."[61] It's unlikely that Atkins made these final payments. When she learned of the seizure of her home, Vaughan told *Jet* magazine that she didn't mind losing the house. "I always had to scuffle for bread," she said. But she hated to lose the memories attached to the house.[62] They represented Vaughan's hopes and dreams of having it all: a rewarding career and a beautiful home, happy marriage, and thriving child. They also symbolized her efforts to realize the idealized version of her life portrayed in the press from the 1940s through the early 1960s, an ideal informed by what society expected of Vaughan and all women. It must have been painful for Vaughan to accept that she could not have this ideal. However, in the coming years, she would find happiness on her own terms, creating a life that better suited her reality as a successful career woman and artist.

Atkins filed for a legal separation on March 20, 1963. "I will surrender the [management] contract if Sarah does not want me to manage her," he told *Jet* magazine. "We do not speak to each other anymore. I feel badly about the breakup of our marriage."[63]

Frustrated, financially and emotionally drained, Vaughan confided in Frank Sinatra. She worked the Riviera in Las Vegas in March, and Herb Mickman recalled, "Sarah told me that she met Frank and it was late at night and they took a walk around the hotel. It was, like, just taking a walk so nobody could see them, and she starts telling Frank, she says, 'My second husband, he went to the bank, he cleaned me out.' He did this, he did that, and Frank says, 'Well, why don't you give me his name, I'll have a couple of guys break his legs.' But she didn't go for that. 'No, I don't think I want that,' says Vaughan."[64]

As Vaughan dealt with the upheaval in her personal life and its inevitable toll, she went back to work. She returned to the daily grind of touring and life on the road, not simply because she had to support the people who depended on her but because emotionally she needed to. Singing had become her way of dealing with life's challenges. Singing, being a musician, symbolized something very special for Vaughan. It represented autonomy, independence, and an opportunity for self-realization. It was the space where she was free to express herself, free to be herself, regardless of what society thought she should or could be. And she fought for this freedom and autonomy her entire life. Whatever might happen in her personal life, singing was her one constant. It was her salvation. And, not surprisingly, her life on the bandstand was also where she forged many of her most rewarding relationships.

As Vaughan went back to work that spring, she returned to Roulette's recording studios. In February and March, she logged five sessions, producing two new albums: *Star Eyes* and *Slightly Classical*. Then Teddy Reig, Roulette's A&R man, went on a Vaughan recording streak. In the span of a month, between May 29, 1963, and the end of June, she participated in eleven studio sessions, seven in Los Angeles and four in Chicago. She stayed in Chicago for another three weeks for a stint at the Edgewater Beach Hotel that began on July 2. This was bassist Charles "Buster" Williams's first gig with the band. He was twenty-one years old and a native of Camden, New Jersey, but he had been working since he was seventeen, first with saxophonist Jimmy Heath, then Gene Ammons, Sonny Stitt, Dakota Staton, and Betty Carter. Vaughan's pianist, Kirk Stuart, heard him backing Betty Bebop at Birdland and introduced himself. "I'm the piano player with Sarah Vaughan," said Stuart, who had been sent on a mission to find a replacement for Richard Davis. "She's looking for a bassist, and she would *love* you! Would you be interested?" He was. Williams never had a formal audition for the trio, but he realized in hindsight that Vaughan had an uncanny ability to hear talent. "She could hear beyond what you were doing," Williams explained. "She could hear your aptitude. She could hear your potential."

"She made me feel comfortable with her from the beginning," Williams remembered. "Now, the first night, the first set we played, it was really amazing. And when we finished the set, she took me up to her suite. And she sat me down and she was telling me how much she loved the way I played. And she was talking about Paul Chambers, who was my hero on bass, and she was talking about all these great bass players and how I was destined to be one of these great bass players. And while she's talking, she rolled a joint. And I had never smoked reefer before. She rolled this joint and she lit up and she took a drive off it and then she passed it to me, and I panicked." His father, however, had prepared him for this moment. Before Williams went on the road at seventeen, his father instilled many life lessons, including how to fake smoking marijuana. His father told him to squeeze the joint tight, put it to his mouth, and pretend to inhale. "When Sarah Vaughan passed me this joint, this is what I did," Williams continued. "But now, she's looking at me, and of course you know, when you're smoking a cigarette or a joint and you suck it, you see the flame at the end gets more brighter. And I'm sucking and ain't nothing getting bright. And she looked, and she said, 'What the hell are you doing?' And she took the joint and she told me, she said, 'Now, this is how you hold it and you smoke this joint.' And she made me smoke this joint."[65]

"So [the] first time I smoked reefer was with Sarah Vaughan. And I was scared to death not to do it," said Williams. But this moment was about more than Vaughan asserting her presence or teaching him how to smoke a joint. Vaughan was sending Williams a message. "She made me feel like it was okay, I mean, 'I'm going to protect you, don't worry. So you can fly, I'm just right here.'"[66] She was telling him that it was safe for him to explore and grow as a musician, to take risks and try new things. It was a pivotal moment in their professional and personal relationship. It was a moment of bonding and trust building. "She never restricted me. She didn't want to hear you playing in a restricted manner. She wanted to hear you growing, exploring. She wanted to hear you being daring," Williams explained. "She wanted you to be free."[67] She encouraged Williams to be open to all of the possibilities before him, to continue learning and moving ahead. "Every time you pick up your instrument, then it has to be an adventure. That's the way I was taught. And that was what Sarah Vaughan initiated, or that was the kind of attitude that she generated. That was the perception that she had, and that's the perception that she wanted those around her to have," he continued. "In other words, what can you do better than you done before? And what can you find that you didn't find before? Not haphazardly or helter-skelter. But based on a confidence and a willingness to take a journey, to explore."[68]

"I was the new guy on the block, and I'm learning the music and I make my mistakes, and she just gives me a big smile," said Williams. "I loved it. I mean she acknowledged everything that you did. If she didn't like it, you knew that. And when she liked it, you knew that too." Pianist Stuart was the musical director, responsible for rehearsing the trio and making sure they were tight. And Chicago native George Hughes was on drums. "But she was always [there], her input was always there because she always made suggestions." Sometimes it was an explicit instruction, but more often than not Vaughan led by example, using musical cues and body language to show her trio what she wanted. "She was always supportive and appreciative of your contribution. And she was so spontaneous that she initiated spontaneity from her musicians," said Williams. She accomplished this by simply being herself. "By being who she was. In other words, she wasn't in a box, so you better not be in a box," Williams explained. "It's not something that you have to say to someone. It's the way you do things. So she was didactic in her excellence."

Vaughan excelled at creating these havens for her and her musicians, spaces where they could be vulnerable, stretch out, and innovate. She fostered a camaraderie and musical intimacy. In many respects, for Williams at least, she often assumed a maternal role, protecting and taking care of her musicians, all while making sure they had what they needed to thrive. After the gigs in Chicago, the trio embarked on a three-month tour of Europe.

They spent a week in France and a month at Tivoli Gardens in Copenhagen, where she and Quincy Jones produced *Sassy Swings the Tivoli,* her first new album for Mercury since leaving Roulette in 1963. Three weeks of one-nighters in England with the Count Basie band followed. While in London, Williams visited the famous Boosey & Hawkes instrument store and fell in love with a bass that he couldn't afford. He returned to the hotel and told Vaughan about the instrument. "Without hesitating, she said, 'Come to the room,' and she gave me the money," Williams recalled. "Our understanding was that I would repay her in installments deducted from my salary, but I don't remember ever seeing any deductions."[69]

Now, more than fifty years later, Williams still plays that bass. "Your relationship with her was not just 'Tonight I'm on a bandstand,'" Williams said. "She was my employer, and at the same time she was a mentor. . . . I don't know about anyone else's relationship with her, but it was very special to me." Most of the musicians who worked with Vaughan expressed similar sentiments. They felt a kinship with her, both musical and personal. They loved and respected her. She played a key, often transformational role in their professional lives. And she helped them in their personal lives. Fostering these relationships with her musicians came easily for her; it was intuitive and second nature, but she still struggled to find a similar kind of love, acceptance, respect, and generosity from the men in her personal life. She knew how to function as a musician, but she didn't know how to function in the role of wife, especially as defined in the 1950s and 1960s. The flashy, often macho men she chose as romantic partners struggled to find their place in her life too. Society dictated that they should be the "man of the house," but this was at odds with Vaughan's powerful personality, stubborn streak, and status as primary breadwinner, internationally famous artist, and genius.

More than two years after she separated from her second husband, C. B. Atkins, her divorce was still not finalized, and tensions between the estranged couple were escalating once again.

Vaughan learned that the IRS would seize their Englewood home on January 20, 1965, and then place it up for auction. In mid-December, before the IRS intervened, she returned to the home to collect her belongings. Atkins was at home, and another ugly confrontation ensued. This time, instead of resorting to violence, Atkins called the police. He insisted that Vaughan broke into his home, even though both her and his name appeared on the title, and took $5,600 in cash, clothing, and furniture. Atkins charged Vaughan with larceny. On December 18, she appeared before an Englewood magistrate, and he issued a summons requiring Vaughan to return to court on January 15 for a preliminary hearing. Just as their failed marriage was about to take another ugly turn, the couple called a truce. Atkins dropped the larceny charges, and they worked toward a divorce settlement.[70] Vaughan was finally free.

11

"The No. 1 Singer of a Decade Ago"

We are very fortunate to have many wonderful singers in America but only a few of these singers attract other singers. Sarah Vaughan is a singer's singer and a musician's singer," said Lady Bird Johnson as she introduced Vaughan in the East Room of the White House on Tuesday, January 12, 1965.[1] President and First Lady Johnson had invited Vaughan and her trio to play at a state dinner honoring the prime minister of Japan, Eisaku Sato. The dinner marked the conclusion of diplomatic talks between the two countries—a celebration of their goodwill and shared desire to improve the world through technology, research, scholarship, and the arts. That night, Vaughan represented the United States' cultural and artistic achievements.

It was her first performance at the White House, and it came during a stressful time in her personal life. She was in the final weeks of her messy, prolonged divorce from Atkins, and it was only days before her scheduled court appearance for his trumped-up burglary charges. Earlier in the day, she and her trio rehearsed. In the evening Vaughan attended the formal dinner, sitting patiently through the gift exchanges, toasts, and idle banter. After the meal, as the president and his guests made their way from the State Dining Room to the East Room, Vaughan excused herself. She changed from a beige lace gown into a beaded gold crepe purchased for the evening, walked to the East Room, and waited for the now-familiar praise of Lady Bird's introduction. She climbed the steps onto the small stage, positioned herself next to the famous Steinway grand piano with carvings of bald eagles on its legs, and sang the Japanese folksong "Sakura." It was a musical ode to cherry blossoms chosen by the first lady to commemorate Japan's generosity and gift of the now-iconic cherry blossoms to Washington, D.C., in 1912.

I knew that song perfectly when I sang it this afternoon but I must admit that tonight I goofed on a few words," she confessed.[2] Pianist Bob James remembered how nervous Vaughan was during both the rehearsal and the concert. "I knew her well enough, having done a lot of shows with her, to know when she was nervous and when she wasn't," he said. "She was quite nervous on that performance day." The enormity of the occasion aside, singing in the East Room was not like working a club or theater. It more closely resembled a living room. It was well lit, and the audience sat in chairs just feet away. Vaughan could see the president and first lady, prime minister, vice president, secretary of state, dozens of other influential politicians and dignitaries, and celebrities like Alfred Hitchcock. "If we were in a jazz club or wherever we would be around the world, in her world, she's totally comfortable and confident," explained James. It didn't matter if there were other jazz superstars, celebrities, or fans. "In this setting it was not a jazz environment, it was the upper social strata, [and] that, I know, contributed to her nervousness on that occasion."[3] Vaughan did, however, settle into her performance. After overcoming the hurdle of "Sakura," with its unfamiliar lyrics and unusual pentatonic scale, she sang six of her staples and, as she had fifteen years earlier at the supper club in

Miami Beach where she sang "The Lord's Prayer" a cappella, she concluded with a spiritual. As Vaughan sang "Sometimes I Feel Like a Motherless Child," she reminded her audience, full of some of the most powerful men in the world, not only of her range as a vocalist but also that her art was rooted in the aesthetics and practices of the black church, her experiences as a black American. This was black music in the White House.

After her set, Vaughan and her trio took pictures with the president, prime minister, and first lady and joined the party. "At one point in the evening, late after dinner, we saw this tall guy coming over to our table where Sarah and my trio were all seated." James continued, "The big tall guy was Lyndon Johnson coming over to ask Sarah to dance. Of course, Sarah was nervous and extremely excited and proceeded to go up on the dance floor with Lyndon Johnson." As James, who had just turned twenty-five, watched Vaughan dance, he realized he might not have an opportunity like this again, so he followed Vaughan's lead and mustered up the courage to ask Lady Bird to dance. "I had my moment, dancing with the first lady, and it was fantastic, which I will never forget."[4]

"When we were dancing afterward it was just one big happy family—everybody was cutting in on everybody else. Still, I don't think that I've ever been so nervous in my life," Vaughan told Down Beat's Bill Quinn in 1967. "When I danced with Mr. Johnson, I was so tense and stiff that he sort of shook me and asked me what the matter was. I explained that I was nervous and he said, 'Put your head on my shoulder and forget about it.' I just died."[5]

Then Vaughan disappeared. "I found her in this office, which had been turned over to her as a dressing room, and she was sobbing," recalled Bess Abell, President Johnson's White House social secretary. "And I said, 'Mrs. Vaughan, what's wrong? What can I do?' And she said, 'There's nothing wrong. This is the most wonderful day of my life. When I first came to Washington, I couldn't get a hotel room and tonight, I danced with the president.'"[6]

It was a moment of personal triumph and satisfaction. A reminder of how much she, a choir girl from Newark and a black woman born into a racist country, had endured. Being relegated to the balconies of Newark's segregated theaters as a girl. Instructed to look but not touch as her fellow musicians in the Hines band shopped for new uniforms in Philadelphia because blacks were not allowed to try on clothes before purchasing them. Enduring the sooty, terribly hot, and overcrowded Jim Crow car on trains as she toured with the Hines and Eckstine bands. Turned away from white hotels and restaurants and being forced instead to find accommodations on the other side of the tracks, in black communities. Pooling her money with fellow musicians to hire a cab between sets at the Copacabana because the club did not have dressing rooms for its black talent and forbade mingling with white guests. Being chased and beaten by an angry white gang after her shift at Café Society Downtown because they didn't want blacks in their neighborhood. And years later, even after she became a star, exiting through the kitchens of hotels in Miami Beach and Las Vegas because blacks were banned from staying there. She had endured all of this, and on the merits of her talent now found herself performing for a president and prime minister. It was a moment of validation and acknowledgment of her immense talent.

It was also a reminder of the larger social, political, and cultural changes happening in the country. Despite his Texas roots and the not-so-closeted racism in his personal life, President Johnson pursued the civil rights agenda set out by John F. Kennedy before his assassination. Applying the same charm he used to put Vaughan at ease, combined with a deft political savvy, Johnson persuaded reluctant southern conservatives to pass the Civil Rights Act. Signed into law on July 2, 1964, the bill outlawed discrimination based upon race, religion, nationality, and gender; curbed unfair voter registration practices; and ended racial segregation in schools and workplaces serving the general public. It was now illegal to deny service to black Americans in hotels, restaurants, theaters, and stores. Many of the slights and racial injustices experienced by Vaughan and her black contemporaries had been outlawed.

Yet the legacy of racism, its social customs, mind-sets, and institutions, persisted, and Vaughan still encountered prejudice every day. "I know that she was feeling it, the prejudice that was going on all around her," said James. And it must have taken its toll. Because she was black, she was not afforded the same opportunities as her white counterparts, despite her tremendous talent. Had she been white, she likely would have had radio and television shows that she then parlayed into a movie career, just like Frank Sinatra, Bing Crosby, Doris Day, and Rosemary Clooney had done. Given the range, quality, and power of her voice, she could have been an opera singer, but because she was black and poor, without a wealthy benefactor, this path was off-limits too. "I know she had a big love for classical music and legitimacy, what the legitimacy of being an opera singer would have meant," said James. "She knew that she had the instrument vocally to be able to do it, and occasionally she would use it in a way that almost was saying that 'I could do that if I wanted to, just change the repertoire from Gershwin to Verdi and it'd be okay.' So that desire to be legitimate, to be appreciated for the depth of her talent was very deep in her. She lived in a social era in which that kind of recognition was not always there." In the 1940s, 1950s, and 1960s, jazz and other forms of black creative expression simply were not respected in the same way as classical music, the ultimate highbrow music. Black music was undervalued and marginalized, especially when practiced by a black artist. "There was a lot of prejudice around in our field," James reiterated, concluding, "I can only speak to the purity of her passion for music and how it just resonated every time she performed."[7]

Although Vaughan had gained the admiration of world leaders and become a symbol of American cultural and artistic achievement, she still had to fight to be respected by her record labels, both in and out of the studio. By the spring of 1963, she had lost patience with Roulette Records. During her three years at the label, Vaughan recorded thirteen full-length albums, including the classics *After Hours* and *Sarah + 2,* not to mention multiple collaborations with Count Basie. Her single "Serenata" spent six weeks at the bottom of *Billboard*'s Top 100 chart in 1960, and she released another thirty-three singles, enough to fill three albums. But Vaughan had barely seen any royalties for her efforts, and once again she felt exploited. It had become common knowledge that Morris Levy and Roulette had mob affiliations, and in 1986 he was indicted on three counts of racketeering and extortion. He had been working under Vincent Gigante and the Genovese crime family since before 1963.[8]

Vaughan turned to her friend the trumpeter, bandleader, arranger, and now producer Quincy Jones. He was nine years Vaughan's junior, and in their early collaborations, Vaughan took Jones under her wing and mentored him. They first worked together in 1958 on *Vaughan and Violins* for Mercury, then again in 1962 on *You're Mine You* for Roulette.[9] In 1961 Jones became a vice president of A&R at Mercury Records, the first African American executive at a major label. And during the spring and summer of 1963, he facilitated Vaughan's departure from Roulette and return, later that summer, to Mercury.

"I could record anything I wanted to," said Vaughan while discussing the early years following her return to Mercury in 1963 with *Down Beat*'s Quinn.[10] Jones was her producer, and with his bebop roots, he not only understood how Vaughan worked and what she needed to thrive creatively; he also respected her as a musician. "She's a very sensitive chick," he explained in a 1965 installment of "The Quincy Jones Column," distributed by the Associated Negro Press. She absorbed everything in her sonic environment—the bustle of the audience, studio technicians, musicians, and ambient noises like the hum of a light or birdsongs, not to mention every detail of a song: its lyrics, harmonic language, and arrangement. "She thinks just like a violin: if everything isn't smooth from base line to harmonies (she can check them all simultaneously) it's impossible for her to tune out and concentrate on the sound that's made her one of the greatest female vocalists in the world," Jones continued. "She's got to be free from any diversions; be free to just sing, to get that certain sound of hers."[11]

"If I put her in the studio with a good song and a great arrangement, then Sarah is really free," explained Jones in another essay. "And that's what she likes. I've said that Sarah responds to arrangements. She's a very sensitive creature. Some singers have their thing and just blast ahead regardless of what's going on around them. But not Sarah. She uses her voice the way a great jazz musician plays his instrument. I'll tell you, a chick like Sarah makes it all worthwhile. She takes all the pain out of the business, makes up for the dues you've paid. The session will be a ball."[12]

After their first outing, *Sassy Swings the Tivoli,* recorded live during her appearances at Tivoli Gardens in Copenhagen in July 1963, Jones and Vaughan prepared for their first studio sessions together since 1958. Jones paired her with Robert Farnon, whom he considered "one of the greatest string arrangers to ever live."[13] Farnon had been writing for the sixteen-voice Svend Saaby Choir in Copenhagen and suggested including them on the album, which would become known as *Vaughan and Voices.* "That was one of my favorite albums that I've made," Vaughan said to Les Tomkins more than a decade later, in 1977. The combination of strings and orchestra created a rich sonic palette over which Vaughan mixed and blended her voice, not to mention an almost operatic sense of high drama. "Oh, I love [Robert Farnon]," she said.[14] The album *Sarah Vaughan Sings the Mancini Songbook,* a collection of songs by the still relatively unknown Henri Mancini, and *¡Viva! Vaughan,* their take on the bossa nova craze, both followed in 1964. Vaughan's and Jones's recordings together, even their commercial singles, were well produced and well sung, a testament to the artistic integrity of Vaughan and Jones. But they didn't sell.

"There were two guys on the Mercury A&R staff that were real musicians, Hal Mooney and myself," Jones explained. "And we always got jeered at because we were making records like Julius Watkins with eight French horns [*French Horns for My Lady*], and Robert Farnon with Sarah Vaughan. We'd sell, like, 1100 records. We really had to take a lot of shit at those A&R meetings." His colleagues, working with hit makers like Roger Miller, Ray Stevens, and the Angels, accused Jones and Mooney of being "budget busters." In the span of a decade, Vaughan, once a key player in Mercury's commercial success and the prestige of their jazz label, was now a budget buster. The music industry was shifting, and jazz musicians and balladeers like Vaughan were increasingly out of sync with the new youth-oriented market. "So it was a challenge to keep the people that I loved; I saw that I had to generate some sales in some other place so we could keep the Sarah Vaughan thing going. And the first one we did with Lesley Gore did it." "It's My Party" made the sixteen-year-old Gore an overnight pop sensation in 1963.[15]

In early 1965, however, Jones shifted focus and moved to Hollywood to write film scores. "After Quincy Jones left, there was nothing," Vaughan lamented to *Down Beat*'s Bill Quinn while describing the final two years of her Mercury contract.[16] With her strongest advocate and musical kindred spirit gone, she was once again subject to the whims of producers obsessed with the bottom line. They abandoned the sophistication of Vaughan singing jazz or serious pop with classical, often operatic inflections in favor of commercial, middlebrow pop. The results were dreadful. Her next two albums, *Pop Artistry* from 1965 and *The New Scene* a year later, rehashed Top 40 material popularized by others. Her cover of "A Lover's Concerto," a schmaltzy ballad based on Bach's Minuet in G, made a brief appearance on the *Billboard* charts during the spring of 1966; otherwise, the new material fell flat. And Vaughan, once a trendsetter, now chased fads. "There was a lot of commercial pressure from the management and from the record label for her to do more pop stuff," explained pianist James. "I even remember vaguely some of the range of stuff we brought in and the material that she was being asked to do that she wasn't really all too enthusiastic about, sometimes very unenthusiastic about it."[17] The sessions were reminiscent of her struggles with producer Mitch Miller fifteen years earlier.

Vaughan had gained a reputation as an artist who could save bad songs from oblivion and salvage subpar, often overwrought arrangements. Guided by her exceptional instincts, musical knowledge, and phenomenal instrument, she infused songs with her wry sense of humor, carefully selecting notes as she reworked cumbersome melodies or improvised new ones, and, of course, added her trademark vocal swoops, slides, and inflections. While Jones respected and facilitated Vaughan's musicality and creative flights of fancy, his successors did not. They viewed her need to explore and embellish as a "problem" rather than an opportunity. One A&R man "solved the Sarah Vaughan problem" by giving her unfamiliar material, usually the day of the session so that she didn't have time to rehearse (even when she asked for lead sheets in advance), then rushing to get his final take before she had a chance to explore. It was a deliberate move to stifle her creativity, to limit and contain her, and, once again, to exploit her for financial gain. Critic Martin Williams, a fierce advocate of Vaughan, decried it as "an appalling denigration of a great talent and potential."[18]

During her final pop sessions for Mercury, Vaughan did sing straight, for the most part, but the results were uninspired, lacking the usual polish Vaughan, a perfectionist, demanded of herself. And they were still highly stylized, often mannered, covers of the day's mediocre pop hits. She sounded more and more like her imitators and was at risk of becoming a parody of her former self. "I might suggest that if she keeps up this kind of inhibited and stylized performing much longer, her voice may be gone and she won't be able to sound like anyone except her imitators," Williams advised in 1968.[19]

And Williams was in awe of Vaughan's voice. "Her voice has range, body, volume. More important, her control of her voice is phenomenal. Her pitch is just about impeccable, and she can jump the most difficult intervals and land true. No other singer has such an effortless command of dynamics," he gushed in 1967, twenty-five years after Vaughan ventured onto the Apollo's stage for amateur night. "For Sarah Vaughan is in several respects the jazz singer par excellence, and therefore she can do things with her voice that a [classically] trained singer knows simply must not be done. She can take a note at the top of her range and then bend it or squeeze it; she growls and rattles notes down at the bottom of her range; she can glide her voice through several notes at midrange while raising dynamics, or lowering, or simply squeezing." For Williams, Vaughan had "one of the most remarkable voices that any of our popular singers has ever possessed," unrivaled even by her contemporaries on the opera and concert stages.[20]

Yet the popular music of the day, the Top 40 hits favored by Mercury and other record labels, simply could not hold up to the force of Vaughan's voice, talent, or creative ambitions. Unlike the tunes of the newly christened American songbook composed in the 1920s, 1930s, and 1940s by Tin Pan Alley composers and canonized by Ella Fitzgerald's landmark, and very popular, series of songbook albums produced by Norman Granz for Verve, most pop songs of the 1960s and into the 1970s and 1980s lacked the harmonic sophistication, rhythmic nuance, or lyrical wit to accommodate Vaughan. They could not support her spontaneous improvisations and creative flights of fancy or her need to explore and test the limits of her voice. Contemporary songs could not bear the weight of Vaughan's creative vision, nor could they contain her. Even when thwarted by unsupportive record producers, she worked to defy expectations and transcend musical boundaries. And time and again she burst through, venturing far out onto the creative precipice.

"I dare say that what Sarah Vaughan needs from an A&R man is the chance to record material with which she is familiar enough so that she can go just as far out as she wants and use all of the remarkable vocal resources she has," Williams wrote in a 1968 appeal to the music industry. He continued, asserting that Vaughan also needed to be challenged and stimulated by a wide variety of accompaniments, ranging from the intimacy of her trio to the grandeur of a full-scale orchestra. She needed a composer not only familiar with her voice, comedic wit, and dramatic flair, but one who also possessed "the boldness to break through the conventions of popular song and even blues form for her." Williams believed that Vaughan's talent called for a secular oratorio or opera composed specifically for her. And under these circumstances, she would shine, revealing a creativity and skill previously unheard. "But in any case," he concluded, "the last thing in the world Sarah Vaughan needs is another would be 'hit record' which shows a tenth of her talent."[21]

No A&R men rose to Williams's challenge. Mercury did not renew Vaughan's contract when it expired in the spring of 1967, and for the first time since 1946 Vaughan was without a record contract. Without a steady stream of new releases to keep her in the public imagination, her career was at risk. But Vaughan was not the only jazz musician struggling. In 1966, Ella Fitzgerald's contract with MGM, who acquired Verve in 1960, expired, and in 1967 Norman Granz retired, leaving her without a manager and like-minded producer. She was soon picked up by other labels, but the results were mixed at best. She sang gospel, country music, religious Christmas songs, and, like Vaughan, covers of mediocre contemporary hits. Vaughan's old compatriots Billy Eckstine, Earl Hines, Count Basie, and Dizzy Gillespie all struggled too.

"I was, as far as I'm concerned, associated with a terrible record company. All we did was make records—I mean that the company didn't get behind my records and push—there was no promotion," she told Quinn in July 1967, six months after her final session at Mercury. Vaughan understood the power of promotion and knew that if a record company really wanted a hit, they could get one if they spent the money. And unlike 1954 and 1955, when Mercury put the full force of the label behind her to launch EmArcy and make her a pop star with the hits "Make Yourself Comfortable" and "Whatever Lola Wants," and 1959, when she broke through again with "Broken-Hearted Melody," by 1967 Vaughan was no longer a priority. "I'm happy to say that I'm no longer with them—I'm free," she said, and when asked what she planned to do next, she simply replied, "Sing."[22]

When Preach' came to me, I was in a bad situation," Vaughan reflected during the same interview with Bill Quinn in 1967, almost five years after escaping from the abuses of C. B. Atkins. "My second husband had been my manager for some time—I think he was managing himself, not me—and I owed a lot of taxes and other bills. Preach' took over, and now I don't owe Uncle Sam a dime." Clyde Golden, a friend of Wells's who soon joined the couple's inner circle, speculated that Vaughan was $150,000 in debt when she and Wells met in 1962. "Preacher put her back on her feet financially," said Golden. "I could be in the poor house right now," Vaughan confessed. "But, thanks to Preach', I don't have to worry about people wanting money under the table for this and that. I can sing better now because I have no problems; I'm free, single, and 21—and it's a damn good feeling."[23]

Vaughan, as she always did, remained loyal and publicly praised Wells, giving him her unconditional endorsement, as she had with both Treadwell and Atkins before him. Yet unlike Treadwell and Atkins, Vaughan never publicly referred to Wells as her romantic partner. During their years together, she recast her personal story, replacing the sensationalism and domestic fairy tales of the 1940s, 1950s, and early 1960s with stories of her professional accomplishments. On the rare occasions that Vaughan did discuss her personal life, she focused on her role as a mother and daughter. In public, Wells remained her manager, working diligently behind the scenes. "If anything ever happened to Preach', I think that I'd just leave the business," she said in 1967. "I'm sure I couldn't replace him."[24]

Vaughan's musicians saw things differently. They viewed Wells as a nuisance to be tolerated, someone they had to put up with because he controlled the money and paid their salaries. Bassist Buster Williams joined the band in July 1963, when Vaughan's relationship with Wells was still new. He quickly saw that Wells was an opportunist. "He was from Newark and he was street-smart. Sometimes you would call somebody like that a hustler,"

Williams explained. "He always had beautiful clothes, and I never felt that he had Sarah Vaughan's interest uppermost in his heart. I always felt that it was more about his interest."[25] He used his status as Vaughan's manager for financial gain, but also to bolster his personal status and importance. "When Sarah was working, he would talk about himself," said bassist Herb Mickman, who joined the trio in 1965, a year after Williams left to play for vocalist Nancy Wilson. "He'd say, 'We're going to Las Vegas, I'm going to be in Las Vegas.' He never said 'Sarah's going to be there.' In other words, that's how he talked all the time. Like it was his [accomplishment]. And he was just the manager and the lover. He wasn't on the stage or anything."[26]

"[Preacher] carried a gun, and he was very good about the money. He got the money on every job," said Mickman. Wells wore his gun in a holster, under his jacket. "We'd work a club, and we did maybe two nights and he'd come in the office where the manager of the club was, and he had his jacket open so you could see his gun and he'd say, 'I need some money for the two nights.'" The threat of violence was understood. Vaughan had been burned in the past, and Wells made sure it didn't happen again.[27]

Guns, and the violence they represented, had been a constant since her days with the Hines and Eckstine bands. Back then, many musicians carried guns to protect themselves from the physical threats of racism, especially while touring the South. Vaughan described the Eckstine band, in particular, as being very rough and rowdy. And Eckstine, who considered Vaughan a little sister, said that he would "whip her ass" when she stepped out of line.[28] Now, more than twenty years later, this tough-guy mentality still permeated the business. It's likely that the roughness and volatility Wells displayed in clubs seeped into his dealings with Vaughan offstage and behind closed doors. "I was naive and I personally didn't have any bad experiences that left me with extreme bitterness, and I shied away from getting involved in any of the worst of that stuff which I realized later was probably going on the whole time," said pianist James. "He was beating up on us," James explained, referring to the low salaries set by Wells. "Naturally I'm sure he did hit her too. He was a tough guy."[29] Buster Williams agreed. "She always picked the wrong men and they beat her, they cheated her and they demeaned her. It was really, really, really sickening to see. I saw some of that. And it's infamous," he said. "But this was her man, and I sure had nothing to do with it. And I'll tell you this: he always gave me what I needed."[30]

"I knew both sides of him. [Wells] had his good qualities, he was a jovial guy," James continued. "At best, [I had] mixed feelings about him in terms of the quality of his management for her. It was fairly well known to us that he had to have been taking advantage of her and had control over her money and a lot of stuff that he shouldn't have had control over and took advantage of it." His sphere of influence extended to her recording sessions with Mercury. "I think Preacher was also very involved in the decisions that were made on her behalf with recording," he explained. "I remember him . . . not really knowing what he was talking about. Having way too much influence without an understanding of the music but trying to make a buck."[31] Conductor and arranger Lalo Schifrin agreed. In June 1963, eight months after Vaughan and Wells met, Schifrin and Vaughan worked together on her final album for Roulette, *Sweet N' Sassy.* Preacher Wells attended the sessions and acted as Vaughan's go-between. "He was coming with messages the next day, like, 'The arrangement you've done for "More Than You Know," Lalo, is outrageous!' That meant, out of this world," Schifrin explained. "I don't think he knew too much about music. So this had to come from Sarah."[32]

"We were underpaid," said James, laughing. For him, and the other musicians in the trio, this was the clearest indication that things were not aboveboard. "He was taking a lot of money off the top, trying to pay the musicians as little as possible," explained Mickman. "Out of the money he paid me, which was $225 a week, I had to pay my motel bill." The musicians also had to pay for food. Mickman joined the trio in 1965, when he was twenty-five years old, and stayed for three years. He negotiated small raises along the way but still struggled to make ends meet. After pianist James left, Mickman became the group's musical director and assumed a new set of time-consuming responsibilities, for which he didn't receive extra pay. "I made $350 at the end, and that was terrible money," said Mickman. "There were acts in Las Vegas where the sidemen were getting more than that."

Yet Mickman and the other musicians, especially the younger ones, stayed because they were happy to have a steady job and more importantly because the music making was unparalleled. "Sarah was a genius singer," Mickman explained. "It was an absolute thrill for me musically." In 1955, when Mickman was fifteen, he fell in love with jazz, and posters of jazz musicians, including glamour shots of Vaughan, plastered the walls of his childhood bedroom. Now he was working with one of his idols. Through her exploration, her insistence on stretching her boundaries, she opened up his musical horizons, showing him new ways to interpret the standards night after night. "Sarah would change a note in a song, not every night the same one, but it would be such a great note," he said. "Every once in a while she'd change a note, and it would be such a great note I would make a note I'm standing right behind her—of what the lyric was in the song when she sang that note, and as soon as the set would end, I would put down my bass and go over to [the] piano and try to find that note with that chord, because it was so good."[33]

"She wasn't trying to be anybody else," James explained. "She was her own person in sound, in style, in approach. The closer that we could get her to feeling comfortable with that, where she felt relaxed and felt like she could stretch out and do everything she was capable of doing, then we'd just have these amazing moments where the combination of her sound and her music artistry and the sophistication and the subtlety was beyond anything I've experienced since." He left the band in 1968. After four years as her pianist and musical director, his apprenticeship had ended, and he was ready to do more studio work and begin building his own career as a solo artist. "I just loved the fact that I had the chance to work with an artist of that stature," he concluded.

"It's a highlight of my career. I talk about it all the time; I'm very proud of it."[34]

Mickman's departure from the band was more contentious. "I had problems at the end of the job. I didn't get paid, and this Preacher guy took taxes out of my checks and never turned it in to the government," Mickman said. "He was a pretty nasty guy, and they owed me $1,200 at the end and nobody could find him." Mickman approached Vaughan over and over, trying to get paid. "He'll pay you," Vaughan told Mickman, but Wells had disappeared. "Eventually I had to get someone to give her a summons to come at the court and pay me." The entire process took over a year and soured his memories of working with Vaughan. "I didn't listen to her records for a couple of years, and then I started buying them again. Because I just love her singing," Mickman said. "She just didn't handle money, she didn't want to know about contracts or anything. She just wanted to be, just to be music."[35]

By December 1968, Vaughan's relationship with Wells had cooled. In April 1969, she filed a suit in New York Federal Court for a summary judgment against Wells and their management firm, Vaughan Wells Corporation. She asked for $847,000 in damages. She claimed that as her manager he collected $942,040 in earnings on her behalf but only remitted $26,000 to her, pocketing the rest. His commission should have been 10 percent.[36]

It was another contentious end to a partnership mixing romance and business, her third since she married Treadwell in 1946, twenty-two years earlier. It was the third time Vaughan had been blind to the financial misconduct of her managers, and the third time in her career she found herself in dire straits financially. And it wouldn't be the last time she installed a love interest as her manager with mixed results. Lifelong friend and vocalist Billy Eckstine referred to her husband-managers as "damagers," calling attention to the financial, emotional, and physical harm they inflicted on her, not to mention their lack of professional experience or connections in the music industry, requirements for effectively advancing her career. Indeed, Vaughan's insistence on mixing her business and personal interests was one of her biggest blind spots, her Achilles' heel, and most agree that it harmed both her and her career.

Yet Vaughan could not imagine living her life any other way. Music was not just her occupation; it was her life, inextricably intertwined with everything she did. It defined who she was at her very core, and perhaps she struggled to separate her personal and professional identities. Her desire that the man in her life be involved with her music making and her habit of making him her manager too, were merely symptoms of this. Her harshest critics attributed this pattern to a deeper insecurity, asserting that she was a lonely woman in search of constant validation. She needed to be in love and to have a man by her side. Some of her musicians and friends speculated that this behavior stemmed from her uneasy relationship with her father. He was stern and disapproving, so Vaughan sought acceptance elsewhere. Yet others were more generous. "She was like all women, looking for someone to love and to be in her corner, with a closeness, an understanding, and a sharing," said friend Aretha Landrum.[37]

"She wanted her men involved in her life," vocalist Joe Williams explained.[38]

> She knew business but needed someone to take the burden off. She was perfectly able to plan the presentation, the work itself, but she needed someone to deal with promotion and the public. Somebody who would do her the favor of taking the constantly ringing phone out of her ear. Sarah needed someone she could trust—a husband, a lover, a best friend. Someone who was understanding and could alleviate the daily chores. She wanted her man to be involved in her life, and music was her life. If you are close to someone, you are involved in all aspects of that person's life. She needed someone around all the time which is why a manager, with a life of his own, married to someone else, did not work out.[39]

"It's very hard for a woman on her own on the road. You're making a lot of money, and you're a woman with a certain kind of power. There are always guys [who want to use you]. That's their identity," said vocalist Annie Ross of the famed trio Lambert, Hendricks and Ross.[40] "And Sassy was peculiarly trusting, when she first met someone. Her naiveté was part of her charm."[41] Ross circulated in the same circles and knew what life was like for a woman in the industry. She remembers men surrounding her and Vaughan at the bars and after-hours clubs they frequented after work. "There was no shortage of people wanting to take us out," she said.[42] They would flatter the vocalists and buy them drinks. "Men could just wrap her around their finger if they showed attention to her. I'm sure all that stuff, she couldn't resist it," explained bassist Bob Magnusson, who worked for Vaughan during the 1970s, adding, "Everybody wants to be loved. Of course she was loved by [the] multitudes of the world. You want that personal care and love."[43] And given Vaughan's brutal touring schedule, she had few opportunities to meet men not associated with the entertainment industry, outside of the bars and clubs where she worked and socialized. It was the same world that members of her church back in Newark referred to as the "sportin' life," filled with gamblers, gangsters, and hustlers. Men known for being rough, bending the rules, and displaying their own brand of hypermasculinity. But Vaughan was attracted to these men. She was drawn to well-dressed, handsome men, macho men with bravado and style. Men likely to be more invested in the same gender roles that she flouted. She also needed men who could leave their lives to follow her on the road. "They were available. And for the most part they could be charming," said Ross of Vaughan's choices in men, explaining, "You don't have a lot of time to look around [for men] when you're on the road."[44]

By elevating the men in her life to the position of manager, Vaughan formalized their role, giving them more standing and legitimacy, not to mention gainful employment. Combining the role of husband or boyfriend and manager, however, also allowed Vaughan to realize her ideal vision for marriage, an ideal where husband and wife seamlessly blended their professional and personal lives in the pursuit of a common goal: making music. They were equal partners in life, love, business, and music. It was a difficult ideal to achieve. And the emphasis on equality was ahead of its time, a decidedly modern, some might say twenty-first-century, approach to marriage and gender equality. Although comfortable being "one of the guys," Vaughan was a woman, and she enjoyed being a woman. But she also expected the same privileges and considerations granted men. Music, in particular jazz, allowed this. On the basis of her profound talent, she navigated the sexism endemic to the jazz world, earned the respect of her male colleagues, and soon emerged as a leader and standard-bearer. But society as a whole still did not encourage this. Her roles as a musician and ambitious professional woman were still incompatible with society's more general expectations of wives, mothers, and women, both black and white.

There was another dynamic at play in Vaughan's choice of managers, beyond her desire to be a manager's sole focus or her vision of an ideal partnership that seamlessly melded the professional and personal. Her circle of contemporaries knew that, in order to truly succeed, a black artist needed a white manager. Louis Armstrong partnered with Joe Glaser for almost thirty-five years, until Glaser's death in 1969. Nat King Cole's work with Carlos Gastel kept him on the top of the pop charts for almost three decades. Norman Granz revived the careers of Duke Ellington and Ella Fitzgerald, transforming both into international superstars. Not only were there virtually no black managers working in the 1930s, 1940s, and 1950s, but white managers held the keys to access and power in the music industry. In 1980, vocalist Lena Horne confessed that her 1947 marriage to Lennie Hayton, then the musical director at MGM, was motivated more by her desire to advance her career than love. "I callously realized that I would have to associate with a White person to get the thing I wanted professionally," she explained in *Ebony* magazine.[45]

White managers and producers offered to represent Vaughan, but she viewed them all with a deep skepticism and ambivalence. In 1946, she rebuffed John Hammond's offer to make her the next Bessie Smith. In 1951, after Vaughan and Nat King Cole worked the Biggest Tour of '51 together, Carlos Gastel, who helped Cole become the most popular black vocalist in the country, offered Treadwell $100,000 for Vaughan's contract (even though the couple never formalized their business partnership with one). Treadwell refused, believing that he could profit more financially if he continued to manage his wife himself. And in 1958, during the World's Fair in Brussels, George Wein suggested a partnership with Vaughan, but she declined his offer too. Within weeks, Vaughan married C. B. Atkins.

"She didn't want a business manager, she wanted someone to take care of her personally," said Wein. Perhaps she believed that having her husband as her manager allowed her more control of her career. She thought that a personal, romantic relationship offered her more leverage. Some might say that conflating the roles of husband or boyfriend and manager suggests that Vaughan had no real interest in being managed at all. She did not like being told what to do, and she bristled at authority, likely more so when it involved a white man in power. "She was comfortable with somebody that was from the same street she was," explained Wein. "And if she'd had a white manager, she would have—she maybe could not have acted the way she wanted to."[46] It was a veiled reference to Vaughan's drinking and drug use, her partying, which many deemed excessive and a symptom of a greater lack of discipline. Vaughan understood the complex dynamics between white men and black women and was unwilling to sacrifice her autonomy to a white man. Maybe at this point in her career, she simply preferred having black managers and wanted to keep the Sarah Vaughan enterprise within the black community (although, she would have white managers in the 1970s and 1980s). Or perhaps, as Wein suggested, she simply felt more at ease with people with a similar background and lifestyle to hers. People who shared her working-class roots, familiarity with the

nightclub scene, and down-to-earth sensibilities, without the
pretensions of the upper crust or establishment. She surrounded
herself with these people, even though they lacked experience
in management or the music industry. And it's possible that she
simply did not realize what good management, by someone with
a larger vision and far-reaching contacts within the industry,
could do for her career.

Regardless of the motivations behind Vaughan's choices in
managers, by 1967 her career was foundering. That summer, the
Baltimore Afro-American profiled the top-earning black female
vocalists, and Vaughan was no longer in the top tier. Led by Ella
Fitzgerald, the "in crowd" included Pearl Bailey, Diahann Carrol, and Nancy Wilson. They regularly commanded $20,000 to
$35,000 a week at the country's leading clubs and lounges. In
contrast, the "with it" but not "in" vocalists—the second tier,
where Vaughan resided—earned as little as $3,500 for a week
in the same venues and rarely exceeded $10,000. Television ap-
pearances were more lucrative, netting the "big four" $2,000
to $15,000 for a single short performance. Vocalist and actress
Barbara McNair, a relative newcomer, recently received $7,000
for a television stint. "There was a time when 'Sassy' Vaughan
could command that much and more," the *Afro-American*'s
Sam Lacy wrote. "But Sarah, possibly boasting the best voice of
the lot, has suffered a sagging appeal in recent years, no doubt
due to managerial problems."[47] Two years later, while reporting Vaughan's split with Wells and subsequent lawsuit, the *Afro-
American* declared Vaughan "the No. 1 singer of a decade ago."[48]
She had no recording contract, the music industry was shifting
beneath her feet, and she did not have a manager to navigate
these new, choppy waters. Her career was not only in decline
but in jeopardy.

12

"I'm Not a Jazz Singer. I'm a Singer"

In August 1970, Vaughan opened at PJ's on Santa Monica Boulevard in Los Angeles. She seemed uncomfortable and uptight as she began her usual set. The club was unbearably hot, with harsh, unflattering lighting. The sound system didn't work, and, adding insult to injury, it was a sparse crowd. Vaughan did her best to work the room. While singing "Lover Man" she joked about the heat, replacing the opening lyric "I don't know why, but I'm feeling so sad" with "I don't know why, but I'm feeling so hot." The joke fell flat. When the substandard PA system became more than she could bear, she dropped her mic onto the floor and pretended to stomp on it. And she tolerated the chatter of patrons, clinking of glasses, and the clang of the off-key cash register until a waitress walked in front of the stage, mid-song, to serve drinks. Vaughan stopped singing, looked around, and reassessed. She sat down, dangled her legs over the bandstand, and asked for requests. An exquisite reading of "Tenderly" followed.

During the 1960s, PJ's had been a fashionable jazz club frequented by celebrities. By 1970, it was in transition, shedding its jazz roots in favor of a more youthful rock 'n' roll format. As the 1970s progressed, the club, now renamed the Stanwood, would become an incubator for Los Angeles's burgeoning rock scene and a proving ground for bands like Van Halen and Mötley Crüe. That night, however, Vaughan opened for a five-piece Filipino rock band called the Jade.

It was a difficult evening for critic and longtime Vaughan advocate Leonard Feather to watch. "Miss Vaughan still owns the most sumptuous voice ever to emanate from a female larynx," he wrote in his review for *Melody Maker*. For him, her reception at PJ's was an affront to both Vaughan and jazz fans.[1] But it was a sign of the times. The music industry was changing, and despite the protestations of critics and its biggest fans, jazz continued to lose ground as its popularity waned. In the mid-1950s when rock 'n' roll first emerged on the scene, most in the industry did not take it seriously. The songs of Elvis Presley, Chuck Berry, and Little Richard were considered frivolous rubbish that appealed to teenagers. Jazz, on the other hand, was thoughtful, adult music, and few doubted its superiority or its future. But during the 1960s rock 'n' roll overpowered the industry. The Beatles and the Rolling Stones burst on the scene in 1964 during the so-called British invasion. Artists like guitarist Jimi Hendrix infused rock with brilliant virtuosic improvisations previously found only in jazz. Bob Dylan went electric in 1965, modernizing the tough, often moralizing folk music aesthetic. And Dylan, John Lennon, Paul McCartney, and many of their contemporaries were skilled songwriters who captured the social, political, and cultural ethos of the 1960s—one defined by a youth culture with an antiestablishment and counterculture bent. During the 1960s rock matured, becoming a more sophisticated, adventurous, and serious form of creative expression. While it still appealed primarily to young audiences, rock began to interest more and more adults.[2] Critics began taking rock 'n' roll more seriously too.

"The Beatles were just part of what changed jazz in the sixties. Pop-rock, in general, soaked up so much of the cultural atmosphere that it changed everything," explained producer Jack

Tracy. He produced Sarah Vaughan, Dinah Washington, and other jazz artists while working at Mercury in the late 1950s and early 1960s. "Radio stations changed their formats from a mix of different types of music to just rock. But chasing after hot singles was perilous. When Chubby Checker's 'Twist' hit in 1960, record companies spent millions of dollars trying to find artists to record it. But by the time those records came out, the Twist was already passé." As record companies devoted their substantial promotion budgets to searching for the next rock hit, there was, of course, little money left for producing and promoting other talent, including jazz musicians, and Vaughan experienced this firsthand during her final years at Mercury. Labels reassigned their most skilled jazz producers to their rock division, where most floundered, and paired their rock producers with jazz artists, in an attempt to revitalize sales. Over time, there were fewer and fewer producers who specialized in and understood jazz. "I think jazz lost its market when it lost the support of radio," Tracy continued. "Before the Beatles, we had no problems getting jazz played on stations. Not the far-out stuff by artists like Ornette Coleman, of course, but Gerry Mulligan, Quincy Jones, and Dave Brubeck. The Beatles' arrival was a huge game changer. By the mid-sixties, it was almost mandatory for jazz artists to record Beatles songs. But most of their efforts were hopeless."[3]

Count Basie released *Basie's Beatle Bag* in 1966. Ella Fitzgerald recorded contemporary pop and incorporated the latest hits into her live sets. And during her post–Quincy Jones sessions at Mercury, Vaughan recorded *Pop Artistry of Sarah Vaughan* and *The New Scene*; both included covers of Beatles songs and other pop-rock hits, all in a desperate attempt to remain current, to chase the latest fads. But the performances too often fell flat and did not satisfy, not because artists executed the material poorly but because their interpretations seemed irrelevant and out of place. The industry had shifted its focus to the emerging singer-songwriter model. Tunes became indelibly linked to a single artist, and rock musicians didn't need an outsider to cover their songs, to create new interpretations that added nuance and depth, one of the core principles of jazz. They had already created their own singular, iconic performances, defined not only by their signature sound, but also by their image and brand. In response, many jazz musicians tried to modernize their images. Dizzy Gillespie grew sideburns, and Vaughan experimented with short skirts and go-go boots in 1969 while touring Europe. But by now Vaughan and her bebop contemporaries were now in their forties and fifties. Swing icon Duke Ellington was approaching seventy, as was Louis Armstrong, considered by many the father of jazz. After decades of perfecting their craft, of changing the course of American music, none of them were particularly hip or cool anymore.[4]

And jazz itself was rapidly changing as new, competing factions emerged and coexisted, all struggling to find viable audiences in a shrinking cultural space. The modernist beboppers of the 1940s inspired a cohort of hard bop musicians in the mid-1950s. Miles Davis, Horace Silver, Art Blakey, Sonny Rollins, Nina Simone, and others extended the language of bebop by reincorporating elements of blues, gospel, and rhythm and blues into their music. In the late 1950s and into the 1960s, Miles Davis and John Coltrane introduced modal jazz, which used musical modes—alternative, often unusual-sounding scales—to create their harmonic frameworks rather than more typical chord progressions. At the same time, Ornette Coleman and Cecil Taylor, later joined by Coltrane, verged toward the avant-garde with free jazz, a style that abandoned fixed harmonic and rhythmic foundations in favor of collective free improvisation. And in 1967, Coltrane, who had emerged as the popular and charismatic face of jazz's avant-garde movement, died at the age of forty. As the 1960s came to a close, jazz was not only in decline; it was in crisis.[5]

A younger generation of jazz musicians, those born in the 1940s, some fifteen to twenty years after Vaughan, however, searched for ways to maintain jazz's core values while making it more commercially viable. These musicians, who came of age at the same time as rock 'n' roll, formed bands that more closely resembled rock bands. Electric basses, guitars, and keyboards replaced their acoustic counterparts, and these new bands focused on a collective sound rather than the loose spontaneous interactions between soloists and a rhythm section that defined modern, bebop-based jazz combos. They moved away from swing, a lilting pattern of eighth notes, in favor of a backbeat, steady, pounding, very danceable eighth notes in straight time, like rock 'n' roll. While older jazz musicians struggled to keep up with advances in recording technology that defined so many new rock 'n' roll releases, preferring instead a more transparent approach to studio recording, younger jazz musicians embraced recording technology and electronic music. But instead of drawing inspiration solely from rock 'n' roll, they turned to the chromaticism and layered, independent rhythmic lines of funk and soul. These elements added a harmonic complexity and rhythmic sophistication not found in rock 'n' roll while creating a robust foundation for improvisation. Veteran Miles Davis reinvented his sound again and released the groundbreaking, and first commercially successful, fusion album *Bitches Brew*. Alumni of his band, which included the likes of Wayne Shorter, Joe Zawinul, Chick Corea, and John McLaughlin, developed the idiom further, founding their own bands and achieving crossover successes throughout the 1970s. The new music was called jazz rock, then jazz fusion, and eventually simply fusion.[6]

Though Vaughan did not reinvent herself or embrace electronic music, she did mentor the next generation of jazz musicians, several of whom became major voices in these new, more commercial styles. She nurtured them along, showing them the ropes and encouraging their musical exploration, just like the guys in the Hines and Eckstine bands did for her decades earlier. After his four-year tenure as Vaughan's musical director, pianist Bob James did studio work, produced records, and continued to tour. He soon became one of the founding musicians of what became known as smooth jazz, a more mainstream, commercially savvy outgrowth of fusion. Pianist Chick Corea, then twenty-seven and still establishing himself, replaced James in 1968 and briefly toured with Vaughan before joining Miles Davis. After the successes of his collaborations with Davis, Corea founded his own fusion band, Return to Forever, and experienced more crossover successes throughout the 1970s. When Corea joined Vaughan's band, he was already bristling at the formalities and conventions of traditional jazz. Bassist Mickman, who became the trio's musical director after James left, remembered that Corea wore sneakers with his tuxedo. One night Corea put incense inside the piano. "The piano was open and smoke is coming out of the piano, and we start playing," Mickman recalled. "Sarah comes out and after the first tune she turns around, she smells it; she said, 'What the fuck is going on here?' because the piano's smoking." And musically, Corea wanted to explore beyond Vaughan's existing arrangements, prepared by James, to craft new, more experimental introductions for the standards Vaughan sang. One night, Vaughan didn't recognize the tune and sang another tune in the same key. "He would also throw challenges out to her," Mickman explained. "He would play some things and I think she actually liked them. He would throw an unusual chord out to her and she would catch it. She had such a good ear."[7] "The first time I heard her live, Chick Corea was playing piano," bassist Bob Magnusson said. He was twenty-one and wouldn't join Vaughan's trio for another three years. "And he played some really far-out intros and she would just nail it. She didn't care."[8]

"I felt like I was playing, let's say, with Miles Davis," said pianist Jan Hammer. "It was basically [a] pure jazz attitude." He joined the band in 1970 when he was twenty-two and still a student at the Berklee College of Music. He'd listened to jazz while growing up in Czechoslovakia. His mother was a jazz singer too, and he accompanied her as a teenager. This prepared him for his first gig with the band at the Hampton Jazz Festival in Virginia. It was in a big coliseum. There was no real rehearsal, only a sound check. "I had to just jump into the cold water, and it worked out fine," said Hammer. "On a personal level, which was really what moved me very much, I spent my teenage years living in Europe, then eventually moving here, but being on the outside looking through the glass [at] what's going on with the big leagues. I really felt that once I joined Sarah that I actually made it into the next level and they let me into their club," he explained. "It was just fantastic and meeting all her great friends." He met pianist Erroll Garner and vibraphonist Milt Jackson. Duke Ellington introduced himself to Hammer after a gig and complemented him on his playing. In the summer of 1970, a few months into his tenure, drummer Jimmy Cobb, who played on Miles Davis's now-classic album *Kind of Blue*, joined Vaughan's trio. "Playing with him every night was just such a dream come true for me," Hammer said. "All the great, great musicians that I admired, all of a sudden I was sort of joining this club, and it was just a fantastic feeling."[9]

Yet there was a generational gap, a clash of cultures. And Vaughan, like the jazz elders she introduced him to, was old school. She expected the guys in the trio to wear suits, usually a tuxedo and bow tie. Early in Hammer's tenure with the band, Vaughan played the *Tonight Show* with Johnny Carson in New York. Hammer knew that the band would be off camera, so he wore a casual, more relaxed jean jacket. "I was in the hippie times living in New York City, and I said, 'Nobody's going to see me.' Well, that was a bad idea. Never did that again," he remembered, laughing. "I got really, really nailed, and she really takes me hard." Vaughan didn't say much—she didn't have to in order to get her message across. "She had [a] very powerful personality—and sassy," Hammer said.[10]

After a year with Vaughan, Hammer handed in his notice. Like many younger musicians, he was intrigued by electronic music and fusion. He had an opportunity to join the Mahavishnu Orchestra, led by guitarist John McLaughlin. The band, mixing elements of rock, funk, and jazz with Indian and European classical music, broke through, becoming one of the first commercially successful fusion bands. Their albums topped not only the jazz charts but the pop album charts too. Hammer played a Minimoog synthesizer, which allowed him to explore beyond the fixed pitches of the piano by bending notes and creating new, more expressive sounds, much like Vaughan did with her voice. In the years after leaving Vaughan, he continued to tour and began composing film and television scores, including the music for *Miami Vice* in the 1980s. The television show's soundtrack album went quadruple platinum and won a Grammy in 1986. "[Working with Vaughan] was a total life-changing experience," Hammer said. "I don't think I would be where I'm now if I didn't make that first turn with her, that sharp, packing my stuff, leaving Boston, moving and just—it's really worked out great for me, and I'm eternally grateful."[11]

Although Vaughan embraced the experimentation of the younger, often avant-garde-oriented musicians in her band, she did not fundamentally change the way she sang, even as the musical landscape shifted around her. "She was in her own world," said Hammer. "It was more like the traditional '50s, '60s style of approach to music."[12] This more traditional approach to jazz relied on existing pieces of music, standards, as a starting point for an artist's development and expansion. She reimagined, reworked, and recomposed these tunes night after night. But aside from scat pieces like "Shulie a Bop" and "Sassy's Blues" featured in her live sets, Vaughan never assumed the role of singer-songwriter or composed new material in the traditional sense of the word. And she could be stubborn. She had her own creative voice and preferences. Instead, she became a fierce advocate for herself and what she considered high-quality material. Now that she was no longer beholden to record labels, she reaffirmed her artistic agency and insisted on singing only music that she liked and found creatively satisfying, regardless of genre.

"I don't care who writes the music. It just has to be good," she told Tom Mackin of the *Newark Sunday News* in November 1968, almost two years into her new life without a recording contract. "I don't purposely avoid new tunes. I do my own version of 'Yesterday,' the Beatles' song. And I sing 'If I Ruled the World.' But I could never do the noisy, rock 'n' roll kind of thing. 'Tenderly,' 'Misty,' 'Poor Butterfly,' these are the songs I like to do. And I believe they are what people expect me to sing when they come to hear me."[13]

By most measures, she sang jazz during these live performances. But she systematically began to reject this label too. "People call me a jazz singer, but I hate that term. Either one is a singer or one isn't. I like doing all types of material—just as long as it's good," she told *Down Beat*'s Bill Quinn in 1967. "I think in many cases the term jazz is outdated; it doesn't cover the subject accurately. Either a musician is a good musician or he's not."[14] It was a stance that she had been fine-tuning since the early 1950s when die-hard jazz critics and fans first accused her of selling out for singing pop, and along with her disdain for musical labels, it was a position that she reasserted and elaborated on for the remainder of her career. She'd been resisting labels foisted on her by the outside world since 1946 when John Hammond offered to make her a blues singer. And in the years since, her convictions had only become stronger and her desire to obscure all labels even greater.

By privileging quality, musicianship, and talent over genre or style designations, Vaughan sought to transcend these same labels, which were often informed by stereotypical assumptions about race and gender. She did not want to be limited or contained by these preconceptions. She wanted the freedom to create on her own terms—hence her insistence on being considered a "singer" rather than a "jazz singer"; her self-identification as one of the guys, a "musician" and "artist," rather than just another girl singer. Her embrace of the designation "singer" rather than "vocalist" also upended a larger cultural hierarchy that differentiated between highbrow art forms like opera and lowbrow forms of cultural expressions, including jazz. It leveled the playing field and removed questions of her legitimacy altogether. When she made music, she became a woman instead of a black woman; a human being instead of an African American. It released her from social and cultural limitations. It was her way to claim her personhood, and it was a battle she had been fighting her entire career.

It was also a decidedly postmodern approach to art and life, but Vaughan, like many of her contemporaries, was ahead of her time. The music industry, and much of society at large, was deeply invested in labels. Record executives needed them to categorize and market artists. They needed to know where to list Vaughan in their catalogs, which bins to place her albums in in record stores, and which radio stations to send her albums to. And in their eyes, she was still a jazz singer and commercial gamble. Despite her widely acknowledged talent, she remained without a recording contract.

The last time I made a record session was a year ago last February. Isn't that ridiculous?" Vaughan said to critic Leonard Feather in November 1968. Her last sessions with Mercury had in fact been in January 1967. Feather, and the jazz community at large, was appalled. He lamented that acts like the Turtles, Tiny Tim, the 1910 Fruitgum Company, and Engelbert Humperdinck made millions while artists like Vaughan remained without a contract. "The record companies feel a responsibility not to the preservation of art, not to the discriminating record buyer, but solely to their stockholders," Feather concluded. With the exception of "Make Yourself Comfortable," "Whatever Lola Wants," and "Broken-Hearted Melody," all from the 1950s, Vaughan's discs rarely charted within a week or two of their release. "My records may not be hits, but at least they keep on selling," she countered; "they're long lasting, which is not bad; but it seems that's not what the record companies arc looking for."

She still wanted to record, but on her terms. That fall negotiations with a new label failed when her manager, Preacher Wells, demanded what industry insiders believed to be an excessive advance against future royalties. "Isn't it more logical," asked Feather, "to assume that you owe your public a few albums? If you'd just recorded for AFTRA scale, wouldn't that have been better than not being on records at all?"

"I believe so. I guess it was all a mistake," Vaughan replied, in what Feather described as a "soft, diffident quasi-whisper."[15]

Perhaps Wells had overstepped during negotiations. He lacked tact and diplomacy or assumed that he had more leverage than he actually did. After all, he was inexperienced in these kinds of dealings. In 1963, when Vaughan switched from Roulette back to Mercury, he'd only been with her for a few months, and Quincy Jones handled the negotiations. Or perhaps Wells simply got greedy, and his failure to negotiate, to come to a reasonable common ground, combined with financial negligence, contributed to his falling-out with Vaughan. They severed their personal and professional ties soon after. At the same time, Feather's proposal was presumptuous, and it suggested that her responsibility to her fans superseded her responsibility to herself. That she should accept a new kind of exploitation from record labels and the music industry. That there was something virtuous in settling for less than she believed she was worth. And she believed that she was worth a great deal as a vocalist. Yet what if she could have full artistic control? Would it have been worth it then? Despite these setbacks, Vaughan, as she always did, remained optimistic and concluded, "Negotiations are going on now. I should be back in the studios before the year's out."[16]

Nothing came of these negotiations either. She received other offers, but she rejected them all, holding out for another two years. Vaughan didn't step into a recording studio until the fall of 1971, almost five years after leaving Mercury in January 1967. As her recording drought persisted, however, she became more comfortable with her new, contract-free existence. "You know what? I have not really wanted to make records all that much," she told Max Jones in November 1969. "You get no royalties; half the time you're working for gangsters. Who needs it?"[17] During her hiatus from recording, Vaughan came to understand her strength and resilience. And she learned that, despite conventional wisdom, she did not need new records to survive in the music industry. "I'm singing what I want to sing," Vaughan confided in her friend and fellow vocalist Annie Ross during a conversation captured on tape. "I know. But wouldn't it be lovely to have the money [from hit records]?" asked Ross. "Of course,"

Vaughan replied. "But it's not on my shoulders. It's not troubling me. I'm proud of myself because I'm doing goddamn fucking good. Five years I made no records. And five years is when I found out that I had something going on. And I was working. And my salary was going up. I had no records out. I just went on and on and on. I worked."[18]

One night, while I was working at Donte's, Bobby Shad of Mainstream Records came in. He'd been my producer for years and years on Mercury," Vaughan told critic Leonard Feather in 1972. "I said to myself, I'm going to talk to him and we're going to make some records. A week later I was signed to his company." She appeared at Donte's in Los Angeles on October 6 and 7, 1971, almost five years into her recording drought. "People were trying to force me to do material I didn't dig, and I swear I'll never do that again even if I have to take another five years off," she said. "Besides, I just got disgusted with all the hanky-panky in the record business. Seemed like everybody was getting the money but me, so I just gave up."[19]

Shad founded Mainstream in 1964, six years after splitting with Mercury. At first, the label specialized in reissues of jazz from the 1940s and 1950s and rarely issued new releases. In 1971, however, Shad began to build his roster of jazz talent with artists like Vaughan's former drummer Roy Haynes, trumpeters Clark Terry and Maynard Ferguson, and vocalist Carmen McRae. "I don't believe these know-it-alls who tell you good music can't sell," he told Feather. "Maybe we went through a bad period, but now the young kids who have been into rock are getting to realize that they can find something in jazz too."[20] Convinced that jazz was on the cusp of a revival, he needed a marquee performer to carry his label and drive sales, and once again he turned to Sarah Vaughan. Her new manager and love interest, Marshall Fisher, rebuffed his initial overtures, demanding substantial advances, and progress stalled until Vaughan approached him that night in Donte's. "You wanna make a date?" he asked. "Tell me when."[21]

Vaughan had met Marshall Fisher nine months earlier, in January 1971, while playing the Tropicana in Las Vegas. "I don't think I will ever forget," said Fisher during an interview with Gil Noble in 1973, as Vaughan looked on, blushing. "I came to see her as a fan. Strictly as a fan. I've loved her for twenty-six years."[22] He worked a concession stand at the Tropicana, and one night he struck up a conversation with Vaughan's drummer, Jimmy Cobb. "I sure would like to meet her," said Fisher. "C'mon with me," Cobb replied, and he introduced them at the hotel bar.[23] "They shook hands, and according to him, they never released [their] hands," said pianist Michiyo Tanaka, Fisher's future wife. "They shook hands and they held hands for three hours. That is how it started."[24]

Their relationship progressed quickly. "After the show at the Tropicana, a month later, I was in California," Fisher explained.[25] He moved into Vaughan's condo in Los Angeles, and she soon introduced Marshall, a white man seven years her junior, to her friends and family in Newark. "He fit right in. The racial difference didn't mean a thing to Sassy or any of us," childhood friend Aretha Landrum remembered. "He was my favorite."[26]

As usual, Vaughan installed Fisher first as her road manager, then as her personal manager. Like her previous suitors, he had no background in management or the music industry. Unlike her past romantic partnerships, he seemed to have Vaughan's best interests at heart. Datebooks from his years with Vaughan meticulously outlined her gigs, recording sessions, appointments, and what she sang during each television and radio appearance. And tucked inside the pages of the date books were love poems that he penned describing his love for Vaughan.

"Marshall was just like a prince to her," bassist Bob Magnusson said. "The best guy in her life that she ever had."[27] Friend and business associate Larry Clothier agreed: "He was one of the nicest people in the world. Marshall would do anything for Sassy. Sassy wasn't used to that kind of treatment. Marshall would never have hit her in a million years. He took care of her.

Anything she wanted, he tried to do it or to get it for her."[28] And according to Walter Booker, Vaughan's bassist between 1976 and 1978, Marshall was "a hustler for her *music,* not her *money.*"[29]

On November 16, 1971, Vaughan returned to the recording studio for the first time since January 24, 1967. Saxophonist Ernie Wilkins, a Count Basie alum turned arranger, scored the new charts and directed the band, and Shad chose the songs. "My theory with Sarah was to start from scratch and introduce her with new material, not the old songs she's been doing in her nightclub act," he explained to Eliot Tiegel of *Billboard.* "I had to let people know this was a new Sarah, so she sang 'Imagine,' 'Inner City Blues,' and 'Universal Prisoner.'"[30]

The session, which became *A Time in My Life,* was not straight-ahead jazz. Nor was it, by most reckonings, a foray into the commercially successful jazz-fusion style, although it did at times incorporate elements of funk and plenty of electric keyboards and guitars. Instead, it was another outing into the adult contemporary market. It seemed that history was repeating itself, and it must have been terribly disappointing for Vaughan. She had boycotted recording studios for almost five years because producers asked her to record material she didn't like. And now, under the helm of Bobby Shad, she was once again chasing pop hits. She covered John Lennon and Marvin Gaye, Bob Dylan's "If Not for You," Carly Simon's "That's the Way I've Always Heard It Should Be," John Sebastian's "Magical Connection," and Michel Legrand's "Sweet Gingerbread Man." While it was a "new" sound for Vaughan, as Shad planned, the album lacked cohesion and a larger creative vision. The funky undertones of Gaye's anthem "Inner City Blues" remained, but its peppy, polished disco feel was at odds with the serious, social-economic commentary of his original reading. The youthful storytelling of "That's the Way I've Always Heard It Should Be" was perfect for the then-twenty-five-year-old ingénue Simon's debut album but wrong for the more mature, forty-seven-year-old Vaughan, now approaching her third decade in the music industry. And the saccharine

"Sweet Gingerbread Man," complete with sweeping strings and bouncy beat, was out of sync with much of the album, including the more somber and serious "Imagine." It was an eclectic mix of tunes, unified only by the simple fact that they had been hits for someone else. Vaughan sang them well, with an admirable taste, but there was nothing uniquely "Sarah Vaughan" about the album—nothing that could not have been done by a singer with a fraction of her talent and imaginative flare.

"I thought he just picked terrible material," her bassist Bob Magnusson said. "It was all like pop stuff, you know. And when I showed up at the studio, the contractors came over, and they were expecting an electric bass. I didn't know anything about it. I walked in with my fiddle." He assumed it would be an acoustic jazz session, like he played every night. "I was thrilled to get to record with Sarah," Magnusson concluded. "But it wasn't stuff that really, to me, showed who she is."[31]

It's hard to know if Vaughan was truly happy with *A Time in My Life* or Shad's new vision for her. Neither bassist Magnusson nor pianist Bill Mays, the two musicians from her trio to play the session, heard Vaughan complain about the material or otherwise express concern, and she incorporated both "Imagine" and "Universal Prisoner" into her live sets. But this was typical. She rarely complained during recording sessions, and she usually added tunes from her recent albums to her live sets. In public, as she always did, she remained diplomatic, if unenthusiastic, professional, and polite, focusing on aspects of the album that she liked. "I'm pleased with this. Sure it's good," she told *Melody Maker*'s Max Jones in February 1972, two months after the album's release. "With Ernie [Wilkins]'s charts you know the music's got to be bang on."[32]

Critical reception of the album was mixed. The pop-oriented *Billboard* praised *A Time in My Life* as a "super artistic-commercial package" that "should break the charts with sales impact." It never made it onto any of *Billboard*'s charts, but Shad, in full PR mode, insisted that the album, especially its ballads, received strong radio play and sold well.[33] Jazz critic Dan Morgenstern was less positive. He was happy to have Vaughan back on records but condemned Shad's misguided attempts to give Vaughan a "new" image. He worried that the material was beneath her, that it didn't give her the space to stretch her improvisatory chops, which, he believed, ranked alongside those of the finest jazz instrumentalists. "Let's hope Sassy gets a better break next time," he concluded.[34]

Vaughan chose her next project. "Jimmy [Rowles] played me a record by Michel [Legrand], the one with the theme from 'Summer of '42' in it," she told Leonard Feather. The French-born Legrand had just won an Academy Award for his original score for *The Summer of '42* and was an established arranger of both pop and jazz. He had worked with Barbra Streisand, Stan Getz, and Shelly Manne. "I'd never heard writing like that—French horns flying all over the place, and such beautiful writing for strings. I told Bobby [Shad] I wanted to make an album with Michel, and he spared no expense."[35]

It was an ambitious undertaking, recorded over four days in April 1972 in a Los Angeles studio. Legrand conducted a massive ensemble numbering 114 musicians, made up of a thirty-eight-piece band, including eight French horns and a rhythm section of three keyboardists, four bassists, four drummers, and a guitarist; a forty-eight-piece string section; two harpists; and a sixteen-voice choir. Vaughan sang ten of Legrand's original compositions with lyrics by Alan and Marilyn Bergman.

"The first take, as I recall, was 'The Summer Knows,'" said Legrand. "Sarah sang her heart out, and I got swept up in the music too. We finished the song and I glanced around the studio, and nearly all of the musicians had tears streaming down their faces, they were so moved. In all my years of working with solid pros like them I'd never seen anything like it. The same thing occurred during almost every song. Sarah had the power to make us weep one moment then smile the next. She was making music from the skies. From the heavens!"[36] Bassist Bob Magnusson agreed. He was the only member of Vaughan's trio included, and for just three tracks. "[The contractors] didn't know me from

Adam," he said. "So I think she went to bat for me." Magnusson went on to play other studio dates and remembered that this one stood out, for both the quality of the material and the response of the musicians in the room. "They would have certain dates where they would applaud," he continued. "But that was one of those dates. The whole orchestra would get up and applaud Sarah and Michel Legrand. I saw it with Johnny Mandell. Some of the really great writers. Patrick Williams. It was really rare."[37]

"It was a beautiful session, and everybody on it was the best musicians that you could get—Shelly Manne and, I mean, just everybody. It was a touching session; there were tears shed— the guys were so moved. I looked over at Shelly, and tears were running down his face; same with a lot of guys," Vaughan told Les Tomkins in 1977. "But now that I hear the album—in some parts, too much music was written. Good—but for vocal, too much, at times. However I still love it. The songs that Michel writes are absolutely gorgeous."[38]

"I really hope it does well, just so [Shad] gets his money back. My God, if it doesn't he'll fire me!" she joked during an interview with Leonard Feather in 1972 while promoting the album.[39] *Sarah Vaughan and Michel Legrand* crept onto the *Billboard* chart of top LPs at No. 200, on July 1, 1972, shortly after its release. It stayed there twelve weeks, peaking at No. 173. But it didn't generate any hits. Shad didn't fire Vaughan, but their future albums together would be more modest, budget-friendly endeavors, and Shad would continue his pursuit to find the always elusive hit. Tensions between Vaughan and Shad escalated as they tussled over their differing musical goals and visions. And these challenges in Vaughan's professional life would be accompanied by a new, devastating blow in her personal life.

13

"Here I Go Again"

Welcome to the Troubadour," Sarah Vaughan said, as she opened at the Los Angeles club on February 1, 1973. "WE welcome YOU to the Troubadour," someone screamed out. And Vaughan was off. She sang her usual standards, "Misty" and "Funny Valentine"; the Brazilian tune "Wave"; a sampling from her album with Michel Legrand; and her cover of the Carpenters' "Rainy Days and Mondays," featured on her new Mainstream release *Feelin' Good*. She even sang "Broken-Hearted Melody." "She gave a new meaning to the term, 'standing ovation,'" wrote one reviewer, who likened the audience to a jack-in-the-box that kept popping up after each song. "Had there not been a second show that evening, I suspect Sarah Vaughan could have stood up there doing encores until the 2 A.M. closing hour. It was a lovely, truly unforgettable evening."[1]

"She totally destroyed it," said pianist Carl Schroeder, who replaced Bill Mays in June 1972. "The place was packed and she just—I mean it was amazing. They were all like hypnotized."[2] Billy Eckstine, Quincy Jones, Carmen McRae, Della Reese, Taj

Mahal, actress Virginia Caper, record executives, and a host of radio and television personalities sat in the audience. Vaughan followed pop star Billy Paul, whose "Me and Mrs. Jones" had just sold two million copies. Executives from Columbia presented Paul with his platinum record plaque earlier in the night, and it was a pro-Paul crowd. Vaughan seemed determined to win them over. After her set, she walked back to the little dressing room she shared with her musicians, sat on the couch, curled up, and began to cry. Her father had just died.

Asbury Vaughan had been a reserved yet strong-willed man. "My daddy, he was very quiet, I would say. Very strict. That's why I'm such a good girl today," Vaughan said, laughing, during an interview with television host Gil Noble two months later. "He was very strict. Nice, though. Knew everything. There was nothing you . . . He knew everything."[3] Her tone was bittersweet, mixing love with a lifelong frustration. Her father never approved of Vaughan's career choice, and he had not wanted his daughter to be in show business. "It never really got resolved, and it was something she carried with her all her life," Vaughan's friend Robert Richards explained. "In the beginning she was so intent on convincing her father that she could do this that she saved everything she made and she bought them a house in Newark while she herself didn't even have an apartment. You know she was running around sleeping on people's sofas. That girl never left." And that night, as she mourned her father's passing, she never would get his approval or acceptance. "She was always that girl from Newark trying to please her father, which was an impossible task," Roberts concluded.[4]

"We were sitting there [in the dressing room] all very quiet, kind of being with her, for her. Just there, everybody, all the cats and the band and stuff," said Schroeder. The usually private woman, who rarely let her musicians see what was happening behind the scenes in her personal life, allowed herself to be vulnerable in front of her band, the cats and musicians who she exposed herself to musically every night. The people she considered her extended family.[5]

Then Billy Eckstine arrived. There was an awkward silence as he surveyed the dressing room. He saw his musical soulmate and friend of thirty years sobbing, inconsolable. He paused, then said, "I'm glad that motherfucker is dead." Schroeder and the other musicians were shocked. "Oh, Billy," Vaughan replied and started to laugh. "Pretty soon, she's laughing like crazy," said Schroeder. "He did it deliberately because he knew what reaction he would get."[6]

Bassist Ron McClure experienced that evening very differently. It was his second week with the band, and they were playing an arrangement by pianist Jan Hammer. "It was a very difficult [arrangement]. It was a pencil copy. It was not exactly a great-looking chart. And I went to the second ending the first time," McClure explained. It was a big mistake but understandable. He was new to the band. "And she turned around with the microphone—Quincy Jones was in the audience, and the place was packed, and she was a big star and people knew her. She whirled around with the microphone to her mouth and said, 'What's the matter with you, motherfucker, can't you read?' and the place cheered. That was day one. Welcome to my trio." Embarrassed and angry, McClure approached Vaughan's manager, Marshall Fisher, and issued a warning. "If she does it again, I will walk off the stage and you will never see me again," he said. "I am sorry," Vaughan conceded. "I made a mistake."[7]

A decade earlier, Vaughan had reprimanded pianist Ronnell Bright onstage too. She was demure and incredibly polite, bassist Buster Williams remembered. "She said something like, 'I know everything that you're going to do but you don't know what I'm going to do, so you better listen a little more closely,'" Williams said. "And it was so nice, but I mean it was a knife to the heart."[8] Bright, who worked with Vaughan for four years, considered her a friend, not just his employer, and his feelings were hurt. He soon left the band to join Nancy Wilson. According to the bulk of the musicians who worked for Vaughan over the years, however, these public reprimands were out of character. Usually she was more diplomatic in both her requests and praise. Perhaps her outburst at the Troubadour was a symptom of her grief as she processed the death of her father.

"It was probably the loneliest gig I ever did in my life. It really was," McClure said. "She and Marshall, her boyfriend and manager, stayed to themselves. Jimmy Cobb was kind of depressed at that point, I think he was going through a divorce. Carl Schroeder stayed in his room and read books about chess. He would not talk to anybody, and I never saw them except for a gig." It was a far cry from the light-hearted, family-like camaraderie and generosity described by McClure's predecessors and successors. "She was a lot of fun to hang out with after shows," said pianist Bill Mays. He worked with Vaughan for just over a year, before leaving in June 1972. "She would take her sewing machine on the road and would be sewing for her daughter. She liked to play spelling games, get together, drink gin and tonics, and play Scrabble or spill and spell and it was like a family, really."[9] Mays contrasted his time working with Vaughan with his experiences working for Frank Sinatra, who was not friendly and rarely interacted with musicians. With Vaughan, if the band worked a holiday like Thanksgiving or Christmas, she prepared a huge meal for friends and the guys in the trio. She also invited the musicians' families to join them on the road, at her expense. During a gig at the Fairmont Hotel in Dallas in May 1972, Vaughan asked bassist Bob Magnusson if he'd like his fiancée and son from his first marriage to join him during the gig. "They had a nice pool, the weather was nice. I said, 'I'd be thrilled.' She says, 'Marshall, get Janet and Mathew round-trip tickets from San Diego to Dallas,'" Magnusson remembered. His family stayed for a week, then went home. And when he relocated to Los Angeles to rejoin the band in 1975, Vaughan paid the cleaning deposit and first and last months' rent for his apartment, with the understanding that Magnusson would pay her back when he could, without interest. "Yes, she had a great, big, big heart," he said. "Amazingly, she treated us like family, the musicians."[10]

As newcomer McClure tried to find his place in the band, he

worked to balance his new full-time job as a touring musician with his life at home. He had a young daughter to support and was doing his best to make things work with her mother. He disliked the way he was paid and struggled to make ends meet. Like his predecessor, he earned $500 a week, which was a respectable salary. But Vaughan's management withheld half of his salary, calling it "road expenses." He was also disappointed by the music making and disliked the stress and drama that preceded each show. He knew Vaughan's history as an innovator with early beboppers like Dizzy Gillespie and Charlie Parker. While he considered her a phenomenal improviser with a keen harmonic ear—McClure remembered being blown away by her hip, unexpected voicings while she played piano—he was frustrated that she performed the same very limited repertoire every night. "I don't think she cared that much at that point about doing anything new. On the other hand, she was going through the motions," he said. "It was the same every night. We would just have this discussion ten minutes before the show of what order we were going to do the same twenty-two songs in. That was the most dramatic part, trying not to mess up and get the right order and time." He wanted, of course, to avoid another public, onstage scolding.[11]

Vaughan's state of mind and emotional well-being affected everyone in the trio. In the months following the death of her father in 1973, she became temperamental, withdrawn, and detached. "There was a lot of substance abuse going on. . . . [She and Marshall] stayed pretty high most of the time and kept to themselves," said McClure. "I've been clean and sober for twenty-two years, so I know what substance abuse can do to a performer. She was 'in her cups,' and that certainly was part of the problem. It tends to isolate people, and that's partly why this was such an un-fun experience for me. I don't know if she was an alcoholic or an addict, but it seemed that way. Basically, I think Sarah wasn't a very happy person at that point in her life."[12]

After four months, at the end of May, McClure prepared to leave. During a gig in Dallas, he met up with John Giannelli, a local bassist, who asked McClure for career advice. He wanted to know how to get a steady gig like the one McClure had with Vaughan. "You want this one?" McClure asked. He set up an audition. Giannelli played a couple of tunes with pianist Carl Schroeder in the afternoon and planned to sit in with the band that night. "Sarah was playing at the Losers Club, it was called," Giannelli explained. "It's a club in Dallas that—I don't know—I think some heavyweight people owned the place. I went there and it turned out that she was waiting for her money, and they didn't pay her, so she didn't do the gig that night. So just on Carl Schroeder's word, she hired me and I moved to Los Angeles. I was twenty-two."[13]

According to pianist Schroeder, much more happened behind the scenes that night. The Losers Club was owned by Anthony "Tough Tony" Caterine, a member of a Dallas crime family, who also had connections with a New Orleans crime family. He owned clubs and managed talent but also dabbled in smuggling, drug dealing, and credit card fraud. "Yeah, it was a little bit slimy," said Schroeder. "And interesting looking faces of the people that were owners; not what you would call the face of a club owner. Looked like somebody had been a bodyguard or a professional wrestler with the nose thing on the side." Erroll Garner played the first half of the bill, and Vaughan followed. Before her final set of the night, manager Marshall Fisher went downstairs to get paid and came back empty-handed. "Man, these guys are giving me a hard time," he told Sarah and went back, and again he returned without the money.[14] "One of the owners told her he didn't have the money," said Schroeder. "She came to the bandstand and said to us: 'Pack up the drums. Pack up the drums. *Pack—up—the—drums*. We're leaving.'" As the band prepared to leave, with a full house looking on, an angry Vaughan prepared to confront the club owners. "Oh, my God, Sarah, what are you doing? These guys are carrying guns. These guys are mafia guys. They'll kill you," Schroeder remembered saying, his disbelief mixed with a genuine concern for her well-being.[15] But Vaughan had become immune to the threat of guns and would not be taken advantage of. Fisher followed her, but she refused his offers to accompany her inside the club office. "She went in there, and she came out with the money," said Schroeder. "Now what she said or what she did with these guys who were hard, you know, what she did or whether she threatened, I have no idea. She came out with the money. Marshall looked at her, I'm sure she told him [what she said], but I never knew. I sort of didn't want to know. I just thought it was so cool that she could walk in there and bogart those jerks and walk out of there, 'Gimme my money, goddamn it.'"[16] That was the moment Carl Schroeder understood how tough Sarah Vaughan truly was. "She was strong," he said. "She didn't like to be that way, but she could when she had to; she was very strong."[17]

It was a strength at odds with the stories he had heard about Vaughan's abusive romantic partnerships of the 1950s and 1960s. "That she was capable of letting herself be dominated by a person so much so that he would exploit her and physically [abuse her], that persists [as] a mystery to me," said Schroeder. "How someone so strong in her persona on stage, and she was secure also privately. I think she was always herself. She wasn't trying to be nobody. It was something that was a mystery, and I felt lucky because Marshall was with her and that never happened. They never did that."[18]

Soon after bassist John Giannelli moved to Los Angeles in June 1973, the trio went back out on the road, and it was grueling. His first gig was four nights at a motel in San Jose, followed by a week at the Fairmont Hotel in San Francisco. "That was a wild gig because a guy came up on stage during her performance and said that he was her long-lost son," Giannelli said. The man was quickly ushered off the stage, but the band teased Vaughan. On July 4, she played Carnegie Hall for her annual appearance at the Newport Jazz Festival–New York, this time backed by an orchestra conducted by Michel Legrand. They did jobs in Connecticut, Virginia, and Pennsylvania before boarding a plane to the French Riviera for three nights of gigs. Two days later, on

July 24, they performed in Carthage, Tunisia. "We played on this stage with like an old Roman amphitheater," Giannelli said. "It was wild because at nighttime you could hear people chanting in the distance." He wanted to play Dizzy Gillespie's "A Night in Tunisia," which Vaughan and Gillespie recorded together back in 1944, but Schroeder said, "No, I'm only going to play blues and 'I Got Rhythm' changes." "And then we went there, [and] he played 'A Night in Tunisia,'" Giannelli remembered, laughing.[19] A friendly camaraderie and humor had returned to the bandstand. Six months after the death of her father, Vaughan's spirits had improved too, and, as she always did, she kept on working.

On Friday, July 27, they were back in the States for a job in Rochester, Michigan. Then, after a short break, the band flew to Australia on August 7, 1973, for two weeks. They returned to work over the Labor Day weekend, then prepared for two and a half weeks in Japan. They did ten one-nighters, with two shows a night, plus three days taping television shows, before flying back to Los Angeles on October 2. After a short break, the band left for a sixteen-day tour of the United Kingdom. On October 31, they began George Wein's annual tour of Europe, this time performing in Romania, Austria, Yugoslavia, Italy, Portugal, Spain, France, Holland, and Belgium. The band did thirteen concerts in seventeen days, followed by a weeklong cruise on the Southampton Princess. Vaughan had been on the road, working in Europe, for almost seven weeks.

On Saturday, November 10, 1973, in the midst of this tour, Vaughan was scheduled to appear at the Cascais Jazz Festival, fifteen miles west of Lisbon. She'd performed in Venice the previous night and needed to fly to Lisbon that day. Giannelli remembered his trip to the airport. He took a taxi to a gondola, then another taxi to a bus, which then took him to the airport. When he and his fellow bandmates finally arrived at the airport, however, they learned that the plane had already left due to fog. "I'll never forget that," said Darlene Chan, George Wein's employee on the ground. She was the tour's road manager and responsible for making sure everybody arrived in one piece and on time.

When she approached airline representatives, they calmly told her that this was not unusual and that they could travel the next day. "We had a show that night," she said, but they were stuck at the airport. "When they heard she wasn't coming, apparently, they threw the seat cushions down toward the stage," said Chan. The Cascais Jazz Festival took place in a giant pavilion that accommodated ten thousand. Stadium-style seating surrounded the tiny makeshift stage, with extra chairs set up on the arena floor in front of the stage. "That was not a riot, but, for them, that was a big deal," explained Chan. Festival organizers did in fact call in the police to manage the protests.[20]

Vaughan extended her tour, sacrificing her only rest day after crisscrossing Europe for nine one-nighters, in order to honor her commitment in Cascais. Two days later, on Monday, November 12, when Vaughan finally performed, the crowd of ten thousand was restless and noisy. They chatted and walked around as she sang. A television camera crew crowded onto the small stage, leaving Vaughan little room to move, and the sound system was not working. When she launched into "Summertime," the audience applauded in recognition. Vaughan curtseyed and turned, looking at bassist Giannelli as she sang "And the livin' is *not* easy." He grinned back, acknowledging her playful rewriting of the lyrics. Moments later a stagehand snuck past her to replace a microphone. She ruffled his hair, in an exaggerated show for the crowd. Then her mic squealed with feedback. She cried out in exasperation, but kept singing and blowing kisses. The audience finally began to settle and pay attention. She reached down into the depths of her baritone to sing "So hush . . ." but before she could sing "little baby," the microphone hissed and squealed again. Vaughan stifled a scream and laughed in frustration as the crowd whistled and voiced its dissatisfaction. She blew them another kiss. And there was more feedback from the mic. She stopped, raised her finger to her lips, saying "Shhhh. Watch me. Look at me." The crowd applauded, Vaughan giggled and started to sing, but stopped again, seconds later. "I gotta stop and say. I want to tell you something," she said, still fighting with the hum and hisses of the microphone, problems likely exacerbated by the camera crew's sound system. "It is very, very difficult for everybody up here. It's hard for the cameramen. It's hard for me. It's hard for everybody because there is no space." Another round of feedback interrupted her. "So—so—you—you, please, please," she pleaded. "Cause I'd just as soon be at home in bed, than go through this. So be calm. The cameramen, they're having a hard time. They're trying very, very hard." Someone shouted from the crowd with entreaties to keep on singing. "Yes, I know, honey," Vaughan replied and delved right back in as if nothing had happened. Many lesser performers would have lost focus, crumbled under the circumstances, but Vaughan, who was physically, mentally, and emotionally exhausted, remained calm and poised. For the next three (uninterrupted) minutes she delivered an emotionally wrenching performance. When she finished, the audience gave her a standing ovation. It was the response she needed, a source of validation that motivated and drove her, much as it had at the Troubadour ten months earlier, to keep on singing, working night after night.

"[Touring] takes a lot out of you, and she had to give in her performance all the time, and you just get tired," Chan explained. "It's tough on the road and sometimes I think she did feel alone— not alone like in a room by herself, but just like 'Okay, this is all on me' kind of thing. And she'd get tired and she'd get snappy and she'd just get—she could be difficult."[21]

Seven weeks earlier, on Monday, September 24, 1973, as she toured Japan, producer Bobby Shad captured Vaughan performing before a live audience. It was a return to familiar territory, harking back to the live club dates Shad recorded at Mr. Kelly's and the London House in Chicago in 1957 and 1958. After her forays into Top 40 pop, the dates were her first strictly "jazz" album for Mainstream. Yet Vaughan disliked the choice of venue: the Sun Plaza Hotel in Tokyo. "I didn't really like doing it there because those Japan audiences are kind of quiet.

They're very good: They love you and all that, but they're just a quiet type of audience," she explained to *Melody Maker*'s Max Jones. They were more reserved than the boisterous crowds she encountered in Europe, and they didn't give her much energy to feed off. "At the end I had to stick in a 'Bye Bye Blackbird' to get a little something out of them. Then they really came to life."[22] Most of the set, in fact, was requests from the audience, and, in spite of Vaughan's concerns, they loved her. "A girl came up and sat with her on the edge of the stage," bassist Giannelli remembered. "The girl was crying on her shoulder, watched her singing. I remember that part of it because the Japanese people just loved her to death. It was just a wonderful, wonderful concert."[23]

Live in Japan, the two-disc set of her free-ranging interpretations of standards and newer, contemporary tunes, was released three months later, in December. "People liked it, and, of course, she sang great. That was just another day at the office for her. That wasn't an exceptional concert in the sense of a special night," said pianist Schroeder. "She worked at very, very high—whatever that level was, that was pretty much every night. And then occasionally she would go somehow even further, or some nights, maybe she wasn't feeling it quite as much, but she'd always respond to the crowd. . . . She brought it all. As good as that is, and I never listen to it, that was another day at the office for her."[24] But this day at the office had been recorded, and it was her first live album since 1963, when Quincy Jones recorded her in Copenhagen at Tivoli Gardens. Critics considered *Live in Japan* her best work in years, and it put her back on the jazz radar.

Buoyed by these successes, Shad planned another live album, this one with Vaughan's friend and pianist Jimmy Rowles. The nightclub chosen by Shad, however, was too loud, so Vaughan and Rowles's regular trio, bolstered by trumpeter Al Aarons and saxophonist Teddy Edwards, retreated to a studio. The session was more exploratory and experimental than her usual nightclub sets. Instead of standards, she sang contemporary tunes, mixing straight-ahead singing with extended stretches of free improvisation. She didn't scat in the conventional sense of the word; rather, she let her voice meander and explore, becoming more fully instrumental. Often the horns simultaneously improvised behind her in a style reminiscent of both the collective improvisation of 1920s New Orleans jazz and the more avant-garde improvisations of free jazz. The results were complex and layered, an often dissonant collection of tones and timbres. *Sarah Vaughan and the Jimmy Rowles Quintet* was an intriguing album, albeit imperfectly realized, that provided a glimpse into what could have been a new direction for Vaughan. But it was a missed opportunity, as almost no one heard the album.

"I think that's one of the best albums she ever made," Rowles told Dan Morgenstern in 1984. The ensemble, in fact, recorded three additional tracks that Shad did not include on the album. And when he released it almost a year later, in December 1974, it was not widely distributed and soon disappeared from record stores. Rowles was furious when he saw the album credits. "I almost jumped over [Bobby Shad's] desk at him because we did 'Morning Star,' and it was my tune with Johnny Mercer's lyrics, and he put down W. C. Handy," Rowles explained. Shad probably misattributed the song in order to avoid paying Rowles publishing royalties. "Boy, he's a *bad* cat. I'd like to meet him again some time. I've got sharp toes."[25]

"We're not talking about Columbia records anymore," pianist Schroeder explained. "This was kind of [a] fly-by-night operation." Before joining Vaughan, he recorded two albums with Vaughan's former drummer Roy Haynes, both on Mainstream with Shad. "They were, you know, uniformly wretched," he said. And since his years at Mercury, Shad had earned a reputation for his less than scrupulous business practices, as Jimmy Rowles so colorfully illustrated. "When I went with [Sarah], she had just recorded with Bob Shad, of Mainstream records, just signed a contract," Schroeder continued. "So that automatically meant she was going to get screwed again."[26]

Carl Schroeder was right. Mainstream was most definitely not Columbia. It lacked the clout, resources, and distribution network of Columbia, or Mercury for that matter. But the larger agendas at the labels were the same. Both Mitch Miller and Bobby Shad wanted to make money. Once again, Vaughan found herself negotiating the competing demands of commercial viability and artistic integrity, those familiar tensions between pop and jazz. Shad skillfully straddled this divide at Mercury, thanks to Vaughan's dual contract with the label's jazz subsidiary, EmArcy. Now, twenty years later, as the market for jazz dwindled, Shad's task was more difficult. And Vaughan's tolerance for bad material had evaporated. She'd grown tired of Shad's relentless pursuit of pop success and his oft-repeated refrain: "Let's find a hit." "What's a hit?" she asked during an interview with *Down Beat*'s Arnold Jay Smith in 1977. "'The Lord's Prayer' is a hit! And why are others making all the bread? The producers and executives didn't make all of this music. We did. I think we should be making more money than we are. But that sounds like an old story." She didn't care about making what she called "hitty records." "It makes the money go up a bit. But you know, with this new contemporary stuff I'm not heartbroken if I don't have a hit," she explained to Max Jones in 1973, in what had become a familiar refrain. "It's Bobby (Shad) who bothers more about it than I do. I'd rather do what I want to do than look for a new hit record."[27]

Her next album was the final straw. *Send in the Clowns,* another collection of disco- and funk-inspired covers geared to the adult contemporary market, was recorded on April 16, 1973, but not released until February 1975. She confided to friends, and later publicly, that she despised the material. And she hated the album's cover art: an over-the-top photo of a clown wearing a black-, red-, and white-striped suit with lace ruffles at the collar and sleeves; afro-style hair framed a chalky whiteface with smeared accents in red and blue; and an oversized pirate hat with giant red pompoms at the corners completed the look. It was dreadful, with unfortunate echoes of blackface minstrelsy, and the image did not align with the sophisticated, black-tie elegance that Vaughan presented onstage. "Sassy sued us for some kind of cover that Bobby didn't really have any control over," said Molly Shad, Bobby Shad's wife. "She just tried to find problems all of the time."[28] As the label's president, Shad did, in fact, make these decisions. Vaughan filed the lawsuit in March 1975. Even though her contract didn't expire for another eighteen months, she sued Mainstream for a release, $8,333 in back pay, and $200,000 in general and punitive damages.[29] She also charged that Mainstream produced and distributed an album, *Sarah Vaughan: Live at the Holiday Inn Lesotho,* whose title inaccurately described the album's origins and that Shad had obstructed and thwarted her career. He threatened to "break her" in the industry by "keeping her off labels."[30]

It was another contentious split with a dysfunctional record label, and Vaughan must have been disappointed. She'd gone five years without a contract because she was tired of singing material she didn't like. She wanted artistic control. But during her three and a half years at Mainstream, she encountered the same pressures to sing subpar material, usually backed by threats and intimidation from producers in search of commercial gain, as she had at Columbia and Mercury. She also endured poor production values, limited distribution, and meager promotion budgets, not to mention Shad's ethically dubious financial dealings, much as she had during her years with Musicraft and Roulette.

Two years after leaving Mainstream, in the spring of 1977, Vaughan revealed the extent of her contempt for and frustration with record labels and their executives and producers. Despite Shad's threats to ruin her recording career, she had signed with Atlantic, headed by Ahmet Ertegun, in 1976, and she was now in the midst of working on her first project for the label, an album of Paul McCartney and John Lennon tunes. "This is the most exciting album I have ever made in my life, because I was involved," she told *Down Beat*'s Arnold Jay Smith. "I was *really* involved in this album. I could say, 'No, I don't like that,' and they would take it out. In fact, they are going to start mixing when I get back home to California and I will be there to help." She was invigorated by the creative process, and her enthusiasm was unmistakable. She had partnered with her longtime arranger Marty Paich and his son, David, an up-and-coming keyboardist on the studio scene who would soon make his mark with the rock band Toto. The sessions mixed her traditional jazz roots with new, more modern sounds. It was a coming together of youth and maturity, and she was clearly thrilled and invigorated by the collaboration. Then, in an unusually candid assessment, she added, "It's the first time I have ever been so involved with an album. Before this I would go into a studio less than a slave."[31]

It was a striking analogy, one that called attention to the industry-wide exploitation of musicians by record labels while simultaneously acknowledging the underlying institutional racism of the industry. By speaking openly about slavery and its legacy, she exposed the complex intersections between race and gender in the United States and the uneasy power dynamics that they created, especially between a white man and a black woman. She reminded fans of the challenges that she encountered every day as a black woman and how, throughout her thirty-five-year career, she had fought to be taken seriously and treated with respect, as an equal, both in and outside of the recording studio.

Despite her enthusiasm for the Beatles project, Atlantic scrapped the album and ended her contract.[32] They explained that the album didn't have any hit material. "I don't know how they can recognize hits in advance," she lamented to Les Tomkins while touring London in June 1977. Maybe they wanted her to make a rock 'n' roll album, she speculated. She didn't know, but in the face of yet another disappointment she insisted that she made a beautiful album. "I've proven myself. I don't give a damn about record companies anymore," she said with her typical firmness and a resolve that had only grown during the past decade. And then she reasserted her determination to persevere, returning to the same coping strategy she had used her entire career when confronted with challenges—be it the disapproval of her father or an evolving music industry that threatened to make her irrelevant. "Listen, I gave up making records for five years— that's how much I am against making things that I don't approve of. So now—here I go again."[33]

14

"The Marian Anderson
of Modern Jazz"

On March 27, 1974, Sarah Vaughan turned fifty. It was a personal milestone, celebrated publicly. Governor Ronald Reagan presented Vaughan with a proclamation from the state of California, her new home, as did Los Angeles mayor Tom Bradley.[1] President Richard Nixon sent Vaughan his birthday wishes, writing, "These wishes come to you from the heart of a nation that respects and honors your talent."[2] And a month earlier, on February 26, Congressman Thomas Rees of California paid tribute to Vaughan in the House of Representatives. "She is a legendary figure in the entertainment world, one who bridges gaps—generation and otherwise—incorporating into every performance a special warmth and rare depth of feeling which can only be accomplished by one who is blessed with 'soul.' I am of course, referring to Sarah Vaughan, whom many call 'The Divine Sarah.' . . . It is my pleasure to report to you that on March 27, 1974, this giant of the music industry—this lovely, talented lady—will mark an important milestone in her life—the celebration of her 50th birthday," he said. Rees praised her artistry, international appeal, and role as "an official ambassador of good will for the United States," adding, "Sarah Vaughan has been called 'the greatest singer in the world' by Tony Bennett and many other greats of the entertainment world. If music is, indeed, the universal language, 'The Divine Sarah' is a linguist without peer. She is not merely a vocalist; she is a brilliant interpretative musician able to improvise, leave her audience breathless with her fantastic versatility, whether in person or via her many recordings."[3]

"Imagine what it feels like to have your birthday permanently recorded in the Library of Congress," Vaughan told reporter Bill Pollock. "I don't much care about New Year's Eve, but I do care about my birthday."[4] It was a satisfying moment, perhaps a moment of vindication, for the vocalist, who at times felt underappreciated, especially by record executives. These public proclamations confirmed what she had come to understand about her legacy and status as an artist. "Over the years, though, I've recorded some pretty bad songs, trying to get a hit, and they keep haunting me," she explained to Leonard Feather in April 1974. She was referring to "Broken-Hearted Melody," of course. "It's nice to have a hit, but I'm lucky; I don't need it. Billy Eckstine and I have a lot in common; he always works and does very well, with or without a big record. To be a legend is what keeps you going. When I was completely off the record for those four or five years, that's when I realized I must be a legend, too. It sure is a nice feeling to know that people will remember you after you're gone—that you'll manage to be a little bit of history."[5]

Soon after her fiftieth birthday, buoyed by this new awareness of her place in music history, not to mention the wisdom that comes with a half century of living, Vaughan embarked on two new projects that would determine the course of the rest of her career. The first was an unexpected silver lining, a postscript of sorts, to her contentious years at Mainstream.

During the recording sessions for her final album at the label, she discovered the new Steven Sondheim tune "Send in the Clowns," and she was intrigued. That night, she phoned friend Robert Richards to tell him about her day in the studio. "It was terrible, terrible. I just hated the songs. I don't like them, I don't ever want to hear this record," he remembered her saying. "But you know, there was one song that I think it's a good song but I didn't have time." She didn't have time to delve in and explore, to put her distinct stamp on the tune. "I think that's a good song," she said. "I'm going to learn that song."[6]

Pianist Carl Schroeder remembered a similar conversation. They were working Mr. Kelly's in Chicago in April 1974 and listened to her Mainstream master. "You know, it's nice," said Schroeder.[7] But Vaughan didn't like Paul Griffin's funk- and disco-infused arrangement. "I despised [it]," she told Jay Scott of the *Globe and Mail* a decade later. "I never even heard the arrangement; I was dubbed over it. It was too fast. You could dance to it. Nobody dances to 'Send in the Clowns.'"[8]

"Sass, did you ever hear the original version?" Schroeder asked during their rehearsal at Mr. Kelly's. "Send in the Clowns" was the signature song from Steven Sondheim's new musical, *A Little Night Music,* which won a slew of Tony awards weeks earlier. "I'd be interested," she said. "Marshall, can you get me a copy of 'Send in the Clowns,' like a lead sheet, the actual lead sheet?" Schroeder asked. "So Marshall comes in with 'Send in the Clowns' and I played through the lead sheet in E-flat major as printed." (The lead sheet was, in fact, in D-flat major.) Vaughan listened, then said, "Yeah, that's how we should do it."[9]

Sondheim wrote "Send in the Clowns" for the musical's lead, Glynis Johns, and tailored it to the limitations of her voice. She had a small range and struggled to sustain long notes, so he composed short, declamatory phrases that ended in consonants built from simple motivic lines. He used the weaknesses of her voice, her uneven vibrato and slight rasp, to enhance the emotional impact of the song and her character's vulnerability. Johns, who had also recently turned fifty, portrayed Desiree Armfeldt, an aging actress with a fatherless daughter at home in the care of her grandmother. Fourteen years after their original affair, she reconnected with the father of her daughter, but he rejected her. "Send in the Clowns" explores the pain of youthful regrets, lost love, disappointment, and the cruel ironies of life.

The parallels to Vaughan's personal life were uncanny, but it was unlikely that these similarities drew her to the song or that she knew the plot of *A Little Night Music.* "The lyrics didn't count that much," explained Schroeder, a sentiment echoed by most of her musicians.[10] Rather, she was drawn to the music: the complexities of Sondheim's harmonic language; the way he built his chords, often layering dissonant tones together; and the shift from D-flat major in the verse to F minor in the bridge. Sondheim also played with meter. He used more difficult compound meters and regularly shifted between $^{12}/8$ and $^9/8$ as the lyrics required. And even though the melody was simple, built from one or two motives stated again and again, it gave Vaughan room to stretch out and explore.[11]

Schroeder wrote Vaughan's arrangement for "Send in the Clowns." He transposed the tune from D-flat major to E-flat major, one of Vaughan's favorite keys. "I played the lead sheet part as written and then I rearranged the bridge, the middle part," he explained, "to make it a little quicker in $^6/8$ and have Walter [Booker], the bass player, play some kind of a counter line, and then we go back to the original [verse]." The arrangement was sparse. Instead of playing thick, layered chords and adding filler between phrases, the pianist played simple, arpeggiated chords. The bassist didn't enter until the bridge, and when he did he played arco, with his bow, rather than the usual, more rhythmic plucking. The drummer also stayed in the background, entering only occasionally to introduce a new timbre or texture that enhanced the song's musical climaxes. "Once she got ahold of that [arrangement], she started singing the heck out of it," said Schroeder.[12]

Vaughan transformed "Send in the Clowns." Whereas Glynis Johns's range barely spanned an octave, Vaughan's spanned nearly four. Johns often cheated. She did not—likely could not—dip down to the lowest notes that Sondheim composed for her. In contrast, Vaughan's interpretation surveyed the full range of her voice. She explored the depths of her baritone and then spiraled up to the heights of her soprano, often in the same breath. And Vaughan slowed the tempo dramatically. When played straight through at a medium pace, the chart clocked in at three and a half minutes. Vaughan nearly doubled that. Her interpretations ran six, often seven minutes. She broke the piece open, adding her trademark vocal inflections. She added melismas and turns, vocal bends and slides. She shifted her timbre from deep and chocolatey to light and silky, almost ephemeral to thick and throaty, and then back again. Sometimes she simply sustained a note, for bars at time, gradually building from soft to loud, a vocal feat that, from a technical standpoint, is incredibly difficult. Other times she experimented with her vibrato or added new vocal turns. When she came to the final reprise of the verse, her trio dropped out. She sang a cappella. In a sense, it was the introduction to her cadenza—that moment in a concerto when the soloist dazzles the crowd with her virtuosity and prowess. Vaughan glided through scales, again demonstrating her range and vocal dexterity. She repeated the final phrase, the hopeful "Maybe next year," over and over, each time adding a new variation and another brilliant vocal feat. In a way, it was the musical realization of the optimism at the center of her personality and worldview.

Vaughan took her listeners on an emotional journey, from a place of pain and heartache to one of optimism and strength. In the musical, Desiree's personal fulfillment, her happy ending, is postponed until the reprise of "Send in the Clowns," when after twists of fate she and her lost love, the father of her child, are reunited. They sing together triumphantly, joyfully. Vaughan, however, accomplished this by herself, on her own terms. In the hands of Sarah Vaughan, "Send in the Clowns" became a vocal tour de force, a vehicle for displaying her vocal mastery and creative vision. She used the same kind of inflections and embellishments that she introduced thirty years earlier. As the spirit, the momentum and energy, of the song grew, so did the intensity of her voice, constantly building until she reached the tune's musical climax. These were all techniques grounded in the black church, the gospel singing of her youth. But now she sang them with an expansive boldness and operatic flair. She transformed a pop song into a vocal masterpiece, a through-composed jazz aria.[13]

"The song belongs to Sarah Vaughan," reviewer Jay Scott wrote in 1984, a decade after she introduced it into her repertoire. "In about six minutes—six minutes replete with references to Gregorian chant and nearly every musical mode since—she communicated a lifetime of lust and longing: she may be the only singer alive capable of compressing *La Traviata* into the space of a show tune."[14]

Other critics disliked the tune. For them, her interpretation of "Send in the Clowns," which had become her obligatory encore, was too mannered, too predictable, and too over-the-top. "'Send in the Clowns,' which has become little more than a vehicle for her vocal high dive, should be given a rest," concluded John Wilson of the *New York Times*. He was a fan of Vaughan's and had been reviewing her performances for more than thirty years. For others, "Send in the Clowns" simply illustrated a larger problem with Vaughan's singing. She was too driven by technique, too enamored with her vocal prowess, so much so that she often lost sight of a song's larger meaning and emotional impact. "The results tend too often to the mannered and even fussy—vocal virtuosity run loose, as a thing in itself," explained John Rockwell, also of the *New York Times*. And Whitney Balliett, the longtime jazz critic for the *New Yorker*, concluded: "She's a person of tremendous technique and talent and probably should have been an opera singer. As a result, she's in the middle between straight pop singing and classical singing, so I find her a kind of freak because she doesn't respect her songs most of the time. Everything is sacrificed to technique and four octaves while the extraordinary voice and lyrics go out the window. I admire her, but she doesn't move me. I have to be moved."[15]

Vaughan didn't care. She clearly enjoyed exploring her voice and showing listeners the remarkable, almost superhuman things she could do with it. And she must have enjoyed the unconditional acceptance and embrace of her fans, despite the disapproval of some critics. By singing this way, she felt empowered and fulfilled as an artist. Confronted by another terrible experience in the recording studio, a bad arrangement fueled by the shortsighted, commercial aims of a record producer, she transformed it into something positive, something truly her own. Once again, she rendered records irrelevant. "Send in the Clowns" became a phenomenon during her live shows, and she sang it her way for seven years before finally recording it again in 1981 with the Count Basie Orchestra. "Send in the Clowns," a song that embraced a woman's maturity and life experiences, became her signature song, a personal anthem of sorts. It replaced "Broken-Hearted Melody" as her most requested song, and in many ways it helped revive her career.

I'm happier than ever and it shows while I'm on the stage," Vaughan told *Ebony*'s Louie Robinson in September 1974. "That's because my personal life is wonderful . . . a great husband, a loving mother, and daughter, many close friends."[16] The previous summer, five months after the death of her father, Vaughan and Fisher bought a house in Hidden Hills, an exclusive, gated community overlooking the San Fernando Valley. Fisher helped her relocate her mother, adopted sister, and twelve-year-old daughter from Newark, and they all lived together as a family in the new house. After years of constant touring combined with bicoastal living, Vaughan was finally reunited with her family.

"Sarah wanted to marry him," Michiyo Tanaka remembered Fisher telling her. "He didn't want to because he had a feeling they would divorce someday."[17] Fisher had been married twice, had three children of his own, and wanted to avoid the legal mess of another divorce. In public, however, Vaughan referred to Fisher as her husband. In him she found a partner completely devoted to her. Someone who loved the music as much as she did. Vaughan was still an intensely private woman, but at fifty she was coming into her own. She began to feel more comfortable in her skin, more comfortable with her role as a public figure. "All of this has helped me to be more at ease with the public than ever," she explained. "Today I talk to people and they talk to me. I love them and I feel their love for me."[18]

"I try to insulate her from all the crap around her, but I stop at the stage," Fisher told Les Tomkins in 1977. "Our philosophy is based on musical integrity. Everything that I do is directed into music—the sound. And I also feel that the best judge of the material that she should do, and the way she should do it, is Sarah. There's simply no other considerations, in my opinion. I work on the perimeter, to direct it all towards making it possible for her to do what she wants to do."[19]

"My career really began when I met Marshall," Vaughan said during the same interview, in a now-familiar show of support for the current man in her life. "I had two husbands that . . . well, that's it, for that subject—I had two husbands, period. Then I married Marshall, and now my business is taken care of. I have an accountant. I don't have to worry about anything. All he wants me to do is sing."[20] This is what Vaughan had always wanted and needed.

"If you don't have your business properly taken care of . . . ," she added, then paused to reflect. "Before, I had accountants, and it was them that told me: 'You're going to get busted for income tax. I'll see you later!' Now I have a very good accountant, and I know I can look back as far as '69, and see where my money went, things like that. He sends me an account every week, a thing at the end of the month; I put 'em in my notebook, and I can find out who got a check or something. I have Marshall to thank for that. It's hard when you've got things on your mind, like: 'Where's my money? I'm working this week, but where's it going? Who's gonna get it? Not me.' Now everything is perfect."[21]

On July 13, 1974, Vaughan launched her second new project after turning fifty, an endeavor that would soon become the third and final crossover phase of her career. She performed a program of American composer George Gershwin's music with the Los Angeles Philharmonic at their summer home, the

Hollywood Bowl, before an audience of 14,336. She collaborated with conductor and pianist Michael Tilson Thomas, the twenty-nine-year-old musical director of the Buffalo Philharmonic Orchestra, who was making his debut at the Hollywood Bowl. The concert, developed by Tilson Thomas, demonstrated the sheer breadth of Gershwin's output, surveying the composer's opera and orchestral works, sweeping film scores, and his deceptively simple, comparatively short songs for musical theater, which soon became part of the American songbook. Tilson Thomas was in search of a vocalist who could sing the material while also demonstrating its potential for further creative exploration. He approached Vaughan. She was excited to participate; she chose arranger Marty Paich for the project, and rehearsals began at her home in Hidden Hills. "We sketched out what the tunes would be, how the medleys would work, and what could happen," Tilson Thomas explained. "Right away I was happy because the arrangements were rich, and Sassy's ideas were terrific."[22]

"Michael Tilson Thomas just had a great admiration for her," said bassist Bob Magnusson. "He could see the genius in her. Sometimes being a jazz artist, you get classical snobs." Magnusson had grown up immersed in the classical tradition. His father was the principal clarinetist with the San Diego Symphony, and before switching to jazz Magnusson played French horn for twelve years. "But Michael, he could see what it was and he would rehearse with her with him playing piano. She would do amazing things, and he would be astounded at it."[23]

"She was very, very nervous, she could get so nervous," Tilson Thomas said, remembering their first rehearsals with the Los Angeles Philharmonic. "We were going to do a medley that began with 'Summertime.' I was supposed to go onstage and start the orchestra, and from offstage Sassy was supposed to sing and then walk onstage singing 'Summertime.' The first time we did it, from offstage came this strangled squeak, which was Sassy trying to get some notes out. Standing offstage, she was paralyzed with fright. We realized that she had to overcome that moment of walking onstage. She was really amazed [to be] doing this with a big orchestra."[24]

She'd performed for large crowds many times. She'd worked with popular music's finest arrangers and composers, including Michel Legrand, Marty Paich, and Henry Mancini, usually backed by an orchestra. And she'd performed in many of the world's finest venues: Carnegie Hall and Town Hall in New York, the Civic Opera House in Chicago, the Royal Albert Hall in London, and the Salle Pleyel in Paris, not to mention the famed opera houses of Italy. But this was her first appearance with a major symphony orchestra in twenty-five years, since 1949, when she and Duke Ellington performed with the Philadelphia Symphony Orchestra at Robin Hood Dell.

Jazz was still set apart from the world of classical music. The symphony orchestra was a revered cultural and musical institution with hundreds of years of history. It represented the establishment, and the classical music that it played, complete with its European pedigree, epitomized highbrow culture. Despite a growing body of criticism and scholarship, jazz, because of its origins in African American aesthetics and its links to nightclubs, still remained, for many in the world of classical music, decidedly lowbrow—an inferior and marginalized outsider. And classical music, its institutions and prestige, had long been off-limits for most black artists. Performing with a symphony orchestra was a big deal for any jazz artist, but perhaps more so for Vaughan, whose parents had dreamed of her becoming a concert artist like her childhood idol Marian Anderson.

Six years earlier, in 1968, a Newark journalist dubbed Vaughan the "Marian Anderson of Modern Jazz."[25] And for years, critics proclaimed that she possessed a "legitimate voice." With her beautiful vocal production, almost four-octave range, and control of both her vibrato and breath, she could have been an opera singer. In 1974, when Leonard Feather asked her if she ever wanted to be an opera singer, she answered, "Yes, I always wanted to; but you have to start early, and I couldn't afford the money for lessons." Learning languages and mastering the classical repertoire all took years of study at a conservatory. Anderson, the first African American woman to sing with the Metropolitan Opera, benefited from well-connected, wealthy patrons. Vaughan did not, so she turned to the world of jazz. "I was thrilled once to receive a telegram of congratulations from Marian Anderson and flattered when [conductor] Zubin Mehta said it was his loss and popular music's gain," she added. "But I think I'm happier where I am. After all, opera can be taught; but what I do I have to feel, which I believe is better."[26]

While opera could have offered Vaughan a certain kind of prestige and respectability, it would have limited her creative freedoms. As a classical musician, she would have been beholden to the score, to the vision of the composer. Even the operas of modernists like Bartok, Berg, and Schoenberg would not have offered her the same opportunities for harmonic exploration, going out to the precipice, as she so often did, especially during the early, most innovative days of bebop. With opera, her artistic license, her personal mandate to craft her own unique vision of music, solely on her own terms, would have been stifled.

Vaughan's debut performance with Tilson Thomas and the Los Angeles Philharmonic received mixed reviews. "For Miss Vaughan, it was a win some, lose some proposition. Her rangy voice with its plush lower register and wistfully warbled top, her improvisatory skills, and her imaginative way with a phrase amply renewed the wonder of tunes like 'Someone to Watch Over Me,' 'Embraceable You,' and 'But Not For Me,'" reviewer Melody Peterson of the *Los Angeles Times* wrote, attributing the effectiveness of the first half in large part to the wonderful arrangements of Marty Paich. "However, Miss Vaughan's encounter with Thomas as piano accompanist in 'Stairway to Paradise,' 'Do It Again,' 'Who Cares?' and 'Fascinatin' Rhythm' seems to have been ill-advised from its inception." Tilson Thomas was not a jazz musician and did not swing, and, like most classically trained musicians, he was committed to stylistically authentic arrangements, including a faithfulness to the songs' original keys, which were unfortunately at odds with Vaughan's range and needs. Her discomfort was obvious. She used a music stand, and before launching into a blisteringly fast "Fascinatin' Rhythm," Vaughan confessed, "I tried to get out of it but Michael wouldn't let me."[27] "Michael was a pusher," explained pianist Carl Schroeder. "He wanted to get it done. It was all in Michael's court. He wanted to have a Gershwin program."[28]

It was an uneasy alliance between their two musical worlds. But Vaughan and Tilson Thomas fine-tuned their collaboration, worked out the kinks, and eventually took the all-Gershwin show on the road. They began in upstate New York with the Buffalo Philharmonic Orchestra, Tilson's home, on October 10, 1975. Four months later, on Sunday, February 1, 1976, Vaughan, Tilson Thomas, and the Buffalo Philharmonic appeared at Carnegie Hall, as part of a concert series celebrating American music and the bicentennial. They performed with the San Francisco Symphony on March 13, and other concerts followed.

A friendship developed between the two artists. After performances they hung out and shared new music. "I'd play Berg, Schoenberg, and Stravinsky," said Tilson Thomas. "I remember playing the last two or three minutes of Berg's Violin Concerto with its wonderfully evolved chords that are as complicated, as beautiful, and as painful as any chords that exist in classical repertory. It's actually a harmonization of a very simple little Bach melody, and the harmonies are way out there. And each time I played it, they'd say, '*Oh no!* Say it isn't so, Michael. Have mercy!'" Although Vaughan was a voracious listener, she had not been exposed to classical music's twentieth-century modernists and their daring, often atonal, harmonic language. "Michael, when you play those chords, I just go out so far," she would say, "and when you stop playing, I come back to the room, and I think: I don't know where I've been for the last five minutes."[29]

In the 1970s, as jazz clubs closed, new performing arts centers, each with its own symphony orchestra, were being built around the country. An abundance of arts funding, from both the public and private sectors, fueled this growth and expansion. "Because of the symphonies in those comparatively small communities, there are more good places to work," Marshall Fisher explained to *Down Beat*'s Arnold Jay Smith in 1977. "Tulsa now has a performing arts center. There are more good halls being built every day all over the country. So we are staying out of the hotels, out of the saloons as much as possible."[30] Vaughan focused more of her energies on concerts with symphony orchestras and began touring the Gershwin program without Tilson Thomas. She expanded her orchestral book, adding new arrangements of material by other composers, including Sondheim's "Send in the Clowns," and incorporated her trio into the act. In 1975, she performed with eight symphony orchestras, usually during their pops concert series, followed by fourteen in 1976 and sixteen in 1977. She continued her work with symphony orchestras throughout the 1980s. Vaughan and her trio played with the Boston Pops directed by the legendary Arthur Fiedler, the Chicago Symphony Orchestra, the Philadelphia Symphony Orchestra, and the National Symphony. They also appeared with dozens of regional orchestras throughout the country—in Louisville, Kansas City, Minneapolis, Houston, Dallas, San Jose, Rochester, Peoria, Toledo, Richmond, and other cities. As she performed with these symphony orchestras, she expanded her reach. She crossed over again, this time introducing the pleasures of her voice and the world of jazz to new audiences: the staid, musical traditionalists who frequented the symphony and performing arts centers.

Yet each time she sang with a symphony orchestra, Vaughan and her trio experienced the clash of musical cultures all over again. "[Arthur Fiedler] didn't really know what Sarah Vaughan was all about," said pianist Schroeder.[31] He met privately with Fiedler for extra rehearsals, playing piano as Fiedler, then in his eighties and approaching his fiftieth anniversary with the Boston Pops, conducted and sang Vaughan's parts, even though he couldn't sing. Another conductor, assuming he knew best, removed all of the "blues" notes from Vaughan's arrangements. "Oh, yes, there's a wrong note there. I had to feex it," Schroeder recalled the French conductor telling Vaughan.[32] Of course, there were no wrong notes; the conductor simply didn't understand that the blues with its flatted thirds, fifths, and sevenths was the core of much jazz and Gershwin too. The conductor's "feexes" transformed Vaughan's arrangements from jazz into something more closely resembling Schubert.

Other conductors struggled to follow Vaughan's trio. Her rhythm section would be in one spot, and the orchestra, sixty or seventy strong, would be three bars ahead. Yet during an extended orchestra interlude, the conductor dramatically waved his arms about. "All the guys in the band are lookin' funny at the conductor," said Schroeder.[33] They were accustomed to the intimacy of their trio and the subtle, almost intuitive style of musical communication they shared. While members of the symphony orchestra were excellent musicians who had devoted decades to mastering the classical repertory, most didn't know how to improvise or swing. To compensate, Schroeder remembered crafting arrangements in $^{12}/_8$ in an effort to notate the feel of a swing rhythm.

At one appearance, they played in an outside amphitheater, as they often did. "We did the rehearsals. Everything was good. We get to the gig. We start the gig. All of a sudden the wind starts blowing. Next thing you know all of the music is flying, like eight feet above the orchestra," reminisced pianist Schroeder, chuckling. "So we're back to playing the trio and there's this music flying around in the sky. And then Sarah turns to the guys. She turns to the cello player on her left and she invites [him to play]." "I don't know the music," he replied. "Just join in," she urged. "You can jam. Just play something."[34]

It didn't occur to her that her request was terrifying for most classical musicians. For them, the score provided security, a safety net. It was their job to faithfully realize the music as written, not use it as a point of departure for musical exploration. But that Vaughan could do this—improvise, spontaneously jam, and sing her way out of trouble with such ease, often in the face of chaos—was a fundamental part of who she was as a musician. It was the source of her freedom. For her, these were basic musicianship skills, and she assumed that her classical counterparts possessed them too. After all, she studied classical piano as a child. In the 1970s, she played piano in her act, often incorporating excerpts from the classical repertory, adding a wink and nod to the audience, as if to say, "I bet you didn't realize I could do that." While rehearsing with symphony orchestras, she could hear, then point out, an out-of-tune violin or trumpet among the sea of instruments. And symphony musicians marveled at her flawless intonation, one of the core yet very difficult skills required of classical musicians. This came easily to Vaughan too. She had perfect pitch.

There were, however, aspects of performing with symphony orchestras that terrified her. She still became terribly nervous before each performance. She fumbled with her microphone and music stand, and often missed lyrics, even though she too had a score in front of her.[35] And she still didn't understand many of the symphony orchestra's traditions and customs. She never quite mastered the art of making her entrance. Instead of walking through the little path made by the first violinists, as soloists usually did, she walked out in front of the orchestra. "Of course the orchestra is set up to about within a foot of the edge of the stage," explained Schroeder. "You're talking about sixty people on stage. So she's got to walk this one foot little crazy walk to get [to the piano and microphone]."[36] It was like walking a tightrope while wearing a glamorous evening gown as several thousand applauded in anticipation. But she didn't know. "The whole spectacle of it broke the ice," said Schroeder. "In one sense it was accidental, but in another it was almost deliberate, because then she could feel that she had broken the ice. She could feel comfortable. What could possibly happen after that? . . . But once she hit the stage, forget it, then there was no nervousness."[37]

On the whole, though, Vaughan loved singing with symphony orchestras. She loved the way her voice sounded backed by the full force of a sixty-piece ensemble, the mixing and melding of timbres as dozens of lush strings, horns, and woodwinds bathed her voice in a way that only a symphony orchestra could. Vaughan must have also appreciated the approval and acceptance, the legitimacy, that performing with symphony orchestras represented. That she, a jazz musician from Newark, had been welcomed into the hallowed halls of classical music, whose roots were steeped in the traditions and institutions of Europe. She also finally realized her childhood aspirations. In 1976, critic Leonard Feather asked her again if she ever sang opera. "No, I just always thought about it. I don't think even my mother realized that," she reiterated, adding, "But now that I'm making these appearances with the symphonies I feel as though I'm doing it anyway."[38]

Rio—the greatest place I think I've ever been on earth," Vaughan proclaimed in the documentary *Listen to the Sun*. After following Vaughan as she performed in Newport, Philadelphia, and Houston in August 1977, filmmaker Thomas Guy and his crew joined her for a week in Rio de Janeiro in October. It was the end of a three-week tour of Mexico, Columbia, Ecuador, Peru, Chile, Argentina, and finally Brazil, and her third tour of Brazil in six years. *Listen to the Sun* gave audiences a glimpse into her life behind the scenes as she traveled, rehearsed, and interacted with the press and her fans, and it was clear that Vaughan had come to love Brazil, its music, food, language, and people. "Let me tell you, the audiences in Brazil, they are the greatest audiences I have ever seen. I don't believe them. I don't believe that people like me that much," she confessed in a private conversation with Milton Nascimento, a prominent Brazilian guitarist and singer-songwriter, a week after her show at Rio's Hotel Nacional on October 21. "When I saw you there at the thing, I saw something that I never saw in my life," he agreed. "The music comes out in Rio," she concluded, perhaps referring to Rio's rich musical heritage and the inspiration she felt there.[39] "Whenever she sings, her soul comes out of her mouth," explained a concertgoer interviewed by Guy, and the woman sitting next to him agreed. "That's right, that's right," she said. "We really love her."[40]

This trip to Brazil was different. After gigs in São Paulo, Rio de Janeiro, and Vitória and a vacation with her trio, Vaughan prepared to enter the recording studio. It had been four months since Atlantic scrapped her Beatles album and canceled her contract, and she hadn't signed with a new label. She decided to take matters into her own hands. For the first time in her career, she would produce her own album. She was no longer beholden to record executives motivated more by financial gain than artistry. She would have full creative control to choose who she worked with, what she sang, and how she sang it. And in recent years, she had become fascinated by Brazilian music. While much of the new popular music being written in the United States buckled under the force of Vaughan's voice and her constant need to explore and delve deeper, Brazilian popular songs could support Vaughan's creative vision. This growing repertoire of contemporary pop music was known for the richness of its harmonic and rhythmic language, and it offered Vaughan a new, dynamic sound world to discover. Given the high esteem in which Brazilians held Vaughan, she had her pick of the country's finest musicians and composers. They brought songs to her like the Magi bestowing gifts, hoping that she would do them the honor of singing their compositions.

She hired the influential singer, composer, and producer Aloysio de Oliveira to organize the five days of sessions. Born in 1914, Oliveira had played a pivotal role in bringing Brazilian music to an international audience, first as a member of the Bando da Lua that toured with Carmen Miranda for twenty-six years until her death in 1955, and then as a producer and composer who collaborated with bossa nova greats, including Antonio Carlos Jobim. Oliveira was an elder statesman within the Brazilian music community and capable of bringing together the country's finest musicians for Vaughan's sessions. On October 31 and November 3, she recorded with Nascimento, who made his international debut on Wayne Shorter's 1974 album *Native Dancer* and would go on to work with Paul Simon, George Duke, Quincy Jones, and Duran Duran. On November 4, she worked with keyboardist Jose Roberto Bertrami, founder of the trio Azymuth, which mixed Brazilian samba and bossa nova with jazz, funk, and folk rock.

On November 5, she collaborated with Dorival Caymmi, a driving force in the bossa nova movement and considered by many a grandfather of Brazilian popular music. And finally, on November 7, during her last day in the studio, she paired with Jobim, the most influential and famous composer in Brazil. He introduced international audiences to the bossa nova with his compositions "The Girl from Ipanema" and "Corcovado" in the 1950s.

Unlike many of her past recording sessions, producers did not rush Vaughan to cut costs or limit her creative freedom. She had time to immerse herself in the material. On October 29, she held a two-hour, free-ranging rehearsal with Nascimento. On first hearing, a recording of the rehearsal could be mistaken for a party. The room was crowded. People laughed and talked as a piano played in the background. The pianist, likely Bertrami, was running through the chord changes for "Bridges (Travessia)," composed by Nascimento. Then Vaughan began to hum, quietly in the background, and Nascimento joined her. She was learning the melody, feeling out the tune. At one point she chose one of her exquisite notes, something not found in the original, and emphasized it until the pianist incorporated the new harmonization into the arrangement. Moments later, she ran through another set of chord changes as she composed what would become her cover's unique tag. After ten minutes, she began to sing the tune's English lyrics. Nascimento joined her, singing in Portuguese, and she said, "English lyrics, kid." "What key is that in?" he asked. "Put it in G. How about G?" she replied. They ran through the song four more times. There was a flurry of conversation and laughter between takes as the musicians shared their ideas. After thirty minutes Vaughan was done, but the music making continued for another hour as the arrangement took shape. Nascimento sang his part again and again, the percussionists joined in, and Vaughan, who could be heard chatting away in the background, occasionally returned to sing. The pace was leisurely, the mood joyful and light-hearted. The entire process was organic and spontaneous, a coming together of musical minds—the kind of music making that Vaughan loved.[41]

During her five days in the studios of Rio de Janeiro, Vaughan recorded more than a dozen songs, plenty for her new album, which would be titled, appropriately, *I Love Brazil!* It would be the first of three albums of Brazilian music that Vaughan would release in the coming years. Singing Brazilian songs would become another important creative outlet for Vaughan, and she would become known as one of their finest interpreters. But when Vaughan returned home in November 1977, she had no way to manufacture or distribute the album. For this, she would need to ally herself with a new record label. She turned to Norman Granz, Ella Fitzgerald's longtime producer and manager, whom she had known since 1948 when she and Charlie Parker headlined one of his popular Jazz at the Philharmonic tours.

In 1973, thirteen years after selling Verve Records to MGM, Granz founded Pablo Records. He hoped that the new label would bolster the careers of his favorite jazz musicians who struggled to find recording contracts as the industry changed. "It's criminal that someone like Sarah Vaughan was allowed to go without making a record for five years," Granz explained in 1971, as he began to dip his toes back into record producing. "The record companies have changed. Executives today are only concerned with the fact that they can gross $9 million with the Rolling Stones. They forget that a profit is still a profit, and that you're still making money if you only net $9,000. I keep telling people that, and they think I'm crazy."[42] Like Bobby Shad of Mainstream, Granz believed that jazz was on the cusp of a resurgence. Unlike Shad, Granz was committed to recording traditional, more mainstream acoustic jazz. At first, he recorded musicians that he managed: Ella Fitzgerald, Count Basie, Duke Ellington, Oscar Peterson, and Joe Pass. His friends. Artists who during the 1940s, 1950s, and early 1960s had fueled his career as a record producer and concert impresario. Now a wealthy man, he wanted to give back to the community who had given him so much. For Pablo, he produced albums in line with his larger vision for jazz. He still favored down-and-dirty jam sessions where musicians spontaneously improvised on standards, chorus after chorus. Although record sales rarely reached even his modest expectations, Granz distributed promotional discs to reviewers and disc jockeys in order to keep artists' names in the public eye. As the 1970s progressed, he expanded the label's roster beyond this core group of musicians, termed "Pablovians" by critic Gary Giddins, to include Dizzy Gillespie, Zoot Sims, Milt Jackson, Clark Terry, and, in the spring of 1978, Sarah Vaughan.

After signing with Pablo, Vaughan leased *I Love Brazil!*, which she owned, to Norman Granz for three years, and it was finally released in July 1979. More than a year earlier, however, on April 25, 1978, Vaughan stepped into the studio with Oscar Peterson on piano, Joe Pass on guitar, Ray Brown on bass, and Louis Bellson on drums for her first session produced by Granz. They recorded nine tracks of standards, five with the full ensemble and the remaining four with Vaughan in a duet with each member of the quartet, including an unconventional pairing with drummer Bellson. They worked quickly, producing the album that would become *How Long Has This Been Going On?* in a single day.

All-star albums featuring a collection a marquee artists jamming were a staple of Norman Granz's catalog. Fans loved hearing their favorite artists on one album, working and creating together, and they made sense financially. But they also presented challenges. There were too many egos in the studio, and the music often suffered. As the headliner of *How Long Has This Been Going On?*, Vaughan, technically speaking, was the musical leader of the session. She expected to be in control, and as she usually did, she suggested chord changes for pianist Oscar Peterson to play behind her. This irritated Peterson, a star in his own right with his own distinct musical voice. "Oscar said to me, 'If she touches that keyboard again, I'm walking out,'" Granz told his biographer, Tad Hershorn, in 2001.[43]

Although critic Gary Giddins disliked this hasty recording schedule (in his opinion, three tracks merited retakes), he hailed the album's release in October as "cause for breaking out the champagne for two reasons—it's one of the best albums she's ever made, and it documents another, if not a new, side of Sarah

Vaughan." After her years with Mainstream singing primarily contemporary pop, Vaughan finally reestablished her jazz footing on wax. It was a relaxed session, reminiscent of her days with Charlie Parker and Miles Davis. She was swinging and adventurous, and she embraced the blues. "I can't think of another Vaughan album with such an abundance of blues locutions, variations, and riffs," wrote Giddins, concluding, "It will be interesting to see if she continues to work with producer Norman Granz, because if he parades the entire Pablo stock company through her sessions (including, one hopes, a set of Benny Carter arrangements), he will be mining the most valuable lode since Ella Fitzgerald discovered songbooks."[44]

How Long Has This Been Going On? was nominated for a Grammy in February 1979, Vaughan's third nomination. (Her second nomination was for *More Sarah Vaughan Live in Japan,* released by Mainstream after she sued for a release from her contract.) *I Love Brazil!* received a nomination in 1980, and critic Leonard Feather deemed it one of the top ten jazz records of the 1970s.[45] Critics praised Vaughan's choice of material and ability to capture the essence of Brazil without losing her own distinctive take on the material. She recorded a follow-up album, *Copacabana,* during her next tour of Brazil in 1979. And her next studio session for Pablo, a collection of Ellington songs, received another Grammy nomination, her fifth, in 1981.

Vaughan had successfully weathered the difficult years a decade earlier, as the musical landscape seemed to shift around her, and emerged a stronger, more resilient and determined performer. She was back in the recording studio. She continued to tour internationally to great acclaim. And thanks to her successful concerts with symphony orchestras, which were both financially lucrative and prestigious, she was no longer beholden to the week-in, week-out grind of the nightclub circuit for her livelihood. She was singing what she wanted, how she wanted to.

15

"I'm Just Coming into My Prime"

just got married and I'm still goo, goo, ga, ga," Vaughan told audiences on June 23, 1978, as she opened her annual concert for the Newport Jazz Festival–New York at Carnegie Hall.[1] But she hadn't married Marshall Fisher. She'd married Waymon Reed, a trumpeter in the Count Basie band. They first met in 1970, during a cruise of the West Indies. "But it didn't get heavy until about a year ago," Reed explained during an interview with *Jet* magazine on his wedding day.

"Yeah, we met again in Disneyland last year," said Vaughan.[2] Basie's band played the amusement park for a week, beginning on August 21, 1977. "I just went down to catch the opening show down there. And every time—I used to see him off and on, and in my mind I said, *mmmm-hmmm!* So this time it was *mm-hmm* worked," she confessed during an interview with *Tonight Show* guest host Sammy Davis Jr.[3] Vaughan and the trio then toured with Count Basie's band in March and April 1978. "Waymon Reed was a man who saw an opportunity and gave her what it was that she needed, what she felt she needed at that point," pianist Carl Schroeder explained. "It was a secret for a while, and once Marshall found out, he disappeared immediately."[4]

The romance between Fisher and Vaughan had cooled and, in recent years, evolved into a close friendship. Fisher spent more and more time on the road doing advance work for the band. He drove the truck that hauled the sound system, gear, and extra luggage between gigs and directed setup before Vaughan and the trio arrived. During performances, he worked the sound board, and when the band flew, he carried the sound system on the airplane. "He did all this work because nobody else would do it. He was devoted," said Schroeder.[5] But it meant that he and Vaughan spent less time together. They only saw one another during gigs and gradually grew apart. Vaughan likely wanted more attention, companionship, and focus on her daily needs while touring. Perhaps she also missed the giddy feeling that comes with a new romance, and she looked elsewhere.

Fisher was heartbroken, and broke as well. If he had married Vaughan, as she wanted, Fisher would have left the relationship with a sizeable settlement. He was proud of the work that he had done as Vaughan's manager and believed that he facilitated her resurgence in the 1970s. (Pianist Schroeder agreed.) But, after seven years, he left with nothing. He was homeless, and Vaughan's bassist, Walter Booker, took him in, letting him stay at his recording studio, Boogie Woogie Studio, in New York. A year and a half later, in September 1979, Fisher went to hear Booker and Jimmy Cobb play at the Tin Palace, and he met Michiyo Tanaka, a Japanese pianist who had recently moved to New York. They soon married, much to Vaughan's surprise. Cynthia Coleman, Booker's girlfriend, broke the news to Vaughan. Tanaka remembered Coleman saying that Vaughan was "in shock" after hearing the news of her marriage to Marshall.[6] She also heard through the grapevine that Vaughan had removed Fisher from all of her photos. "Marshall always loved her even after breaking up with her. I was jealous," said Tanaka. For the first seven years of Tanaka's marriage to Fisher, he talked about Sarah Vaughan. "I was so jealous because he mentioned Sarah like it was a present tense."[7]

On Tuesday, June 13, 1978, Vaughan, now fifty-four, married Waymon Reed, who was sixteen years her junior, at the Chicago home of a friend. Unlike her wedding to C. B. Atkins twenty years earlier, also in Chicago, she was surrounded by friends and family, including her mother and daughter. *Jet* magazine reported that Vaughan wore a pink chiffon gown and cried into her bouquet as the groom awkwardly placed the ring on her finger. "Waymon called me about three weeks ago from Tokushima, Japan, and asked me to marry him," she told the magazine. He was on tour with the Basie band, days before an earthquake. "I don't know whether the earthquake started because he proposed or because I said 'yes,'" she joked. The couple planned to live in her Hidden Hills home, and they would honeymoon in the Bahamas when their work schedules permitted. (She would receive an honorary doctorate from Northwestern University on Saturday, June 17, and open the Newport Jazz Festival the following Friday.) And when asked what the future held, she said, "Ummh, well . . . oh honey, I don't know! I'm just so happy I can't even think straight yet." Then, with her characteristic optimism and insistence on living in the present, she added: "You'll see lots of things happening now for Sarah Vaughan Reed."[8]

Reed quit his job with the Basie band and joined Vaughan on the road, and her trio became a quartet. "He was an adequate trumpet player, but that was the least of his many talents. His job was to keep her happy and supply her with that," said Schroeder, adding, "Waymon, well, he was just a snake. He was just promoting himself, that's all."[9] Within six months, after yet more symphony appearances, the summer festival circuit, and another tour of England and Eastern Europe, Reed wanted to become the leader of the band and persuaded Vaughan to fire bassist Walter Booker and drummer Jimmy Cobb. "I really think Waymon was jealous of Jimmy Cobb and me being so close to her," Booker explained. "We had a pact, and he was the outsider all the time."[10] Schroeder, the group's musical director, resigned in solidarity. He had no interest in breaking in a new rhythm section. Cobb had been with Vaughan for nine years, Schroeder seven, and Booker three. It was the end of an era. The trio that supported Vaughan during her career renaissance of the 1970s had disbanded.

"Walter and Jimmy, their level was as high as Sarah's in some moments. I was kind of a fly on the wall going 'Oh, this is so cool, everyone's playing their ass off over here.' I felt very lucky and still do," said Schroeder. "It's funny that something like that, something that's extramusical, could dictate something happening to the music that was such high quality." The men in Vaughan's personal life wielded tremendous power and influence, and for Schroeder this was her greatest weakness, a weakness at odds with the perfection that he heard in her voice. "To see a flaw like that which wasn't visible to the public, so the public could appreciate it like Judy Garland or Billie Holiday, whose flaws were visible on stage. [It] made her that much more human and more easy to empathize with," he continued. She was a human soul with flaws. "I attribute it to her humanity. That's what makes it so fantastic. [She had] a high level of ability to sing and to create and she was still a mess like you and me!"[11]

Jimmy Cobb didn't know that he had been let go from the band until his replacement, drummer Roy McCurdy, called him. "I called Jimmy Cobb and asked him about it because I didn't want to just go and take a job that he had been working on," McCurdy explained. "We talked about it and he said, 'Yes, go ahead and take it.'"[12] Pianist Mike Wofford and bassist Andy Simpkins joined McCurdy in the new trio and began rehearsals at Vaughan's home in Hidden Hills. "Waymon conducted those rehearsals," Wofford said. "Sarah would be there and she would sing some and she would listen, and if she really wasn't happy with the tempo or something she would mention it and talk about it. But for the most part, she just stayed out of the picture and let us learn the stuff on our own."[13]

In March, after a month of rehearsals, the band went on the road. In the midst of a sixteen-stop tour with vocalist Mel Tormé and saxophonist Gerry Mulligan, Vaughan made three separate appearances at Carnegie Hall within the span of ten days. While it was common to program classical musicians this way, in cycles of concerts (pianist Arthur Rubinstein, for instance, played ten Carnegie Hall recitals in less than five weeks to celebrate his seventy-fifth birthday in 1961), this was the first time that a jazz musician received similar treatment. "I felt that for once I'd like Sarah to be acknowledged as the great artist that she is," said impresario George Wein.[14]

"[It] is a nice step for jazz," Vaughan told Mary Campbell of the Associated Press. "But I'm worried. I usually play Carnegie Hall once a year, not three times in a week. When I think about it, my stomach jumps. I always get nervous before concerts, but this is different."[15] It was an honor, a career retrospective of sorts, and an opportunity to demonstrate her breadth as a performer. On Wednesday, March 21, she shared the bill with Tormé and Mulligan in a nod to the cool jazz and pop aspects of her career. On Friday, March 23, she invited two daring, experimental vocalists, Betty Carter and Herb Jeffries, to join her in what critics viewed as a tribute to her modernist, more avant-garde roots. And a week later, on March 30, for the final concert, she performed with the Count Basie Orchestra, harking back to her days in the big bands. All of the concerts sold out, and Wein added an additional show on March 21.

The concert with Carter and Jeffries was exceptional, but the other two did not live up to expectations. Aside from her exhilarating duets with Carter and Jeffries, she did not collaborate with her fellow headliners. And instead of demonstrating her range, she sang the same repertoire, with similar arrangements, each night. Detractors worried that she was in a rut, simply going through the motions. Several critics pointed to her new trio, still struggling to gel, as the source of her problems. They missed her old trio. "Something was amiss, and expressed itself in uncertain pacing, an undercurrent of tension. Exaggeration of the less enchanting traits of her style at the expense of the felicities," Richard Sudhalter of the *New York Post* wrote. "Her longtime accompanying trio, billed on the printed program, had been replaced—and from the look and sound of things, at very short notice. They were reading, watching for cues from Sarah and her husband and musical director, Waymon Reed, featured on fluegelhorn. They were coping, but cautiously."[16] Vaughan seemed strained, working overtime simply to hold things together. She relied on her trademark vocal virtuosity as a prop rather than a tool for exploration and discovery. Perhaps her unease with her new trio also contributed to the lack of variety in her programming. Regardless, her concert cycle at Carnegie Hall, a unique opportunity to shine, failed to live up to its potential.

With time, the trio improved and began to click musically. Offstage, however, the new band still struggled as tensions escalated between the trio and Waymon Reed. As musical director, Reed wanted to assert his dominance over the trio. "Sass was really close to all the musicians," explained drummer McCurdy. "So we'd come down in the morning and we'd get breakfast sometimes in the hotel and sit there and talk and all that kind of stuff. And I remember one time [Reed] came down and told me—he came down and Sass was sitting having breakfast with the musicians, and he says, 'You know, you're not supposed to sit at the same table with Sass. You can't sit at the same table with her.' Things like that, just strange stuff. Or 'You can't talk with Sass. You have to talk to me first and I'll pass things along to her.'"[17] It was reminiscent of efforts by her past husbands, especially Atkins, to control and isolate her, to distance her from her musicians and support network. And it was at odds with her egalitarian approach to making music, one of the core principles of jazz. Reed also begrudged the trio their high salaries, another one of the ways that Vaughan demonstrated her respect for the musicians she worked with.

Reed's behavior became increasingly erratic. Her trio saw him run uncontrollably, for no visible reason, down an airport concourse, then collapse. Another time, after a disagreement with Vaughan, he ran into a busy street, stopping traffic while yelling "Kill me! Kill me!" A confrontation with an airline representative over seat assignments became so heated that the desk agent challenged Reed to a boxing match. Arguments between Reed and Vaughan became more volatile. There were more concerns about physical abuse. And, according to rumors, Reed hit Vaughan's mother.[18] Friends suspected mental illness.

"I just couldn't get along with him because his personality was just too strange and he acted too strange all the time and he just wanted you to do things that just were ridiculous," McCurdy remembered. "So right after the Playboy Jazz Festival that was it for me. They let me go from the band, and it wasn't a musical thing. I talked to Sass, she said it was nothing musical, it was just personal between her—she was so involved with her husband in that time and we couldn't get along, so it was just time to move on. So I did."[19] He'd been with the band for less than six months. Pianist Mike Wofford lasted until the end of the year, but then he left too, and the trio was in transition again.

Vaughan's insistence on involving her husband in her career, constantly supporting and advocating for him, also harmed her efforts in the recording studio. On August 13, 1979, Vaughan and Norman Granz began their second collaboration together: a two-album collection of Duke Ellington songs. As he had in 1957 when recording Ella Fitzgerald's groundbreaking Ellington songbook on Verve, Granz backed Vaughan with a variety of combos, both big and small. But the first session got off to a bumpy start. Granz enlisted Benny Carter to write arrangements for a twenty-two-piece ensemble that included a full complement of strings, French horns, harp, reeds, guitar, and her trio. Vaughan asked that space be left in the arrangements for Reed to solo. Granz didn't honor her request, but instead of him telling her in advance, she discovered the omission the day of the session, after the arrangements had been completed and the musicians hired. She scrapped the six tracks recorded that day, and they remained unreleased until 2013. It was an expensive decision, one that probably damaged her working relationship with Granz and, according to many, hurt the project. Two days later she returned to the studio to record three of the same songs, this time backed by a ten-piece jazz ensemble. Similar sessions with a quintet and a new ten-piece combo followed on August 16 and 27, and all included Reed. Then the production moved to New York. On September 12 she recorded four new big band arrangements by Billy Byer and four tunes backed by another octet the next day. The final two sessions took place in Los Angeles on January 22 and 23, 1980. The first was with a blues-inflected band, and the second with a duet pairing piano and guitar.

"I really love Norman; he's done so much for jazz," Vaughan told Leonard Feather in March 1980. "The only thing is, you just don't argue with him. You pick up the phone and keep saying 'Yes, Norman.' It's always a battle with him, because he just wants me to come in, look at a bunch of sheet music he has laid out, pick out some songs, and jam. Well, I don't want to spend the rest of my life doing that. . . . It's time for a change in jazz, instrumentally and vocally. Instead of everybody just jamming for fifteen choruses, there should be music written out for a few choruses, then solos for a few, alternating. It seems to me that just jamming is beginning to go out of style."[20]

"Why should I hate the word jazz? That's where I started, and that's one of the things I still do," she added when Feather asked her if she resented the jazz label. "What I *don't* want to be called is a blues singer, although on one recent session Norman even had me doing that: I sang Duke Ellington's 'Rocks in My Bed' with some old time blues musicians."[21] Backed by an ensemble including bluesmen Eddie "Cleanhead" Vinson on saxophone and vocals, pianist Lloyd Glen, and electric guitarist PeeWee Crayton, Vaughan adopted the role and mannerisms of a blues singer, even calling out words of encouragement and approval as her new bandmates soloed. She sang dutifully, but it was completely out of character with who she was as a musician, and the track was an anomaly, out of sync with the rest of the project. In the end, it was another old-school blues jam session. It's unclear if Vaughan was satisfied with the results. "Well, I tried so hard before Duke passed to do an album with his orchestra. But we never made it," she said while publicizing the *Duke Ellington Songbook*. "So now, I um, I think it is a nice album."[22]

By the time Vaughan finished the recording session for the *Duke Ellington Songbook,* Reed was no longer touring or playing with Vaughan. On January 31, 1980, when Vaughan performed at Avery Fisher Hall in New York, she told audiences that Reed was back in Los Angeles awaiting a kidney operation. One week later, on February 7, her concert at the Hollywood Bowl started thirty-five minutes late due to the sudden illness of Reed after his release from the hospital. She dedicated the concert to him and, in his absence, plugged his new record, *46th and 8th*.

Before returning to Los Angeles for her performance at the Hollywood Bowl, Vaughan taped two episodes of *The Dick Cavett Show* scheduled for broadcast March 6 and 7, 1980. She was distracted and uneasy as she answered the usual questions about her newest album, her early days on the road with Charlie Parker and the other beboppers, her childhood aspirations, and her future plans. And then suddenly, without prompting, she added: "Well, you know, my husband is in the, umm . . . ," she paused, collecting herself. "My husband and I, we, um, he plays trumpet. Waymon. And we usually work together. He would have been here today, but he's in the hospital. But we have combined our little things together. And he . . ." "You are known as a great team," Cavett prompted, helping Vaughan through the moment. "The Quartet and I. It's Waymon. . . . We had a lot of nice little things we had together," she said, slipping into the past tense with a grim finality, before quickly correcting herself. "That we are doing together. He was taken sick."[23]

Seconds later, Vaughan giggled, and the tone of the conversation returned to lighter talk-show banter. But it was an unusually candid exchange for the publicly reserved, often evasive singer. She was vulnerable and worried about her husband's declining health. She was also sad, almost resigned. Perhaps she realized that their working relationship, which she clearly valued, and their marriage, despite its many incompatibilities and volatility, was over. And it must have been disappointing. Marriage was still a cultural ideal and expectation, viewed by many as a prerequisite for happiness, especially for women. But Vaughan's search for a partnership of equals living and making music together, the companionship and contentment that this represented, continued to elude her. Her quartet was once again a trio. She and Reed did not perform together again. The couple soon divorced, and Reed passed away from cancer three years later, on November 25, 1983.

"It's been a life of laughs and tears," Vaughan reflected in 1981, in the wake of her divorce. "The only thing I regret is that I married unhappily three times. Singing has given me my greatest pleasure. Sometimes I feel that singing is the only thing I've got that keeps me going. I mean there are problems and then there are problems. The only thing that allows me to forget the problems is to keep singing." It was a strategy that she had been using for almost forty years. It got her through the ups and downs of the music industry and the death of her father, not to mention the emotional and financial devastation of her failed marriages. But the rigors of life on the road were beginning to take their toll. "I just can't work steady night after night, anymore. I can't get along with people if I'm tired. I turn crabby. Then I must go out on stage and smile and look happy. That's hard. I'd rather be sick and stay home."[24]

It was before dawn on Thursday, January 28, 1982. Vaughan had just taken a red-eye from sunny Los Angeles to a cold and icy Philadelphia. John Schreiber, of George Wein's Festival Productions, the same production company responsible for the many incarnations of the Newport Jazz Festival and Vaughan's tours of Europe, waited with a limousine at the airport to take her to Wilmington, Delaware. Vaughan was singing two shows at the Grand Opera House that night. The engagement had been booked nine months earlier as part of a four-concert series celebrating the great American song composers, and Schreiber, recently promoted to producer, decided to pair Vaughan with George Gershwin.

"She gets off the plane and she's just in a bad mood. She clearly hasn't slept [when] she arrives in Philadelphia," said Schreiber. He knew Vaughan and had worked as a road manager for her tours sponsored by Wein. "We have to drive forty-five minutes to Wilmington, and I'm sitting in the back of the limo with her and I go, 'I am so excited that you're here and I just can't wait to hear the Gershwin program.' And she looked at me, she's perked up and she went, 'Gershwin program? What do you mean?' And I go, 'Well, you know, it's Sarah Vaughan sings Gershwin.' And she said, 'Not as far as I'm concerned. I'm going to do my show.' And I go, 'Didn't Frank [Vaughan's agent, Frank Rio] tell you?' And it's advertised as Sarah Vaughan sings Gershwin. She looked at me and she said, 'That's your problem, not mine.'"

"I'm petrified, and I'm a kid," recalled Schreiber, who was twenty-seven at the time. "I haven't been producing that long." He dropped Vaughan at her hotel and waited for the New York offices of Festival Productions to open. "What are you talking about, what do you mean Gershwin? Who said anything about Gershwin?" Marie St. Louis, Festival Production's longtime booker, asked when Schreiber called. "Marie! Don't you know?" he said. "No, I don't know anything about that, that doesn't make any sense to me," she replied. "How could you tell those people she was going to sing Gershwin?" Nowhere in Vaughan's contract did it stipulate that she would sing Gershwin. "My star is saying forget it, my colleagues in the office totally do not have my back, so I'm fucked," Schreiber explained. "And Sarah's asleep, because she has to rest up." And both shows were sold out.[25]

Vaughan arrived at the Grand Opera House at 5:00 P.M. for her sound check, only to discover a television crew waiting to tape the rehearsal. She wasn't happy. "My drummer's not here. This is gonna sound terrible without my drummer," she complained. Vaughan wanted to control how her music was presented and disseminated. She was a perfectionist and disliked sharing performances that she considered flawed or compromised with audiences. Casually clad in a knit cap, white blouse, black boots, and bright red pants, with a cigarette in one hand and microphone in the other, Vaughan scatted a few bars accompanied by her pianist. After the rehearsal she consented to a short interview with the television crew, then learned that the segment would not air until the following week. "That's ridiculous," she said. "If I had known that, I wouldn't have done it."[26]

Gary Mullinax, a reporter from the *Wilmington News Journal*, watched all of this as he waited in the wings for his interview. According to Mullinax, she sighed and groaned her disapproval throughout, leaning her elbows on a table and occasionally putting her head down. She said that she was getting the flu. "Then she explained why she's hated Wilmington for more than thirty years," he wrote. "The first time I came through here in the '40s I saw the whipping post," Vaughan recalled. Delaware was the last state in the country to use whipping posts to punish criminals, both black and white. The state finally abolished the laws in 1972, but public floggings took place until 1952, and in 1963 a judge sentenced a man responsible for a $4 robbery to twenty lashes, though the governor overturned the sentence. It was an embarrassing episode in Delaware's recent past, and a practice that Vaughan likely associated with racial discrimination. It was during this same 1944 stop in Wilmington that Vaughan and her bandmates encountered the racist shoeshiner at the train station, stood up for themselves, and then had to flee town. Although Wilmington tore down its whipping post in the early 1970s, the memory still haunted Vaughan in 1982. "I can still see that thing," she told Mullinax. "I hate it."[27]

It was an inauspicious start to Vaughan's interview, and she was living up to her reputation for being difficult and evasive with the press. She was grumpy and short-tempered as she answered the usual questions about her early career, life offstage, and continuing dislike of labels. Then the conversation turned to that night's performance at the Grand Opera House, part of its Tribute to the American Popular Song series. "I don't know about no Gershwin tonight. I wasn't told," she said. "It puts me in a bad position."[28]

Producer Schreiber visited Vaughan's dressing room before the show. "I know you weren't planning on singing any Gershwin, but could you do part of the set? Could part of the set be Gershwin?" he asked one last time, hoping to persuade her. "No, I don't think so. I've just been singing a lot of Gershwin lately. I'm fed up with Gershwin," she said. The day before flying to Philadelphia, Vaughan had been in rehearsals with conductor Michael Tilson Thomas for another all-Gershwin program with the Los Angeles Philharmonic. After her two shows in Wilmington on Thursday night she would play New York on Friday and Saturday before returning to Los Angeles for more rehearsals with Tilson Thomas. On Monday and Tuesday, February 1 and 2, she would sing Gershwin with the Los Angeles Philharmonic, and this time it would be recorded. "I just want to do my show," she told Schreiber. "Believe me, it will be fine. Don't worry about it."[29]

"She gets on stage, the audience is going crazy," Schreiber remembered. "She's just blowing the roof off the place, and there's no Gershwin, at all. And she's singing 'Alone Again, Naturally,' and the woman who works at the Grand Opera House looks at me and goes, 'I didn't know that Gershwin wrote "Alone Again, Naturally."' I'm like, 'I don't know, maybe he did. Who knows.'" He had decided not to tell the Grand's management about his challenges with Vaughan.[30]

"Are you all having a good time tonight?" Vaughan asked midway through her set. The audience answered with a resounding "Yes!" "You know, I know it was advertised that I was supposed to sing Gershwin tonight. I hope you don't mind that I sing the songs that I like best to you," she explained. The audience cheered, and she continued, "And for those of you who were looking for Gershwin and aren't getting any, it's not John Schreiber's fault I'm not singing Gershwin tonight. Just know that, ladies and gentlemen." Of course, no one in the audience knew who Schreiber was. Vaughan finished her show and received her usual curtain calls and sang her usual encore, "Send in the Clowns." "Great, we did it," Schreiber thought. "We dodged a bullet. Everybody had a ball. Who cares about the Gershwins."[31]

Monday morning, the Grand Opera House's marketing director called Schreiber. "I need you to read something," she said. The *Morning News* had run an editorial with the unfortunate headline "Disappointed at the Grand" that charged the theater with shortchanging patrons. They had been promised Vaughan singing Gershwin and didn't get it. The paper condemned both the faulty communications between the management and the star and Vaughan's inflexibility. "With four decades of singing popular music behind her including a lot of Gershwin (as in four-LP sides of 'Sarah Vaughan Sings George Gershwin'), one might feel that Miss Sassy could have interpolated at least one Gershwin song in her program without a whole lot of 'notice,'"[32] wrote the *Morning News* editorial team. Someone must be held responsible, they insisted. Two weeks later, in a letter to the newspaper, John Schreiber, representing Festival Productions, took full responsibility for the mix-up. "Needless to say, the contract was not renewed," he said.[33]

It was soon revealed that the Vaughan controversy was part of an ongoing feud between the *Morning News* and local arts organizations, who charged the paper with biased and sensational reporting in service of its own agenda. But the damage had already been done. Gary Mullinax's unflattering, judgmental profile was syndicated and bolstered perceptions of Vaughan, who loathed interviews, as a difficult, temperamental artist. And it was yet one more incident in a series of incidents that prompted promoter and producer George Wein, whose career spanned more than sixty years, to consider Vaughan the most difficult artist he worked with. His memories of their many conflicts often overshadowed his enjoyment of her recordings, even though he adored her voice. "When she was good, she was very good," he wrote in his memoir, "and when she was bad, it was miserable."[34]

"She was difficult," agreed Darlene Chan, the Wein employee Vaughan requested to accompany her on her European tours in the late 1960s and 1970s. "Also very sweet. Sometimes I was hoping for a day when you wake up [and] it was nice Sass. I have to say, being on the road and the schedule that we kept is grueling for anybody." After more than forty years in the business, Chan understood that all artists had good and bad days. But it was also well known that Vaughan abused her body. She drank, sometimes to excess, and used drugs, and this likely influenced her day-to-day temperament. "I think sometimes it made her a little difficult for us to deal with on a person-to-person level, but it never, to my knowledge, really affected her singing," explained Chan. And Vaughan could be stubborn. When she didn't want to do something, she would figure out ways to get out of it, Chan remembered. Vaughan disliked television crews recording her shows. Although the terms of her contract had already been agreed upon, Vaughan, believing she was being taken advantage of, wanted extra money for the television performances. In Spain, during the 1970s, Vaughan saw broadcast trucks outside of her venue and assumed that they planned to tape her show. They did not, but she refused to go on and reduced the Spanish promoter, the local presenter with a financial stake in the concert, to tears. During a tour of London, Festival Productions booked Vaughan into the Dorchester, a five-star luxury hotel, and she insisted that her trio stay there too. "There wasn't any way we could afford to put the guys in the Dorchester," Chan explained. "She wasn't getting off the bus, she wasn't doing anything until all the guys, all of us were in the Dorchester with her." Vaughan wanted Chan and the trio, her guys, nearby. And in the end, they all stayed at the Dorchester.

Vaughan liked having Chan, another woman, with her on the road. Chan understood what it was like being surrounded by men for weeks at a time. "I think she thought I took care of her, which I tried to," said Chan. Yet Vaughan disliked it when she became friendly with the guys in the band. "I think she felt I was siding with them," Chan explained. "She wanted it to be [that] she was the boss and everybody else was her people." Her relationship with Vaughan deteriorated further when Wein placed

Vaughan and Carmen McRae on the same tour and assigned Chan to manage them both. "That didn't sit well with her, and after that we didn't get along so well," Chan said.[35]

Robert Jones, another road manager employed by Festival Productions, had a very different experience. He toured with Vaughan in the 1980s and took pride in anticipating her needs. After his first tour with Vaughan, he learned that she was concerned with the sound, in particular the sound she heard through the monitors. She wanted a good microphone, so he began packing a backup mic in his kit of supplies to use in an emergency. He also brought an extra cymbal stand in case the drum kit provided by the venue didn't have enough. And he knew that Vaughan, who perspired profusely while onstage, must have Kleenex. "Not handy tissues, AVC tissue or something," Jones explained. "You had to have Kleenex." He brought those too, and every time he saw a spare box of Kleenex, he tucked that into his bag of supplies. Anything to make life as easy as possible for Vaughan and her musicians. Like Chan, he tried to shield them from the controlled chaos of touring. This could include a sudden change in venue, like the time promoters in Italy decided to move a concert, after patrons had started arriving, from a small indoor theater to a nearby park. The change in venue required a team of men to carry a grand piano, drums, and sound equipment across the grounds. Or when she couldn't find her passport before a flight from Rome to Nice. "Don't worry," he told a flustered Vaughan. Jones called the hotel, and they found the passport and airmailed it to Nice the next day. In the meantime, he helped Vaughan negotiate customs, passing out publicity photos to the officials in immigration as onlookers exclaimed, "It's Sarah Vaughan!"

"I never had an ounce of problems with Sarah," said Jones. "I just loved being with her." They got along well. She was kind to him and his family. During a tour of Finland, while en route to the airport in Helsinki, Jones remembered Vaughan telling him, "Well, I want to give you something when we get onto the plane." "So, when I got on the plane, she came up and gave me two ballpoint pens, gold pens. I was stunned," he recalled. Then she said, "You are the best person I've ever had to deal with, because I never had to deal with you."[36]

Pianist Carl Schroeder viewed conflicts between Vaughan and presenters—be it a promoter, producer, or club owner—as part of the territory. The needs and priorities of the star, the artist, did not always align with those of the presenter, who, like the talent, wanted to create good music but was also concerned about the bottom line, his profit. According to Schroeder, Vaughan's requests were modest. To do her job well she wanted a good venue; adequate publicity; a functioning sound system so that she could hear herself; a suitable piano, drum set, and mic; and a dressing room, ideally with air conditioning. It was the presenter's responsibility to provide these. "Nah, she wasn't that high-demanding," said Schroeder. "[But] Sarah was not going to get run over. . . . She was stronger than any, any anybody. She had developed that kind of strength. So she would get after George [Wein] to get what she wanted."[37]

"She took care of the band," said bassist John Giannelli. He traveled with a huge, fiberglass bass trunk and remembered Vaughan tipping the airport skycaps $20 to insure that it got on the plane. "She always had a good rapport with the skycaps and everything everywhere," he explained. "She treated people nice." But she could become firm, very assertive when she needed to. During a gig at Mr. Kelly's in Chicago in April 1974, someone stole Giannelli's amplifier. "So she got real strong with the club owner and got the money right away, and somebody shipped me a new amplifier from Los Angeles. Hop by bus the next day."

Schroeder remembered a gig at the Hyatt Regency O'Hare, again in Chicago, with a piano that simply would not stay in tune. Vaughan sang opening night and received her usual standing ovations. But she refused to sing Tuesday night and left a full house waiting for her arrival, even though the hotel management promised to replace the piano by Wednesday. "She locked herself in the bathroom of her suite," said Schroeder. "The manager came knocking on the door, but she stayed in the bathroom. We left the next day. The hotel evicted her." Then the hotel hired Carmen McRae to replace Vaughan.[38]

"I thought things were rough in the old days, but they're getting weirder and weirder every day," Vaughan told Eleanor O'Sullivan of the *Asbury Park Press* days before her trip to Wilmington, Delaware, in 1982. "I signed this contract last year and in the rider the promoter put in, 'We don't supply this and we don't supply that, only soda and beer, and if you want whiskey, bring it yourself, and if you want a towel backstage, you have to pay a $5 deposit.' All these do's and don'ts. He doesn't know all I want to do is to sing and get the hell out of there. Promoters are nuts. They don't know anything. They're talking about towels. If I want a towel, I'll bring a Kleenex."[39]

"I think she saw me as what I was, which was a promoter," explained John Schreiber. "I often felt with Sarah like I was suffering for the sins and indignities that'd been laid on her through the decades by horrible managers. I showed up and I'm innocent, I love you, you're the greatest. And she's thinking back to some terrible thing that happened in 1959 based on the work of some dreadful manager."[40]

Vaughan had weathered more than her share of challenges, those inflicted by managers but also by the industry at large: Club owners who refused to pay her after she packed the house. Mobsters that insisted she continue on at their club despite other commitments or suggested that she not play a rival venue, requests all backed by implicit threats of violence. Record executives who wanted to control her creatively but not pay her royalties. White promoters who sabotaged the work of their black counterparts in an effort to enter the lucrative field of promoting black artists themselves, a tactic that sparked the controversy in Atlanta during the Biggest Show of '51. Segregated clubs that didn't have dressing rooms for the black talent. Lounges in segregated hotels that were happy to profit from her singing but unwilling to let her stay at their hotel.

"Prejudice is only the first step, [it's] being black twenty-four hours a day," explained George Wein, who married a black woman in 1959. "It isn't that people you're with are prejudiced against you. They may be your friends. But you're still black and they are white. And you have to have a really mature look of things to be—to not let those things disrupt you or upset you, and I don't think Sarah could do that."[41]

Vaughan didn't publicly discuss until the late 1970s and early 1980s the racism she experienced throughout her career. During her *Dick Cavett Show* appearance in 1980, the same appearance where she discussed Waymon Reed's failing health, Cavett encouraged her to share stories of the racial intolerance she confronted during her days with the Billy Eckstine band. She told him of the white man who threw chicken bones back into the Jim Crow train car and the band's retaliation, of rude southern whites requesting songs, and how she carried a hatpin, rather than a gun, to protect herself. The studio audience laughed as she pretended to get the hatpin from her purse and feigned a stabbing motion while saying "Ha, ha, ha." "You've left your mark all over America," said Cavett. "I've left my mark all over America," she replied, then her tone became more serious and matter of fact. "You know, they really are unpleasant things to talk about, but that was the way of life then."

The conversation turned to the prejudice she encountered as a child in New Jersey and her fascination with the segregated bathrooms and water fountains during her first tours of the South. "It's surprising when you first see that," Cavett observed. "Yes. I used to take pictures. I still have some pictures of those sort of things," she explained. "It's good that so much of that has passed," said Cavett, a politically liberal white man. His empathy for Vaughan was genuine, but, like so many white Americans, he wanted to believe that segregation, discrimination, and the pain of racism were a thing of the past. Vaughan disagreed. "Yeah," she replied, her voice now quiet, "It's still here, though." "You're still finding it," said Cavett, acknowledging her point of view. "It's a little better," she conceded.[42]

Vaughan encountered other, more mundane slights in her day-to-day life as a professional musician. She would fly in for a gig and proceed to the designated hotel only to find that a room had not been booked. Or a promoter would forget to hire a car to pick her up after her performance, forcing Vaughan to wait an hour and half and then call a taxi herself. Decades of slights, some intentional, resulting from social customs, and others simply oversights, shaped Vaughan. They were part of her experience. She internalized them and developed a healthy skepticism for authority and institutions of power.

"My sense always was that she was mistrustful of the promoter class," Schreiber explained. The people with the power. "She tolerated her presenters and her promoters. And yet she understood that, of course, they were the vehicle or they were the agent by which she got to do the thing that she was always struggling to get. And when she was on stage, it was otherworldly, it was magical."[43]

These new tunes have me a nervous wreck," Vaughan told *Down Beat*'s James Liska. "I like new tunes. But they make me nervous. I can't help it." She and Michael Tilson Thomas were rehearsing for another set of Gershwin concerts with the Los Angeles Philharmonic on February 1 and 2, 1982, nearly eight years after they first developed the program together in 1974.[44] Since then she had performed with dozens of symphony orchestras. PBS produced three television specials of Vaughan singing the program with symphonies, including *Rhapsody and Song: A Tribute to George Gershwin*, which won an Emmy in 1981. This time CBS planned to record the program for a new album, and Vaughan was excited but nervous.

"One night I got drunk just thinking about it. In my own house. I just went into the living room and drank me some cognac. Went to take a sip. Took sips," Vaughan laughed as she told the story. "Before Sarah goes on, she's real nervous," Tilson Thomas confirmed. "But the minute she's on—" "I'm so nervous right now and I'm always nervous before a show," Vaughan interrupted. "Barbara McNair made a statement in *Jet* magazine that people who were nervous before they went on must be insecure. I don't know why she said that. Carmen [McRae] says the same thing. Before I go on, I'm real nervous, and it lasts until I get the reaction from the audience." After forty years in the business, she still cared what an audience thought, and she went out every night hoping to win them over. She believed that once an artist lost this drive to satisfy their audience, they should retire. "Of course, sometimes it gets worse," she explained. "People sit out there and stare at you and don't applaud. Then I start shortening up my show because I think they don't enjoy what I'm doing and I want to get the hell off of there. And then when I come back and sign autographs, the say 'I've never heard you better.' Then I'm saying, 'Why do you do that to me, you all? I thought you hated me out there.'"[45]

"Oh, come on now, just sixteen lousy bars," said Tilson Thomas, bringing Vaughan back to their rehearsal of their new introduction for "The Man I Love." "That could be 16 messed-up bars," she said as she studied the score, contemplating how she would reimagine the tune's introduction. "I'm gonna have all this music on stage with me, you know." "Anything you'd like on stage is fine," Tilson Thomas assured her. "You see? No sacrifice is too great for my art."[46]

The concert began with a flourish. The orchestra played the dramatic overture from *Porgy and Bess*. The audience applauded and cheered, and then Vaughan seamlessly launched into a medley of favorites from the opera. At first her voice sounded strained, likely from nerves, but true to form, after more enthusiastic applause, she loosened up. Her voice became both lighter and richer, more flexible and malleable. She worked her way through seventeen Gershwin standards. On some tunes she was an operatic diva, with a sumptuous, expansive voice backed by the full forces of the orchestra; on others a swinging girl singer with a big band. Sometimes she assumed the role of musical theater songstress, especially when accompanied by the precision of the classically trained Tilson Thomas on piano. Other times, however, she improvised, relishing her role as a master of jazz. She stretched out and explored the harmonic language of a song, uncovering new, unexpected territory. She scatted with enthusiasm on up-tempo choruses. She sang wordless countermelodies she composed for the slower, contemplative ballads. And she embellished the existing melodic lines with her now-trademark vocal inflections. Sometimes she took on all of these musical personas within a single number, as she did with the new arrangement for "The Man I Love." It became a ten-minute, through-composed tour de force that demonstrated both the genius of her musical mind and the sheer brilliance and scope of her voice. Everything about the concert was distinctly Sarah Vaughan. She was not contained by musical genres or labels, nor was she pressured to score a big hit. She was simply free to sing.

She repeated the same program the next night, February 2, and then producers from CBS entered the editing suite to choose which takes to include on the album *Gershwin Live!* "I knew the girl who was one of the producers on it," explained Vaughan's longtime friend Robert Richards. "When they all got together to listen to the [two] nights, nobody could come to any kind of agreement which one was the best. One liked night one, one liked [night two]." They reviewed each number on the program, and there were no obvious flaws in either take. Both performances were wonderful. "So they put [two] things up on the wall and threw darts," said Richards.[47]

"The Concert of the Year Is Now the Album of the Year!" CBS Records proclaimed in print ads announcing the release of *Gershwin Live!* three months later. "On May 15, Sarah Vaughan, The Queen of Jazz, will appear at Avery Fisher Hall celebrating her 40th anniversary as a performer," an ad in the *New York Times* added. "But you can hear Sarah Vaughan anytime on her spectacular new CBS Records release, *Gershwin Live!*"[48] Robert Richards attended the Lincoln Center concert and visited Vaughan backstage. The dressing rooms at Avery Fisher Hall had two rooms: one for entertaining guests and a second, private space for the artist to get dressed. When Richards arrived, Vaughan took him back into the second room. "Then we locked ourselves in the bathroom," said Richards. Vaughan held *Gershwin Live!* in her hands.

"I'm just gonna scream I'm so excited," she said, then screamed. "Wait till you hear this, I'm just thrilled with it." "We played a couple tracks of it, then she had to go back to her guests out there," Richards reminisced. "She loved that record."[49]

At last, Vaughan had recorded an album that realized her musical goals and vision. Unlike far too many of her earlier recordings, *Gershwin Live!*, the culmination of her work with Michael Tilson Thomas, represented a true collaboration of music equals. And performing with the Los Angeles Philharmonic in their symphony hall must have fulfilled many of her long-held desires for legitimacy, respect, and acceptance by the cultural elite. In January 1983, *Gershwin Live!* was nominated for a Grammy award. After six nominations, three of them lost to Ella Fitzgerald, she finally won her first Grammy.

I did a concert last week in Boston with Wynton Marsalis. He is an absolute genius. He's so good, I can't tell you in words how good he is," said Vaughan when asked about up-and-coming jazz talent by Jay Scott.[50] She and Marsalis had performed with the Boston Pops at Symphony Hall on May 1, 1984. It was her second appearance with the orchestra, Marsalis's first, and their first time working together. Weeks earlier the twenty-two-year-old Julliard-trained trumpet player had won two Grammys, one for best jazz instrumental soloist for his album *Think of One* and a second for best classical soloist with an orchestra for his album of trumpet concertos by Haydn, Hummel, and Leopold Mozart. He was the first artist to win in both jazz and classical music categories in the same year. That night in Boston, Marsalis played Haydn's Concerto for Trumpet in E-flat, then after intermission joined Vaughan for two numbers during her set. The concert placed jazz and classical music on an equal footing. It was a coming together of an established yet still very active jazz legend with one of jazz's brilliant new voices, who would soon elevate the status of jazz within the American cultural landscape. The evening was a symbolic meeting of the past and present, with a glimpse into the future.

The days leading up to Vaughan's appearance with the Boston Pops had been difficult. On April 28, her performance at a ball celebrating the city of Rochester's sesquicentennial was delayed nearly an hour because the hall did not have a suitable piano. A grand piano was secured from the nearby Eastman School of Music to replace the venue's untuned upright Everett, but the incident rekindled assertions that Vaughan was difficult and temperamental. She countered these allegations with a simple, "No, it means I don't sing with a lousy piano."[51] On April 30, the day before her appearance in Boston, she attended funeral services for her friend of forty years and frequent collaborator Count Basie. The legendary bandleader passed away on April 24 at the age of seventy-nine. Then she flew to Boston from New York, and after she settled into her hotel room on the twenty-fifth floor, a fire alarm went off. She walked down twenty flights of stairs before learning that it had been a false alarm.[52]

The next day, she was in good spirits and looking forward to that day's work. The orchestra applauded when she arrived at rehearsal. Vaughan sat at the piano as Marsalis played through his encore, the flashy "Carnival of Venice." She hugged Marsalis and conductor John Williams as her trio set up, then she ran through that night's numbers. "Some performers give very little at a rehearsal, but Vaughan gets so caught up in the sensation of singing that even when she seems intent on doing a simple run-through, she ends up improvising and stretching her voice," critic Gary Giddins wrote in the *Village Voice*.[53]

In the evening, she strode onto the stage with her usual confidence, wearing a billowing orange gown with gold brocade. She began her set with an up-tempo "Just Friends" backed by her trio, whom she introduced, followed by her well-known ice-breaker. "And in case you don't who I am, I'm Dolly Parton!" she said, while thrusting out her chest. Then she gave her audience a survey of her forty-two year career, a lesson in jazz history. She sang "Body and Soul," the tune that began it all on that fateful night at the Apollo Theater's amateur night in 1942. She sang "Misty," the Erroll Garner tune she debuted in 1958 on *Vaughan and Violins* and helped make a standard. "I Hadn't Anyone Till You," another gem from her live 1963 album *Sassy Swings the Tivoli* and her most recent album with Count Basie, followed.

Then Marsalis returned to the stage. He and Vaughan shook hands. Vaughan kissed him on the cheek and turned to the audience while shrugging her shoulders and winking as if to say, "Oooh, I just kissed this very handsome young man." The audience laughed as John Williams eased the orchestra into the introduction to "September Song." Marsalis noodled behind Vaughan as she sang the tune, often incorporating his motivic lines into her interpretation. An easy give-and-take, a spontaneity, developed between the artists. Vaughan finished her chorus and passed the baton to Marsalis, and it quickly became clear that his solo that night was identical to the one trumpeter Clifford Brown crafted thirty years earlier when he and Vaughan recorded the track for Mercury on the iconic album *Sarah Vaughan*. For Marsalis, like Dianne Reeves and so many other aspiring jazz musicians, the album had piqued his interest in jazz and played an important role in his musical education. "He kept apologizing because he was playing [Clifford's solo] note for note," Vaughan told Scott days later. "He said, 'I'm not copying it or anything; I just love this solo.' I said, 'Relax, I don't blame you.'"[54]

Jazz artists often paid tribute to one another by quoting material, and it was common practice for jazz novices to transcribe solos that they admired. They took the solos apart, studied the riffs and harmonic language to understand how an admired master moved through musical time. It was a didactic technique that helped young musicians learn how to improvise and craft their own solos.[55] In this case, however, with the benefit of hindsight, Marsalis's performance also symbolized a larger shift in the musical landscape and jazz's place within it. In December 1954, when Vaughan, Brown, Herbie Mann, Paul Quinichette, Joe Benjamin, Roy Haynes, and Jimmy Jones gathered in Mercury's studios to record their album, the session was described as an intimate after-hours session—that magical, almost mythical, space where musicians were free to create and explore unfettered by commercial constraints. Jazz was the music of jam sessions and nightclubs. Now, thirty years later, the same music was being performed in the grandeur of Symphony Hall. By recreating Clifford Brown's solo on "September Song," Marsalis in effect granted it the same seriousness and legitimacy as the classical music he recreated in the first half of the program. In a sense, Vaughan and her music had come full circle.

Despite her "legitimate" voice, Vaughan spent much of her career in search of legitimacy, a respect for her talent regardless of the kind of music she sang. That night in Boston, as critic Giddins sat in Vaughan's dressing room, a reporter seeking an interview confessed that she knew nothing about jazz or Vaughan and hoped that Vaughan would help her get through. "Honey, I'm not going to be your teacher," said Vaughan, as she politely showed the reporter to the door. Then she turned to Giddins and asked, "Do you think they'd send someone out to interview Beverly Sills with a line like that?"[56] For decades, she had been fighting the pervasive belief that classical music, and the musicians who performed it, was inherently superior to jazz and jazz artists. And while she had an unwavering belief in her talent, at times she too viewed the world of classical music with awe and reverence. It had its own unfamiliar customs, traditions, and repertoire often deemed off-limits to black artists. Her respect and admiration for Marian Anderson and Leontyne Price was a tribute to their talent, but also an acknowledgment that they had found ways to break into that world. By 1984, however, ten years after her first Gershwin concert with Michael Tilson Thomas and the Los Angeles Philharmonic, after dozens of concerts with symphony orchestras across the country, television specials with prominent orchestras, and her Grammy-winning *Gershwin Live!*, the symphony orchestra as an institution had lost much of its mystique. "They make it easy," Vaughan said of her experience singing with the Boston Pops. "Those musicians wouldn't be up there if they couldn't read, you know, and Williams is one of the best. I used to think all symphony conductors knew what they were doing. I know better now."[57]

"I studied classical music because so many black musicians were scared of this big monster on the other side of the mountain called classical music," said Marsalis, expressing a similar sentiment, two weeks before his performance with Vaughan and the Boston Pops. "I wanted to know what it was that scared everybody so bad. I went into it and found out it wasn't anything but some more music. After you sit up there and play all those scores, you find out that classical musicians are just like all other musicians—most of them are mediocre and a handful are excellent."[58] Whether they played classical music or jazz, they were all musicians.

"Sarah Vaughan is the greatest there ever was. She understands harmony and sings notes other singers don't sing," Marsalis told Giddins the morning after their performance in Boston. The night before, after "September Song," Vaughan and Marsalis launched into an up-tempo "Autumn Leaves." Vaughan scatted. Marsalis looked on, smiling, as she executed a slow, controlled swoop from the bottom of her range to the top. He smiled again when she made an unexpected chord substitution, incorporating an angular, chromatic figure into her scatting. He took a blisteringly fast solo, and then he and Vaughan traded fours, as if in a jocular banter, until the end of the tune. "She sang something on the bridge to 'Autumn Leaves' I couldn't believe," Marsalis reflected. "I thought 'Damn!'"[59]

It was just another night at work for Vaughan. As had become her custom, she finished her set with "Send in the Clowns," her jazz aria. It was her moment to become an operatic diva. She transformed the pop song, infusing it with her gospel and jazz roots, into something extraordinary, distinctly Sarah Vaughan. And that night, as she had for the past decade, she did it in Symphony Hall. As she sang with symphony orchestras across the country during the third crossover phase of her career, she introduced jazz to new audiences, those more comfortable in the staid elegance of a concert hall than a nightclub. With these concerts, Vaughan, and others, helped jazz along on its journey toward legitimacy, its entrance into the academy. Three years later, in 1987, Marsalis cofounded Jazz at Lincoln Center, and in the subsequent years the organization presented concerts, developed education programs, and built new venues that physically and symbolically canonized jazz as a prestigious high art. In the span of Vaughan's career, jazz had emerged as America's classical music.

I just keep going," Vaughan told Jay Scott, the reporter for the *Globe and Mail,* during her stop in Toronto the following week. She was reflecting on her career and the many changes she had weathered in the industry. "Indefinitely?" asked Scott. "Will you be touring when you're Alberta Hunter's age, in your late eighties?" "Nooooo. I'll only come out for special events," she replied, laughing. "To tell you the truth, I'm getting sick of being on the road. I want to make records, but I don't have the pep for the stage—though once I'm out there, and they're screaming and hollering, I love it. But I need a change. I've got tired of going out, singing, coming off, going to the next town, going out, singing, getting off, the same routine. For 42 years. So my 43rd year will be a change."[60]

Five weeks earlier, on March 27, 1984, Vaughan turned sixty, a milestone she joked about during her sets, and she was having a very good year. She'd just starred in one of American Express's popular "Do you know me?" commercials with pianist Billy Taylor. She signed a contract with Quincy Jones's record label, Qwest, and toyed with the idea of making an album of country and western music. On May 17, she would record a duet with singer Barry Manilow. The commercially successful yet often derided pop star recruited Vaughan and a handful of other jazz musicians to work with him in his own quest for greater legitimacy and respect. The jazz-inspired *2:00 A.M. Paradise Café* went platinum, spawned a behind-the-scenes documentary, and earned both Manilow and Vaughan a Grammy nomination for their collaboration on "Blue." On June 30, in Dusseldorf, Germany, she sang a cycle of philosophical poems written by Pope John Paul II, translated into English by Gene Lees and arranged by conductor Lalo Schifrin. She debuted the work in a concert billed as "One World, One Peace" and then entered the recording studio. The sessions resulted in what is perhaps one of her most eclectic albums, *The Planet Is Alive . . . Let It Live!: Sarah Vaughan Sings Pope John Paul II.* On Sunday, July 8, her concert with Wynton Marsalis and the Boston Pops was broadcast on PBS's popular *Evening at the Pops.* And on July 22, she appeared on an all-star television tribute celebrating the upcoming Olympic Games. "This is my year," she said. "The jobs are coming in and I'm making them. Hey, I'm just coming into my prime."[61]

Despite tiring of life on the road, Vaughan kept on singing, working, and pushing herself. "As soon as you retire, you die," she said in 1980, and it was a mantra that guided the final years of her career.[62] In 1986, during an appearance on Marian McPartland's popular radio program *Piano Jazz,* McPartland suggested that Vaughan was at her peak, and Vaughan, then sixty-two, responded, "Oh no, I'm not at the peak. I've got much more to do. Whatever that is, but there's more to do, I'm sure." This too had become a familiar refrain. In January, she recorded a new album of songs from *South Pacific* with opera singer Kiri Te Kanawa and actor Mandy Patinkin, which also became a television special. The following year, 1987, she stepped into the recording studio again to collaborate with producer Sergio Mendes on *Brazilian Romance,* which earned a Grammy nomination, her ninth. She taped the television special *Sass and Brass,* which aired on Cinemax in March. And she continued to tour, making her usual rounds of the nightclubs, symphony halls, and festivals at home and abroad.

"I'm slowing down because I'm getting sick of the road," Vaughan said again in 1988. That year alone she'd toured Australia and New Zealand, Europe, and Japan, in addition to her usual gigs in the United States. But this time she seemed to mean it. "I pick my places now. It took a long time to be able to do that. Twenty years ago, I said, 'Where's the work?' If anybody had told me then that I'd be off for three months, I'd have said you've got to be kidding, I'd starve to death. But after forty-six years, I saved my money pretty well." She began spending more time doing things that she enjoyed, without the pressures of getting onstage night after night. "When I'm off the road, I like to travel, just go where I like. I like to ride trains," she said. "When I can do what I want to do in this business, then I'm a star. Not the glamour part."[63]

Vaughan's mind was at peace, and she seemed satisfied with what she had done and accomplished, with the career she'd had. And the outside world continued to honor her life in music. That spring she was inducted into the American Jazz Hall of Fame, and eight months later, in January 1989, the National Endowment of the Arts designated her one of their Jazz Masters. Then on February 22, 1989, she received a Lifetime Achievement Grammy, alongside her friends Dizzy Gillespie, whom she had known since 1942, and opera singer Leontyne Price.

On Saturday, June 24, 1989, Vaughan began her annual tour of summer jazz festivals when she performed at the Fourth Annual Great Words Jazz and Blues Festival in Mansfield, Massachusetts. The next night, Sunday, she returned to the Hampton Jazz Festival in Newport News, Virginia, for the fourth time. But her show was a disappointment. She started fifty minutes late, played a spotty set, and she was out of sorts, repeatedly complaining about the hot lights and sound quality. On Monday night she was in Toronto to open the inaugural du Maurier Downtown Jazz Festival. She was back to her usual charming, witty self as she crafted comedy bits on the fly. She joked about her age, now sixty-five, insisting that she had no intentions of retiring. Two songs into her set she discovered that her tissue box was not in its proper place on the piano. "I don't have my Kleenex!" she announced, feigning exasperation. Without her Kleenex, she explained, she was just like Linus without his blanket in Peanuts. "I'll go crazy!" she said. And when her Kleenex arrived, she frantically pulled countless tissues from the box, littering the stage.[64] She toyed with the audience throughout her set, adding an element of unpredictability and spontaneity to her otherwise predictable show. And she sang wonderfully. "Be reassured," wrote Geoff Chapman of the *Toronto Star*. "Those subtly smoky tones, the faultless vibrato and low-register resonance are fully intact, the vinyl victories of the past still justified."[65]

On Wednesday, June 28, she was in New York for the JVC Jazz Festival, and her mood had turned again. Promoter George Wein remembered visiting her backstage at Carnegie Hall. He wanted to offer her a hug and wish her luck. The first thing she said to Wein was "Why do you pay Ella more than you pay me?"[66] "I was so mad at her," Wein said. "That's all she could think of. And the fact that Sassy worked for me like twenty, thirty, forty concerts a year and Ella worked for me one concert a year. [It] never entered into her head that I was a main source of Sassy's income, but she just heard that maybe I paid Ella on one night more money than she got."[67] Ella Fitzgerald was the bigger star, and she could command more, and her public performances were less and less frequent. Fitzgerald, now seventy-one, diabetic, and recovering from heart bypass surgery, had to sit while performing, and doctors limited her to a single show a month. When she performed at the JVC festival the previous Sunday, she had the entire bill to herself.[68] Her ticket price was $40. The ticket price for Vaughan's show on Wednesday was $35, and she shared the bill with the Milt Jackson Quartet.

Wein left Vaughan's dressing room and didn't plan to stay for the show; he was too angry. Their relationship spanned thirty-seven years since she first played his club Storyville in 1952. He booked her on the first Newport Jazz Festival in 1954 and almost every one since, not to mention its many domestic and international spin-offs. Perhaps Vaughan's outburst, her seeming lack of appreciation for Wein's efforts and loyalty, was her coming to terms with the simple fact that Ella would always be the bigger star. Or perhaps she simply did not feel well. On his way out of the hall, Wein stopped at the sound booth to make sure everything was fine. "The first number she [sang], she was absolutely terrible," said Wein. It confirmed his fears that Vaughan was going to have a bad night. "I stayed there for a few minutes, and by the third number the magic took over, and I could forgive her for anything when the magic took over."[69]

Of course, the audience in the hall knew nothing of her argument with Wein, and critic John Wilson considered it another impressive showing. "Miss Vaughan," he wrote, "was in charge from the moment she stepped on the stage to parade before her cheering admirers and then, finding her glass of water misplaced on a small table, she angrily wrestled the table to one side of the stage, knocking her microphone to the floor in the process." Then she sat down and calmly began her set. She scatted on "Sweet Georgia Brown," moved on to the languorous ballad "Island," her Gershwin medley, and her usual encores "Misty" and "Send in the Clowns" to close. "Brilliant as she is as a singer," Wilson concluded, "Miss Vaughan has become much more than that—a superb entertainer who keeps her audiences' reactions in constant flux between the miracles of her voice and comedy bits that her audiences know by heart, but which they always respond to, as when she sings the male part in a 'Misty' duet with herself and sounds like a macho Ink Spot."[70]

Two days later she was scheduled to depart for a Wein-sponsored fifteen-engagement tour of Europe. It was the same circuit of festivals and halls that she had been doing for more than thirty years. She canceled, and no one knew why. "She just decided she didn't care what happened," said Wein. She left her trio musicians, the concert presenters, everyone, in the lurch. "It was a disaster; her fans in Europe were looking forward to her appearance. I had a lot of problems with various festivals in Europe who blamed me for her cancellation."[71] Wein asked for a doctor's note to appease promoters and protect himself financially. Vaughan resisted, but finally, two weeks later, she presented Wein with a note from a doctor in Virginia with a diagnosis of arthritis in her right hand. "Even after I received it many of the promoters were unsympathetic," he said.

That summer, Robert Richards remembered Vaughan calling

him as she prepared to leave for a gig nearby. She was looking forward to the day. She hired a car to drive her, and her mother packed her a lunch. Two of Richards's friends attended the concert. They told him that Vaughan was unbelievable, that she had the audience screaming for more. Then his friend asked, "Well, what happened to her arm?" "What do you mean?" Richards responded. "Her arm was in a sling," his friend said. Vaughan had mentioned nothing to him. Richards called her. "My friends loved you and were wondering what happened to your arm," he began. Then there was silence. "I could tell she wasn't telling the truth because it was a long pause while she made something up. She said, 'Oh, I accidentally got it caught in the door when I got out of the car, and I had a doctor come and he said I should have it in a sling.'"[72] He knew not to push her, to let her tell him things on her terms. Only later did Wein and the rest of the world learn that in June Vaughan began treatment for a malignant tumor in her hand.[73] She had cancer and kept it a secret, even from her closest friends.

But she continued to work. On Tuesday, August 1, 1989, she played Ravinia to rave reviews. That weekend, she sang in Atlanta at their annual jazz festival. On Friday, September 1, she returned to the Hollywood Bowl for the first of two appearances with the Los Angeles Philharmonic, this time conducted by Marty Paich. Before the concert, Mayor Tom Bradley proclaimed September 1 "Sarah Vaughan Day." But that night Vaughan's usually polished stage persona began to falter. Her set at the Hollywood Bowl lacked focus and continuity. She could no longer reach the soaring, lyrical soprano of her youth. And she confessed, several times, to the audience of nearly twelve thousand, that she was terribly nervous. There were moments of brilliance, flashes of the old Vaughan, but on the whole, according to Don Heckman's review in the *Los Angeles Times,* "listeners at Friday's program heard only a mild, pastel version of Vaughan's once bold and colorful style."[74]

Days later, Vaughan was diagnosed with lung cancer.[75] The malignant tumors in her right hand, the same hand she bandaged and placed in a sling, had in fact metastasized from the cancer in her lungs. With hindsight, all of the signs had been there. Her musicians remembered her struggling to catch her breath as she walked the long concourses in airports. Sometimes she complained that her chest hurt while she sang. Yet she still sounded phenomenal. In the fall, as she began treatment, she insisted on working. On Tuesday, October 10, she opened at Blues Alley in Washington, D.C. That week she sang two shows a night, at eight and ten, adding a midnight show on Friday and Saturday. Then she traveled to New York for a week at the Blue Note. She missed opening night, October 17, but sang the rest of the week through Saturday. Throughout the week, old friends like trombonist Clifton Smalls, whom she worked with in the Earl Hines band in 1943, visited her in her dressing room, but she revealed nothing. She made a flurry of phone calls, and at times seemed upset. On Sunday, she arrived at the club in the afternoon. Then she left. She couldn't sing. Instead, she summoned Robert Richards and other close friends to her hotel room and finally told them that she had lung cancer.

Years later, vocalist Ann Hampton Callaway realized that she had attended Vaughan's last night at the Blue Note. "What I remember," said Callaway, "what was interesting about her presence was she was wearing an aqua gown and she was not wearing shoes. And I sat there close to the front, in the middle, right in front of the stage and I thought, 'Oh, goddesses don't wear shoes.' It seemed to make perfect sense." Callaway, then thirty-one, listened and absorbed everything she heard. "I was stunned by the intensity of her emotions and how when she sang 'Send in the Clowns' there was this gravitas that was quite extraordinary," she explained. "It was as if she was trying to tell us everything she'd ever learned and express everything she'd ever felt. Like, 'I just want you to know who I am. I don't have much more time, but I want to say what I've learned.'"[76]

Sarah Vaughan would never sing in public again. After her Blue Note appearances, she wanted to go on a cruise and asked Richards to join her. "It was horrible, horrible," said Richards. "She was very sick. She ran out of medication. I was running around trying to get prescriptions filled, and they wouldn't fill them."[77] She was in terrible pain and never left her cabin. Her body was failing her. She had scheduled appearances at Yoshi's in San Francisco and George's in Chicago for November. At the end of October, as her health declined, she did not cancel them, choosing instead to postpone them until the spring. Press releases explained that she was halting her heavy touring schedule while she recovered from a recurrence of the cancer in her hand. She planned to resume live performances in February.[78]

"Time is a funny thing," Vaughan wrote in a column for *USA Today* published on January 26, 1990. She marveled at the passage of time. Forty-seven years ago, as a teenager just starting out, her future felt vast and unlimited. And now, months, years, and decades later, she realized that it was gone in the blink of an eye. She reflected on her career, explaining that when she won the Lifetime Achievement Grammy the previous spring, she struggled to comprehend that she had already produced an entire lifetime of work. "I just don't think about a legacy. . . . I just take one day at a time and, when I work, I live very much in the present," she wrote. "Today, as always, I just do what I've been doing: singing, recording, performing."[79]

She still considered singing, the process of making music, to be special. It represented freedom and an opportunity for self-determination and ultimately self-realization. People came together, and differences in class, race, gender, and age momentarily disappeared. The previous year, before her health deteriorated, Vaughan contributed to Quincy Jones's album *Back on the Block*, which brought together three generations of musicians from jazz, pop, R & B, funk, and rap. She sang on three tracks. She collaborated with Chaka Khan on "Setembro (Brazilian Wedding Song")" and Ella Fitzgerald, Dizzy Gillespie, Miles Davis, James Moody, and George Benson on "Birdland," and on "Wee B. Dooinit" she joined Fitzgerald, Siedah Garrett, Bobby McFerrin, Al Jarreau, and Take 6. "There we were, musicians of different generations, and yet we were so gloriously in the moment, making music," she wrote, explaining that differences in age and style disappeared during the sessions. "But that's how it's supposed to be, and for me, it's always been like that."[80]

Vaughan's ability to live in the moment, to focus on the present, especially when she sang, was the key to her longevity as an artist. Without it, the disappointments of her romantic life, the daily injustices of racism and sexism, the whims of record producers, and the ups and downs of the music industry, not to mention the daily grind of touring and performing, could have crushed her. And she approached death the same way. Taking it one day at a time, all while trying to do what she loved best: sing.

Epilogue: "The Greatest Vocal Artist of Our Century"

I t was in October of 1942 when I stepped up on the stage of Harlem's Apollo Theatre on amateur night, a shy 18-year-old, and sang 'Body and Soul,'" Vaughan continued in her piece for *USA Today*. "I remember the feeling of triumph when I won the contest (first prize, $10), and thinking to myself, 'I really can do this. I really can move people with my singing.'"

In the years since, she had traveled the world, singing to hundreds of thousands. Her forty-seven years in music had been a whirlwind of wonderful musicians, family, friends, loving audiences, successful recordings, honors, and adventures. She expressed her gratitude to her fans, who she believed had given her far more than she had ever given them. And then she closed her essay, her final farewell, proclaiming one last time, "I think today I'm singing better than ever. And I believe with all my heart that the best is yet to come."[1]

Without yielding any of her typical (almost defiant) optimism, Vaughan thanked her fans and, in a sense, said goodbye. But she never revealed that she was dying from lung cancer. At the end of February, newspapers across the country reported that Vaughan had been admitted to Cedars-Sinai Medical Center for treatment of the cancer in her hand. A hospital spokesperson said that the cancer was not serious and that Vaughan expected to leave the hospital soon. A month later, in March, similar reports circulated again. Vaughan was resting at home after another hospital stay and planned to return to work on April 2 for her recording session with Quincy Jones and George Duke.

"Producer George Duke and I did our best to keep Sarah Vaughan alive by planning a Brazilian LP; it was her favorite kind of music," Quincy Jones wrote in his autobiography. They first worked together in Paris in 1958, when he produced *Vaughan with Voices*. "She wanted to sing Ivan Lin's 'Dinorah.' George and I played songs on cassette while she lay in a hospital bed at Cedars [Sinai Hospital] dying of cancer."[2] They tossed around ideas and worked out lead sheets as Vaughan's mother, daughter, and old friend June Eckstine, Billy Eckstine's first wife, looked on, helplessly. "There was nothing they could do, but she was determined to make a record. Determined," said Richards, concluding, "Singing was everything. She was a singer."[3]

In the final months of her life, Vaughan was in and out of the hospital and continued to keep the public, and many of her longtime friends, in the dark. Vocalist Carmen McRae visited Vaughan at home near the end. They reminisced about their careers, shared experiences, and friendship, dating back to the 1940s. "She never said a word about anything, but you could see she wasn't herself," said McRae. "She was in pain from walking up the steps." Vaughan was a private woman, and according to her manager, Harold Levy, the man responsible for circulating press releases, she didn't want people to know how much pain she was in.[4] "Word was kept away from us," explained vocalist Joe Williams, another longtime friend. He first worked with Vaughan during the grueling Birdland Tours with the Count Basie band in the 1950s. "That's probably how she wanted it. She was always in charge, that girl."[5]

Billy Eckstine, however, did know that his musical soulmate, his dear friend since 1942, was very sick. And Vaughan desperately wanted to see him. "Is B. coming?" she asked every day. Richards called Eckstine two, perhaps three times, asking him, then pleading with him to come for one last visit. It would make her so happy, he said. But Eckstine refused. "No, I can't," he said. "I can't see her like this."[6]

Complications forced Vaughan to return to the hospital on Saturday, March 31. She missed her recording session on Monday and decided the next day that she would be more comfortable at home. As she left the hospital for the last time, when no more could be done, she called Jones and reassured him, "Don't worry, I won't disappoint you. I can sing lying down."[7]

Sarah Lois Vaughan died on Wednesday, April 4, 1990, at 9:20 P.M. Her mother and daughter were at her side. She was sixty-six.

When the city of Newark learned of Vaughan's passing, it draped city hall in purple bunting and flew flags at half-mast. On Sunday, April 8, the New Jersey Symphony Orchestra presented a farewell concert in her honor. And on Monday, her funeral was held at Mount Zion Baptist Church, where it had all begun. "A Newark girl comes home, having gone full circle, and what a circle that has been," said the Reverend Granville Seward as he addressed nearly a thousand mourners who crowded into the church to pay their respects. Speakers broadcast the service to hundreds more gathered outside, and then they all watched as a horse-drawn carriage carried Vaughan through the streets of Newark one last time.[8]

In the coming months and years, there would be more memorial concerts as her friends, the musicians who worked with her, paid tribute to her life in music. Then the musical tributes, songs and albums began to appear. In 1990, Vaughan's former pianist Bob James composed "Wings for Sarah." "It was my tribute to a memory that I had that I learned so much from," he explained. "I learned many, many, many things from her, but one of the things I felt that I learned the most was about tempo." Vaughan loved to sing ballads very slowly, slower than James had ever done before. "Sometimes I felt like I could take a nap in between beat one and beat two," he joked. "And it still might not be slow enough for her." It was his job to set the tempo of each tune as he played his introduction. If he got it right, she would be comfortable, settle in, and explore. "But if I got it wrong, I would get the wings," he said. Vaughan kept time with her shoulder blades and arms. If she was unhappy with a tempo, she'd gently move her arms and elbows up and down, to show the trio, who was behind her, where the beats should be going, which tempo was right for her. "So having had such fond memories of that and learning the power of setting [the] tempo right and attributing it all to Sarah Vaughan, I decided somewhere down the line to write a song about it called 'Wings for Sarah,'" James said. "It was also about the time that I was imagining her in heaven, hopefully listening to this piece."[9]

In 1991, Carmen McRae, Vaughan's friend since 1943, re-leased *Sarah: Dedicated to You.* After singing a dozen of Vaughan's best-known and best-loved tunes, all backed by pianist Shirley Horn, McRae concluded with a new tune, "Sarah," penned by Carroll Coates. She sang of Vaughan's time on earth, the power and meaning of her voice, then imagined Bessie Smith and other vocal greats welcoming Vaughan to heaven. The album was a love letter to her dear friend. "I am honored to have the opportunity to pay homage to such a great lady," wrote McRae in the album's liner notes. "I miss you, Sass." McRae was devastated by Vaughan's passing; her health soon declined, forcing her to retire, and *Dedicated to You* was her last album. In 1993, both Dizzy Gillespie and Billy Eckstine passed away, followed by McRae in 1994 and Ella Fitzgerald two years later. It was the end of an era.

In the coming decades, there would be more tribute albums to Vaughan, this time from the next generation of vocalists, those who had grown up listening to Vaughan. They loved her voice and what she did with it, and they learned from her example. Dianne Reeves released *The Calling: Celebrating Sarah Vaughan* in 2001. Reeves began listening to Vaughan as a high schooler in the 1970s, when her uncle gave her a copy of *Sarah Vaughan,* and she credits this album with helping her define her voice and use it as an instrument, all while inspiring her to take herself seriously as a musician. Reeves had only one conversation with Vaughan, backstage at a Cannonball Adderley tribute concert in 1975, and Reeves, then only eighteen, didn't realize that she had been speaking with her idol. Three years later, she opened for Vaughan at a festival in Wichita, Kansas. She was now twenty-one and working with trumpeter Clark Terry, who had told Vaughan about the promising young vocalist. "I remember being on stage and [I] looked out, she's sitting out [there]—I could see something sparkling," Reeves said. "I was like, 'Oh my God.' I started singing everything I knew and Clark started laughing, because I wanted to impress her. I finish, and she walks backstage, and she looks at me and she says, 'As long as I live, I don't ever want you opening for me again,' and then walks off. I was in tears."[10]

It was a crushing experience, but it was also an endorsement, a thumbs-up of sorts. Reeves possessed a range, technical facility, and mastery of her voice reminiscent of a much younger Vaughan, and the veteran singer was competitive. That night she schooled Reeves. "I just remember leaving without being able to speak to anybody of what I just heard," Reeves explained. She was in awe of Vaughan's breath control; the suppleness of her voice, how she would bend a note and then take it higher and higher; how she got inside of a song's harmonies; the intimate conversation she had with the other musicians onstage; and, perhaps most important, the unwavering respect that those same musicians had for Vaughan.[11]

"She was always reaching. That was important to me," said Reeves. "She always had a conversation, musically, with the musicians. She wasn't afraid to work with anybody, because for her every musician has their harmonic vocabulary, their approach. Because of that, I love working with different people, because it's like, 'Oh, I didn't hear it like that,' and then you find yourself in this new place and you start creating in this other way and you're hearing their stuff in a totally different way, and you're going,

'Well, I didn't hear it like that.' Just keeps going on and on. This fearlessness of being able to go into all of these different kinds of ways of thinking about music, to me, was probably the greatest inspiration."[12]

There were other, more practical lessons too. Reeves learned that she should sit while singing ballads. "She let me know that your voice doesn't have to get old," said Reeves, who heard Vaughan perform when she was in her fifties and sixties, and, miraculously, her voice seemed to improve with age. And by observing Vaughan and her contemporaries, Reeves came to understand her priorities as a musician and the kind of career she wanted to have. "When I did my first record contract, I asked for artistic freedom from the very beginning," explained Reeves. This was in 1981, a year before Vaughan recorded *Gershwin Live!* and only four years after she organized the sessions for *I Love Brazil!*— albums where Vaughan finally had the artistic control and freedom that she had fought for her entire career. Reeves had seen record producers try to water down talent, including Vaughan's, stripping it of its richness and power, its complexity, and agency so that it would fit into the little space where they needed it to be. "That is just not cool," Reeves remembered thinking, and she became determined not to let this happen to her.[13]

"What [Vaughan] was and what she did was outrageously powerful, and she was a woman," said Reeves. Vaughan seized her power. She was true to herself in a world that didn't always want her to be, paving the way for future generations of vocalists to do the same. "There was a point in my life—I love her so much—that I realized even when I started singing as Dianne Reeves, the person, and Dianne Reeves, the singer and the person . . . ," Reeves explained, then paused. "[Singing] is the one thing that nobody could take away. This was the ship. I'll stand in it. This is my power, is my superhero suit, and you can't take that away from me."[14]

When I was three years old, I was scat singing to Sarah Vaughan and Ella albums," said Ann Hampton Callaway, remembering her family's love of jazz as she grew up in Chicago in the 1960s. Callaway, who released *From Sassy to Divine: The Sarah Vaughan Project* in 2014, also considers Vaughan a role model. Like Vaughan, Callaway plays piano, and Vaughan helped her understand that "you don't have to be the chick singer; you really know what you're talking about, you know what key you sing a song and you know the changes, you know a lot more musically." She admired the emotional intensity and sensuality of Vaughan's singing and how she brought disparate musical elements together into a single musician. "One of the things that I was very captivated by was the sound of her voice. I loved classical music, and I loved pop music, and I loved jazz music. She seemed to combine all of those. She had almost an operatic approach sometimes, and her voice had all the colors. I'd like to say that her voice was very orchestral. She had many colors in her voice and could bring out the cellos for one song, flutes for another, and the trumpets for another," said Callaway, adding, "She gave me a palette. She gave me the sense of the voice as not just one sound. That it is a . . . there are so many different colors to the human voice that you can use to express feeling and story."[15]

Callaway also learned from Vaughan's live albums. She loved when Vaughan made mistakes and fixed them on the spot, like she did when she stumbled over the word "Parthenon" on *Sarah Vaughan After Hours at the London House* or her impromptu tribute to Ella Fitzgerald when she forgot the lyrics to "How High the Moon" from *Sarah Vaughan at Mr. Kelly's*. "There was a sense that you can make a mistake as a singer and it's okay," said Callaway. "That you can just make fun of yourself. You can be funny and make up new lyrics in the moment, and as long as you know how to do that, you never ever have to have stage fright." Vaughan showed her how to believe in herself, how to trust her musical toolbox, and the value of living in the moment. "One of the greatest freedoms in my career is that I am never worried about—I mean, I am always going to do my best and sing a song and honor the song, but if I screw up, I make up new lyrics just like Sarah."[16]

"I think subliminally I picked up when I was studying her . . . that she has [a] star quality she owned," continued Callaway. "There are the two types of singers: owners and renters. Renters are like, 'Oh, maybe I'll do this, this seems like an interesting song.' Then there are singers like, 'This is how I feel. This is what I mean. This is what I have to say.' She will get up to a microphone, and whatever she said, whatever mood she was in, however much sleep she had or little sleep she had, or how many cocktails she had, she got up to a microphone and would still be Sarah Vaughan."[17]

And Vaughan has influenced the newest generation of singers, young women who never saw Vaughan perform live but continue to listen to and learn from her. "She was one of my mom's favorite singers. So I don't remember a time she wasn't a part of my life and what I lived," explained Cécile McLorin Salvant, a promising new star on the jazz scene with a voice that many liken to a young Sarah Vaughan's. Born in 1989, only months before Vaughan passed away, she remembered hearing Vaughan's voice as her mother cooked dinner and cleaned the house and as her family hung out on Sunday afternoons, listening to the same song over and over. She associates Vaughan with those sweet memories of her childhood. "And I think that's definitely part of my love and attachment to her, is that element of—it feels like I'm going home."

As a teenager, Salvant was interested in classical singing, but then she found herself drawn to Vaughan's voice. "I was just in awe, and I wanted to sing just like her," she said. "That's what I wanted." Like countless vocalists before her, she was fascinated by Vaughan's vocal control, her vibrato, the endless spectrum of colors and timbres she created, her harmonic and rhythmic approach, and, of course, her virtuosity, how she could go anywhere with her voice. She was also intrigued by Vaughan's ability to sound like a crooner. She could sing with the same power and force as a man. "I thought, 'This is just the best voice.' That just feels good to listen to."[18]

Vaughan will continue to influence future generations of singers. In 2012, the New Jersey Performing Arts Center in Vaughan's hometown of Newark launched the Sarah Vaughan International Jazz Vocal Competition. Each year, thousands of aspiring vocalists from around the world, all of them women, submit audition tapes and videos, hoping that they will get their big break, just like Vaughan did in 1942 when she stepped onto the stage of the Apollo Theater in Harlem. "It keeps the flame alive," said John Schreiber, once a road manager for Vaughan and now the CEO of the performing arts center and the competition's cofounder. "It's important that young singers and young musicians understand her legacy, appreciate her contributions, and have opportunities to aspire to be great and unique. I think that's what this does. [The] young women who participate, I'm terribly moved by each of them. They're genuinely honored to be participating in a competition with Sarah's name on it. They all understand who she is and [that] she's on the pantheon."[19]

And this cycle of influence and inspiration continues on a smaller scale too, in intimate neighborhood clubs when a vocalist decides to sing a set in tribute to Sarah Vaughan, or when a young woman posts a video of herself online singing "Whatever Lola Wants," copying every detail of Vaughan's cover, because she loved the way that Vaughan sang the tune and how singing like Vaughan makes her feel empowered, bold, and confident.

"Sarah Vaughan is quite simply the greatest vocal artist of our century," proclaimed composer Gunther Schuller in 1980 as he introduced her to audiences at the Smithsonian's National Museum of American History. "Her art is so remarkable, so unique that it, *sui generis,* is self-fulfilling and speaks best on its own musical artistic terms. It is—like the work of no other singer—self-justifying and needs neither my nor anyone else's defense or approval."[20] And now, as the twenty-first century is well under way, Vaughan is still making her mark. Her legacy continues not just in the vocalists who honor her but also in her fans. Her legacy lives on in the listeners who cherish her albums,

in their childhood memories of aunties and grandmothers playing Vaughan whenever they visited. In a young couple's memories of falling in love. Or in a college student playing cribbage
with her roommates. And as these memories fade, new ones
are made as the next generation of listeners discovers Vaughan
for the first time, buys her records, plays her at their wedding,
or simply enjoys her voice on a lazy Sunday afternoon. Sarah
Vaughan can be heard on the radio, in television commercials,
and in the grocery store as we shop. Hers is a voice that has become a part of our sonic landscape, a part of our daily lives. It
is a voice for the ages that forever changed the way we hear and
appreciate the human voice in song.

Acknowledgments

This project began during my days as a graduate student at
the University of Pennsylvania and would never have happened
without the support, guidance, and continued encouragement
of Carol Muller and Guthrie Ramsey Jr. They taught me how to
think about music, race, and gender, and for that I am grateful.

As a young scholar just beginning my journey into the world
of Sarah Vaughan, I was fortunate to discover the wealth of resources at the Institute of Jazz Studies at Rutgers University's
Newark campus. In the years since, its staff, in particular Tad
Hershorn, Joe Peterson, Elizabeth Surles, and Vincent Pelote,
has helped me navigate its holdings, all while generously sharing
their enthusiasm and expertise. A travel grant from the Morroe
Berger–Benny Carter Research Fund facilitated my work at the
Institute of Jazz Studies.

I have also appreciated the assistance of Loren Schoenberg
and Ryan Maloney at the National Jazz Museum in Harlem,
Tom Ankner at the Charles F. Cummings New Jersey Information Center, Thomas Tierney at the Sony Music Archives Library, Maristella Feustle of the Willis Conover Collection at the

University of Northern Texas, Jacqueline Thornburg of the LBJ Presidential Library and Museum, and Vickie Wilson of Johnson Publishing Company, as well as the librarians, archivists, and sound technicians at the Performing Arts Reading Room of the Library of Congress, the Schomburg Center for Research in Black Culture, the New York Public Library for the Performing Arts, the Paley Center for Media, the Jazzinstitut Darmstadt, the University of Pennsylvania, and the University of Washington.

I owe a special thanks to the friends and musicians who discussed their memories, experiences, and impressions of Sarah Vaughan. I enjoyed these conversations, and even though only a fraction of what we talked about appears in print, their contributions shaped the manuscript and brought Vaughan, the artist and woman, to life. In particular, I would like to thank vocalists Dianne Reeves, Ann Hampton Callaway, and Annie Ross. Their insights shifted my perspective and helped me more fully understand what it is like to be a singer and touring musician and what made Vaughan so extraordinary. I also thank Robert Richards, Michiyo Tanaka Fisher, Carlton Schroeder, and Frank De La Rosa for sharing rare videos, private recordings, unpublished notes, and their personal memorabilia with me. This project benefited immeasurably from the kindness and generosity of spirit of each person I spoke with.

This book could not have become a reality without my literary agent, Matt McGowan. He possessed a keen understanding of its objectives, saw its potential, and skillfully found it a good home.

I am also indebted to everyone at Ecco. My editor, Denise Oswald, has been patient, given me extra time when I needed it, and, most important, offered thoughtful, spot-on feedback. She, along with Emma Janaskie, Emma Dries, Rachel Meyers, Ben Sadock, and the rest of the team at Ecco, has made this an enjoyable and rewarding process.

My research assistant, Kelsey Cloonan, has been indispensable. She tracked down leads, visited libraries and archives, scoured the secondary literature, and prepared more than six hundred endnotes. She has been my eyes and ears on the ground on the East Coast, making it possible for me to spend more time with my family in Seattle. She is a bright, capable, and talented young woman, and I am excited to see what her future holds.

I thank Julie Bradley, Beth Maxey, Chris Robinson, Jennifer Lin, Sara Smith, Susan DeMattos, and Judith Tick. They each offered a different kind of support—intellectual, emotional, or practical, and sometimes all three. I am thankful for my wonderful nanny, Aryka Olson Lucey, who cared for my son during the first two years of his life. Knowing that he was in loving, capable hands made it possible for me to pursue my dreams and aspirations. I also appreciate the devoted teachers at Bright Horizons Redmond, especially Sharon, Kelsey, Karen, Orit, Sarah, and Sol.

And finally, this project would have been impossible without the unconditional love of my family. My parents, Joyce and Cecil Hayes, taught both my brother and me how to be curious, creative, and engaged. They have always stood behind me emotionally, physically, and, in the early days, financially as I battled poor health and struggled to find my way. Even after I opted out of a traditional academic career, my father encouraged me to get my work and ideas out into the world. My brother, John, has been both an ally and friend, and I consider myself lucky and proud to have him as a brother. My in-laws, Dick and Peggy Kramer, have been kind, supportive, and tremendously patient, delaying vacations to accommodate this book's deadlines. I also thank Peggy for donning her editor's hat and reading my proposal and first chapters. But most of all, I thank them for their son, Nicholas. He has been my greatest advocate, friend, and confidant. He knows little about music or writing but understands that I needed to write this book to find my voice and thrive. I am forever grateful for his love, compassion, generosity, and skills as a co-parent to our son, Jack, the light of both of our lives.

Notes

Prologue
1. James Liska, "Sarah Vaughan: I'm Not a Jazz Singer," *Down Beat*, May 1982.
2. Max Jones, "Going Over Common Ground," *Melody Maker*, July 4, 1981, 26 26, 35.
3. Guthrie P. Ramsey Jr., *The Amazing Bud Powell: Black Genius, Jazz History, and the Challenge of Bebop* (Berkeley: University of California Press, 2013), 8.
4. Ibid., 1–12, 54–57; Scott Knowles DeVeaux, *The Birth of Bebop: A Social and Musical History* (Berkeley: University of California Press, 1997).

Part I: An Artist Is Born, 1924–1947
1. "Sarah Vaughan Waxes Two Xmas Songs," *Pittsburgh Courier*, November 22, 1947, 16.
2. The description of Vaughan's Town Hall performance on November 8, 1947, is based upon the live recording of this concert. Sarah Vaughan and Lester Young, *One Night Stand: The Town Hall Concert 1947*, Blue Note CDP 7243 8 32139 2 4, compact disc.
3. Michael Levin, "Vaughan Great, But Lester Slips," *Down Beat*, December 8, 1947, 7.

Chapter 1: "There Was No Sign of Any Kind of Voice"
1. Kevin Mumford, Newark: *A History of Race, Rights, and Riots in America* (New York: New York University Press, 2007), chapters 1–2; Brad Tuttle, *How Newark Became Newark: The Rise, Fall, and Rebirth of an American City* (New Brunswick, N.J.: Rivergate, 2009); Clement Alexander Price and

New Jersey Historical Society, *Freedom Not Far Distant: A Documentary History of Afro-Americans in New Jersey* (Newark, N.J.: New Jersey Historical Society, 1980), 77–80.

2. Leslie Gourse, *Sassy: The Life of Sarah Vaughan* (New York: C. Scribner's Sons, 1993), 7.

3. Barbara Gardner, "Sarah," *Down Beat*, March 2, 1961.

4. Barbara Kukla, *Swing City: Newark Nightlife, 1925–50* (Philadelphia: Temple University Press, 1991), 166–167.

5. Matthew Seig, dir., *Sarah Vaughan: The Divine One*, VHS (New York: BMG Video, 1991).

6. Kukla, *Swing City*, 167.

7. Sarah Vaughan, "Interview One: Musical All My Life," interview by Les Tomkins, May 31, 1977, transcript on the National Jazz Archive website, http://www.nationaljazzarchive.co.uk/stories?id=43.

8. Ibid.

9. Kukla, *Swing City*, 167–168

10. Sarah Vaughan, interview by Marian McPartland, *Piano Jazz*, NPR, January 17, 1986, available online at http://www.npr.org/2008/07/18/92646654/sarah-vaughan-the-divine-one.

11. "Sarah Vaughan: She Is Most-Imitated Singer as Well as Most Controversial," *Ebony*, September 1949, 29–30.

12. Seig, *Sarah Vaughan*.

13. Max Jones, *Jazz Talking: Profiles, Interviews, and Other Riffs on Jazz Musicians* (Boulder, Colo.: Da Capo, 2000), 261.

14. Seig, *Sarah Vaughan*.

15. Kukla, *Swing City*, 132.

16. Ibid., 168.

17. Ibid., 132.

18. Ibid., 168.

19. Ibid., 81.

20. Vaughan, interview by Tomkins, part 1.

21. Gourse, *Sassy*, 15–16.

22. Vaughan, interview by McPartland.

23. Richard Carlin and Kinshasha Conwill, *Ain't Nothing Like the Real Thing: How the Apollo Theater Shaped American Entertainment* (Washington, D.C.: National Museum of African American History and Culture through Smithsonian Books, 2010), 91.

24. "Cootie Williams Band Heads Apollo Revue," *New York Amsterdam News*, October 17, 1942. The circumstances leading up to Vaughan's Apollo appearance remain unclear. Some report that she went to the amateur-night competition intending to accompany a girlfriend on piano and at the last minute decided to sing herself (Gourse, *Sassy*, 16). Another account says that she was inspired to compete after a friend won second prize. And Vaughan herself, in a 1943 interview, said that her friend "Jabo" Smith, a trumpeter at the Alcazar, advised her to go see Cleota Rogers, Cooper's assistant, to set up an audition for the amateur night so that she could get her big break (Carolyn Dixon, "Great Career Forecast for Sarah Vaughan," *New York Amsterdam*

News, January 30, 1943). In a 1948 piece she penned for the National Negro Press Association, Vaughan wrote that she entered the contest on a dare from friends, "on the condition that these friends would be in the audience to cheer me on" (Sarah Vaughan, "Career Began on Dare: Ex-Baptist Choir Singer Names Her Favorite Vocalists," NNPA, May 1, 1948), while her mother and her friend Robert Richards say that Vaughan's October 1942 appearance was in fact her second or third attempt, not her first as so often told.

Although we may never know what prompted Vaughan's efforts, once she decided to compete, she was pragmatic. In her 1977 interview with Les Tomkins, she explained, "When I entered show business at eighteen, it was unplanned. It just happened. Oh, in the back of my mind I wanted to be in show business, but I always thought: 'Silly girl, it'll never happen.' So then I did the Amateur Hour at Apollo just to get the ten dollars, which was the first prize. A week at the theatre went with it, but I wasn't even worried about that. I just wanted that ten dollars, because that was a lot of money." Sarah auditioned for emcee Ralph Cooper and was scheduled to perform the same week that the Earl Hines band headlined, but the program ran long, and she was bumped to the next week.

25. Ralph Cooper, *Amateur Night at the Apollo: Ralph Cooper Presents Five Decades of Great Entertainment,* with Steve Dougherty (New York: HarperCollins, 1990), 155.
26. Ibid.
27. Ibid.
28. Jones, *Jazz Talking,* 237.
29. Kukla, *Swing City,* 168.
30. Cooper, *Amateur Night,* 153.
31. Gardner, "Sarah," 20.
32. Vaughan, interview by McPartland.
33. Stanley Fields, "Only Human," *Daily Mirror,* November 30, 1954.
34. Vaughan, interview by McPartland.
35. Stanley Dance, *The World of Earl Hines* (New York: Scribner, 1977), 282.
36. Ibid.
37. Jones, *Jazz Talking,* 237.
38. Eileen Southern and William Clarence "Billy" Eckstine, "'Mr. B' of Ballad and Bop," *The Black Perspective in Music* 7, no. 2 (Autumn 1979): 197–198.
39. Jones, *Jazz Talking,* 237.
40. Southern, "'Mr. B' of Ballad and Bop," 198.
41. Jones, *Jazz Talking,* 237.
42. Ibid.
43. Barry Ulanov, "The Human Sarah: Her Life Is Pitched in the Middle Key but Her Singing Scales the Heights," *Metronome,* October 1949.
44. George Kanzler, "Sarah Vaughan: Newport Jazz Festival Pays Special Tribute to 'The Divine One,'" *Star Ledger,* June 23, 1974.
45. "Earl Hines Captures Harlem; Predict a New Record," *Chicago Defender,* January 23, 1943.

46. Carolyn Dixon, "Great Career Forecast for Sarah Vaughan," *New York Amsterdam News,* January 30, 1943.

47. Ibid.

48. "4 Shot in Savoy by Wild Jitterbug," *Chicago Defender,* February 20, 1943.

49. "On Leave and Off Leaves: We're Speaking of Ruby Blakley, Madelyn Green [*sic*], Song Chirpers," *Chicago Defender,* March 13, 1943.

50. Travis Dempsey, *An Autobiography of Black Jazz* (Chicago: Urban Research Institute, 1983), 317.

Chapter 2: "Ah *Mon Vieux,* This Chick Is Groovy!"

1. Max Jones, *Jazz Talking: Profiles, Interviews, and Other Riffs on Jazz Musicians* (Boulder, Colo.: Da Capo, 2000), 260.

2. Rory O'Connor, "A Joyful Noise," *New York Woman Magazine,* clip folder, Institute of Jazz Studies, Rutgers University, Newark, N.J.

3. Guthrie P. Ramsey Jr., *The Amazing Bud Powell: Black Genius, Jazz History, and the Challenge of Bebop* (Berkeley: University of California Press, 2013), 54–56.

4. Jones, *Jazz Talking,* 260.

5. Matthew Seig, dir., *Sarah Vaughan: The Divine One,* VHS (New York: BMG Video, 1991).

6. Barbara Gardner, "Sarah," *Down Beat,* March 2, 1961, 21.

7. Dizzy Gillespie, *To Be, or Not . . . to BOP: Memoirs,* with Al Fraser (Garden City, N.Y.: Doubleday, 1979), 189.

8. Leonard Feather, "Sara Vaughan: She's a Musicians' Singer, but the Public Lovers Her Too, and So Does Leonard Feather Who Tells You All About Her," *Metronome,* July 1, 1946, 21. The quote cited is, in fact, Feather reminiscing in 1946 about the first time he heard Vaughan in April 1943. His original review, appearing in *Metronome* in June 1943, read: "Next came Earl's new girl, Sarah Vaughan. Here is a real find. You can tell she's a musician from the way she sings little phrases that betray her feeling for chord changes and her innate accuracy of pitch. She did nicely with 'Heard the Song Before' and 'Taking a Chance on Love,' arranged by Dick Vance and Don Redman, respectively, and followed up with a socko version of 'Body and Soul.'" Leonard Feather, "Earl Hines: New Finds with Hines," *Metronome,* June 1, 1943, 21.

9. Jones, *Jazz Talking,* 238.

10. Ibid., 261.

11. Ibid., 260.

12. Scott Knowles DeVeaux, *The Birth of Bebop: A Social and Musical History* (Berkeley: University of California Press, 1997), 152.

13. Seig, *Sarah Vaughan.*

14. Gillespie, *To Be, or Not . . . to BOP,* 189.

15. John Malachi, interview by Bryant DuPre, May 6, 1983, transcript, Jazz Oral History Project, Institute of Jazz Studies, Newark, N.J., 2:47.

16. Gillespie, *To Be, or Not . . . to BOP,* 189.

17. Malachi, interview, 2:45–2:47.

18. Mark S. Foster, "In the Face of 'Jim Crow': Prosperous Blacks and Vacations, Travel and Outdoor Leisure, 1890–1945," *The Journal of Negro History* 84, no. 2 (1999): 143.

19. DeVeaux, *Birth of Bebop,* 249.

20. Ibid.

21. Cary Ginell, *Mr. B: The Music and Life of Billy Eckstine* (Milwaukee, Wisc.: Hal Leonard, 2013), 62.

22. DeVeaux, *Birth of Bebop,* 249.

23. Butch Lacy, interview with author, June 1, 2016.

24. Gillespie, *To Be, or Not . . . to BOP,* 176–177.

25. Ibid., 193.

26. Ibid.

27. Sarah Vaughan, interview with Dick Cavett, *The Dick Cavett Show,* March 6 and 7, 1980.

28. Mike Wofford, interview with author, October 16, 2014.

29. Sarah Vaughan, "Interview Two: A Beautiful Session," interview by Les Tomkins, May 31, 1977, transcript on the National Jazz Archive website, http://nationaljazzarchive.co.uk/stories?id=389.

30. Gillespie, *To Be, or Not . . . to BOP,* 193.

31. Vaughan, interview by Tomkins, part 2.

32. Ibid.

33. Ibid.

34. Jones, *Talking Jazz,* 238.

35. DeVeaux, *Birth of Bebop,* 334. When Eckstine started singing with Hines, he made $10 a night, and when he left the band in 1943, he earned $30 a night.

36. Ibid., 337; Malachi, interview.

37. Miles Davis and Quincy Troupe, *Miles: The Autobiography* (New York: Simon & Schuster, 1989), 9.

38. Vaughan, interview by Tomkins, part 1.

39. "At Metropolitan," *Cleveland Call and Post,* November 18, 1944.

40. Southern and Eckstine, "'Mr. B' of Ballad," *The Black Perspective in Music* 8, no. 1 (Spring 1980): 57.

41. Jones, *Talking Jazz,* 241.

42. Vaughan, interview by Tomkins, part 1. Vaughan expressed similar sentiments in Dizzy Gillespie's memoirs: "I don't think the band was any experiment; it wasn't no experiment; they were just playing music that they knew. They weren't experimenting or anything. If it didn't work, it just didn't work. But it worked. They were getting out there and playing what they knew to play. We tried to educate people. We used to play dances, and there were just a very few who understood who would be in a corner, jitterbugging forever, while the rest just stood staring at us. But we didn't care, we didn't care. Maybe, we just knocked each other out. Yeah, we had lots of fun." Gillespie, *To Be, or Not . . . to BOP,* 192.

43. Gillespie, *To Be, or Not . . . to BOP,* 192.

44. Ibid., 189.

45. Vaughan, interview on *The Dick Cavett Show.*

46. Davis and Troupe, *Miles,* 97.

47. Jones, *Talking Jazz,* 238.

48. Don Gold, "Soulful Sarah," *Down Beat,* March 30, 1957.

49. Jill Jonnes, *Hep-Cats, Narcs, and Pipe Dreams: A History of America's Romance with Illegal Drugs* (New York: Scribner, 1996), 119–139.

50. Carl Schroeder, interview with author, October 23, 2015.
51. Vaughan, interview by Tomkins, part 1.
52. Jones, *Talking Jazz*, 238.
53. Gillespie, *To Be, or Not . . . to BOP*, 192.
54. Vaughan, interview by Tomkins, part 2.
55. Malachi, interview, 2:67. For more on the sexual harassment experienced by female musicians, see Sherrie Tucker, *Swing Shift: "All-Girl" Bands of the 1940s* (Durham, N.C.: Duke University Press, 2000).
56. Malachi, interview.
57. Judy Carmichael, interview with author, September 29, 2014.
58. Ibid.
59. "Wax for Eckstine's Ork," *Down Beat*, July 1, 1944.
60. Vaughan, interview by Tomkins, part 1.
61. Malachi, interview, 2:60; and Leonard Feather wrote: "Moreover, both [Eckstine] and Billy Shaw, his personal sponsor and biggest booster up at the William Morris office, were so enthusiastic about Sara Vaughan, the girl singer with the band, that they managed with some difficulty to persuade DeLuxe reluctantly to cut one side featuring her instead of Billy on vocal." Leonard Feather, "Billy Eckstine: Brand New Band Draws Loot; It's Commercial, Artistic to Boot; A-minus Musically, 1 Commercially," *Metronome*, January 1, 1945, 12.
62. Malachi, interview, 2:60.
63. Vaughan, interview by Tomkins, part 1.
64. Leonard Feather, review of "I'll Wait and Pray," sung by Sarah Vaughan, *Metronome*, July 1, 1945, 18.
65. Leonard Feather, "Stage Show Reviews: Billy Eckstine, Dizzy Heights," *Metronome*, November 1, 1944, 22.
66. Ginell, *Mr. B*, 65. According to Billy Eckstine's son Ed, "Pops had no respect for Leonard Feather and basically thought he was an asshole who was a thorn in his side and a forced necessary evil in his life and the lives of black musicians of his generation. He hawked his 'sad-ass, corny tunes' that Pop refused to record, but humored him nonetheless because he had seven mouths to feed and the power of Leonard's pen could hinder the process of he and others he loved and respected from getting gigs. And they weren't always that plentiful" (Ginell, *Mr. B*, 64).
67. Leonard Feather, *The Jazz Years: Earwitness to an Era* (New York: Da Capo, 1987), 100.
68. "That Ain't Hay, Billy: Certainly Not at $2,000 per Disc," *Chicago Defender*, March 31, 1945.
69. Robert Greenfield, *The Last Sultan: The Life and Times of Ahmet Ertegun* (New York: Simon & Schuster, 2011), 100.
70. Vaughan, interview by Tomkins, part 1.

Chapter 3: "I'm Not Singing Other People's Ideas"
 1. Leonard Feather, "Sara Vaughan: She's a Musicians' Singer, but the Public Loves Her Too, and So Does Leonard Feather Who Tells You All About Her," *Metronome*, July 1, 1946, 48.

2. Leslie Gourse, *Sassy: The Life of Sarah Vaughan* (New York: C. Scribner's Sons, 1993), 38.
3. "Sarah Loaded—But No Peace," *New York News,* April 10, 1955.
4. Count Basie, *Good Morning Blues: The Autobiography of Count Basie,* with Albert Murray (New York: Random House, 1985), 270.
5. Ibid., 271.
6. Sarah Vaughan, "Interview One: Musical All My Life," interview by Les Tomkins, May 31, 1977, transcript on the National Jazz Archive website, http://www.nationaljazzarchive.co.uk/stories?id=43.
7. Harry Belafonte, *My Song: A Memoir,* with Michael Shnayerson (New York: Alfred A. Knopf, 2011), 56.
8. Vaughan, interview by Tomkins, part 1.
9. Marianne Ruuth, *Sarah Vaughan* (Los Angeles: Holloway House, 1994), 152.
10. Feather, "She's a Musicians' Singer," 48.
11. Ibid.
12. "Sarah Loaded—But No Peace," *New York News,* April 10, 1955.
13. Feather, "She's a Musicians' Singer," 48. A copy of Vaughan's contract with Musicraft Records (archived in the Institute of Jazz Studies special collections) confirms that her agent at this time was Howard Richmond.
14. Barry Josephson and Terry Trilling-Josephson, *Cafe Society: The Wrong Place for the Right People* (Urbana: University of Illinois Press, 2009), 203.
15. Alvin Moses, "Gossips Type Rochester: Critics Ignore Muriel 'Gaines' Art," *Chicago Defender,* July 27, 1946.
16. Josephson and Trilling-Josephson, *Café Society,* 204.
17. Ibid., 203.
18. Ibid., 204.
19. Vaughan, interview by Tomkins, part 1.
20. Gourse, *Sassy,* 43.
21. Vaughan, interview by Tomkins, part 1.
22. Ibid.
23. John Gennari, *Blowin' Hot and Cool: Jazz and Its Critics,* Kindle ed. (Chicago: University of Chicago Press, 2006), chapter 1, location 686.
24. Chris Albertson, *Bessie* (New Haven, Conn.: Yale University Press, 2003), xiv, quoted in John Gennari, *Jazz and Its Critics,* chapter 1, note 61, Kindle location 5823.
25. Vaughan, interview by Tomkins, part 1.
26. Ibid.
27. Gennari, *Jazz and Its Critics,* chapter 1, location 352–944.
28. Eric Porter, *What Is This Thing Called Jazz?: African American Musicians as Artists, Critics, and Activists* (Berkeley: University of California Press, 2002), 69–72; Scott DeVeaux, *The Birth of Bebop: A Social and Musical History* (Berkeley: University of California Press, 1997).
29. Evelyn Brooks Higginbotham, *Righteous Discontent: The Women's Movement in the Black Baptist Church, 1880–1920* (Cambridge, Mass.: Harvard University Press, 1993), 185–188.
30. Leonard Feather, "Sarah Doesn't Dig Bessie," *Metronome,* March 1949, 18–23.

31. Michael Levin, "Downtown Café Society Floor Show Offers Value," *Down Beat,* August 26, 1946, 3.
32. As per Vaughan's contract with Musicraft Records, dated May 8, 1946, located in the Institute of Jazz Studies' special collection Musicraft Records, Inc., Records; "Vaughan for the Money! Sarah Signs Fine Pact with Wax Co.," *Pittsburgh Courier,* June 13, 1946.
33. Feather, "She's a Musicians' Singer," 49.
34. Michael Levin, "Downtown Café Society Floor Show Offers Value," *Down Beat,* August 26, 1946, 3.
35. Gourse, *Sassy,* 47. While Garry remembered being present at this incident, along with bandleader J. C. Heard, newspaper reports did not mention them and focused instead on Vaughan, George Treadwell, and Naomi Wright.
36. "Sarah Vaughan Mobbed in Village: Hoodlums Hit Cafe Society Singing Star," *New York Amsterdam News,* August 17, 1946; "Barbarism Flare in Greenwich Village Terrorizes New Yorkers," *Baltimore Afro-American,* August 24, 1946; "Singer Slugged by NY Thugs," *Baltimore Afro-American,* August 24, 1946; "Hoodlums Assault Three Entertainers," *Chicago Defender,* August 24, 1946; "Hoodlums Bring Lynch Spirit into N.Y. City; Entertainers Are Beaten," *Cleveland Call and Post,* August 24, 1946; "Citizens Protest 'Village' Terror," *New York Amsterdam News,* August 24, 1946; "Billy . . . Rowe's Note Book: Strictly Personal," *Pittsburgh Courier,* August 24, 1946; "Mob Spirit Flares in New York City," *Norfolk Journal and Guide,* August 24, 1946; Horace Carter, "4 Whites Gang Slam Stewart: Village Attacks Move to 52nd St., Musician Knocked Down, Kicked," *New York Amsterdam News,* September 7, 1946; Michael Levin, "Sarah Vaughan Beaten Up by Gang," *Down Beat,* August 26, 1946; "New Yorkers Ask Protection in City's Greenwich Village," *Baltimore Afro-American,* August 31, 1946; Gourse, *Sassy,* 46–47; and Barney Josephson, in Josephson and Trilling-Josephson, *Café Society,* 204.
37. Music, "Girlish Voice," *Time,* July 1, 1946.
38. "Sarah Vaughan Sparks Café Society Show," *Down Beat,* March 25, 1946, 3; E. B. Rea, "Encores and Echoes," *Baltimore Afro-American,* April 6, 1946; E. B. Rea, "Encores and Echoes," *Baltimore Afro-American,* April 20, 1946.
39. Feather, "She's a Musicians' Singer," 48.
40. Sarah Vaughan, "How He Proposed," *Tan Confessions,* November 1, 1950, 3.
41. Advertisement, *New York Amsterdam News,* January 18, 1947, 21.

Chapter 4: "The Most Talked About Voice in America"

1. E. B. Rea, "Encores and Echoes," *Baltimore Afro-American,* March 22, 1947.
2. Travis Dempsey, *An Autobiography of Black Jazz* (Chicago: Urban Research Institute, 1983), 246.
3. Sarah Vaughan, in Don Gold, "Soulful Sarah: A Success As A Pop-

Jazz Singer, She Seeks Greater Accomplishment," *Down Beat,* May 30, 1957, 13.

4. Sarah Vaughan, interview with Dick Cavett, *The Dick Cavett Show,* March 6 and 7, 1980.

5. Hoe [pseud.], "Vaughan Wows Them at 11:60 Club Jazz Concert," *Down Beat,* April 23, 1947, 13.

6. Don [pseud.], "11:60 Club Clicks with Opera House Concert," *Down Beat,* May 21, 1947, 15.

7. Stand-alone photo, *Chicago Defender,* May 17, 1947.

8. Johnny Sippel, "Night Clubs-Vaudeville: Follow-Up Reviews," *Billboard,* May 31, 1947.

9. Gold, "Soulful Sarah," 13.

10. Elena Razlogova, *The Listeners Voice: Early Radio and the American Public* (Philadelphia: University of Pennsylvania Press, 2011), 132–141; Ben Yagoda, *The B-Side: The Death of Tin Pan Alley and the Rebirth of the Great American Song* (New York: Riverhead, 2015), 130.

11. Dale Harrison, "All About the Town," *Chicago Sun,* May 27, 1947; Leonard Feather, "He Lit Up the Vast Wasteland," *Los Angeles Times,* August 1, 1982.

12. Dave Garroway, *The Dave Garroway Show,* NBC Radio, September 21, 1947. This and other quotes are based on my transcription of the broadcast, a recording of which exists in the Music Division of the Library of Congress.

13. Richard Dyer, *White* (London: Routledge, 1997), 14–15.

14. Sarah Vaughan, "Interview One: Musical All My Life," interview by Les Tomkins, May 31, 1977, transcript on the National Jazz Archive website, http://www.nationaljazzarchive.co.uk/stories?id=49.

15. "Sarah Vaughan, Singing Favorite, 'Billboard' Choice," *Los Angeles Sentinel,* April 8, 1948; "Music: Promising Tag to Torme and Vaughan," *Billboard,* April 3, 1948, 17.

16. "Jazz at the Philharmonic," *Cincinnati Enquirer,* April 18, 1943, Sunday edition, Kentucky edition.

17. Harold V. Cohen, "The Drama Desk," *Pittsburgh Post-Gazette,* April 24, 1948, 12.

18. R. McB [pseud.], "Hot Jazz, Bebop Rock the Pabst," *Milwaukee Journal-Sentinel,* May 5, 1948, 26.

19. "Sarah Vaughan Scores Big Hit at the Strand," *New York Amsterdam News,* May 22, 1948.

20. "Wonder If He Took 'Lord's Prayer,' Too," *Baltimore Afro-American,* March 20, 1948; "Thieves Show Preference for Sarah Vaughan Discs," *Chicago Defender,* March 27, 1948.

Part II: A Star Is Born, 1948–1958

1. "Sarah Vaughan Captures Broadway Swing Throngs," *Chicago Defender,* July 10, 1954, national edition.

2. "Detective Watching La Vaughan's Clothes," *Philadelphia Tribune,* September 1, 1953.

3. Sarah Vaughan, *Perdido! Live at Birdland, 1953,* Natash Imports, 1992, CD.
4. Ibid.
5. Herm Schoenfeld, "Night Club Reviews: Birdland, N.Y.," *Variety,* September 2, 1953.
6. Alvin Webb, "Sue Sarah Vaughan Husband for 250G's: Unprovoked Assault on Sarah's Fan," *New York Amsterdam News,* April 4, 1953.
7. Arnold de Mille, "On the Spot," *Chicago Defender,* April 11, 1953, national edition.
8. Ibid; Webb, "Sue Sarah Vaughan."
9. "Sarah Vaughan's Mate Denies Slashing Man," *Baltimore Afro-American,* April 11, 1953.
10. James Hicks, "Big Town," *Baltimore Afro-American,* April 18, 1953.
11. "Sarah Vaughan's Hubby Beats Rap: Treadwell's Victim Fails to Testify," *New York Amsterdam News,* April 18, 1953.

Chapter 5: "The Girl with the Magic Voice"

1. "Vaughan's Disc Soars," *Chicago Defender,* August 28, 1948, 9. It's difficult to know the accuracy of these sales figures. At times, the black press exaggerated record sales in order to elevate the stature and successes of prominent African Americans. Later estimates, probably generated by Vaughan's marketing team, suggested that she sold three million copies of "It's Magic." This is unlikely.
2. "Television Review: Tele Followup," *Variety,* September 15, 1948, 30.
3. "Sarah Vaughan Sues Wax Firm for $3,117 Back Pay," *Afro-American,* October 23, 1948, B6.
4. Sarah Vaughan, "Interview Two: A Beautiful Session," interview by Les Tomkins, May 31, 1977, transcript on the National Jazz Archive website, http://nationaljazzarchive.co.uk/stories?id=389.
5. "Musicraft Snag Ends, Vaughan in Col Term Deal," *Variety,* March 23, 1949.
6. "Sarah Vaughan Files Suit Against Record Company," *New Journal and Guide,* February 19, 1949; "Sarah Vaughan Files Suit Against Musicraft Disks," *New York Amsterdam News,* February 19, 1949.
7. "Sarah Vaughan Cuts for Columbia," *Billboard,* February 5, 1949.
8. "Battle for Discs Ends: Sarah Cuts Musicraft Ties, Eyes More $$$," *Baltimore Afro-American,* March 26, 1949.
9. "La Vaughan Gets Musicraft Pact Release: Waxes for Columbia," *Billboard,* March 26, 1949.
10. Marc Myers, *Why Jazz Happened* (Berkeley: University of California Press, 2012), 73–80, 92.
11. "Theatre in Brief," *Norfolk Journal and Guide,* April 23, 1949.
12. "MIX," "Record Reviews," *Down Beat,* November 3, 1950.
13. "MIX," "Record Reviews," *Down Beat,* October 6, 1950.
14. "Sarah Vaughan Platter Made in 24 Hours," *New York Amsterdam News,* August 12, 1950.
15. "Record Review," *Down Beat,* December 1, 1950, 15.
16. Charles Granata, *Sessions with Sinatra: Frank Sinatra and the Art of Recording* (Chicago: Chicago Review Press, 2003), 73.

17. Rosemary Clooney, *Girl Singer: An Autobiography* (New York: Bantam Doubleday, 2000), 74.
18. Granata, *Sessions,* 69.
19. Gourse, *Sassy,* 76.
20. Arnold Jay Smith, "Sarah Vaughan: Never Ending Melody," *Down Beat,* May 5, 1977, 17.
21. Ben Yagoda, *The B Side: The Death of Tin Pan Alley and the Rebirth of the Great American Song* (New York: Riverhead, 2015), 23.
22. Sarah Vaughan contract sheet, Sony Archives, accessed September 29, 2015.
23. Ted Fox, *In the Groove: The People Behind the Music* (New York: St. Martin's, 1986), 50.
24. "Diskery Pacts Full DJ Skeds for Top Stars: Columbia Revamps Spinner Promotions Thru 'A-B-C' Jocks," *Billboard,* December 30, 1950.
25. "La Vaughan Gets Col. Billy," *Billboard,* January 13, 1951.
26. Mitch Miller, "The State of Records," *Metronome,* November 1, 1952.
27. Yagoda, *The B Side,* 23–27, 133; Granata, *Sessions,* 68–70; Miller, "State of Records."
28. Columbia Records Advertisement, *Billboard,* January 17, 1953, 30.
29. "Mix," *Down Beat,* June 30, 1950.
30. "Record Review of Columbia 39576, 'I Ran All the Way Home' and 'Just a Moment,'" *Down Beat,* November 16, 1951.
31. Leonard Feather, "The Blindfold Test: Garroway Laments Sarah's Lapse," *Down Beat,* May 7, 1952.
32. Frank Stacy, "Nat Cole Talks Back to Critics," *The Capitol,* April 1946, quoted in Yagoda, *B-Side,* 125.
33. Quoted in Daniel Mark Epstein, *Nat King Cole* (New York: Farrar, Straus & Giroux, 1999), 223.
34. Quoted in Carl Ginell, *Mr. B: The Music and Life of Billy Eckstine* (Milwaukee, Wisc.: Hal Leonard, 2013), 107–108.
35. Nat Hentoff, "Sarah's Answer to Critics: Sing Best Way I Know How," *Down Beat,* April 4, 1952.
36. Ibid.

Chapter 6: "She's Vaughanderful. She's Marvelous"

1. Sarah Vaughan, *I'll Be Seeing You: The Sarah Vaughan Memorial Album,* Vintage Jazz Classics, VJC-1015–2, 1990, CD.
2. Jimmy Jones, interviewed by Patricia Wells, January 8, 1978, reel 3, transcript, 5, Jazz Studies Oral History Collection, Institute of Jazz Studies, Rutgers University, Newark, N.J.
3. Sarah Vaughan, *I'll Be Seeing You.*
4. Stanley Fields, "Only Human," *Daily Mirror,* November 30, 1954.
5. Ibid.
6. "King-Duke Unit Nets $351,550 in 5 Wks.: Giant Arena Package Hits Stride After Slow Road Start; Take in $25G Twice," *Billboard,* November 3, 1951; Hal Webman, "Rhythm and Blues Notes," *Billboard,* November 3, 1951.

7. C. W. Greenlea, "400 Refuse to Attend Jimcrow Concert at Side Door in Atlanta, 4,000 Others Enter," Associated Negro Press press release, November 7, 1951.

8. Ibid.

9. Ibid.

10. Associated Negro Press, "Atlanta Leaders Get Apologies in Municipal Hall Bias," November 14, 1951.

11. Cliff MacKay, "Ellington Plays as Atlantans Enter Back Door: Tear Up Tickets in Disgust over JC Police Rough as They Herd Colored Patrons to Rear; Whites Use Front," *Baltimore Afro-American,* November 3, 1951.

12. Ibid.; Greenlea, "400 Refuse to Attend."

13. Gladys P. Graham, "Jo Baker Target of Bias at Stork Club; Guest of Owner Is Refused Service by Employee; Incident Irks Sugar Ray Robinson, NAACP," Associated Negro Press press release, October 22, 1951.

14. Associated Negro Press, "Duke Ellington Denies 'We Ain't Ready' Story, Tells of Possible Loss of All Band Jobs if He Refused to Play in Atlanta," December 3, 1951.

15. Greenlea, "400 Refuse to Attend."

16. MacKay, "Ellington Plays as Atlantans Enter Back Door."

17. Ibid.

18. Kobena Mercer, "Black Hair/Style Politics," *Out There: Marginalization and Contemporary Culture,* ed. Russell Ferguson, Martha Gever, Trinh T. Minh-ha, and Cornel West (New York: The New Museum of Contemporary Art, 1990), 35–47.

19. Greenlea, "400 Refuse to Attend"; "Atlanta Leaders Get Apologies in Municipal Hall Bias," Associated Negro Press deadline release, November 14, 1951.

20. "'Big Show' Manager Hits NAACP's Lines," *Baltimore Afro-American,* November 24, 1951.

21. Otis N. Thompson, "'We Ain't Ready,' Duke Declares," Associated Negro Press, November 21, 1951, originally appeared in *St. Louis Argus,* November 16, 1951.

22. Associated Negro Press, "Duke Ellington."

23. Daniel Mark Epstein, *Nat King Cole* (New York: Farrar, Straus & Giroux, 1999), 224–227. Dick LaPalm said that the White Citizens Council abducted him in Biloxi during the Biggest Show of '51. However, the WCC was founded in 1954, three years later, in response to the Supreme Court's decision in *Brown v. Board of Education.* It's likely that another white supremacist group was responsible for relocating LaPalm in the middle of the night.

24. Quoted in Maria Cole, *Nat King Cole: An Intimate Biography,* with Louie Robinson (New York: William Morrow, 1971), 125–126.

25. Ibid.

26. Marianne Ruuth, *Sarah Vaughan* (Los Angeles: Holloway House, 1994), 96.

27. Butch Lacy, interview with author, June 6, 2016.

28. "Upcoming Acts," *Miami Daily News,* December 16, 1950; "Sarah

Vaughan Shatters Ban on Sepia Stars at Dixie Celebrity Club: Song
Stylist to Stint Two Weeks," *Atlanta Daily World,* December 21, 1950;
"LaVaughan Headlines Show: Sarah Shatters Precedent; Opens at
Miami Beach Club," *Norfolk Journal and Guide,* December 23, 1950.
29. Advertisement, *Miami Daily News,* December 15, 1950.
30. Leslie Gourse, *Sassy: The Life of Sarah Vaughan* (New York:
C. Scribner's Sons, 1993), 56.
31. George Wein, interview with author, November 18, 2015.
32. Sarah Vaughan, "My Best on Wax," *Down Beat,* April 21, 1950.
33. Ibid.
34. "Raps Critics Who Don't Like Sarah Vaughan's 'Prayer,'" *Philadelphia Tribune,* January 13, 1948.
35. Untitled, *Daily News,* November 14, 1951, included in clip folders for
Sarah Vaughan, Schomburg Center for Research in Black Culture.
36. Farah Jasmine Griffin, "When Malindy Sings: A Meditation on Black
Women's Vocality," *Uptown Conversation: The New Jazz Studies* (New
York: Columbia University Press, 2004), 102–105.
37. Tobin Miller Shearer, "Invoking Crisis: Performative Christian Prayer
and the Civil Rights Movement," *Journal of the American Academy of
Religion* 83, no. 2 (June 2015): 490–512.

Chapter 7: "Sarah Vaughan and Her Pygmalion"
1. E. B. Rea, "Sarah Vaughan at Home," *Baltimore Afro-American,* February 26, 1949.
2. Sarah Vaughan, "The Man Behind Me," *Our World,* March 1951.
3. Freda DeKnight, "Date with a Dish," *Ebony,* January 1952.
4. Alverta Alexander, "Sarah's No. 1 Singer, Never Had a Lesson—She
Just Started and Zoomed; Lauds Her Husband; Would Like Children,"
Pittsburgh Courier, September 16, 1950.
5. Joanne Meyerowitz, "Beyond the Feminine Mystique: A Reassessment
of Postwar Mass Culture, 1946–1958," in *Not June Cleaver: Women
and Gender in Postwar America, 1945–1960,* ed. Joanne Meyerowitz
(Philadelphia: Temple University Press, 1994), 233–234.
6. Al Monroe, "Swinging the News," *Chicago Defender,* August 28, 1948,
national edition, 9.
7. Leslie Gourse, *Sassy: The Life of Sarah Vaughan* (New York:
C. Scribner's Sons, 1993), 56.
8. "Sarah Vaughan's Boxer Routs Holdup Men; Wins Steak Dinner,"
Chicago Defender, June 26, 1948, national edition; "Baron Bows," *Down
Beat,* June 14, 1948, 1.
9. "Phony P.A. Stories Only Hurt Clients," *Down Beat,* October 11, 1948.
10. "The Man Behind the Gal: George Treadwell Quit Band to Pilot
Singer-Wife—It Paid Off," *Baltimore Afro-American,* February 21,
1948; "Hubby Can Take Bow for Guiding Career of Sarah Vaughan,"
Pittsburgh Courier, February 21, 1948; "Husband Keeps Guard on
Vaughan's Career," *Philadelphia Tribune,* February 28, 1949; "Sarah
Vaughan's Husband Is Key That Opens Door," *Cleveland Call and Post,*
February 28, 1948.

11. Sarah Vaughan, "My Biggest Break," *Negro Digest,* July 1, 1949; Sarah Vaughan, "How He Proposed," *Tan Confessions,* November 1, 1950; Vaughan, "The Man Behind Me."

12. Gourse, *Sassy,* 69.

13. Ibid., 68.

14. Ibid., 69.

15. Photograph, *Chicago Defender,* August 30, 1952, national edition, 22; "Picture of Contentment," *Philadelphia Tribune,* August 26, 1952, 12.

16. "In the Clink," *Philadelphia Tribune,* July 14, 1951, 1; "Sarah Vaughan, Buddy Young Nabbed by Police," *Pittsburgh Courier,* July 14, 1951, 6.

17. Conrad Clarke, "Quiz Sarah Vaughan in Dope Case: US Aide Says Singer Wasn't Too Helpful," *Philadelphia Tribune,* April 5, 1952; "Sarah 'Sings' of Dope: Sarah Vaughan Called Before Dope Probers; Songstress Surprise Witness but Won't Say What Happened," *Baltimore Afro-American,* April 12, 1952, 1.

18. "Izzy Rowe's Notebook: Sons and Daughters of Harlem, U.S.A.," *Pittsburgh Courier,* August 22, 1953, 22.

19. Mary Stratford, "Sarah Won't Air Romance with Joe," *Baltimore Afro-American,* February 2, 1957.

20. Sid Shalit, "Second Hearing—Second Sight," *New York Daily News,* January 19, 1952, 1.

21. Sarah Vaughan, "Dark Girls Can Make It Too!" *Tan Confessions,* March 1953, 47.

22. Ibid., 28, 47–48.

23. Sarah Vaughan, interview by Marian McPartland, *Piano Jazz,* NPR, January 17, 1986.

24. Rob Roy, "Jivin' the Jive," *Chicago Defender,* March 20, 1948, 9.

25. Hal Webman, "Music: N.Y. Clique Opens with Big Splash—and Buddy Rich," *Billboard,* December 11, 1948.

26. Gourse, *Sassy,* 58.

27. John S. Wilson, "Capsule Comments," *Down Beat,* February 10, 1950.

28. Ibid.

29. Kathy Davis, *Reshaping the Female Body: The Dilemma of Cosmetic Surgery* (New York: Routledge, 1995), 12.

30. Patricia Hill Collins, *Black Feminist Thought: Knowledge, Consciousness, and the Politics of Empowerment* (New York: Routledge, 2000), 79. Anne DuCille addresses a similar issues in "Toy Theory: Black Barbie and the Deep Play of Difference," in *Skin Trade* (Cambridge, Mass.: Harvard University Press, 1996), 8–59.

31. Kobena Mercer, "Black Hair/Style Politics," *New Formations* 3 (1987): 33, 45.

32. Ibid., 35.

33. Jack Zipes, *Fairy Tales and the Art of Subversion: The Classical Genre for Children and the Process of Civilization* (New York: Routledge, 1991), 3; Cristina Bacchilega, *Postmodern Fairy Tales: Gender and Narrative Strategies* (Philadelphia: University of Pennsylvania Press, 1997), 5–6; Laura Tosi, "Smart Princesses, Clever Choices: The Deconstruction of the Cinderella Paradigm and the Shaping of Female Cultural Identity

in Adult and Children's Contemporary Rewritings of Fairy Tales,"
Miscelánea 24 (2001): 93–106; Marina Warner, *From the Beast to the
Blonde: On Fairy Tales and Their Tellers* (London: Chatto & Windus,
1994), 362–367; Lisa Rettle, "Fairy Tales Re-visited: Gender Concepts
in Traditional and Feminist Fairy Tales," *Arbeiten aus Anglistik und
Amerikanistik* 26, no. 2 (2001): 181–198.

34. For a comprehensive survey of the Pygmalion myth and its many
retellings see Essaka Joshua, *Pygmalion and Galatea: The History of a
Narrative in English Literature* (Burlington, VT: Ashgate, 2001).

35. Martin A. Danahay, "Mirrors of Masculine Desire: Narcissus and
Pygmalion in Victorian Representation," *Victorian Poetry* 32 (1994):
35–53.

36. Shalit, "Second Hearing-Second Sight."

Chapter 8: "Sarah Vaughan Is Finally on the Way to the Pot of Gold"

1. "Sarah Comfortable as New Disc Soars," *Baltimore Afro-American,*
December 18, 1954.
2. "Music-Radio: The Billboard Music Popularity Charts: Popular
Records—This Week's Best Buys," *Billboard,* November 13, 1954.
3. "Music: Retail Disk Best Sellers," *Variety,* November 24, 1954.
4. "Even Sarah Vaughan Has Unreached Goal in Amusement Setup,"
Chicago Defender, December 18, 1954, national edition.
5. *Friday with Garroway,* NBC Radio, December 3, 1954, Library of
Congress, transcribed by author.
6. Herm Schoenfeld, "Music: Jocks, Jukes and Disks," *Variety,*
February 24, 1954.
7. *Friday with Garroway,* December 9, 1954.
8. Johnnie Garry, "Harlem Speaks," National Jazz Museum in Harlem,
oral history/interview, November 29, 2007.
9. *Chicago Defender,* December 18, 1954; *Baltimore Afro-American,*
December 18, 1954.
10. "Television Review: Ed Sullivan," *Variety,* March 23, 1955.
11. June Bundy, "Vox Jox," *Billboard,* May 21, 1955.
12. "Big Clearance Fuss Centers Around 'Lola,'" *Billboard,* April 2, 1955.
13. B. Dietmeier, "Banner Year Ahead . . . Juke Industry," *Billboard,* July
30, 1955.
14. June Bundy, "Diskers & Pubbers Learning Show Scores Don't Pay Off,"
Billboard, July 30, 1955.
15. "'Lola' Draws Ban from KFWB Jockey," *Billboard,* April 16, 1955.
16. "The Billboard 1955 Disk Jockey Poll—Most Played Female Vocalist,"
Billboard, November 12, 1955.
17. "Mercury Plugs Hi-Fi Display," *Billboard,* March 31, 1956; "Packaged
Records: Best Selling Packaged Records—Pop Vocal," *Billboard,* May
26, 1956; "Packaged Records: Best Selling Packaged Records—Jazz,"
Billboard, May 26, 1956.
18. "Sarah Vaughan's New Four-Year Merc Deal," *Variety,* May 23, 1956;
"Other Big Deals for Fem Artists," *Variety,* May 30, 1956; "Music:
Those High-C Phono Figures," *Variety,* May 30, 1956.

19. "Stafford Inks New Col. Pact," *Billboard*, May 5, 1956; "Jo Stafford Signs Contract," *Broadcast Telecasting*, May 7, 1956, 98. Unlike *Billboard* and *Broadcast Telecasting*, *Variety* reported that Stafford earned $60,000 a year for five years—in other words, $300,000 rather than $500,000. "Music: Jo Stafford Gets 60G Deal from Col," *Variety*, May 2, 1956.

20. "Doris Day Signs Disk Pact," *New York Times*, May 11, 1956.

21. Garry McGee, *Doris Day: Sentimental Journey* (Jefferson, N.C.: McFarland, 2005), 27, 30; David Kaufman, *Doris Day: The Untold Story of the Girl Next Door* (London: Virgin, 2008), 214, 220.

22. *Down Beat*, December 29, 1954; "Popular Records," *Down Beat*, February 23, 1955.

23. "Reviews of New Pop Records," *Billboard*, November 6, 1954; "Review Spotlight," *Billboard*, November 6, 1954.

24. Nat Hentoff, "Ella Tells of Trouble in Mind Concerning Discs, Television," *Down Beat*, February 23, 1955.

25. "Music-Radio: RCA Release Date Fracas on Two Tunes," *Billboard*, January 14, 1956.

26. "Second Annual Disc Jockey Poll Shows Strong Recording Trends," *Down Beat*, March 1955.

27. David Brackett, "What a Difference a Name Makes: Two Instances of African-American Popular Music," lecture at the Society for American Music Twenty-Eighth Annual Conference, Lexington, Ky., March 7, 2002.

28. Elaine Tyler May, *Homeward Bound: American Families in the Cold War Era* (New York: Basic Books, 1988), 9–17.

29. Ibid., 26.

30. "Sarah Comfortable as New Disc Soars," *Baltimore Afro-American*, December 18, 1954.

31. "Pop Records: Review Spotlight On . . . ," *Billboard*, June 16, 1956.

32. "Grand Union and Penn Fruit Climb on LP Bandwagon," *Billboard*, June 16, 1956.

33. Stephen G. Meyer, *As Long as They Don't Move Next Door: Segregation and Racial Conflict in American Neighborhoods* (Lanham, Md.: Rowman & Littlefield, 2000), 6–10.

34. Ibid., 95–96.

35. Daniel Mark Epstein, *Nat King Cole* (New York: Farrar, Straus, & Giroux, 1999), 181, cited in Robert M. Fogelson, *Bourgeois Nightmares: Suburbia, 1870–1930* (New Haven, Conn.: Yale University Press, 2007), 122

36. Meyer, 96.

Chapter 9: "The High Priestess of Jazz"

1. Nat Hentoff, "One of Two Record Pacts 'For Me,' Asserts Sarah," *Down Beat*, January 26, 1955.

2. Ibid; Nat Hentoff, "Two Sarah Vaughan's Make Each Other Comfortable," *Record Whirl*, July 1955.

3. Hentoff, "Two Sarah Vaughan's."

4. Hentoff, "One of Two Record Pacts."

5. Hentoff, "Two Sarah Vaughan's."
6. "Jazz Review," *Down Beat*, May 18, 1955.
7. Scott DeVeaux, *The Birth of Bebop: A Social and Musical History* (Berkeley: University of California Press, 1997), 202–235; Robert Walser, *Running with the Devil: Power, Gender, and Madness in Heavy Metal Music* (Hanover, N.H.: Wesleyan University Press, 1993), 55–75; Ingrid Monson, "The Problem with White Hipness: Race, Gender, and Cultural Conceptions in Jazz Historical Discourse," *Journal of the American Musicological Society* 48, no. 3 (1995): 396–422.
8. Dianne Reeves, interview with author, December 15, 2015.
9. "Music-Radio: EmArcy Label Building Up Jazz Catalog," *Billboard*, December 4, 1954.
10. Bob Shad, "Shad Shows Expansion of EmArcy," *Down Beat*, January 25, 1956.
11. Jose [pseud.], "Night Club Reviews: Waldorf-Astoria, N.Y.," *Variety*, June 5, 1957.
12. "Basie, Sarah Balk at Calypso in Waldorf-Astoria Debut," *Jet*, June 20, 1957, 59.
13. Dorothy Kilgallen, "Sarah Vaughan Balks at Calypso," *Washington Post and Times Herald*, June 7, 1957.
14. "Basie, Sarah Balk at Calypso in Waldorf-Astoria Debut," *Jet*, June 20, 1957, 59.
15. "Wows at the Waldorf," *Newsweek*, July 1, 1957.
16. Jose, "Night Club Reviews."
17. Al Monroe, "So They Say," *Chicago Defender*, June 15, 1957.
18. "Sarah, Count Score Solidly at Waldorf," *Pittsburgh Courier*, June 15, 1957.
19. Jose, "Night Club Reviews."
20. "Basie-Vaughan's Boff Biz atop Posh Waldorf; Also 'Mixed' Dancing," *Variety*, June 19, 1957.
21. Herm Schoenfeld, "Music: New York's Jazz-Ma-Tazz," *Variety*, June 19, 1957.
22. "Sarah, Count Score Solidly at Waldorf," *Pittsburgh Courier*, June 15, 1957. A similar sentiment was first expressed in a *Variety* review of the Waldorf concerts: "She's one of the top singers of this day, with the ability to tackle any type of song with this highly developed voice and a style easily appreciated by all. She's as good for the Waldorf as she has been for the Birdland, where she's billed as the 'Divine Sarah.'" Jose, "Night Club Reviews."
23. Leslie Gourse, *Sassy: The Life of Sarah Vaughan* (New York: C. Scribner's Sons, 1993), 91.
24. "Sarah Vaughan Divorced, George Reweds," *New York Amsterdam News*, June 20, 1957.
25. "Sarah Vaughan's 'Ex' and Wife Decide to Live in Jersey Town," *Chicago Defender*, July 24, 1957, daily edition.
26. Masco Young, "The Grapevine," *Pittsburgh Courier*, August 17, 1957.
27. "Sarah Loaded—But No Peace," *New York News*, April 10, 1955.
28. Gourse, *Sassy*, 91–92.

29. Barbara Gardner, "Sarah," *Down Beat,* March 2, 1961.
30. Photo standalone 6, *Pittsburgh Courier,* February 15, 1958.
31. Marc Myers, "Interview: Ronnell Bright (Part 3)," *JazzWax,* April 23, 2008, http://www.jazzwax.com/2008/04/interview-ron-2.html/.
32. Ibid.
33. Pit [pseud.], "Night Club Reviews: Mr. Kelly's, Chi," *Variety,* March 3, 1958.
34. Myers, "Interview: Ronnell Bright (Part 3)."
35. Ibid.
36. Ibid.
37. Ibid.
38. Ibid.
39. Bert Vuijsje, liner notes to Sarah Vaughan, *If This Isn't Love—Jazz at the Concertgebouw,* Dutch Jazz Archives, CD, MCN 1006, 2010.
40. Roy Haynes, email correspondence with author via his agent, Jordan Fritz, April 2, 2014.
41. Roy Haynes, interview by Ted Panken, "2007 Jazziz Article and Four Interviews with Roy Haynes, Who Turns 87 Today," *Today Is the Question: Ted Panken on Music, Arts, and Politics* (blog), March 13, 2006, https://tedpanken.wordpress.com/2012/03/13/a-2007-jazziz-article-and-four-interviews-with-roy-haynes-who-turns-87-today/.
42. Haynes, email with author.
43. "Harlem Speaks: Roy Haynes, April 6, 2005," National Jazz Museum in Harlem, http://www.jazzmuseuminharlem.org/oldsite/archive.php?id=295, accessed September 8, 2016.
44. Roy Haynes, interview by Anthony Brown, May 15, 1994, Smithsonian Jazz Oral History Program, National Museum of American History, Smithsonian Institution, Archives Center.
45. Roy Haynes interview by Ted Panken, "2007 Jazziz Article."
46. Nat Hentoff, "Miles: A Trumpeter in the Midst of a Big Comeback Makes a Very Frank Appraisal of Today's Jazz Scene," *Down Beat,* November 2, 1955, reprinted in Frank Alkyer, Ed Enright, and Jason Koransky, eds., *The Miles Davis Reader* (New York: Hal Leonard Books, 2007), 39.
47. Roy Haynes interview by Anthony Brown.
48. Gourse, *Sassy,* 91.
49. Maurice Burman, "I Love—Yes Love—Mr. B," *Melody Maker,* April 19, 1958.
50. Marc Myers, "Sarah Vaughan: 1958 and 1964," *JazzWax,* November 24, 2008, http://www.jazzwax.com/2008/11/sarah-vaughan-1.html/.
51. Max Jones, "Sarah is a Knock-Out," *Melody Maker,* April 19, 1958.
52. Quoted in Vuijsje, liner notes to Vaughan, *If This Isn't Love.*
53. Myers, "Interview: Ronnell Bright."
54. Gourse, *Sassy,* 93.
55. Ibid., 97–98.
56. "Harlem Speaks: Johnnie Garry, November 29, 2007," National Jazz Museum in Harlem, http://www.jazzmuseuminharlem.org/oldsite/archive.php?id=346/, accessed March 15, 2016.

57. Ibid.

58. Gourse, *Sassy,* 97–98.

59. Photo standalone 18, *Chicago Defender,* November 3, 1958, daily edition.

60. "Harlem Speaks: Johnnie Garry."

61. Penny M. Von Eschen, *Satchmo Blows Up the World: Jazz Ambassadors Play the Cold War,* Kindle ed. (Cambridge, Mass.: Harvard University Press, 2008), location 88–143.

62. Ibid.; "Sarah Wants Trip to Russia," *Toronto Daily Star,* June 15, 1959.

63. Oscar Lopez, "Classics: Expo '58 + Philips Pavilion/ Le Corbusier and Iannis Xenakis," *ArchDaily* (blog), August 25, 2011, http://www.archdaily.com/157658/ad-classics-expo-58-philips-pavilion-le-corbusier-and-iannis-xenakis/.

64. George Wein, *Myself Among Others,* Kindle ed. (New York: Da Capo, 2009), location 2934.

65. Von Eschen, *Satchmo Blows Up,* Kindle ed., chapter 1, location 196.

66. Robert H. Haddow, *Pavilions of Plenty: Exhibiting American Culture Abroad in the 1950s* (Washington, D.C.: Smithsonian Institution Press, 1997), 74.

67. Ibid., 172–174.

68. Wein, *Myself Among Others,* location 2937.

Part III: A Career Is Reborn, 1959–1990

1. Robert Richards, interview with author, July 21, 2015.

2. James Liska, "Sarah Vaughan: I'm Not a Jazz Singer," *Down Beat,* May 1982; Arnold Jay Smith, "Never Ending Melody," *Down Beat,* May 5, 1977.

3. Liska, "Sarah Vaughan."

4. Max Jones, "Sarah Vaughan Says," *Melody Maker,* January 30, 1960, 2, 3.

5. Ibid.

6. Herb Mickman, interview with author, November 20, 2015; Bob Magnusson, interview with author, September 29, 2015.

7. Robert Richards, interview with author.

8. Bob Protzman, "Sarah Vaughan Feels She Deserves More," *Akron Beacon Journal,* June 1, 1978, D-8.

Chapter 10: "They Say You Can't Teach New Tricks to Old Dogs— So Get New Dogs!"

1. "Sarah Vaughan Weds Chicago Sportsman," *New York Amsterdam News,* September 13, 1958.

2. Ibid.

3. Ibid.

4. "Greg Harris Notebook," *Chicago Defender,* September 9, 1958, daily edition.

5. "Sarah Vaughan Weds Chicago Sportsman," *New York Amsterdam News,* September 13, 1958.

6. Marianne Ruuth, *Sarah Vaughan* (Los Angeles: Holloway House, 1994), 101.

7. Leslie Gourse, *Sassy: The Life of Sarah Vaughan* (New York: Da Capo, 1993), 100.

8. "Sarah Vaughan, Singer, Wed," *New York Times*, September 5, 1958; "Marriages," *Variety*, September 10, 1958; "Sarah Vaughan to Clyde Atkins, Chicago, Sept. 4 Bride Is the Jazz Singer, Groom Is a Chi Taxicab Fleet Owner," *Variety*, September 10, 1958.

9. Dorothy Kilgallen, "Martha Raye Dealing for 'Dressler' Role," *Asbury Park Press*, February 24, 1959, 10.

10. Masco Young, "The Grapevine," *Pittsburgh Courier*, February 21, 1959.

11. "Music: Daily News Star Jazz for N.Y. Charity Units," *Variety*, February 10, 1960; "Music: Madison Sq. Garden Hits as Jazz Joint in Sock Daily New Charity Layout," *Variety*, June 8, 1960.

12. "Madison Sq. Garden Hits."

13. Allan Morrison, "Sarah Vaughan Adopts a Baby," *Ebony*, September 1961.

14. "People," *Time*, December 28, 1959.

15. Leonard Lyons, "Lyons Den," *Chicago Defender*, January 14, 1960.

16. Photograph, *Chicago Defender*, June 17, 1961; "Sarah Adopts Baby Girl," *New Pittsburgh Courier*, July 1, 1961, national edition.

17. "Sarah Vaughan Adopts a Baby," *Ebony*, September 1961, 88–94.

18. "Words of the Week," *Jet*, April 28, 1955, 30.

19. "Vaudeville: Atkins, Filho in S.A. Deal," *Variety*, December 30, 1959.

20. "Chatter: Chicago," *Variety*, June 15, 1960; "Vaudeville: Ahmad Jamal Also Gets His Fill of Bonifacing," *Variety*, October 4, 1961; Earl Wilson, "It Happened Last Night," *Morning News*, July 11, 1961; George E. Pitts, "George E. Pitts Sez," *Pittsburgh Courier*, June 25, 1960.

21. "Izzy Rowe's Notebook," *New Pittsburgh Courier*, June 10, 1961, national edition.

22. Gloria Lynne, *I Wish You Love: A Memoir* (New York: Forge, 2000), 122.

23. Gourse, *Sassy*, 109.

24. Richard Davis, interview with author, March 13, 2014.

25. Dorothy Kilgallen, "Voice of Broadway: Connie Francis Next Mrs. Dick Clark?," *Weirton (W.Va.) Daily Times*, June 7, 1961; "Izzy Rowe's Notebook," *Pittsburgh Courier*, October 31, 1959.

26. Teddy Reig, *Reminiscing in Tempo: The Life and Times of a Jazz Hustler*, with Edward Berger (Metuchen, N.J.: Scarecrow, 1990), 60.

27. Edward Berger, *Basically Speaking: An Oral History of George Duvivier* (Metuchen, N.J.: Scarecrow, 1993), 103–104.

28. Gourse, *Sassy*, 104.

29. Reig, *Reminiscing*, 61.

30. Ibid., 114. It's also possible that this incident took place almost a year later in May or June 1963 during her Los Angeles recording sessions with the Gerald Wilson Orchestra. She was now involved with John "Preacher" Wells, known for carrying a gun, and in the midst of a messy separation from Atkins. A gossip column reported: "Sarah Vaughan's dramatic battle with her estranged husband, C. B. Atkins, on a Hollywood street the other day ended making fans for him, because he didn't strike back. The row was caused by his desire to see the daughter they adopted during the happier phase of their marriage, and when he stopped by Sassy's recording studio to let her know he'd picked up the

little girl for an outing, the singer flew into a rage that amazed a couple of dozen onlookers." Dorothy Kilgallen, "Voice of Broadway," *Monroe (La.)-News-Star,* June 20, 1963, B-10.

31. Barbara Gardner, "Sarah," *Down Beat,* March 2, 1961.

32. Gourse, *Sassy,* 108.

33. "Harlem Speaks: Johnnie Garry, November 29, 2007," National Jazz Museum in Harlem, oral history/interview.

34. Ibid.

35. Gourse, *Sassy,* 108.

36. "Vaudeville: Vaude, Café Dates," *Variety,* July 26, 1961; "Sarah Faces Knife, 3-Month Idleness," *Baltimore Afro-American,* August 5, 1961; Al Monroe, "So They Say," *Chicago Defender,* August 1, 1961, 16; Al Monroe, "So They Say," *Chicago Defender,* August 2, 1961, 16; Ol' Nosey [pseud.], "Everybody Goes When the Wagon Comes," *Chicago Defender,* August 19, 1961, 10.

37. Dorothy Kilgallen, "Sarah Vaughan Hits Marital Discord," *Asbury Park Evening Press,* October 19, 1962, 25.

38. "Sarah Vaughan Issues Warrant for Husband's Arrest; He Is Questioned by Police in Threats to Kill," *Philadelphia Tribune,* October 20, 1962.

39. Dave Hepburn, "Sarah Vaughan Sorry Police Grabbed Hubby: The Battling Love Birds," *New York Amsterdam News,* October 27, 1962.

40. Kilgallen, "Sarah Vaughan Hits Marital Discord."

41. Masco Young, "The Grapevine," *Pittsburgh Courier,* November 24, 1962.

42. Bob Queen, "Sarah Vaughan's Hubby Threatens to Kill Her, But They Kiss and Make Up," *Pittsburgh Courier,* October 27, 1962.

43. Chet Coleman, "'Divine One' and Spouse Lectured to by Magistrate: Throng of Several Hundred Stands Outside Station," *Philadelphia Tribune,* October 23, 1962.

44. Queen, "Sarah Vaughan's Hubby"; Coleman, "'Divine One' and Spouse Lectured"; "Music: Sarah Vaughan Springs Spouse After Jailing Him," *Variety,* October 24, 1962.

45. Chet Coleman, "Was the Arrest of Sarah Vaughan's Husband Just a Publicity Stunt?," *Philadelphia Tribune,* October 23, 1962.

46. Masco Young, "The Grapevine," October 2, 1962.

47. Duke Bryant, "Unhappy About Vaughan," *Philadelphia Tribune,* October 23, 1962.

48. Dorothy Kilgallen, "Sarah Vaughan's Sad Story Is Out," *Washington Post and Times-Herald,* November 20, 1962.

49. Hepburn, "Sarah Vaughan Sorry."

50. "Sarah Vaughan Asks Divorce," *New York Times,* November 3, 1962; "Sarah Claims Life Threats, Asks Divorce," *Telegram,* November 3, 1962; "Sarah Asks Divorce From Atkins Both as Husband, Manager," *Chicago Defender,* November 5, 1962; "Money Behind Divorces of Dandridge, Vaughan," *Chicago Defender,* November 12, 1962.

51. Herb Mickman, interview with author, November 20, 2015.

52. "Sarah Seeks Divorce; Atkins Hints at Reunion," *Jet,* November 22, 1962, 58.

53. Izzy Rowe, "Izzy Rowe's Notebook: Sons and Daughters of Harlem," *New Pittsburgh Courier*, November 24, 1962, national edition.
54. Dorothy Kilgallen, "Terrail Rates 1–1 with Ava Gardner," *Asbury Park Evening Press*, December 8, 1962.
55. Art Peters, "Dinah Peacemaker as Sarah and C. B. Atkins Collide at Birdland: 'Divine One,' Feuding Hubby," *Philadelphia Tribune*, December 25, 1962.
56. "Atkins Free on $10,000 Bond; Hubby Shoots at Singer Sarah Vaughan in Englewood Home," *New Pittsburgh Courier*, February 2, 1963; "Sarah Vaughan Hubby in Shooting Spree, Jailed," *Chicago Daily Defender*, January 28, 1963.
57. "Battle of Sarah and Mate Due in Court After Wild Fight and Shooting Scrape," *Chicago Defender*, February 2, 1963, national edition.
58. "Atkins Free on $10,000 Bond."
59. "Sarah's Popularity Up Despite Marital Woes," *Baltimore Afro-American*, August 3, 1963.
60. "Sarah Vaughan, Mate Feud," *Baltimore Afro-American*, January 2, 1965; "Sarah Vaughan in Another Legal Hassle with Husband—He Charges Her with Larceny," *Norfolk Journal and Guide*, January 9, 1965.
61. "Will Seek Legal Separation from Sarah—Atkins," *Jet*, March 28, 1963, 62.
62. "Seize Sarah's $50,000 Home for $19,000 in Texas," *Jet*, March 21, 1963, 58.
63. "Will Seek Legal Separation from Sarah—Atkins," *Jet*, March 28, 1963, 62.
64. Herb Mickman, interview with author.
65. Buster Williams, interview with author, September 4, 2015.
66. Ibid.
67. Liner notes, *Jazz Icons: Sarah Vaughan Live in '58 & '64* (Naxos, 2007), DVD.
68. Buster Williams, interview with author.
69. Liner notes, *Jazz Icons*.
70. "Sarah Vaughan, Mate Feud," *Baltimore Afro-American*, January 2, 1965; "Sarah Vaughan in Another Legal Hassle."

Chapter 11: "The No. 1 Singer of a Decade Ago"

1. Dorothy McCardle, "The Word Was Sakura; Sarah Sang It," *Washington Post* and *Times Herald*, January 14, 1965.
2. Ibid.
3. Bob James, interview with author, November 16, 2015.
4. Ibid.
5. Bill Quinn, "Sassy '67," *Down Beat*, June 27, 1967.
6. Gardiner Harris, "The Underside of the Welcome Mat," *New York Times*, October 10, 2008; "The White House, President Lyndon B. Johnson, Daily Diary," Tuesday, January 12, 1965, archived at the LBJ Presidential Library and Museum.
7. Bob James, interview with author.

8. George Anastasia, "Extortion Case Ties Music-Industry Executive with Mob," *Philadelphia Inquirer,* June 25, 1987.

9. Quincy Jones, *The Complete Quincy Jones: My Journey and Passions: Photos, Letters, Memories & More from Q's Personal Collection* (San Rafael, Calif.: Insight Editions, 2008), 21.

10. Quinn, "Sassy '67."

11. "The Musical Side of Sarah," *Pittsburgh Courier,* October 9, 1965.

12. Quoted in Jones, *Complete Quincy Jones,* 35–36. Jones made similar observations in Quincy Jones, "Sarah Makes It All Worthwhile," *Melody Maker,* October 12, 1963.

13. Jones, *Complete Quincy Jones,* 34.

14. Sarah Vaughan, "Interview One: Musical All My Life," interview by Les Tomkins, May 31, 1977, transcript on the National Jazz Archive website, http://www.nationaljazzarchive.co.uk/stories?id=43.

15. Jones, *Complete Quincy Jones,* 35–36.

16. Quinn, "Sassy '67."

17. Bob James, interview with author.

18. Martin Williams, "Some Notes on a Singer. Before It's Too Late," *Jazz Journal,* July 1968, 36–37.

19. Ibid.

20. Martin Williams, "Words for Sarah," *Saturday Review,* August 26, 1967, 18.

21. Williams, "Some Notes on a Singer," 36–37.

22. Quinn, "Sassy '67."

23. Ibid.

24. Ibid.

25. Buster Williams, interview with author, September 4, 2015.

26. Herb Mickman, interview with author, November 20, 2015.

27. Ibid.

28. Dizzy Gillespie, *To Be or Not . . . to BOP: Memoirs,* with Al Fraser (Garden City, N.Y.: Doubleday, 1979), 192; Max Jones, *Jazz Talking: Profiles, Interviews, and Other Riffs on Jazz Musicians* (Boulder, Colo.: Da Capo, 2000), 238.

29. Bob James, interview with author.

30. Buster Williams, interview with author.

31. Bob James, interview with author.

32. James Gavin, liner notes, *Sarah Vaughan: Sweet 'N' Sassy,* EMI Records, Ltd., 7 2435–31793–2, 2001, compact disc.

33. Herb Mickman, interview with author.

34. Bob James, interview with author.

35. Herb Mickman, interview with author.

36. "Sarah Vaughan Sues Former Mgr. Wells," *Variety,* April 16, 1969.

37. Leslie Gourse, *Sassy: The Life of Sarah Vaughan* (New York: C. Scribner's Sons, 1993), 126.

38. Marianne Ruuth, *Sarah Vaughan* (Los Angeles: Holloway House, 1994), 104.

39. Ibid., 113.

40. Gourse, *Sassy,* 110.

41. Ibid.
42. Annie Ross, interview with author, September 22, 2015.
43. Bob Magnusson, interview with author, September 29, 2015.
44. Annie Ross, interview with author.
45. Lena Horne, "Lena on Her Loveless Childhood, Her Durable Beauty, Sex and the Older Woman, Her Life's Triple Tragedy," *Ebony,* May 1980, 44; James Gavin, *Stormy Weather: The Life of Lena Horne* (New York: Atria, 2009), 240–241.
46. George Wein, interview with author, November 18, 2015.
47. Sam Lucy, "Ella's In Crowd," *Afro-American,* June 10, 1967.
48. "Singer Sarah Vaughan Sues Manager for 847G," *Afro-American,* April 26, 1969.

Chapter 12: "I'm Not a Jazz Singer. I'm a Singer"

1. Leonard Feather, "Caught in the Act: Sarah Vaughan," *Melody Maker,* August 22, 1970.
2. Gary Giddens and Scott DeVeaux, *Jazz* (New York: W. W. Norton, 2009), 530–536; Peter Keepnews, "Jazz Since 1968," in *The Oxford Companion to Jazz,* ed. Bill Kirchner (Oxford, UK: Oxford University Press, 2005), 488–501.
3. Quoted in Marc Myers, *Why Jazz Happened* (Berkeley: University of California Press, 2012), 170–171.
4. Giddins and DeVeaux, *Jazz,* 530–532.
5. Ibid., 530–536; Keepnews, "Jazz," 488–501.
6. Giddins and DeVeaux, *Jazz,* 534–536.
7. Herb Mickman, interview with author, November 20, 2015.
8. Bob Magnusson, interview with author, September 29, 2015.
9. Jan Hammer, interview with author, November 5, 2015.
10. Ibid.
11. Ibid.
12. Ibid.
13. Tom Mackin, "Newark's 'Divine Sarah,'" *Newark Sunday News,* November 10, 1968.
14. Bill Quinn, "Sassy '67," *Down Beat,* July 27, 1967.
15. Leonard Feather, "LP Scene Is Not Sarah's Groove," *Los Angeles Times,* November 3, 1968; reprinted as "Jazz Scene: Time for the Recording Famine to Come to an End," *Melody Maker,* December 7, 1968.
16. Ibid.
17. Max Jones, "Why Miss Vaughan Isn't Recording," *Melody Maker,* November 1, 1969.
18. Sarah Vaughan, Annie Ross, Marshall Fisher, unidentified man, conversation recorded by Marshall Fisher, undated, shared with author by Michiyo Tanaka Fisher.
19. Leonard Feather, "Sweet Sarah," *Melody Maker,* October 14, 1972.
20. Leonard Feather, "Jazz Scene: Shad Bobs Back," *Melody Maker,* June 3, 1972.
21. Ibid.
22. "Sassy: A Tribute," *Like It Is with Gil Noble,* WABC-TV, reaired January 30, 2011. This tribute to Vaughan, which included footage from

a 1973 interview, was originally aired in April 1990 and can be found on YouTube at https://www.youtube.com/watch?v=sYCYSXaQVFc.

23. Leslie Gourse, *Sassy: The Life of Sarah Vaughan* (New York: C. Scribner's Sons, 1993), 136.
24. Michiyo Tanaka Fisher, interview with author, October 28, 2015.
25. "Sassy: A Tribute," *Like It Is.*
26. Gourse, *Sassy,* 137.
27. Bob Magnusson, interview with author.
28. Gourse, *Sassy,* 138.
29. Ibid., 137.
30. Eliot Tiegel, "Sarah Vaughan, Michel Legrand Mainstream's New Jazz Team," *Billboard,* May 27, 1972.
31. Bob Magnusson, interview with author.
32. Max Jones, "Sweet Sarah," *Melody Maker,* February 5, 1972.
33. "Distributors Ordered Double on Second Album," *Billboard,* May 27, 1972.
34. Dan Morgenstern, "Review," *Down Beat,* March 30, 1972.
35. Leonard Feather, "Jazz Scene: Sweet Sarah," *Melody Maker,* October 14, 1972.
36. Michel Legrand, liner notes to *Sarah Vaughan with Michel Legrand,* Heritage Jazz 513001X, 1992, compact disc.
37. Bob Magnusson, interview with author.
38. Sarah Vaughan, "Interview Two: A Beautiful Session," interview by Les Tomkins, 1977, transcript on the National Jazz Archive website, http://www.nationaljazzarchive.co.uk/stories?id=389.
39. Feather, "Jazz Scene: Sweet Sarah."

Chapter 13: "Here I Go Again"

1. Gene Robertson, "On the Beam," *Sun Reporter,* February 10, 1973.
2. Carl Schroeder, interview with author, October 23, 2015.
3. "Sassy: A Tribute," *Like It Is,* WABC-TV New York, reaired January 30, 2011.
4. Robert Richards, interview with author, July 21, 2015.
5. Carl Schroeder, interview with author, October 23, 2015.
6. Ibid.
7. Ron McClure, interview with author, October 28, 2015.
8. Buster Williams, interview with author, September 4, 2015.
9. Bill Mays, interview with author, September 14, 2015.
10. Bob Magnusson, interview with author, September 29, 2015.
11. Ron McClure, interview with author.
12. Ibid.
13. John Giannelli, interview with author, November 14, 2015.
14. Carl Schroeder, interview with author, September 29, 2015.
15. Leslie Gourse, *Sassy: The Life of Sarah Vaughan* (New York: C. Scribner's Sons, 1993), 168.
16. Carl Schroeder, interview with author, September 29, 2015.
17. Gourse, *Sassy,* 168.
18. Carl Schroeder, interview with author, September 29, 2015.

19. Ibid.
20. Darlene Chan, interview with author, November 20, 2015; "Cascais Jazz 1973: Sarah Vaughan," *Jazz No País Do Improviso* (blog), October 29, 2009, http://jnpdi.blogspot.com/2009/10/cascais-jazz-1973-sarah-vaughan-fonte.html.
21. Darlene Chan, interview with author.
22. Max Jones, "Sarah: Searching for that Natural Sound," *Melody Maker,* November 17, 1973.
23. John Giannelli, interview with author.
24. Carl Schroeder, interview with author, October 23, 2015.
25. Jimmy Rowles, interviewed by Dan Morgenstern, September 27, 1984, transcript, Jazz Studies Oral History Collection, Institute of Jazz Studies, Rutgers University, Newark, N.J., 85.
26. Carl Schroeder, interview with author, September 29, 2015.
27. Arnold Jay Smith, "Never Ending Melody," *Down Beat,* May 5, 1977; Max Jones, "Sarah: Searching for that Natural Sound," *Melody Maker,* November 17, 1973.
28. Gourse, *Sassy,* 147.
29. Ibid.; "Litigation Blues," *Down Beat,* May 8, 1975.
30. "Sarah Vaughan Suit Asks Mainstream for $200,000," *Jet,* April 10, 1975.
31. Smith, "Never Ending Melody."
32. "News," *Down Beat,* June 14, 1977.
33. Sarah Vaughan, "Interview Two: A Beautiful Session," interview by Les Tomkins, 1977, transcript on the National Jazz Archive website, http://www.nationaljazzarchive.co.uk/stories?id=389.

Chapter 14: "The Marian Anderson of Modern Jazz"

1. "Music Records: L.A. Salutes Sarah," *Variety,* March 27, 1974; Leonard Feather, "Sarah's High Road from Harlem," *Los Angeles Times,* April 14, 1974.
2. Jennings Parrott, "Honcho Not So Macho in Dealings with Wacs," *Los Angeles Times,* March 29, 1974.
3. "Congress Pays Birthday Tribute to Top Entertainer Sarah Vaughan," *Tri-State Defender,* March 23, 1974.
4. Bill Pollock, "Sarah Vaughan's Gift of Music," *Herald-Examiner,* undated, clip folder, Institute of Jazz Studies, Rutgers University, Newark, N.J.
5. Feather, "Sarah's High Road from Harlem," reprinted in Leonard Feather, *The Pleasures of Jazz: Leading Performers on Their Lives, Their Music, Their Contemporaries* (New York: Horizon, 1976), 110.
6. Robert Richards, interview with author, July 21, 2015.
7. Carl Schroeder, interview with author, October 23, 2015. The specific timeline for "Send in the Clowns" remains unclear. Denis Brown's discography suggests that the session took place sometime in 1974, in Los Angeles. According to Vaughan's datebooks, however, she recorded the tune on April 16, 1973, in New York, the day after she finished two weeks at Mr. Kelly's in Chicago. Carl Schroeder remembers his

rehearsals with Vaughan taking place at Mr. Kelly's, when the band shared the bill with Freddie Prinze, which they did April 8–20, 1974.

8. Jay Scott, "Sarah Vaughan Is Ready for Some Changes," *Globe and Mail*, May 7, 1984.

9. Carl Schroeder, interview with author, October 23, 2015.

10. Ibid.

11. For discussion of Stephen Sondheim's musical language, see Steven Swayne, *How Sondheim Found His Sound* (Ann Arbor: University of Michigan Press, 2007), 66, 107, 120.

12. Carl Schroeder, interview with author, October 23, 2015.

13. I thank Dianne Reeves for helping me understand how Vaughan's singing, especially her interpretations of "Send in the Clowns," was informed by her experiences singing in her church choir.

14. Jay Scott, "Sarah Vaughan: The Most Accomplished Voice in Jazz," *Globe and Mail*, May 3, 1984.

15. Carl Schroeder, interview with author, October 23, 2015; John S. Wilson, "Jazz: Sarah Vaughan and Zoot Sims," *New York Times*, February 1, 1982; John Rockwell and John S. Wilson, "Jazz: Sarah Vaughan's Old Standards: Albert Dailey, Solo Pianist," *New York Times*, July 4, 1981; Ernie Santosuosso, "He Writes Grace Notes about Jazz," *Boston Globe*, May 25, 1980.

16. Louie Robinson, "Divine Sarah: The Inimitable Miss Vaughan Is an All-Time Star Without a Hit, a Queen Without a Country," *Ebony*, April 1975.

17. Michiyo Tanaka Fisher, interview with author, October 28, 2015.

18. Robinson, "Divine Sarah."

19. Marshall Fisher, "Interview Three: Our Philosophy," interview by Les Tomkins, 1977, transcript on the National Jazz Archive website, http://www.nationaljazzarchive.co.uk/stories?id=390; Robinson, "Divine Sarah."

20. Sarah Vaughan, "Interview One: Musical All My Life," interview by Les Tomkins, May 31, 1977, transcript on the National Jazz Archive website, http://www.nationaljazzarchive.co.uk/stories?id=43.

21. Ibid.

22. Leslie Gourse, *Sassy: The Life of Sarah Vaughan* (New York: C. Scribner's Sons, 1993), 149.

23. Bob Magnusson, interview with author, September 29, 2015.

24. Gourse, *Sassy*, 149–150.

25. Tom Mackin, "Newark's Divine Sarah," *Newark Sunday News*, November 10, 1968.

26. Feather, "Sarah's High Road."

27. Melody Peterson, "Gershwin Music at the Bowl," *Los Angeles Times*, July 15, 1974.

28. Carl Schroeder, interview with author, October 23, 2015.

29. Gourse, *Sassy*, 151–152.

30. Arnold Jay Smith, "Never Ending Melody," *Down Beat*, May 5, 1977.

31. Carl Schroeder, interview with author, October 23, 2015.

32. Gourse, *Sassy*, 154.

33. Carl Schroeder, interview with author, October 23, 2015.
34. Ibid.
35. Leonard Feather, "Music Review: Vaughan, Philharmonic Bowl," *Los Angeles Times,* August 23, 1976.
36. Carl Schroeder, interview with author, October 23, 2015.
37. Carl Schroeder, interview with author, September 29, 2015.
38. Leonard Feather, "Jazz: Symphonies Beckon to Sarah," *Los Angeles Times,* April 18, 1976; Leonard Feather, "Sarah Vaughan: Dreams of Singing Opera," *Washington Post,* April 19, 1976.
39. From a recording made by Marshall Fisher on October 29, 1977, in Rio de Janeiro; copy provided by Michiyo Tanaka Fisher; transcription by author.
40. Thomas C. Guy, prod., *Listen to the Sun* (New Jersey: NJPTV, 1978).
41. The description of this rehearsal is based on the recording made by Marshall Fisher on October 29, 1977, in Rio de Janeiro.
42. Tad Hershorn, *Norman Granz: The Man Who Used Jazz for Justice* (Berkeley: University of California Press, 2011), 338.
43. Ibid., 361.
44. Gary Giddins, "Soulfully, Sarah Vaughan," *Village Voice,* October 20, 1978.
45. Leonard Feather, "Top 10 Jazz Records for the 1970s," *Los Angeles Times,* December 30, 1979.

Chapter 15: "I'm Just Coming into My Prime"

1. Associated Press, "Festival Off to a Jazzy Start," *White Plains (N.Y.) Journal News,* June 24, 1978, 4.
2. "Sarah Vaughan, Jazzman Waymon Reed, Tie Knot," *Jet,* July 6, 1978.
3. Sarah Vaughan, interview with Sammy Davis Jr., *Tonight Show,* NBC, October 2, 1978.
4. Carl Schroeder, interview with author, September 29, 2015.
5. Ibid.
6. Michiyo Tanaka Fisher, email message to author, November 5, 2015.
7. Michiyo Tanaka Fisher, interview with author, October 28, 2015.
8. "Sarah Vaughan, Jazzman Waymon Reed, Tie Knot," *Jet.*
9. Carl Schroeder, interview with author.
10. Leslie Gourse, *Sassy: The Life of Sarah Vaughan* (New York: C. Scribner's Sons, 1993), 183.
11. Carl Schroeder, interview with author.
12. Roy McCurdy, interview with author, November 4, 2015.
13. Mike Wofford, interview with author, October 16, 2014.
14. John S. Wilson, "A Singer's 4 Concerts in 10 Days," *New York Times,* March 18, 1979.
15. Mary Campbell, "3 Carnegie Concerts Set for Jazz Singer," *Asbury Park Press,* March 21, 1979.
16. Richard M. Sudhalter, "Sarah Vaughan Heats Up," *New York Post,* March 23, 1979.
17. Roy McCurdy, interview with author.
18. For more on Waymon Reed's unpredictability see Gourse, *Sassy,* 185–196.

19. Roy McCurdy, interview with author.
20. "Vaughan Returns for an 'Encore,'" *Los Angeles Times*, March 9, 1980.
21. Ibid.
22. Sarah Vaughan, interview with Dick Cavett, *The Dick Cavett Show*, March 7, 1980.
23. Ibid.
24. Ed Levitt, "Fabled Sarah Vaughan Still a Jazz Master," *Dallas Times Herald*, July 5, 1981.
25. John Schreiber, interview with author, January 7, 2016.
26. Gary Mullinax, "Sarah Vaughan Talks Backstage," *Wilmington News Journal*, January 31, 1982.
27. Ibid.
28. Ibid.
29. John Schreiber, interview with author.
30. Ibid.
31. Ibid.
32. John Schreiber, "Letter to the Editor: Ms. Vaughan Said No," *Wilmington Morning News*, February 15, 1982, main edition.
33. John Schreiber, interview with author.
34. George Wein, *Myself Among Others*, Kindle ed. (New York: Da Capo, 2009), location 7540.
35. Darlene Chan, interview with author, November 20, 2015.
36. Robert Jones, interview with author, December 18, 2015.
37. Carl Schroeder, interview with author.
38. John Giannelli, interview with author, November 14, 2015; Gourse, *Sassy*, 168; Laura Schmalback, "'Sassy' End to Mellow First Night," *Des Plaines (Ill.) Herald*, November 12, 1976.
39. Eleanor O'Sullivan, "Miss Vaughan: I'm No Star," *Asbury Park Press*, January 28, 1982, main edition.
40. John Schreiber, interview with author.
41. George Wein, interview with author, November 18, 2015.
42. Sarah Vaughan, interview on *The Dick Cavett Show*.
43. John Schreiber, interview with author.
44. James Liska, "Sarah Vaughan: I'm Not a Jazz Singer," *Down Beat*, May 1982.
45. Ibid.
46. Ibid.
47. Robert Richards, interview with author, July 21, 2015. Richards remembered three nights of performances when in fact there were only two.
48. Display ad 64, *New York Times*, May 9, 1982, D22.
49. Robert Richards, interview with author.
50. Jay Scott, "Sarah Vaughan Is Ready for Some Changes," *Globe and Mail*, May 7, 1984.
51. Sally Kalson, "Simply Sarah: Vaughan to Bring Divine Voice Here," *Pittsburgh Post-Gazette*, August 31, 1984, 27.
52. Gary Giddins, *Faces in the Crowd: Players and Writers* (Oxford: Oxford University Press, 1992), 93; Steve Orr, "More Than 1,000 Guests Hear

Sarah Vaughan, Gap Mangione at Rochester's Sesquicentennial Ball," *Rochester Democrat and Chronicle*, April 29, 1984, 14.

53. Giddins, *Faces in the Crowd*, 94.

54. Scott, "Sarah Vaughan Is Ready for Some Changes."

55. Paul F. Berliner, *Thinking in Jazz: The Infinite Art of Improvisation* (Chicago: University of Chicago Press, 1994), 95–99.

56. Giddins, *Faces in the Crowd*, 98.

57. Ibid., 94.

58. Al Hunter, "Marsalis' Playing Is Sharp: Trumpeter Breathes New Life into Music," *Wilmington Sunday News Journal*, April 15, 1984, F2.

59. Giddins, *Faces in the Crowd*, 96.

60. Scott, "Sarah Vaughan Is Ready for Some Changes."

61. Marshall Fine, "Sarah Vaughan Still Going Strong in Jazz," *Poughkeepsie Journal*, November 2, 1984, 49.

62. Janos Gereben, "Views Reviews Previews: Ms. Vaughan Discusses Toes, Interviews, etc." *Oakland Post*, July 11, 1980.

63. Brian Lanker, *I Dream a World: Portraits of Black Women Who Changed America*, ed. Barbara Summers (New York: Stewart, Tabori & Chang, 1989), 134.

64. Mark Miller, "Jazz Festivals 1989 Vaughan Triumphs Again," *Globe and Mail*, June 28, 1989.

65. Geoff Chapman, "Sarah Kicks Off Festival with Stellar Repertoire," *Toronto Star*, June 27, 1989.

66. Wein, *Myself Among Others*, location 7542.

67. George Wein, interview with author.

68. James T. Jones, "Like Ella, This Jazz Fest Can Still Swing," *USA Today*, June 28, 1989, final edition.

69. George Wein, interview with author.

70. John S. Wilson, "Jazz Festival; Vaughan: A Diva; Jackson: Dour," *New York Times*, June 30, 1989, late edition.

71. Wein, *Myself Among Others*, location 7554.

72. Robert Richards, interview with author.

73. Zan Stewart, "Chick Corea Named Top Keyboardist; Sarah Vaughan to Resume Tour in February," *Los Angeles Times*, January 3, 1990.

74. Don Heckman, "Jazz Review: A Version of Sarah Vaughan," *Los Angeles Times*, September 4, 1989.

75. Myrna Oliver, "Sarah Vaughan, 'Divine One' of Jazz, Dies at 66," *Los Angeles Times*, April 5, 1990.

76. Ann Hampton Callaway, interview with author, June 6, 2016.

77. Robert Richards, interview with author.

78. Stewart, "Chick Corea Named Top."

79. Sarah Vaughan, "Seems Like Yesterday, Not 47 Years," *USA Today*, January 26, 1990, final edition.

80. Ibid.

Epilogue: "The Greatest Vocal Artist of Our Century"

1. Sarah Vaughan, "Seems Like Yesterday, Not 47 Years," *USA Today*, January 26, 1990, final edition.

2. Quincy Jones, *Q: Autobiography of Quincy Jones* (New York: Three Rivers, 2002), 316.

3. Robert Richards, interview with author, July 21, 2015.

4. James T. Jones, "Vaughan Kept Illness Secret," *USA Today,* April 6, 1990, final edition.

5. Ibid.

6. Robert Richards, interview with author, July 21, 2015.

7. Jones, *Q*, 316.

8. "Rights for Sarah Vaughan Held in Newark Hometown," *Jet,* April 30, 1990, 52–54.

9. Bob James, interview with author, November 16, 2015.

10. Dianne Reeves, interview with author, December 15, 2015.

11. Ibid.

12. Ibid.

13. Ibid.

14. Ibid.

15. Ann Hampton Callaway, interview with author, June 6, 2016.

16. Ibid.

17. Ibid.

18. Cécile McLorin Salvant, interview with author, June 6, 2016.

19. John Schreiber, interview with author, January 7, 2016.

20. Gunther Schuller, *Musings: The Musical Worlds of Gunther Schuller* (New York: Oxford University Press, 1989), 102–103.

Index

Aarons, Al, 293–94
Abell, Bess, 245
Academy Awards (1961), ???
Academy of Music (Philadelphia), 67
Adams Theater (Newark), 19
Adderley, Julian "Cannonball," 171, 189, 190, 361
Adler, Richard, 168
African Americans. *See also* racism; segregation
  in Chicago, 83–84
  civil rights and, 143–44, 181–82, 246–47
  housing segregation, 180–82
  in Newark, 15–17, 19–20
"After Hours," 122
After Hours (1961), 227, 248
After Hours at the London House, 198–200, 222, 363
Akron Beacon Journal, 216
Alcazar (Newark), 24–25
All-Star Jazz Concert (1945), 67
Amateur Night at the Apollo (Harlem), 28–31, 357, 372–73n

American Express, 348
American Federation of Musicians, 58, 107, 111
American Idol (TV show), 30
American Jazz Hall of Fame, 350
Ammons, Gene, 51, 59, 80, 237
Amsterdam, 203–5
Anderson, Marian, 22–23, 143, 308–9
  at the Apollo, 9
  "Ave Maria," 120
  at Lincoln Memorial, 23, 143
  "The Lord's Prayer," 142
  Vaughan's admiration for, 9, 76, 120, 217, 309, 346
Andre, Miguelo, 100
Andrews, Julie, 157
"And This Is My Beloved," 164
Apollo Theater (Harlem), 27–35, 40–41, 81
  Amateur Night at, 28–31, 357, 372–73n
"April in Paris," 186–87
Archway Supper Club (Chicago), 220

Armstrong, Louis, 83, 261, 268
  Hot Five and Hot Seven Sessions,
    33, 83
Arrio, Martinez, 194
arts funding, 310–11
Asbury Park Press, 338
ASCAP, 168–69
Associated Negro Press (ANP),
    132–33, 134–35
"As You Desire Me," 112
"A-Tisket, A-Tasket," 20, 207
Atkins, Clyde B.
  arrest of, 230–31, 232
  divorce from Vaughan, 233–36,
    240–41, 243–44
  domestic violence of, 229–34,
    254, 390–91*n*
  gambling of, 226
  marriage to Vaughan, 216,
    219–20, 222–24, 228, 229–30,
    233–34, 262
  personal management of
    Vaughan, 220–21, 224–26,
    228–29, 235–36
Atkins, Deborah Lois, 223–24, 230,
    233, 286, 305, 323
Atlanta Municipal Auditorium,
    132–36
Atlanta Musicians Protective
    Association, 133
Atlantic Records, 195, 296–97, 315
Auld, Georgie, 61, 76, 189
Australia, 290, 349
"Autumn Leaves," 347
"Ave Maria," 120–21
Avery Fisher Hall (New York), 329,
    342
Azymuth, 315–16

Back on the Block, 355–56
Bailey, Pearl, 263
Baker, Josephine, 19, 134, 135, 143,
    210
Baker, La-Vern, 175
Balliett, Whitney, 304
Baltimore Afro-American, 80, 104,
    133–34, 135, 152, 233, 263
Baron von Ludwig (dog), 97, 145, 148

"Bashful Matador, The," 175
Basie, William James "Count,"
    66–67. *See also* Count Basie
    Orchestra
  death of, 344
  Holiday and, 73
Basie's Beatle Bag, 267
Bates, Clayton "Peg Leg," 130
Beatles, the, 266–67, 296–97
beauty and race, 152–53, 157–60
bebop, 4–5, 12–13, 38–40, 51, 74,
    96–97
Bechet, Sidney, 209, 210, 211
Beckles, Lionel, 230
Beiderbecke, Bix, 83
Belafonte, Harry, 68, 191
Bellson, Louis, 318
Benjamin, Joe, 185–86, 196, 345
Bennett, Tony, 117, 190, 300
Benson, George, 355
Berger, Edward, 226, 228
Bergman, Alan, 280
Bergman, Marilyn, 280
Berklee College of Music, 270
Berlin, 163
Bernhardt, Sarah, 93
Berry, Chuck, 266
Berry Brothers, 140
Bertrami, Jose Roberto, 315–16
big bands, 21
Biggest Show of '51, 129–39,
    142–43, 262, 338
Billboard, 23, 85–86, 95, 107, 112,
    120, 163, 166, 171, 172, 214,
    221, 248, 250, 278, 279
Billingsley, Sherman, 134
Birdland (New York), 99–101, 103,
    150, 163–64, 183, 222, 234–35
birth of Vaughan, 15
Bishop, Wally, 205
Bitches Brew, 269
"Black Coffee," 112
black femininity, 157–58, 175–76
black hairstyles, 158–59
Blakey, Art, 51, 268
Block, Martin, 116
"Bluebird of Happiness, The," 20
Bluebonnets, the, 50

Blue Note (to New York), 190, 354–55
blues, 3–4, 73–76, 91–92
Blues Alley (Washington, D.C.), 354
"Body and Soul," 30–31, 344, 374n
Bonneville Dam, 88–89
Boogie Woogie Studio (New York), 322
Booker, Walter, 278, 302, 322, 323–24
Boosey & Hawkes, 240
Boston Plaza (Newark), 25
Boston Pops, 343–48, 346, 349
Boswell, Connee, 167
Bracket, David, 174
Braddock Hotel (Harlem), 66
Bradley, Tom, 299, 353
Brazilian music, 6, 314–19
Brazilian Romance, 349
Bright, Ronnell, 196–202, 203, 206, 220, 226, 285–86
Brockman, Gail, 37
"Broken-Hearted Melody," 213–17, 221, 236, 253, 283, 300
Brooks, Evelyn, 31
Brooks, Phyllis, 17–18, 20
Brown, Clifford, 185–86, 189, 198, 346
Brown, Inez, 224
Brown, Ray, 318
Brown v. Board of Education, 382n
Brubeck, Dave, 193, 208, 267
Buddy Kaye Quintet, 108
Buffalo Philharmonic Orchestra, 310
Burman, Maurice, 202
Burton, Linn, 85, 86, 94
bus touring, 42, 131
Byas, Don, 205
"Bye Bye Blackbird," 293
Byer, Billy, 328

Café Society (New York), 69–74, 76–81, 114, 152, 246
Callaway, Ann Hampton, 354, 362–64
Calling, The: Celebrating Sarah Vaughan, 360–61

Calloway, Cab, 37
Campbell, Floyd, 84
Campbell, Mary, 325
cancer of Vaughan, 353–54, 357–59
Caper, Virginia, 284
Carmichael, Judy, 56–57
Carnegie Hall (New York), 132, 289, 308, 310, 321, 325–26, 351
Carpenter, Charles, 136–37
Carpenter, Thelma, 66, 100
Carrol, Diahann, 263
Carson, Johnny, 271
Carter, Benny, 227, 319, 327
Carter, Betty "Bebop," 3, 237, 325
Cascais Jazz Festival, 290–92
Cash Box, 121, 166
Caterine, Anthony "Tough Tony," 288
Catlett, Sid, 63
Cavett, Dick, 18, 48, 84, 329–30, 339
Caymmi, Dorival, 316
Cedars-Sinai Medical Center, 358, 359
Celebrity Club (Miami Beach), 140–41
"C'est La Vie," 171
Chambers, Paul, 238
Chan, Darlene, 290–91, 292, 334–36
Chapman, Geoff, 351
Checker, Chubby, 267
"Cherokee," 40
Chicago, 83–94, 197, 237–39
Chicago Cardinals, 220
Chicago City Hall, 219
Chicago Civic Opera House, 85, 308
Chicago Defender, 34, 36, 85, 147, 155, 166, 235
Chicago Savoy, 35–36
Chicago style, 83–84
Chicago Sun, 87
Chicago Symphony Orchestra, 230, 311
Chicago Theatre, 97, 147–48, 149
Chick Webb Orchestra, 28, 29, 207
childhood of Vaughan, 15–24

China Theater (Stockholm), 203
Chordettes, the, 178
"Christmas Song, The," 114
Christy, June, 208
Cincinnati Enquirer, 96
"City Called Heaven, A," 121
Civil Rights Act of 1964, 246–47
Civil Rights Act of 1968, 181–82
civil rights movement, 143–44, 181–82, 246–47
Clark, June, 32–33
Clark Monroe's Uptown House (Harlem), 39–40, 80
classical music, 307–14, 346–47
Clooney, Rosemary, 117–18, 119, 156, 174
Clothier, Larry, 277
Club Silhouette (Chicago), 88
Coates, Carroll, 360
Cobb, Jimmy, 150, 271, 277, 286, 322, 323–24
Coker, Henry, 197
Cole, Maria, 181
Cole, Nat King, 85, 114, 120, 126, 261
    Biggest Show of '51, 129, 130–31, 134–35, 137–38, 262
    housing segregation, 180–81
Coleman, Cynthia, 322
Coleman, Ornette, 267, 268
Collins, Fred, 100–101
Coltrane, John, 268
Columbia Records, 110–23, 164, 171–72, 173
Columbo (TV show), 222
"Come Along with Me," 164–65
"Come On-A My House," 117–18, 119
Comfort, Joe, 227
commercialism, 33, 49–50, 115, 125–28
Concertgebouw (Amsterdam), 204–5
Condon, Eddie, 83
"Confess," 177
Conover, Willis, 208, 209
Continental Records, 61, 63, 65

contralto, 1, 112–13
Cooper, Al, 32
Cooper, Bob, 208
Cooper, Ralph, 28, 29–31, 373n
Cootie Williams Band, 29, 80
Copacabana, 319
Copacabana (New York), 67–68, 246
Corea, Chick, 269–70
Count Basie Orchestra, 72, 73
    at the Apollo, 28
    Basie's Beatle Bag, 267
    Vaughan and, 57, 66–67, 190–93, 248, 305, 321–22
    at Waldorf Astoria, 190–93
Crawford, Ray, 197
Crayton, PeeWee, 328
Crosby, Israel, 149
"Cross Over the Bridge," 177
Culley, Wendell, 197

Dagmar, 119
Dale, Ted, 141–42
Dameron, Tad, 155
Damn Yankees (musical), 168, 170
Damone, Vic, 108
Dandridge, Dorothy, 100, 190
"Danny Boy," 20
"Dark Girls Can Make It Too!", 152–53, 158
Daughters of the American Revolution, 23
Davis, Miles, 115, 124, 268, 355
    Bitches Brew, 269
    Corea and, 270
    Gillespie in St. Louis, 51–52
    Haynes and Vaughan, 201
    Kind of Blue, 271
Davis, Modina
    Atkins and, 220, 228–29, 230
    hairstyles of Vaughan, 155–56
    Treadwell and, 149, 194, 195–96
Davis, Richard, 196–97, 200, 202, 226, 237
Davis, Sammy, Jr., 171, 321
Day, Doris, 97, 108, 112, 120, 171–72, 190
death of Vaughan, 359

Decca Records, 167, 168, 173
Dedicated to You, 360
"De Gas Pipe She's Leakin' Joe,"
    117, 118–20, 191
DeLuxe Records, 58–59, 65
dental work, 155
De Paur, Leonard, 142
Dick Cavett Show (TV show), 18,
    48, 84, 329–30, 339
Diemer, Kees, 205
Diggs, Pancho, 21, 25
"Dinorah," 358
Dion, Celine, 30
disc jockeys (DJs), 86–88, 94–95,
    167. *See also specific DJs*
Doctor Pygmalion (Maltz), 157
"Don't Blame Me," 11
Donte's (Los Angeles), 276
Dorchester Hotel (London), 335
Dorsey, Tommy, 34, 67
Down Beat, 3, 12, 58, 76, 78, 80,
    84–85, 86, 95, 115–16, 118,
    123–24, 125, 126–27, 148, 156,
    172–73, 186–87, 189, 214, 220,
    228, 245, 248, 250, 273, 295,
    296–97, 311, 340
Downbeat (New York), 66
Drifters, the, 195
drugs (drug use), 54, 151–52, 238,
    262, 335
Duke, George, 315, 358
du Maurier Downtown Jazz
    Festival, 350–51
Dun, Bob, 167
Duran Duran, 315
Durham, Pop, 25
Dutch AVRO Television, 204
Duvivier, George, 227
Dyer, Richard, 92–93
Dylan, Bob, 266, 278

early life of Vaughan, 15–24
Eason, Leon, 24
"East of the Sun," 62
"Easy Come, Easy Go Lover," 164
"Easy to Love," 227
Ebony (magazine), 146, 224, 225,
    261, 305

Eckstine, Billy
    background of, 40
    cancer of Vaughan, 358–59
    death of, 360
    death of Vaughan's father, 285
    Feather and, 61, 376*n*
    formation of band, 49–58
    in Hines band, 19, 30–31, 33–34,
        36, 39–41, 43, 45–49
    "I Love You," 124–25
    sexism of, 53–54, 55
    solo career of, 126
    touring the South, 45, 46, 47,
        48–49
    Vaughan at the Apollo, 30–31,
        33–34
    Vaughan in the band, 10, 49–59
    Vaughan's departure from band,
        62–63, 65, 66, 69
    Vaughan's husband-managers
        and, 258–59
Eckstine, June, 358
Edgewater Beach Hotel (Chicago),
    237
Edwards, Teddy, 293–94
Ellington, Edward Kennedy
        "Duke," 116, 268
    at the Apollo, 28
    Biggest Show of '51, 129, 130,
        131, 134–37
    Duke Ellington Songbook, 327–29
    Granz and, 261
    Hammer and, 271
    Musicraft recording contract, 76
    "Perdido," 116
    at Ravinia, 230
Ellis, Herb, 198
elocution lessons, 153–55
Emancipation Proclamation, 16
EmArcy, 164, 171–72, 175, 183–90,
    295
embodiment and race, 90–94
Englewood home, 222–23, 233,
    235, 241
Epstein, Daniel Mark, 137
Ertegun, Ahmet, 296–97
Esquire, 81
"Eternally," 222

European tours, 163, 201–12, 239–40
"Experience Unnecessary," 170–71
Explosive Side of Sarah Vaughan, 227

Fair Housing Act of 1968, 181–82
Fairmont Hotel (Dallas), 286
Fairmont Hotel (Philadelphia),
    139–40
Fairmont Hotel (San Francisco), 289
Falk, Peter, 222
Famous Door (New York), 66
fan clubs, 97
Farnon, Robert, 249–50
"Fascinatin' Rhythm," 309
Feather, Leonard
    blindfold tests, 75–76, 124
    Eckstine and, 61, 376n
    recording sessions, 60–62, 77–78
    Vaughan and, 41, 60–62, 66, 68,
        75–79, 208, 266, 274–75, 280,
        300, 308–9, 314, 328, 374n
Feelin' Good, 283
female musicians, 40, 42–44, 55–56
femininity, 157–58
Ferguson, Maynard, 276
Festival Productions, 330–40
Fiedler, Arthur, 311
Fields, Herbie, 85
Fields, Sidney, 32
fiftieth birthday of Vaughan, 299–300
Finland, 336–37
Fisher, Marshall, 276–78, 285,
    288–89, 305–6, 311, 321–23
Fitzgerald, Ella, 5, 20, 156, 253,
    263, 267
    at the Apollo, 28–29, 32
    "A-Tisket, A-Tasket," 20, 207
    death of, 360
    Gillespie and, 43
    Granz and, 207–8, 252, 253, 261
    recording choices and race, 173
    Vaughan and, 95, 192, 205, 207,
        208, 351, 355
Flamingo (Las Vegas), 222
Fontainebleau Hotel (Miami
    Beach), 201, 221, 235
Ford, Mary, 176
Forrest, Helen, 65, 156

46th and 8th, 329
Fox, Ted, 119
Frank Music, 168–69
Freeman, Buzz, 149
French Riviera, 289–90
Frigo, John, 198
*From Sassy to Divine: The Sarah
    Vaughan Project,* 363

Gabor, Donald, 61
Gale, Alan, 140–41
gambling, 43
G&R Records (Newark), 26
Gardner, Barbara, 228, 229–30
Garner, Erroll, 101, 189, 207, 208,
    271, 288, 344–45
Garrett, Siedah, 355
Garroway, Dave, 84–91, 93–94,
    124–25, 139, 143, 147, 164
Garry, Johnnie
    Atkins firing of, 228–29
    racist assault on, 378n
    subway attack on, 78–79
    Treadwell and Vaughan, 80,
        147–48, 149, 150, 155, 165–66
    Vaughan and European tour,
        206–7, 209
    Vaughan and "The Lord's
        Prayer," 141
Gastel, Carlos, 181, 261, 262
Gaye, Marvin, 278
George Treadwell and His Allstars,
    115
George Treadwell Orchestra, 80–81
Gerald Wilson Orchestra, 390n
Gershwin, George, 306–10, 331–34,
    340–43
Gershwin Live!, 342–43, 346, 362
Getz, Stan, 280
Giannelli, John, 287–91, 293, 337
Gibbs, Georgia, 171, 175
Gibson, Ginny, 168
Giddins, Gary, 318–19, 344, 346, 347
Gigante, Vincent, 248
Gillespie, John Birks "Dizzy," 10,
    67, 81, 115, 268, 355
    "A Night in Tunisia," 62, 290
    death of, 360

in Eckstine band, 50–52, 53–55, 375n
in Hines band, 37, 38–40, 43, 46–47
Lifetime Achievement Grammy, 350
Musicraft recording contract, 76
recording sessions, 61–62, 63
Vaughan and Atkins, 219, 223
"girl singers," 33, 91–93
Glaser, Joe, 261
Glen, Lloyd, 328
Globe and Mail, 301, 348
Gold, Don, 84, 86
Golden, Clyde, 254
Goodman, Benny, 72, 83, 95, 208
Gordon, Dexter, 51, 59, 96
Gore, Lesley, 250
Gormé, Eydie, 166
Gould, Mike, 228
Gourse, Leslie, 26
Graham Auditorium (Newark), 21
Grammy Awards, 319, 343, 350, 355
Grand Terrace Ballroom (Chicago), 33
Granz, Norman, 96, 207–8, 211–12, 252, 253, 261, 317–19, 327–28
Great Migration, 15–16
Great Words Jazz and Blues Festival, 350
Green, Al, 63
Green, Benny, 37
Greene, Evelyn, 18
Greene, Madeline, 34, 36, 40, 50
Griffin, Farrah, 143
Griffin, Paul, 301
Griffith, Andy, 166–67
Gross, Walter, 89
guns, 36, 228, 255–56, 288–89
Guy, Thomas, 314

Haitian Moon Dancers, 190–91
Haley, Bill, 174
Hammer, Jan, 270–72, 285
Hammerstein, Oscar, 89
Hammond, John, 69, 71–74, 91, 119, 262, 273

Hampton, Lionel, 28
Hampton Jazz Festival, 270, 350
Hancock Park Property Owners Association, 180–81
Handy, W. C., 294
Harmonicats, 85
Harris, Benny, 50, 53–54
Harrison, Dale, 87–88
Harry James Orchestra, 65, 156
Hawkins, Coleman, 30
Hawkins, Erskine, 19
Haymes, Dick, 89, 108
Haynes, Roy, 185–86, 197, 200–202, 276, 294, 345
Hayton, Lennie, 261
Hazel, Marian "Boonie," 56
Heard, J. C., 70, 78–79, 80
Heath, Jimmy, 237
Heath, Ted, 202, 203
Heckman, Don, 353
Hendrix, Jimi, 266
Henke, Mel, 85
Hentoff, Nat, 126–27, 173, 183, 184, 185, 187, 201
Hepburn, Audrey, 157
Herd, Eugene "Fats," 101
heroin, 54
Hershorn, Tad, 318
"He's Got the Whole World in His Hands," 23
"He's My Guy," 186
"Hey, Naughty Papa," 171, 175
Hicks, James, 104
Hidden Hills home, 305, 307, 323, 324
highbrow/lowbrow values, 2, 6, 217, 273
Hines, Earl "Fatha," 32–44, 53, 83
Vaughan and racist incident, 46–49
Vaughan at the Apollo, 30, 31, 32–34
Vaughan's trial period with band, 34–36, 37
Vaughan with the band, 10, 19, 37–44, 354
Hinton, Milt, 45
Hitchcock, Alfred, 244

Holiday, Billie, 30, 69–70, 72, 73
Hollywood Bowl, 307–10, 329, 353
Hope, Bob, 76
Horn, Shirley, 360
Horne, Lena, 143, 261
hot jazz, 72
housing segregation, 180–82
Houston, Whitney, 30
Howard, Bob, 20
"How High the Moon," 192, 203,
   205, 207, 223, 363
"How Important Can It Be,"
   167–68, 173, 178, 190
How Long Has This Been Going On?,
   318–19
"How Much Is That Doggie in the
   Window," 166, 177
Hubbard, Eddie, 86
Hudson, George, 51
Hughes, George, 239
Humperdinck, Engelbert, 274
Humphries, Frank, 67
Hunter, Alberta, 348
Hyatt Regency O'Hare (Chicago),
   337–38
Hydeaway (Newark), 25

"I Can't Give You Anything but
   Love," 227
"I Cover the Waterfront," 11–12
"I Cried for You," 12, 25, 100–101
"Idle Gossip," 163, 167
"If Not for You," 278
"If This Isn't Love," 192, 203, 205
"If You Could See Me Now", 155
"I Get a Kick Out of You," 100
Illinois Children's Home and Aid
   Society, 223
"I'll Know," 120
"I'll Wait and Pray," 59–60, 63, 65,
   97
"I'll Walk Alone," 52
I Love Brazil!, 314–18, 319, 362
"I Love the Guy," 116, 121
"I Love You," 124–25
Images, 184, 189
"Imagine," 278, 279
"I'm Glad There Is You," 186

"Inner City Blues," 278
"Interlude," 62
Internal Revenue Service (IRS),
   235–36, 241
In the Land of Hi-Fi, 124, 171, 190
"I Ran All the Way Home," 121,
   122, 129
Irelan, Charles M., 151–52
"It Happened Again," 175
"It Might as Well Be Spring,"
   89–90, 93, 121
"It's Easy to Remember," 164
"It's Magic," 107–10, 380n
"It's My Party," 250
"It's You or No One," 107

Jackson, Mahalia, 143
Jackson, Milt, 271
James, Bob, 244, 245, 247, 250,
   255–58, 269–70, 359–60
James, Etta, 175
James, Harry, 65, 156
James, Joni, 167
Japan, 290, 292–93, 319
Jarreau, Al, 355
Jazz at Lincoln Center, 348
Jazz at the Philharmonic, 96, 207,
   208, 317
Jazz Club USA (radio program), 208
jazz critics, 123–27, 184. See also
   specific critics
jazz experimentation, 1–2, 37–40,
   51–53
jazz fusion, 269, 278
jazz rock, 269
Jeffreys, Herb, 73
Jeffries, Herb, 325
"Jelly, Jelly," 33
Jet (magazine), 138, 191, 234, 236,
   321, 323, 340–41
"Jim," 186
Jim Crow laws, 15, 16, 44–48,
   132–39, 180, 210, 246, 339
Jobim, Antonio Carlos, 315, 316
"Johnny Be Smart," 171, 174–75
John Paul II, Pope, 348–49
Johns, Glynis, 301–3
Johnson, Budd, 51

Johnson, Edmund, 103–5
Johnson, Hugh, 167
Johnson, Lady Bird, 243–46
Johnson, Lyndon, 181–82, 245–47
Johnson, Pete, 70
Johnson, Willie, 24
Johnson, Ziggy, 84
Jones, Jimmy, 96, 129, 149, 185–86, 196, 345
Jones, Max, 4, 23, 30, 42, 203, 214, 275, 279, 293
Jones, Quincy, 240, 248–50, 251, 267, 275, 293, 348, 355, 358
Jones, Robert, 336–37
Jones, Ruth, 194–95
Jones, Thad, 197
Jordan, Louis, 41
Josephson, Barney, 69–71, 81
"Just a Moment More," 121, 122
"Just Friends," 123, 344
JVC Jazz Festival, 351–52

Katz, Dick, 198
Kaye, Sammy, 120
Kelly, Grace, 144
Kelly, Wynton, 197
Kennedy, John F., 246
Kenton, Stan, 193, 202
Kessel, Barney, 96, 227
Kessler Air Force Base, 137–38
Khan, Chaka, 355
Kilgallen, Dorothy, 191, 221
Kind of Blue, 271
King, Ben E., 195
King, Martin Luther, Jr., 143, 210
King, Peggy, 166
King, Teddi, 174
Kipling, Rudyard, 94
Kirby, George, 140
Kirby, John, 67–68, 89
Kitt, Eartha, 100
Kleenex, 336, 338, 350–51
Knokke, Belgium, 206–7
Krupa, Gene, 83
Ku Klux Klan, 46

Lacy, Butch, 46, 139–40
Lacy, Sam, 263

Laine, Frankie, 114, 117
Lambert, Hendricks & Ross, 260
Landrum, Aretha, 228, 259, 277
Lane, Earl, 231–32
Langford, Frances, 76
LaPalm, Dick, 137–38, 382n
Larks, Mello, 168
Las Vegas, 139, 222, 226, 236, 255, 277
Laurel Garden (Newark), 21
Lawrence, Jack, 89
Lawrence, Steve, 166
Lee, Julia, 75
Lee, Peggy, 67, 95, 113, 156
Lees, Gene, 348–49
Legrand, Michel, 278, 280–81, 283, 289, 308
Leiber, Jerry, 195
Lennon, John, 266, 278, 296–97
Levin, Michael, 12, 76, 78
Levy, Harold, 358
Levy, Morris, 100, 222, 248
Levy, Stan, 96
Lewis, Meade Lux, 72
Lewis, Rudy, 195
Leyden, Norman, 115
Library of Congress, 300
Lieberson, Goddard, 114
Lin, Ivan, 358
Lincoln, Abraham, 16
Lincoln Memorial, 23, 143
Lindy Hop, 21
Liska, James, 214, 340
Listen to the Sun (documentary), 314–15
Little Night Music, A (musical), 301–2
Little Richard, 266
Little Rock Nine, 211
Live in Japan, 292–93
London, 163, 201–3
London House (Chicago), 198–200, 222, 363
"Lord's Prayer, The," 114, 141–44, 244–45
Los Angeles Philharmonic, 306–10, 333, 340–43, 346, 353
Los Angeles Times, 309, 353

Losers Club (Dallas), 288–89
Louis, Joe, 84, 152
"Lover Man," 63, 104, 203, 207, 265
"Lover's Concerto, A," 250
"Lover's Quarrel," 122–23
"Love You Madly," 130–31
Lowe, Mundell, 227
Lubinsky, Herman, 26
"Lullaby of Birdland," 186
lung cancer of Vaughan, 353–54, 357–59
lynchings, 46, 69–70
Lynne, Gloria, 223, 225–26, 231
Lyons, Leonard, 223

McCarthy, Jim, 148
McCartney, Paul, 266, 296–97
McClure, Ron, 285–88
McConnell, Shorty, 12, 37, 53–54
McCurdy, Roy, 324, 326, 327
McFerrin, Bobby, 355
McGhee, Howard, 51
McIntyre, Carl, 24–25
MacKay, Cliff, 135
Mackin, Tom, 272–73
McLaughlin, John, 269, 271–72
McNair, Barbara, 263, 340–41
McPartland, Jimmy, 83
McPartland, Marian, 20, 27, 32, 349
McPhatter, Clyde, 195
McRae, Carmen, 196–97, 276
  cancer of Vaughan, 358
  death of, 360
  Vaughan and Atkins, 228, 230
  Vaughan and touring, 336, 338
  "Whatever Lola Wants," 168, 169
MacRae, Gordon, 108
Madison Square Garden (New York), 222
"Magical Connection," 278
Magnusson, Bob, 215, 260, 270, 286, 307
  Vaughan and Fisher, 277
  Vaughan and recording, 279, 280–81
Mahavishnu Orchestra, 271–72

Mainstream Records, 276, 283, 292–96, 300–301, 317, 319
Make Believe Ballroom, 116
makeup, 155–56
"Make Yourself Comfortable," 163–67, 173, 176–80, 182, 183
Malachi, John, 43–44, 51, 56, 59–60, 101, 149, 202
Malotte, Albert Hay, 142
Maltz, Maxwell, 157
"Mama Will Bark," 119
managers. See also specific managers
  Vaughan's choice of, 258–63
Mancini, Henri, 249, 308
"Mandalay" (Kipling), 94
Mandell, Johnny, 281
"Man I Love, The," 11, 341, 342
Manilow, Barry, 348
Mann, Herbie, 185–86, 198, 345
Manne, Shelly, 280, 281
March on Washington (1963), 143
Marie Bryant Dancers, 130
marijuana, 54, 151–52, 238
Marsalis, Wynton, 343–48, 349
Martin, Tony, 76, 108
Mary Elizabeth Hotel (Miami), 140–41
master recordings, 110–11, 112–13
May, Elaine Tyler, 179
Mays, Bill, 279, 283, 286
Mays, Willie, 181
"Me and Mrs. Jones," 284
"Mean to Me," 11, 63, 130, 203
media, 77–78, 79–80, 87, 145–48
Mehta, Zubin, 309
Mello-Larks & Jamie, 168
Melody Maker, 202, 203, 214, 266, 279, 293
Mendes, Sergio, 349
Mercer, Johnny, 294
Mercer, Kobena, 158–59
Mercury International Convention, 201–2
Mercury Records, 114, 163–80, 183–90, 219, 240, 248–53, 267, 274–75, 345–46
Merrill, Bob, 166, 173
Metamorphoses (Ovid), 154

Metronome, 34, 41, 60–61, 66, 68, 75, 77–78, 95, 122, 125
Metropolitan Opera, 309
MGM Records, 101, 113, 129–30, 167, 253, 261, 317
Miami Daily News, 140
Miami Vice (TV show), 272
Mickman, Herb, 215, 233–34, 236, 255, 256–58, 270
Miller, Mitch, 114–22, 127, 174, 191, 250, 295
Miller, Roger, 250
Milt Jackson Quartet, 351
Milwaukee Journal-Sentinel, 96
Minton's Playhouse (New York), 39–40
Miranda, Carmen, 315
"Misty," 344–45, 352
modal jazz, 268
"Mona Lisa," 114
Monroe, Vaughan, 174
Monroe's Uptown House (Harlem), 39–40, 80
Montgomery bus boycott, 210
Moody, James, 355
Mooney, Hal, 249–50
Moore, Johnny, 195
Morales, Noro, 100
More Sarah Vaughan Live in Japan, 319
"More Than You Know," 256
Morgan, Jaye P., 171
Morgenstern, Dan, 279–80, 294
Morrison, Allan, 224
motherhood and Vaughan, 223–24
Mötley Crüe, 266
Mount Zion Baptist Church (Newark), 17, 18, 19, 22, 27, 35, 121, 142, 359
Mr. Kelly's (Chicago), 197, 292, 301, 337
"Mr. Sandman," 178
"Mr. Wonderful," 171, 174
Mulligan, Gerry, 189, 267, 325
Mullinax, Gary, 332
Municipal Auditorium (Atlanta), 132–36
Murder, Inc. (film), 222

musical education of Vaughan, 25–26, 38–39
musical labels, 4–5, 6
Music Makers Club (Columbus), 97
Musicraft Recordings, 76–77, 80–81, 87, 108–11
Music USA (radio program), 208
Myers, Marc, 197, 200
My Fair Lady (musical), 157
"My Favorite Things," 227
"My Tormented Heart," 122

NAACP (National Association for the Advancement of Colored People), 77, 133, 134, 136–37, 182
Nascimento, Milton, 314, 315–16
National Endowment of the Arts, 350
National Records, 63
National Youth Administration, 26
Native Dancer, 315
"Nature Boy," 114
Navarro, Theodore "Fats," 51
"Never," 171, 175
Newark, 15–17, 19–20
Newark Arts High School, 23–24
Newark clubs, Vaughan singing in, 24–27
Newark Sunday News, 272–73
Newark YMCA, 21
New Jersey Afro-American, 25
New Jersey Performing Arts Center, 365
New Jersey Symphony Orchestra, 359
"New Look," 98, 155
Newport International Youth Band, 209
Newport Jazz Festival, 193, 209, 226, 289, 321, 323, 330
New Scene, The, 250, 267
"New Sound," 13, 94, 98
Newsweek, 191–92
New Year's Eve Day recording session (1944), 61–62, 65
New York Amsterdam News, 35, 77, 79, 103, 104, 220, 233

New Yorker, 304
New York Herald-Tribune, 153, 159
New York News, 195
New York Post, 326
New York Symphony, 150
New York Times, 220, 304, 342
New Zealand, 349
nickname of Vaughan, 33, 144, 202
"Night in Tunisia, A," 62, 290
1910 Fruitgum Company, 274
Nixon, Richard, 299
Noble, Gil, 277, 284
No Count Sarah, 222
Nola Studio (New York), 61
Northwestern University, 323
"No Smoke Blues," 61–62, 65
novelty songs, 114, 116, 117, 119,
    121–22, 166

Oasis (Los Angeles), 113
Odeon (London), 202–3
"Old Devil Moon," 165, 192
Oliveira, Aloysio de, 315–16
Olympic Games, 349
Onyx Club (New York), 66, 67
opera, 6, 308–9, 314
Orchestra World, 95
Orpheum Theatre (Newark), 19
O'Sullivan, Eleanor, 338
Otis, Clyde, 214, 223
"Our Waltz," 222
Our World (magazine), 149
"Out O' Breath," 122
overdubbing, 115, 166, 176, 177–78
"Over the Rainbow," 192, 204, 207

Pablo Records, 317–19
Page, Patti, 100, 121, 156, 166, 176,
    177–78
Paich, David, 297
Paich, Marty, 297, 307, 308, 309,
    353
Paramount Theatre (New York),
    113
Paris, 100, 163, 308, 358
Parker, Charlie "Yardbird," 10, 63, 99
    drug addiction of, 54, 58
    in Eckstine band, 50–52

in Hines band, 37, 38–40, 47
    personal quirks of, 58
    Vaughan and touring, 96, 317
Parthenon, 198–99
Parton, Dolly, 344
Pass, Joe, 318
"Passing Strangers," 203
Pate, Johnnie, 198
Patinkin, Mandy, 349
Patterson and Jackson, 130
Paul, Billy, 284
Paul, Les, 176
"Perdido," 116, 123, 130, 165
Peterson, Melody, 309
Peterson, Oscar, 208, 317, 318
Philadelphia Symphony Orchestra,
    113, 308, 311
Philadelphia Tribune, 142, 231,
    232–33
Phillips, Flip, 96
piano, 17, 20–21, 39
Piano Jazz (radio program), 349
pitch, 1, 117, 251
Pittsburgh Courier, 10, 95, 192
Pittsburgh Post-Gazette, 96
PJ's (Los Angeles), 265–66
*Planet Is Alive . . . Let It Live!: Sarah
    Vaughan Sings Pope John Paul II*,
    349
Plantation Club (Los Angeles), 62
Plantation Club (St. Louis), 51
Playboy Jazz Festival, 327
"Polka Dots and Moonbeams," 165
Pollock, Bill, 300
"Poor Butterfly," 192, 273
Pop Artistry, 250, 267
pop music, 5–7, 22, 102, 167
Porgy and Bess, 341
Potter, Tommy, 96
Powell, Bud, 210
Presley, Elvis, 214, 266
Price, Leontyne, 346, 350
Prima, Louis, 28
Prinze, Freddie, 397*n*
Proctor's Theater (Newark), 19
Progressive Talent, 224–25
Protzman, Bob, 216
Pygmalion, 154, 157, 159–61

Queen, Bob, 25
Quinichette, Paul, 185–86, 198, 345
Quinn, Bill, 245, 248, 250, 253, 254, 273

race
  beauty and, 152–53, 157–60
  embodiment and, 90–94
  femininity and, 157–58
racism, 44–48, 73–74, 78–79, 90–94, 132–40, 180–82, 209–11, 246–47, 338–40
Radio Record Shop (Newark), 26
Rainey, Gertrude "Ma," 74–75, 91
"Rainy Days and Mondays," 283
Ramsey, Guthrie, Jr., 4
rape, 55–56
Ravinia Festival, 230, 353
Raye, Martha, 76
Reagan, Ronald, 299
Reconstruction, 16
red hot mamas, 74–75
Reed, Susie, 70, 71
Reed, Waymon, 326–30
  marriage to Vaughan, 321–22, 323–24
Rees, Thomas, 299 300
Reeves, Dianne, 188, 345, 360–62
Reig, Teddy, 45–46, 226–28, 237
Return to Forever, 270
Reuther, Wyatt, 101
Rhapsody and Song: A Tribute to George Gershwin, 340
Rhumboogie Club (Chicago), 84–85
Richards, Robert, 118, 215
  cancer of Vaughan, 352–55, 358–59
  Vaughan and death of father, 284
  Vaughan and Hammond, 72
  Vaughan and recordings, 300–301, 342–43
Richmond, Howard, 69, 76, 377n
Rio, Frank, 331
Rio de Janeiro, 314–17
Riviera (Las Vegas), 236
Riviera Club (St. Louis), 51–52
Roach, Max, 63, 189
"Road to Mandalay, The," 94

Roberts Show Lounge (Chicago), 225
Robeson, Paul, 71, 143
Robin Hood Dell (Philadelphia), 113, 143, 308
Robinson, Chris, 369
Robinson, Jackie, 181
Robinson, Louie, 305
Robinson, Ray, 134
"Rock It for Me," 20
rock 'n' roll, 216, 266–69
"Rocks in My Bed," 328
Rockwell, John, 304
Rodgers, Richard, 89
Rodney, Red, 96
Rogers, Cleota, 372n
Rogers, Timmie, 130, 140
Rolling Stones, 266, 317
Rollins, Sonny, 268
Romance on the High Seas (film), 107, 108
Rosie the Riveter, 97
Ross, Annie, 228, 260, 275–76
Ross, Hudson, 87
Ross, Jerry, 168
Roulette Records, 184, 222, 226, 237, 240, 247–48, 256, 275, 296
"Route 66," 114
Rowles, Jimmy, 280, 293–94
Roxy Theatre (New York), 66, 134
Royal Albert Hall (London), 163, 308
royalties, 109, 110–11, 118, 164, 195, 248, 274, 275, 294
Rutgers University, 18
Ruyter, Michiel de, 205

Sablon, Jean, 76
Sacks, Manie, 112, 114, 115
St. Louis, Marie, 331
St. Louis Post-Dispatch, 96
"Sakura," 244
Salle Pleyel (Paris), 163, 308
Salvant, Cécile McLorin, 364
San Diego Symphony, 307
San Francisco Symphony, 310
"Sarah," 360

Sarah: Dedicated to You, 360
Sarah and Dizzy, 180
Sarah Vaughan (album), 184–88, 198, 360–61
Sarah Vaughan: Live at the Holiday Inn Lesotho, 296
"Sarah Vaughan and Her Pygmalion," 154–61
Sarah Vaughan and Michel Legrand, 280–81
Sarah Vaughan and the Jimmy Rowles Quintet, 293–94
Sarah Vaughan at Mr. Kelly's, 197, 222, 363
Sarah Vaughan at the Blue Note, 190
Sarah Vaughan International Jazz Vocal Competition, 365
Sarah Vaughan Sings the Mancini Songbook, 249
Sarah + 2, 227, 248
Sass and Brass (TV show), 349
"Sassy's Blues," 272
Sassy Swings the Tivoli, 240, 249, 293, 345
Sato, Eisaku, 243, 244
"Saturday," 165
Savoy Records, 26
"Say You'll Wait for Me" (Los Angeles), 122
Schiffman, Frank, 30
Schifrin, Lalo, 256, 349
Schoenfeld, Herman, 102, 165
Schreiber, John, 330–40, 365
Schroeder, Carl, 286, 290
  "Send in the Clowns," 301–2, 396–97n
  Vaughan and death of father, 283–85
  Vaughan and Parker, 54
  Vaughan and presenters, 337–38
  Vaughan and recording, 293–95, 301–2
  Vaughan and Reed, 321–22, 323, 324
  Vaughan and symphony orchestras, 310, 311–13
  Vaughan at Losers Club, 288–89
Schuller, Gunther, 365

Scott, Eileen, 167
Scott, Hazel, 70
Scott, Jay, 301, 304, 343, 345, 348
Sebastian, John, 278
Sedaka, Neil, 214
segregation, 16, 19, 44–48, 90–91, 132–40, 180–82, 210–11, 246–47, 339
Send in the Clowns, 295–96
"Send in the Clowns," 300–305, 311, 347, 352, 354, 396–97n
"September Song," 186, 345, 346, 347
"Serenata," 222, 248
set list, 206
Seward, Granville, 359
sexism, 56–58, 119
Shad, Bobby, 188–90, 201–2, 276, 292–96
  recording sessions, 165–66, 185–86, 278–81, 292–94
Shad, Molly, 296
"Shake Rattle and Roll," 174
Shank, Bud, 208
Shaw, Artie, 76
Shaw, Arvell, 205
Shaw, George Bernard, 157
Shearer, Tobin Miller, 144
Sherman, Al, 88
Sherman Hotel (Chicago), 85–86
Shore, Dinah, 112, 168–70
Shorter, Wayne, 269, 315
"Shulie a Bop," 165, 272
"Signing Off," 61–62, 65
Sills, Beverly, 346
Silver, Horace, 268
Silver Slipper (San Diego), 62
Simon, Carly, 278
Simon, Ernie, 86, 87–88
Simon, Paul, 315
Simone, Nina, 143, 210, 268
Simpkins, Andy, 324
Sinatra, Frank, 34, 67, 112, 113, 119, 120, 126, 190, 236, 286
Sing Along with Mitch, 122
"singer" label, 273–74
singing style. *See* vocal style
Sippel, Johnny, 85–86

Skateland (Newark), 21, 25, 29
Slater, Fred "Duke," 219
slavery, 16, 44, 297
Slightly Classical, 237
"Slowly with Feeling," 171, 175
Smalls, Clifton, 354
Smith, Arnold Jay, 118, 295,
    296–97, 311
Smith, Bessie, 72, 74–75, 91
"Smooth Operator," 221
solo career of Vaughan. *See also*
    specific albums and songs
  career is reborn, 213–17
  in Chicago, 83–94
  choice of personal managers,
    258–63
  crossover phase, 101–3
  growing popularity, 95–97,
    145–46
  jazz critics and, 123–27
  launch of, 65–81
  a star is born, 99–105
  Treadwell's makeover, 154–61
  underemployment, 66–69
  Vaughan's voice and Garroway,
    86–94
"Sometimes I Feel like a Motherless
    Child," 142, 245
"Sometimes I'm Happy," 204
Sondheim, Steven, 300–302
"Sophisticated Lady," 227
South, touring in the, 44–49, 51,
    132–39
South Pacific (musical), 349
Spain, 335
Spotlight (New York), 66
Stafford, Jo, 97, 117, 120, 171–72
"Stairway to Paradise," 309
Star Eyes, 237
Starlight Roof (New York), 190–93
Stars of Jazz (TV show), 100–101
State Department, U.S., 209, 210,
    211
State Fair (film), 89
Staton, Dakota, 237
Steele, Larry, 230
Stevens, Ray, 250
Stewart, Rex, 73

Stewart, Slam, 79
Stitt, Sonny, 237
Stoller, Mike, 195
Stork Club (New York), 134
"Stormy Weather," 61
Storyville (Boston), 141, 143, 144,
    196, 211, 351
Strand Theatre (New York), 97, 113
"Strange Fruit," 69–70
Streisand, Barbra, 280
Stuart, Kirk, 237, 239
Stuff Smith Trio, 67
Stump and Stumpy, 130
Sudhalter, Richard, 326
Sullivan, Ed, 108, 113, 167
"Summer Knows, The'", 280–81
Summer of '42, The (film), 280
"Summertime," 291–92, 307–8
Sun Plaza Hotel (Tokyo), 292–93
Svend Saaby Choir, 249
"Sweet Georgia Brown," 352
"Sweet Gingerbread Man," 278,
    279
Sweet N' Sassy, 256
symphony orchestras, 306–14,
    340–43

Take 6, 355
Talmadge, Art, 166, 171, 219–20
Tanaka, Michiyo, 305–6, 322–23
Tan Confessions, 81, 149, 152–53,
    158
Taylor, Billy, 348
Taylor, Cecil, 268
Ted Heath and His Music, 202, 203
Te Kanawa, Kiri, 349
"Tenderly," 89, 117–18, 203, 207,
    265
Terry, Clark, 276, 361
"Thanks for the Memory," 198–200
"That's the Way I've Always Heard
    It Should Be," 278
"There Are Such Things," 34
"There Goes My Baby," 195
"These Things I Offer You," 121,
    122, 164
"They Were Doin' the Mambo," 174
"Thinking of You," 116, 121

Think of One, 343
Third Ward, Newark, 16–17, 20, 21
Thirteenth Amendment, 44
"This Ole House," 174
Thomas, John Charles, 142
Thompson, Lucky, 51
Three Deuces (New York), 66, 79
Tiegel, Eliot, 278
Tilson Thomas, Michael, 217,
    307–10, 333, 340–43, 346
Time (magazine), 80
"Time and Again," 67
Time in My Life, A, 278–80
Tin Pan Alley, 252
Tiny Tim, 274
Tivoli Gardens (Copenhagen), 240,
    249, 293, 345
Toast of the Town (TV show), 108, 167
Today Show (TV show), 87, 125
Tomkins, Les, 19, 48, 72, 109, 249,
    281, 297, 306, 373*n*
tone, 1, 59–60, 112–13
Tonight Show (TV show), 271, 321
"Too Young," 114, 126
Tormé, Mel, 76, 325
Toto (band), 297
Town Hall (New York), 9–13
Tracy, Jack, 124, 125, 266–67
train touring, 42, 43, 47–48
Treadwell, Fayrene Williams, 194
Treadwell, George, 145–52
    assault charges against, 103–5
    divorce from Vaughan, 193–94,
        195–96
    marriage to Vaughan, 80, 81, 105,
        148–52, 160
    music management of, 194–96,
        197, 221
    personal management of
        Vaughan, 119, 130, 142,
        145–49, 164–65, 202
    publicity campaigns, 146–49,
        152–58, 160–62
    recording sessions, 80–81, 115
    remarriage of, 194
    subway attack on, 78–79
Treniers, the, 223
Tropicana (Las Vegas), 277

Troubadour Club (Los Angeles),
    283–85
Tucker, Frank, 25
Turtles, the, 274
Tuskegee Airmen, 79
"Tweedle Dee," 175
Twentieth Century Fox, 113
2:00 A.M. Paradise Cafe, 348

Ulanov, Barry, 34
"Underneath the Overpass," 117
"Unforgettable," 114
Universal International, 113
"Universal Prisoner," 278, 279
USA Today, 355, 357–58

Valentine, Jerry, 59–60
Van Halen, 266
Varese, Edward, 209
Variety, 102, 146, 163, 165, 166,
    170, 178, 192–93, 197, 220
Vaughan, Ada, 15, 16–17, 22–24,
    27, 75, 284, 305, 314, 323, 327
Vaughan, Asbury, 15, 16–17, 22–23,
    27, 75, 284–85
Vaughan, Deborah Lois. *See* Atkins,
    Deborah Lois
Vaughan and Violins, 248, 249,
    344–45
Vaughan Wells Corporation, 258–59
Vaughan with Voices, 358
Verve Records, 207–8, 252, 253,
    317, 327
Veteran's Club (Harlem), 103–4
Village Voice, 344
Vinson, Eddie "Cleanhead," 328
Viva! Vaughan, 249
vocal blackness, 86–94
vocal codes, 90–92, 177
vocal lessons, 23, 154
vocal style, 59–60, 71, 75–76,
    102–3, 176–77, 251–52, 304
vocal whiteness, 90–94
Voice of America, 208, 209

Walden, A. T., 133
Waldorf Astoria (New York),
    190–93, 221, 223

Waller, Thomas "Fats," 20
"Wallflower, The (Dance with Me, Henry)", 175
"Waltzing Down the Aisle," 167–68, 173, 175
Washington, Dinah, 156, 175, 189, 220, 223, 232, 234–35
Washington Post and Times-Herald, 191, 233
Waters, Ethel, 41, 61–62, 74–75
Watkins, Julius, 249–50
Watkins Hotel (Los Angeles), 150
Webb, Alvin, 104
Webb, Chick, 28, 29, 207
Wein, George, 262–63, 334, 335–36, 338–39
   cancer of Vaughan, 353
   Vaughan and "The Lord's Prayer," 141
   Vaughan and touring, 290, 330
   Vaughan at JVC Jazz Festival, 351–52
   Vaughan at World's Fair, 209, 211–12, 262
Wein, Joyce, 212
Wells, John "Preacher," 234–35, 254–59, 263, 274–75
Wells, Patricia, 130
Wess, Frank, 197
Weston, Paul, 117
We the People (TV show), 113–14
"Whatever Lola Wants," 168–70, 173–74, 175–76, 365
"Whatever Will Be, Will Be (Que Sera, Sera)", 172
"Whippa-Whippa-Woo," 116
whipping posts, 332
White, Josh, 70
White Citizens Council (WCC), 382*n*
White House, 243–47

white managers, 261–63
Wilkins, Ernie, 278, 279
Williams, Charles "Buster," 237–41, 254–55, 256, 285
Williams, Charles "Cootie," 29, 80
Williams, Joe, 191, 220, 259, 358
Williams, John, 66, 344, 346–47
Williams, Martin, 251–53
Williams, Mary Lou, 70
Williams, Patrick, 281
Wilmington Grand Opera House, 330–34
Wilmington News Journal, 332, 334
Wilson, Annette, 149
Wilson, John, 156, 304, 352
Wilson, Nancy, 255, 263, 285
Wilson, Rossiere "Shadow," 37, 50, 51, 53–54
Wilson, Teddy, 76
"Wings for Sarah," 359
"With My Eyes Wide Open I'm Dreaming," 177
WMAQ, 88–89
WMCA, 77
Wofford, Mike, 48, 324, 327
World's Fair (1958), 208–12, 262
World War II, 97, 98, 179
Wright, Naomi, 78–79
Wright, Ray, 167

"You Are My First Love," 52
Young, Lester, 9, 10, 12
"Young Woman Blues," 75
You're Mine You, 248
"You're My Baby," 221–22
"You Taught Me to Love Again," 123

Zawinul, Joe, 269
Zimmer, Graeme, 97